Churchill and Eden at War

Elisabeth Barker

ISBN 0 333 23467 7

First published 1978 by
MACMILLAN LONDON LIMITED
4 Little Essex Street London WC2R 3LF
and Basingstoke
Associated Companies in Delhi Dublin
Hong Kong Johannesburg Lagos Melbourne
New York Singapore and Tokyo

Printed in Great Britain by
THE ANCHOR PRESS LTD
Tiptree, Essex

For K.

Contents

CONTENTS

Foreword

Working on this book has been for me a journey of exploration. I wanted to satisfy my own personal curiosity about the wartime relations between two men who, in different degrees, so greatly influenced the lives of a whole generation, including my own (b. 1910). Until a few years ago I had been in the sloppy habit of attributing everything that 'Britain' did in the Second World War to 'Churchill', without bothering to think much how decisions were actually reached. Then, when I did some detailed research in the official British documents on Austria and south-east Europe, I realised that in the field of foreign policy Eden had a great deal to do with decision-making, that he was quite often at odds with Churchill and that Churchill did not always win.

In his introduction to his great work, *British Foreign Policy in the Second World War*, Sir Llewellyn Woodward wrote that 'Mr Eden . . . was able to balance, and often to correct, Mr Churchill's rapid approach and equally rapid conclusions.' He also wrote that Eden was 'a realist . . . inclined by temperament to think in terms of distant consequences and ultimate considerations'.[1] With the deepest respect for the official British historian, it seemed to me that there was rather more to it than that, and that if the various aspects of wartime foreign policy were examined specifically from the point of view of the relationship between the two men a more complex picture would appear; that sometimes it was Eden who was rapid in his conclusions and Churchill who was the realist, and that there was a continuing dialogue or argument between them, in which they often changed roles.

It also seemed to me that there was a marvellous chance to try to re-create their relationship as it developed – at certain times, almost hour by hour. This was because of Churchill's overpowering impulse to communicate every idea, fear or hope and to relieve frustration or anxiety by dictating a minute; and he then expected a reply in writing. Churchill's minutes – often very brief – are in themselves fascinating reading, pithy, dramatic, angry, pathetic and funny in turns; Eden clearly did his best to respond in kind, so through the minutes alone a good deal of the relationship could be seen.

Then, too, there were Eden's irritated or long-suffering pencilled scrawls on minutes or telegrams from Churchill, which were not meant for Churchill's eyes. For instance, when Churchill accused the British ambassador in Moscow of 'cringing' before Molotov, Eden scribbled in the margin 'Yet no one is more effusive to the Russians than P.M.'[2] Or there was the extraordinary doodle which Churchill drew on a minute from Eden about changes in the exiled Greek government; it looks like an inextricably tangled ball of twine, and perhaps represented Churchill's view of Greek politics.[3]

Of course these minutes do not convey more than a part of the whole relationship; there were also arguments in the War Cabinet or the Defence Committee; private talks, sometimes over a quiet dinner; weekends at Chequers; telephone conversations, sometimes transatlantic. Glimpses of these can be seen in the official documents and also in Eden's own war memoirs, *The Reckoning*, especially when he quotes from his own diary. These are important, showing that an explosion of rage on Churchill's part could quickly be followed by reconciliation and was often not taken very seriously by Eden. It would be fascinating to know how much more is revealed in the rest of Eden's diary, which presumably may be made available one day to his official biographer.

Yet there is such a vast volume of material already available in the documents in the Public Record Office that it seems unlikely that the overall pattern would be greatly changed. Here I have been very fortunate in that I have been able to see the Avon Papers, released in 1978, at a very early stage, so as to fill out or modify the picture I had already built up by long research in the Prime Minister's papers and the Foreign Office documents released in 1971.

I also quickly saw that it was essential to look at the Churchill–Eden relationship in the context of the War Cabinet, and to find out how far Churchill could or could not be controlled by his Cabinet colleagues; the roles of the Labour leaders, Attlee and Bevin, and the support they sometimes gave Eden against Churchill, were particularly interesting. Research in the War Cabinet minutes, confidential annexes and memoranda led me back to the months *before* Eden became Foreign Secretary, to the time of Dunkirk and to Churchill's confrontation with Halifax and Chamberlain at that extremely dangerous moment, when the course of British and perhaps world history could so easily have been changed if Churchill had failed to get his way. To me, a good deal of this was new, and it seemed to show how important it was for Churchill to have a man with whom he was in sympathy, and on whose personal loyalty he could count, as Foreign Secretary.

The great bulk of this book is therefore based on the documents in the Public Record Office. These are quoted by permission of H.M. Stationery Office. I am most grateful to the Keeper of the Public Record Office and also, personally, to Mr Duncan Chalmers, Principal Assistant Keeper, Modern Records, to Mr R. R. Mellor and to Miss Carol Dimmer for the kind an generous help they gave me; it has been most valuable.

I have, of course, tried to consult those who worked with Churchill or Eden in one capacity or another during the war years. I should particularly like to thank Mr Harold Macmillan, Lord Strang, General Sir Ian Jacob, Sir John Colville and Sir Frank Roberts. (Lord Strang's unpublished special University of London lecture of March 1965 is a masterly brief survey of the Churchill–Eden relationship in the war years and I am most grateful to him for lending me a copy of the text.) I had hoped to see Lord Avon himself, but this was not possible; I should, however, like to thank Lady Avon for helpful advice.

I owe sincere thanks to the publishers, Macmillan : to Alan Maclean for badly needed encouragement to tackle a daunting job; to Richard Garnett for friendly and sage advice and criticism; to Honor Burgess for brilliant detective work in spotting errors and inconsistencies of detail, including one historical howler. (But for any errors which escaped her microscope, I take full responsibility.)

Finally, this book is *not* meant to be an attempt to rewrite the history of British foreign policy in the war years. That would be idiotic presumption. It has the narrower aim of looking at the Churchill–Eden relationship in three main contexts. There are their differences over de Gaulle; their differences over Roosevelt, shown in the particular cases of Spain and Portugal, Italy, and Greece; their baffled efforts to deal with Stalin, illustrated in the particular cases of the Soviet frontier question, Poland, Czechoslovakia, and the Balkans. In their arguments over these things can, I think, be found the seeds of some of the great British post-war problems : the clash between a shrunken Britain and a resurgent Gaullist France; the pursuit of a vanishing special relationship with the U.S., combined with recurrent Anglo-American commercial wrangles, for instance over civil aviation; the cold war with the Soviet Union in its various forms and phases.

I hope, too, that I may have communicated a small part of the interest and pleasure that I myself got from reading the documents. I sometimes disturbed the calm of the P.R.O. with involuntary cackles of laughter and once had to spend some hours holding back tears over that tragedy of seemingly wasted heroism, suffering and human lives, the Warsaw rising. But that, I suppose, has nothing to do with the writing of history.

PART ONE
Churchill and Eden

CHAPTER ONE

Partners or Prima Donnas?

Churchill was a man who set great store by his personal relationships, and never more than in the Second World War, his time of severest strain, blackest fears, highest hopes, greatest achievements, but also most agonising frustrations and even humiliations. Some people have seen his wartime relationships with his nearest collaborators in terms of master and loyal servants. On one side of his work, the shaping of military strategy, it has been shown that this was not so; the British Chiefs of Staff could be very stubborn and in the last resort Churchill would not go against them. On the other side, the forming and carrying out of foreign policies, it is still fairly common to see Churchill as the powerful mastermind, Anthony Eden as his loyal right-hand man. One intelligent observer saw it as a man–woman relationship, in the sense of a partnership between a dominant, aggressive, 'male' personality and a submissive 'feminine' personality, the one complementing the other as in the Victorian ideal of marriage.[1]

Perhaps at moments Churchill himself saw it in this light. At others he certainly did not; even more certainly, Eden did not. Their wartime relationship is extraordinarily well documented in their frequent and very revealing minutes to each other and in other recorded exchanges. These show that, if the Prime Minister's relations with his colleagues were all in some degree unequal, those with his Foreign Secretary were less unequal than others.

A year after he had been voted out of power in the 1945 general election, Churchill wrote to the Secretary to the Cabinet that he was being 'pressed from many quarters' to give his account of the British war story:

> I should like to tell the story so far as possible in my own words written at the time. As you know, a great part of my work was done in writing (dictated typescript) and I should scarcely need to publish any documents other than those I have composed myself. . . . In telling a tale the words written in the circumstances of the moment are of far greater significance than any paraphrase of them or subsequent composition.[2]

At this time Churchill seems to have felt that his own minutes could themselves tell the story. But when he came to write his war history he did in fact very often resort to 'paraphrase' and 'subsequent composition', banishing his minutes – or such of them as he decided to publish – to the end of the volume as appendices. This must have been partly because his creative drive as writer and historian took charge and, together with a certain natural egoism, compelled him to reshape the story with broader brush-strokes and more glowing colour. But it must have been partly because he quickly saw that his own minutes, alone, did *not* tell the whole story.

To read these minutes today is to be tempted to think that Churchill, in writing them, felt that he was doing two creative acts at one time: dictating the course of future historical events by making them happen, and also dictating the history of the Second World War as it would eventually be written. He once wrote to Stalin that a question in dispute should be left to the verdict of history: 'But remember, if I live long enough I may be one of the historians.'[3]

Yet a close look at the Churchill minutes shows that they were seldom simple commands which dictated events. More often they were requests for information, sharp or kindly criticisms of action or inaction, fairly tentative suggestions, sometimes outbursts of ill-temper or frustration or hurt feelings. They certainly expected an answer, usually a very quick answer, and sometimes the answer 'No.'

From Eden Churchill quite often got the answer 'No,' expressed in many different ways according to each man's temper at that particular moment. Eden was 'feminine' enough to take careful notice of Churchill's moods and sensitive spots, to try to avoid direct confrontations (unless Churchill was in a distant country or at the far end of a long-distance telephone line), to save Churchill's face, and so to say 'Yes, but not in that way,' or 'Not just yet,' or 'Not in present circumstances, but things may change,' rather than to give a hard, unsweetened 'No.' The fact remained that Eden could show great tenacity, even obstinacy, in defending his department – from the end of 1940, the Foreign Office – against attack, and his own policies, or the Office's, against Churchill's more aggressive impulses or higher flights of fancy. Whether Eden's policies were always wiser is another question.

In the last years of peace Eden was very far from unequal in relation to Churchill, in terms of British politics. Churchill had been out of office for ten years by 1939, and had quarrelled with the establishment of the

Conservative Party who thought him a wild and dangerous man. His personal followers in the House of Commons were very few indeed and not particularly influential; the most energetic was Brendan Bracken. When the war started he was already sixty-four.

Eden was twenty-two years younger. On the other hand, he lacked Churchill's extraordinary physical and mental energy, recuperative power and stamina. After a very bad flight home from Moscow in 1935 he was seriously ill and an invalid for several months.[4] During the war he suffered from gastric ulcers. But by the time the war began he had already made a brilliant political career, starting as Parliamentary Under-Secretary in 1931, then becoming Lord Privy Seal in charge of League of Nations affairs and soon after, in 1935, Foreign Secretary. His resignation in February 1938 – on the eve of Hitler's forcible annexation of Austria – was basically caused by Neville Chamberlain's determination to follow his own foreign policy behind Eden's back, whether towards Mussolini, Hitler or Roosevelt. In the end Eden found this personally humiliating, unbearably so.

However, the manner of his resignation was so restrained and polite that he remained popular with rank-and-file Conservatives, as also with many Liberal and Labour supporters, and had not broken irreparably with the party leadership. A pro-Chamberlain Conservative M.P., Henry (Chips) Channon, who disliked Eden, wrote in his diary that Eden would not be 'bitter', 'firstly because he is a gentleman, and secondly because he is too shrewd a statesman to burn his boats irretrievably. Already there is talk of his coming back . . . in the autumn.'[5] Eden himself certainly hoped to return to office soon, and according to Oliver Harvey, his former principal private secretary, had on occasions to be restrained by his friends from eating humble pie so as to get back.[6] His group of followers in the House of Commons – called by Tory opponents 'the Glamour Boys' – numbered between twenty and thirty and included some influential people such as Leo Amery and good orators such as Duff Cooper.

In the last years before the war, therefore, most people would have rated Eden's political prospects far more highly than Churchill's. A leading member of the orthodox Conservative establishment, Lord Halifax, even discussed privately the idea of Eden's becoming prime minister, though he dismissed it because he thought him 'too sensitive, not tough enough to be P.M.'[7]

As war came closer, Eden offered to undertake important diplomatic missions while outside the government – in the spring of 1939 to the Soviet Union,[8] in the following August to Turkey.[9] Both ideas were rejected by Chamberlain as unduly provocative to the dictators; for the same reason he would not have Eden back in the government.

Eden's 'provocativeness' had by 1939 been highlighted by his increasingly close comradeship with Churchill in opposing appeasement of the dictators. Churchill had watched Eden's career at the Foreign Office with sympathy, writing later that Eden, as Lord Privy Seal, won his reputation at Geneva by rallying the nations of Europe against one dictator (Mussolini): 'He was a devoted adherent of the French Entente ... he was anxious to have more intimate relations with Soviet Russia. He felt and feared the Hitler peril. It might almost be said that there was not much difference of view between him and me, except, of course, that he was in harness.'[10] When Eden became Foreign Secretary, however, he wrote to his wife: 'I think you will now see what a lightweight Eden is.'[11] But in his war history he wrote that he was 'in close sympathy' with Eden as Foreign Secretary: 'He seemed to me the most resolute and courageous figure in the Administration.' He added that he and Eden 'corresponded freely' and that he always supported Eden in the House 'when he took resolute action, even though it was upon a very limited scale', knowing that 'he would act more boldly if he were not enmeshed'.[12] In August 1937 the two saw a good deal of each other at Cannes; it was probably then that Churchill joined Eden in backing No. 17 at the roulette table, with brilliant success – an incident which Churchill recalled in the War Cabinet in the darkest days of 1940.[13]

On his side, Eden in office was courteously noncommittal in his response to Churchill's wilder ideas. In September 1937 Eden was trying to grapple with the problems of the Spanish Civil War, in particular the activities of Italian submarines clandestinely attacking merchant ships carrying cargoes to republican Spain. Churchill wrote to Eden proposing a private arrangement with the Turkish leader, Kemal Atatürk, to introduce Royal Navy personnel with four-inch guns on to tankers and merchantmen leaving the Black Sea: these would thereafter 'offer themselves' to the pirate submarines and then 'get a few'. 'This', Churchill wrote, 'is a dodge which comes off best when it is first tried, but is very good then.' He coupled the dodge with an invitation to Eden to dine with him and Lloyd George. Eden referred the idea to Duff Cooper, then at the Admiralty, who replied sarcastically that it would be admirable 'if it were our policy to expedite the outbreak of war'. He added that he did not envy Eden the proposed dinner and implied that Churchill was still living in the earlier world war.

Eden replied to Churchill politely that he was just going to attempt negotiations with the Mediterranean powers (at Nyon) to deal with the submarine problem; this made it impossible for him to accept the dinner invitation. Thereafter, Churchill wrote to Eden to congratulate him on his (apparent) success at Nyon: 'It was very good of you, when you are so busy, to write to me.'[14]

So at this time Eden was very much on the inside track, Churchill the outsider.

Eden's resignation in 1938 caused Churchill deepest gloom. He wrote later: 'My heart sank, and for a while the dark waters of despair over-whelmed me. . . . From midnight till dawn I lay in my bed consumed by emotions of sorrow and fear. . . . He seemed to me at this moment to embody the life-hope of the British nation. . . . Now he was gone . . . I . . . saw before me in mental gaze the vision of Death.'[15] These melo-dramatic words must have conveyed a real emotion; but Churchill also feared that Eden had failed to present the grounds for his resignation properly, so damaging their joint cause. From then on the two men worked fairly closely together in the House of Commons and outside it. The Eden and Churchill groups jointly tabled a resolution in the House on 29 March 1939 after Hitler's entry into Prague. It bore thirty-six signatures, the vast majority of them Eden's followers.

But during the next threatening months Churchill's political star rose again. It was Churchill whom Chamberlain, on 1 September, after Hitler's attack on Poland, invited to enter the government. Churchill agreed with-out comment, but later wrote to Chamberlain suggesting that the Liberal leader, Sir Archibald Sinclair, and Eden should be included also – as he put it, to bring down the Cabinet's average age to fifty-seven and a half.[16]

This, at least, was Churchill's account; Eden's was a little different, in that Churchill had at the outset asked whether Eden was to be invited to join. In the event, Chamberlain's invitation did not reach Eden until 3 September – the offer of the post of Dominions Secretary, without a seat in the War Cabinet but attending War Cabinet meetings. This aroused no enthusiasm in Eden who felt his position anomalous as a spectator of War Cabinet proceedings without a real part in them.[17] But he did the job, kept in touch with Churchill and bided his time.

The outbreak of war, therefore, weighed down the political balance be-tween the two men heavily on Churchill's side. It is difficult to explain on purely rational grounds how this happened. In retrospect it is rather more surprising that Britain should actually have gone to war in Sep-tember 1939, when no British territory or territory of major strategic importance to Britain was directly threatened, than that there should have been a long period of appeasement; equally surprising that in June 1940 there was no visible or audible British demand for negotiation with the enemy. Both things can perhaps only be explained by the extraordinary personality of Churchill and the myth that had grown up round him in the years between the two wars. In the First World War his wife had written to Asquith that, whatever faults he might have in his colleagues' eyes, 'he has the supreme quality which I venture to say very few of your present or future Cabinet possess – the power, the imagination, the deadliness, to fight Germany'.[18]

In the 1930s he seemed to embody the warlike, daring, defiant strain which had been almost bred out of the average Englishman. His 'power, imagination and deadliness' had become not just a legend but a living force as a result of Hitler's rise. It must have been one of the factors pushing the peace-loving Chamberlain to make the terribly painful decision to declare war and later to hand over power to Churchill and back him in defiance of Hitler in the summer of 1940. It would be fanciful to suggest that if Churchill had not existed Britain would not have gone to war in 1939. But when de Gaulle once said to him, 'In a manner of speaking, you personally *are* the war,'[19] his words had perhaps a deeper meaning than he intended.

Eden, young as he was, had also become something of a legend. As a very young man he had served with courage in the First World War, and had then earned international fame before he was forty. He had good looks, great charm, a soft and pleasing manner. But his legend, though glamorous, was more conventional, less potent and a good deal less deadly than Churchill's. If in January 1939 Halifax had privately discussed Eden as a possible Prime Minister, in May 1940, when Chamberlain had to go, Eden was out of the picture. The choice was between Halifax himself and Churchill. Churchill was willing to serve under Halifax, but Eden (according to his own account) backed up the orthodox Conservative, Sir Kingsley Wood, in advising him not to agree to this but to remain silent if asked.[20] The credit for this advice was also claimed for Brendan Bracken by Beaverbrook.[21] Both claims may be true. Churchill, once Prime Minister, offered Eden the post of Secretary of State for War, which he accepted, though, as he wrote later, he knew that his position would be difficult since the state of the army was inglorious and relations with Churchill might be 'choppy'.

Although Eden added that in practice Churchill was 'indulgent' to him, and that no two men could have worked more closely together,[22] things clearly *were* choppy during the following months. Although membership of the Defence Committee, presided over by Churchill and acting as a sort of inner War Cabinet, gave Eden more power than before, he soon found himself in trouble with Churchill over the conflict of priorities between the needs of the army in Britain and in the Middle East, with Churchill giving first claim to Britain and Eden pressing the claims of the Middle East.

There were problems, too, over Churchill's personal relations with the Chief of the Imperial General Staff, Sir John Dill, and the Middle East Commander-in-Chief, General Wavell. Eden's description of Dill's difficulties throws light on his own methods of handling Churchill: 'While he was always correct in his attitude to the Prime Minister, he was not so ready to adapt his moods to those of Churchill which could succeed each other with a bewildering if engaging rapidity. Dill never lacked personal charm but it was not in his character to be aware of it, still less to employ it to ease any discussion about which he cared.'[23] When Wavell first met Churchill, Eden observed that 'the Commander-in-Chief was not a man who could be drawn out, or one to make a special effort to please'.[24] Eden, on the other hand, tried to please, knew his own charm, used it, studied Churchill's moods and reacted to them with skill and good timing to win his point. He did his best to defend the generals against Churchill's blasts, which he felt to be unjust – so much so that Chamberlain once said to him with 'wry sympathy', 'I'm sorry, Anthony, that all your generals seem to be such bad generals.'[25]

The Churchill–Eden relationship survived these initial clashes over policy and persons, perhaps because of its well-grounded intimacy. In August 1940 Churchill was already mooting the idea of Eden's becoming Foreign Secretary in succession to Halifax, who never got on well with Churchill – he thought it his mission to restrain him[26] – and who was not liked by the Labour leaders and the anti-appeasers because of his close association with Chamberlain. After more bickering between Churchill and Eden over strategy in the Middle East and Greece, the changeover took place in December. Eden welcomed it in his heart, feeling that 'my responsibility must be greater as Churchill's colleague at the Foreign Office, than as his subordinate with the army'.[27]

Eden therefore believed that in returning to the Foreign Office he was regaining something of the old equality in his relations with Churchill. Churchill believed that the change would please Eden who, he wrote later, was like a man going home.[28] But he had firm ideas on the question of equality. In implied criticism of Chamberlain's practice as Prime Minister, he wrote later that 'the Foreign Secretary has a special position in a British Cabinet. He is treated with marked respect in his high and responsible office, but he usually conducts his affairs under the continuous scrutiny, if not of the whole Cabinet, at least of its principal members. . . . The supervision is, of course, especially maintained by the Prime Minister, who personally . . . is responsible for controlling, and has the power to control, the main course of foreign policy.' Churchill added that there should be harmony of outlook and even of temperament between Foreign Secretary and Prime Minister.[29]

Certainly Churchill, throughout his partnership with Eden, saw himself as controlling foreign policy, often not only in its main course, but in its details, to an extent which must equally often have irked Eden. For a man who with some reason regarded himself as unusually experienced and skilful in foreign affairs, who was regarded by some of his contemporaries as over-sensitive to criticism, and who later earned a reputation as a prima donna,[30] Churchill's constant incursions into his territory and periodic nagging and niggling must have been especially hard to bear.

Yet he did bear it, usually with good grace. There were two reasons. It cannot be doubted that there was real and deep friendly feeling between the two men. Eden quoted approvingly Herbert Morrison's description of their relationship as that of father and son.[31] Of course not all sons love their fathers but Eden also wrote that he grew to love Churchill through their general agreement and occasional differences.[32] He also gave many instances of Churchill's occasional outpourings of warm affection or repentance for bad temper, his sudden flashes of humour which disarmed ill-feeling and made all well. On his side Churchill, especially in times of particular strain or exhaustion, obviously came to rely more and more on Eden for sympathy, a ready responsiveness and congenial company. Beaverbrook might be his oldest and closest crony but Eden was a far more constant companion in wartime, in both senses of the word 'constant'.

Within the upper ranks of the Conservative Establishment there were from time to time rumblings of discontent, even revolt, against Churchill's highly personal war management. Eden does not ever seem to have wavered in his political loyalty, however often he let the Foreign Office see his fits of frustration and irritation at the Prime Minister's whims. At a particularly bad period in the war the elder statesman, Lord Salisbury, pressed for a radical reorganisation in the defence field – which would have meant a serious weakening of Churchill's position. He wrote to Eden : 'If he is not careful Winston will be in his grave or in a lunatic asylum.' Eden was not tempted into betrayal. He merely instructed his officials to send Salisbury formal thanks.[33]

If real friendship was one reason why the Churchill–Eden relationship stood the strains of war, the other was Churchill's nomination of Eden as his successor in the event of his own death – a step taken in response to a request from King George VI in June 1942. In any other politician this would have looked like a shrewd move by the Prime Minister to secure Eden's personal loyalty, while making sure that there could be no other political rival to himself than Eden – no rival who might have been a much more dangerous threat than Eden ever was. Tory critics of Churchill who, when his political stock was low, discussed ousting him always thought that Eden would not be a satisfactory replacement, so they had to put up with Churchill.[34]

Eden's own political stock slumped in the summer of 1941 because of his personal sponsorship of the Greek campaign, even though his enthusiasm for it had almost certainly been first fired by Churchill's own eagerness for a Balkan front against Hitler, and even though Churchill 'covered' Eden in the House of Commons. But Eden's reputation revived, so that his appointment in November 1942 as Leader of the House of Commons was accepted without question. Yet he was never a threat to Churchill. Beaverbrook wrote in late 1942 of Eden as 'heir to Churchill's throne', adding, 'he is the most popular of the Ministers, after Churchill. And it must be said that he comes a long way after Churchill.'[35]

If Churchill had wanted to be Machiavellian in naming Eden as his heir, he would have been temperamentally incapable of keeping it secret. His real motive was certainly the very simple one that there was no other leading Conservative who would be accepted by the Labour Party, and no Labour minister who would be accepted by the Conservatives. Eden, as Churchill wrote to the king, was the outstanding minister in the largest political party in the House of Commons.[36]

In making Eden Leader of the House a few months later, he laid a very heavy and time-consuming burden on an already overworked man, which made the Permanent Under-Secretary at the Foreign Office, Sir Alexander Cadogan, complain bitterly in his diary of the impossibility of discussing matters with the Foreign Secretary. Churchill clearly could not understand that a man so much younger than himself could lack his own strength and power of recuperation, or that by over-straining him he was gaining a rather unfair advantage in his long wrangles with him over foreign policy.

But Eden on his side got some gain from his Leadership of the House, even if it drained his physical energy. His close contact with parliamentary opinion made it easy for him to use the threat of trouble or even a revolt in the House as a means of stopping the Prime Minister doing things Eden disliked. His good relations with the Labour leaders, Attlee and Bevin, enabled him to use them as allies in the War Cabinet against Churchill's wilder or more dangerous plans, especially when Churchill was out of the country and Attlee took the chair at Cabinet meetings. And Eden also knew when he could count on Labour sympathy in the House.

Another card in Eden's hand was his friendliness – at that time – with leading journalists, based on his personal charm, willingness to seem to seek their views, and championship of the anti-appeasement cause in the pre-war years. One most independent-minded journalist said many years later, half joking, that he had then had almost a passion for Eden; another, in those days on the far Left, said Eden had stood for what he and his friends believed in.[37] On the other hand Churchill, though he had practised journalism, never called a meeting of lobby correspondents and apparently only gave one wartime Press conference in London, which was a bad failure.[38] He was, however, on good terms with the Press magnates – according to Harold Macmillan, 'partly because he had a high opinion of their influence and partly because he had depended upon them in certain periods of his life for a substantial part of his income'.[39]

On Churchill's side was his extraordinary power of using words to sway both Parliament and people, his precious gift of oratory. Eden lacked this. His speeches were dull and unadventurous in their wording and were later described by one historian as cliché-ridden;[40] a senior Foreign Office official said that he removed any striking phrase from any speech that had been drafted for him.[41] By contrast, his minutes to Churchill were written in a limpid, direct style – perhaps a response to the Prime Minister's own way of writing.

On Eden's side was the fact that he had at his back, urging him on and keeping him up to the mark, the Foreign Office, an institution with a great tradition of confidence in its unique wisdom and experience in its own special field. (At times this confidence might be misplaced, but it was the self-assurance which was important to Eden.) After he became Leader of the House, tied down in the Commons on at least three days in the week,[42] more and more of the work fell on his senior officials, especially Cadogan who also, in Eden's absence, represented the Foreign Office in dealings with Churchill, who at such times took over with some glee the role of Acting Foreign Secretary. Cadogan had no hesitation in standing up to Churchill or urging Eden to do so. Eden knew that if he gave way too easily to Churchill he might lose his own department's respect, which he valued very highly.

For much of the time, and especially after he became Leader of the House, Eden was the protagonist of the ideas and policies of his department, unless they happened to run up against his personal principles or prejudices, rather than their creator. His own officials did not regard him as an originator of policy, rather as a man with a very keen and accurate sense of timing and a skilful negotiator.[43]

Churchill liked to carp at the Foreign Office, taunting them for long-windedness[44] and for producing documents where odd and even paragraphs gave both sides of the case. He also liked to give little curtain lectures on the art of diplomacy as he saw it, particularly on the importance at certain times of doing nothing and keeping silent: 'It always seems to me that so much of diplomacy consists of waiting. . . . There should be intervals.' To one unfortunate diplomat he wrote: 'I do not understand this extraordinary itch to be doing something every day.'[45]

But the prestige of the Foreign Office was such, and Churchill's rather grudging respect for it sufficiently strong, for him to refrain from using his own personal advisers as rival policy-makers. He very often discussed foreign questions in a general way – perhaps over dinner – with Professor Lindemann (Lord Cherwell), but did not use him in any real sense as an adviser. The one exception was when Lindemann – in Eden's absence – persuaded him to support the Morgenthau Plan for the 'pastoralisation' of Germany when this was unexpectedly put forward by the Americans at the 1944 Quebec conference.

Another exception was that after the fall of France Churchill gave special duties to his old friend of the Secret Intelligence Service, Major Desmond Morton, in relation to France, and used him as a go-between in his dealings with de Gaulle. But when Eden objected this arrangement gradually lapsed, which caused Morton some distress.[46]

Eden for his part took good care to ward off any interference in the handling of foreign policy, except from Churchill himself. When Eden first got the job of Foreign Secretary Churchill arranged that Halifax, while ambassador in Washington, would still have a place in the War Cabinet whenever in London; this helped to make Halifax go quietly. But Eden wrote to Churchill a few days after taking over to ask him to 'make it plain that responsibility for advising the Prime Minister and War Cabinet on the conduct of foreign policy is that of the Foreign

Secretary and of the Foreign Secretary alone. This responsibility extends, of course, to the whole sphere of foreign policy. . . . We can none of us wish to re-enter a period of divided responsibility in foreign policy. . . .'[47]

As for Lord Cherwell, Eden did not lightly forgive him his interference over the Morgenthau Plan. When, a few months after the 1944 Quebec conference, Morgenthau was again pressing his views on harsh treatment of Germany and Cherwell backed them in minutes to Churchill, Eden wrote to Cadogan: 'I resent, perhaps too readily, Lord Cherwell's interference in our affairs;' he seemed to him 'to show little understanding of our problems and to be obstinate, even obtuse'.[48]

The man who had the most serious chance of interfering in foreign policy from the sidelines was Churchill's old crony, Beaverbrook. Yet in 1942 Eden used him with some skill as an ally in his efforts to overcome opposition from prominent Conservatives – and, at first, from Churchill himself – to an Anglo-Soviet treaty. Later in the war Beaverbrook's ardent pro-Russian feelings were sometimes a nuisance, though not a serious threat, to Eden.

Churchill enjoyed talking to Beaverbrook but would not let him influence decisions in which he was not concerned as a minister. In April 1945 Churchill wrote to Eden: 'I had a long talk with Max the other night because I like to hear the Russian case stated at its maximum. I thought you might be interested to read his notes.'[49] Perhaps Max was responsible for some of Churchill's violent swings of feeling for and against the Soviet Union. But there is little sign that Eden feared or resented him. In the latter part of the war Beaverbrook's defiant stand against all real or imagined American efforts to enslave Britain and break up the Empire came in useful, up to a point, in stiffening Churchill's defence of British interests against Roosevelt. Eden sometimes thought Beaverbrook made tactical mistakes or went too far, but on balance found him a healthy influence.

So Eden was very much better off than the wretched U.S. Secretary of State, Cordell Hull. Churchill very seldom did things behind Eden's back or over his head; he kept him informed and when possible consulted him in advance. (He liked to have his own sources of political information, independent of the Foreign Office, but that was rather different.) Roosevelt, on the other hand, worried very little about informing or consulting his elderly and somewhat crotchety Secretary of State unless he wanted to make use of him in frustrating Churchill or keeping the U.S. Congress sweet. Bypassing Hull, he relied heavily for advice on foreign problems on his friend, Harry Hopkins, and his old naval crony, Admiral William

Leahy, and liked to take one or other with him on his foreign missions. He was determined whenever possible *not* to take Hull with him to such meetings; Churchill took Eden with him whenever political issues were at stake, unless Roosevelt vetoed this in order to exclude Hull.

If Eden was lucky in this respect, he suffered sometimes from Churchill's overpowering impulse to go personally to the main scene of drama, especially if there was any physical danger involved, as in Egypt after the fall of Tobruk or in Athens during the civil war of December 1944. This meant that he did not let Eden do as many foreign trips on his own as he would have liked. After the Yalta conference in February 1945, for instance, it had been arranged that Eden should go alone to Athens, but he was again baulked by Churchill. Cadogan noted in his diary, 'Anthony of course delighted at the idea of a trip on his own and not as a member of the Prime Minister's suite. But the P.M. evidently had second thoughts about allowing Anthony to go gathering laurels on his own, and announced that he would come with us tomorrow – to Anthony's rage and horror. It's rather like travelling with Melba and Tetrazzini in one company.'[50]

But at other moments Churchill – when Eden was thwarted by someone other than himself – could be warmly sympathetic. After the launching of *Overlord*, Churchill rushed to visit the troops in France as soon as he possibly could, and was enormously exhilarated. Eden was longing to follow in his footsteps, if possible accompanying King George VI. But there was no room for him in the party. He wrote to Churchill on a slip of paper: 'My little jaunt is off. . . . But I shall swim to Cherbourg. . . .' Churchill wrote back: 'I will arrange it in a little while. . . . I am so sorry. W.'[51]

Eden was a naturally ambitious and perhaps vain man, always eager to be 'doing something', as Cadogan complained,[52] and was bound to be frustrated and irked by the fact that it was Churchill who got the foreign trips and the limelight. He grumbled to Cadogan once about 'the P.M.'s galumphing about and meddling with everything'.[53] But he swallowed his bile, partly because of real affection for Churchill, partly because of Churchill's self-mockery: 'I see what you mean – you think I would be like a fat old bluebottle on a cowpat,' or 'There is old Anthony thinking all I want is a joy ride. He has got it all wrong . . . I bear no rancour.'[54]

Finally, there was for Eden the prospect of the succession – and Churchill was apt to joke about this, too, telling Eden that he himself must be allowed to go where he liked and anyway, if he was killed, 'it would have been a good way to die and I should only have come into my inheritance sooner'.[55]

Within this broad framework of mutual affection, irritation, anger and tolerance, the dialogue between Churchill and Eden over foreign policies, disclosed in their wartime minutes rather than their memoirs, was a series of serious and sometimes sharp arguments over the options open to Britain in the war years. At home, Churchill's mastery of any situation was strictly bounded by pressures from the Chiefs of Staff, from Eden and the Foreign Office, from the Labour leaders and others in the War Cabinet, from the Conservative Party establishment, by Parliament and the Press. In foreign affairs he was bounded by the steady dwindling of Britain's military and economic strength in relation to the rapid rise of the power of the two great Allies, the United States and the Soviet Union.

The options open to the British, therefore, narrowed steadily as the war went on. But real choices, on matters vitally important not just for the war itself but also for the post-war world, continued to confront them. If they made fewer wrong choices and more sensible choices than they might have done, this was partly due to the Churchill–Eden dialogue.

Eden himself, just before his death, pointed to three major blunders made by Britain's enemies: Hitler's attack on Russia, the Japanese attack on the Americans at Pearl Harbor, and 'the extraordinary action of Hitler and Mussolini after Pearl Harbor' in declaring war on the United States.[56] If Hitler, Mussolini and the Japanese warlords had been subjected to the same pressures as Churchill and, like Churchill, had freely though grumblingly accepted them, they might never have committed these blunders, and Britain might never have survived. The great thing in war is to make fewer mistakes than the enemy.

PART TWO

Churchill, Eden, de Gaulle

CHAPTER TWO

De Gaulle or Pétain?

One of Churchill's wartime staff, the perceptive John Colville,[1] wrote later that 'Churchill attached paramount importance to personal contacts in politics and especially in foreign affairs.'[2] He added that it would be wrong to assume that Churchill's friendships were political, even though their inspiration might be so; he was naturally affectionate, and it was difficult for him not to become fond of people once he had come to know them, and his liking for Roosevelt, as later for Truman and Eisenhower, was entirely sincere.[3]

The three most important foreign policy issues which faced Churchill and Eden during the war were Britain's relations with the United States, the Soviet Union, and western Europe, notably France; or, since Churchill thought in terms of personal contacts, with Roosevelt, Stalin and Charles de Gaulle. From the point of view of winning the European war, Roosevelt and Stalin were, of course, very much more important than de Gaulle. However useful the contribution of the French armed forces and the French Resistance may have been from 1943 on, it was very small compared with the Soviet and U.S. roles in the defeat of Hitler. In the longer perspective of the role of France and its neighbours in post-war Europe, relations with de Gaulle could be of great significance, both for the British and for other Europeans.

This, at least, was the opinion of the Foreign Office and of Eden from quite early on. Churchill, channelling his main energies into winning the war, took a much less urgent interest in the future of France. Moreover, though to him 'the United States' meant 'Roosevelt' and 'Russia' meant 'Stalin', he strongly resisted the idea that 'France' meant 'de Gaulle'. This was partly because of his friend Roosevelt's personal feud with de Gaulle. But it was also because he could never get from de Gaulle the kind of personal response he looked for in his contacts with Allied leaders – a spontaneous human warmth, a willingness both to make and to appreciate a generous gesture, the shared joke, a somewhat romantic sense of comradeship-in-arms. Even from Stalin he seemed to get these things at times, though many unpleasant things as well.

From de Gaulle he very seldom got such responses, even when he made a special effort to bury hatchets and restore peace and friendship. He also obviously had his own idea of what a French patriot and gallant soldier ought to be; General Giraud and General Georges were much nearer to it than de Gaulle who, as the war went on, increasingly assumed a cold reserve, a high dignity, the well-timed rebuff or calculated insult, as the right weapons for a French leader in circumstances which he saw as humiliating. If, as Colville wrote, Churchill was naturally affectionate, de Gaulle certainly was not, at least in his dealings with his allies. Churchill would have liked to like de Gaulle, but de Gaulle would not let him.

Churchill's own sense of hierarchy and code of behaviour impelled him to show respect or deference and to be lavish in his gratitude where these seemed due; he also expected the same respect or gratitude from others. He got little of either from de Gaulle who thought such things contrary to the honour of France.

Eden seems to have found it much easier to admire de Gaulle and to forgive his extreme 'awkwardness' and often baseless suspicions of Britain, and was much less influenced by Roosevelt's preconceptions and prejudices than Churchill. The official British historian, Sir Llewellyn Woodward, described the differences between Churchill and de Gaulle as 'sharp' and wrote that 'in his attitude towards General de Gaulle the Prime Minister seemed at times to the Foreign Office to show less than his usual generosity. . . . He came understandably, though without full cause, to distrust and suspect his political aims.'[4] This seems rather an understatement. Desmond Morton, who watched the two men at close quarters, wrote later of Churchill: 'He never liked de Gaulle. Those two wildly differing personalities were never likely to see eye to eye. . . . He supported him very grudgingly. . . . Winston never believed that de Gaulle in person would rule France after the war. . . . He stuck to de Gaulle because he failed to find an older soldier, let alone a known French politician, to take his place.'[5]

The official historian of S.O.E.'s work in France gave a different summing up: 'Churchill's temper was as strong and as hasty as the General's own, and their relation during the war was one of amity punctuated by intermittent rows, some of them of substantial size. But they always healed their quarrels.'[6] The documents of the case certainly bear out the quarrels but from 1942 on reveal little of the amity. At times Churchill was not only angry with de Gaulle but showed positive dislike, tempered by a certain unwilling admiration. De Gaulle's own memoirs suggest that this dislike, along with an even more grudging admiration, were fully reciprocated.

Eden's unhappy task was to try to mollify first one, then the other, prevent an irreparable breach and work for compromises which would save face on both sides – and, if possible, save Roosevelt's face too, though Eden refused to give this such high priority as Churchill did. He liked the General well enough to exert his charm and conciliatory skills willingly; he probably got pleasure from trying to make Churchill go against Roosevelt's wishes. Between the wars he had been, as Churchill put it, 'a devoted adherent of the French Entente', and accepted without question the strongly held conviction of his senior officials that a strong and friendly France was a vital British long-term interest. The fall of France had made this, for the Foreign Office, an article of faith which it would be heresy to question. William Strang,[7] who played a leading part in shaping policy towards de Gaulle, was a firm believer. Churchill accepted the faith but would not agree that it meant backing de Gaulle through thick and thin.

Churchill's first impressions of de Gaulle, in the first half of June 1940, were good. He took Eden with him to visit the French Prime Minister, Paul Reynaud, Marshal Pétain and General Weygand on 12 June when, as Churchill told the War Cabinet, it was clear that France was near the end of organised resistance. Pétain, according to Reynaud, had made up his mind that peace must be made with the Germans. Weygand said that if the present position of the French forces collapsed, he would not be responsible for any attempt to carry on the struggle, though he would serve under any other officer. But, Churchill told the Cabinet, de Gaulle 'was all in favour of carrying on guerrilla warfare. He was young and energetic and had made a favourable impression. . . . It seemed probable that if the present government collapsed, M. Reynaud would turn to General de Gaulle to take command.'

Eden, for his part, said French politicians favouring a deal with the Germans might be strong enough to overthrow Reynaud. Churchill told the Cabinet there might then be two French governments, one which made peace and one which organised resistance in the colonies and with the fleet and carried on guerrilla warfare. From what he had said earlier about de Gaulle, it looked as though he might have had de Gaulle in mind for the second sort of government.[8] De Gaulle himself said two years later that it was on this occasion that he had decided to carry on the fight in Britain.[9]

Four days later de Gaulle was in London on a mission from Reynaud and found himself involved in a project to issue a declaration on Anglo-

French Union which might dramatically halt the disintegration in France. Leo Amery, Secretary of State for India but passionately interested in Europe, was pressing some such move on Churchill. Sir Arthur Salter, distinguished economist turned senior government official, had a hand in it. De Gaulle was drawn in by Jean Monnet, then French economic representative in London, later founding father of the European Communities, and his colleague René Pleven.[10] On 16 June Churchill told the War Cabinet that he had seen de Gaulle who had urged that some very dramatic move was essential to give Reynaud the essential support to keep his government in the war, and said this might be a proclamation of indissoluble union. Halifax reported that Sir Robert Vansittart, diplomatic adviser to the government, de Gaulle, Monnet, Pleven and Desmond Morton of Churchill's staff had drafted a proclamation and de Gaulle wanted to take it back with him that night.

Churchill admitted that 'his first instinct had been against the idea' but he was encouraged to find a body of opinion in the War Cabinet in favour. The Cabinet approved the draft, authorised de Gaulle to take it back to Reynaud, telephoning him in advance in time for his crucial government meeting at 5 p.m., and suggested that Churchill and the Labour and Liberal Party leaders should meet Reynaud as quickly as possible.[11]

It was all too late to stop the rot. Reynaud resigned and the next day Pétain formed a government. De Gaulle returned very briefly to France, realised there was nothing he could do there, and came back to England.

By then it must have been obvious that this relatively junior general had political as well as military potential. The War Cabinet was probably not surprised when in the late morning of 18 June they were told by the Minister of Information, Duff Cooper, that de Gaulle had given him the text of a broadcast he wanted to make, saying that France was not defeated and inviting all French soldiers to rally to him. Churchill was not there, and Chamberlain was in the chair; the War Cabinet agreed that 'it was undesirable that General de Gaulle, as *persona non grata* to the present French government, should broadcast at the present time, so long as it was still possible that the French government would act in a way conformable to the interests of the Alliance'. (In other words, it was hoped that Pétain might strike a hard bargain with the Germans and at least keep the French fleet out of German hands.) But in spite of this decision, later in the day 'the members of the War Cabinet . . . were consulted again individually . . . and it was agreed that General de

Gaulle should be allowed to broadcast, which he accordingly did the same evening'.[12]

Since Churchill had not been at the morning meeting, it seems likely that he was responsible for this change of heart. Eden *had* been there but had presumably not opposed the decision against the broadcast.

Four days later the War Cabinet, with Churchill in the chair, again discussed whether de Gaulle should broadcast. The Admiralty was anxious not to upset the feelings of the French navy and was against. Lord Lloyd, who had just visited Bordeaux, said he had been told by many French officers there that, but for de Gaulle's earlier broadcast, they would never have known of the opportunity to continue the struggle alongside Britain. For the Foreign Office, Lord Halifax said he was in favour. It was agreed that de Gaulle should broadcast.[13]

On the next day, Sunday, 23 June, in the light of the armistice concluded between Pétain and the Germans, de Gaulle broadcast that a French National Committee was to be formed in agreement with the British government, and a statement was also broadcast that the British government would recognise 'such a provisional French National Committee' fully representing independent French elements. But the War Cabinet had not yet decided on this and as from midnight the British statement was banned from the air and the late editions of the newspapers, on Halifax's instructions. Perhaps Churchill had out-distanced the Cabinet.[14]

But by 28 June the situation had grown clearer and Halifax proposed that, following a further broadcast by de Gaulle, a statement should be made that 'His Majesty's Government recognise General de Gaulle as the leader of all free Frenchmen, wherever they may be, who rally to him in support of the Allied cause'. The Cabinet, with Churchill in the chair, agreed.[15]

So within ten days of de Gaulle's first broadcast he had achieved recognition by the British government on very broad and vague terms which could well justify him in believing he would soon be accepted as an Allied leader on equal terms with the exiled governments already based in London. Churchill's impetuosity had certainly been a major factor; Halifax was a little more cautious but on the whole the Foreign Office had been ready to pin their faith on de Gaulle. To give his cause the necessary financial, material and legal backing, an agreement was negotiated with him. (For the Foreign Office, Strang was deeply involved.) On 5 August Churchill told the War Cabinet of minor difficulties which had arisen (one was the British refusal to guarantee the exact frontiers of any country) and how they were being solved. The Cabinet gave its approval.[16]

As a result of this agreement, Britain started subsidising and supplying the de Gaulle movement; a year later the annual cost was reckoned at about £8 million a year. Of this about £380,000 was credited to the movement each month, of which £170,000 was, by September 1941, earmarked for Free French West Africa. The rest was accounted for by armaments and supplies provided by the British service departments.[17]

The total cost to Britain of backing de Gaulle was therefore small; but so also, in those early days, had been the response to de Gaulle's appeal to the French to follow him. Not surprisingly, Churchill, always an optimist, went on hoping that at least some elements in the Pétain regime in Vichy would come over to the Allied side bringing French North Africa with them. After all, both Pétain and General Weygand, now Pétain's representative in North Africa, had been famous Allied commanders in the First World War. On 23 and 25 July – before the agreement with de Gaulle had been signed – Churchill sent minutes to Halifax proposing that he should send a secret message to Weygand.

> I want to promote a kind of collusive conspiracy with the Vichy government whereby certain members of that government, perhaps with the consent of those who remain, will levant to North Africa in order to make a better bargain for France....

Halifax thought it was too early, and doubted whether Weygand was the right man : 'I should have thought rather that we should have to find suitable leaders in France who are not identified either with the old regime or with the present Vichy government.'[18]

But Churchill persisted in his idea. At the end of August 1940 de Gaulle had his first success in the French empire, when French Equatorial Africa and the Cameroons declared for him. In September, however, came the Dakar operation – the first in which de Gaulle and the British co-operated – which ended badly. This did not make Churchill turn against de Gaulle; he told the House of Commons early in October that the government 'have no intention whatever of abandoning the cause of General de Gaulle until it is merged, as merged it will be, in the larger cause of France'. This, of course, left it open to Churchill to contact other French elements if he could find them but safeguarded de Gaulle's position. The worst effect of the Dakar fiasco, from the General's angle, was the suspicion by some of the British, still more the Americans, that the failure was due to leaks or worse from de Gaulle's London headquarters. This gave

Roosevelt a stick he was to beat de Gaulle with for a long time to come.

In October Churchill was pursuing his efforts to get a message through to Weygand. At the end of the month he proposed to Halifax that de Gaulle should be told that 'we have communicated with General Weygand, or tried to. In view of our relations with de Gaulle, and engagements signed, he has a right to feel assured we are not throwing him over.'[19]

De Gaulle might not like this, but there was not much he could do about it. The Americans, who maintained relations with Vichy, were in a stronger position to help or hinder. That autumn Roosevelt instructed the diplomat Robert Murphy to make an 'inspection tour' of French North Africa, and to report directly to him, bypassing the State Department Murphy learnt in Algiers in December that Weygand had received Churchill's message promising British support if he acted, but had sent it to Pétain in Vichy, considering 'such furtive manoeuvres behind Pétain's back a reflection on both Churchill's intelligence and honour', adding, 'This confirms my distrust of Churchill's judgement.'[20]

Churchill was trying to contact Pétain as well as Weygand. At the end of the year Eden replaced Halifax as Foreign Secretary and Churchill gave instructions that Eden was to be kept in continuous touch with this matter. Eden's first proposal was not a happy one. On 10 January 1941 he suggested that Churchill should ask Roosevelt to instruct his new ambassador in Vichy, Admiral William D. Leahy, to pass a message to Pétain.[21] Eden at this stage obviously did not know about Leahy's warm sympathy with Pétain and the Vichy government and his ingrained, childish suspicion of Britain.

Roosevelt sent the instructions to Leahy, whose reaction, as reported by Eden to Churchill, was crushing: 'Marshal Pétain has not the slightest intention of going to North Africa or of transferring his government. . . . I trust that the present message as well as future ones can be altered in form before delivery.'[22] Meanwhile, from Weygand – who obviously thought he could get something out of Churchill's message – came a request for supplies, linked with a vague promise that Morocco would one day resume the fight.[23]

De Gaulle thought that he could now get into the act. At the beginning of February he proposed to Eden that Free France – his own movement – should borrow or buy on credit arms, ammunition and petrol from the U.S. and keep them ready for shipment to North Africa immediately Weygand decided to fight, at which point the Free French would 'join those under the command of General Weygand and . . . all the partisans of Free France in North and Occidental Africa would help in strengthening his authority in these territories'. This looked like an offer to place himself under Weygand's command. Desmond Morton minuted to Churchill that this proposal was of great interest and should be examined in detail without delay. But Eden wrote to de Gaulle stressing the difficulties and concluding in lukewarm words: 'The idea is an interesting one and if there were any variant of it which seemed likely to be practicable, I should be glad to discuss it at any time with you.' Churchill adopted Morton's suggestion that a special committee should examine the idea.[24]

De Gaulle also suggested that he himself should send a letter to Weygand and produced a text. The Foreign Office wanted Churchill to press the General to phrase it more warmly, but Churchill left it unchanged.[25] So at this stage de Gaulle was still thinking of an alliance with Weygand, and the Foreign Office still had hopes that this might succeed.

Churchill, however, was impatient and was beginning to get fed up with Weygand, thinking Weygand's request for supplies no fit response to his own message. He minuted to the Foreign Office in mid-February:

> We have made Weygand great offers to which we have had no reply. . . . Our attitude . . . should not be one of approach to him. Until he has answered through some channel or other the telegram I sent him he ought not to be given supplies. Not one scrap of nobility or courage has been shown by these people so far, and they had better go on short commons till they come to their senses.

Even more angrily he minuted to the Chiefs of Staff: 'It is impossible to base a policy upon this grovelling crowd. . . . For the present our attitude should remain reserved and indeterminate.'[26]

The Americans were all for sending supplies to Weygand, but certainly not through de Gaulle. Murphy, who had a long talk with Roosevelt in the autumn of 1940, wrote later that 'the French Africa policy of the U.S. government . . . became the President's personal policy. He initiated it, he kept it going, and he resisted pressures against it, until in the autumn of 1942 French North Africa became the first major battleground where Americans fought Germans.' But to Murphy Roosevelt 'barely mentioned Charles de Gaulle'. He had apparently 'already decided that he need not consider him a major factor in French affairs. The President's only reference to him was to say that the ill-fated attempt to capture Dakar confirmed his poor opinion of de Gaulle's judgement.' Murphy added that Roosevelt never lost this distrust of de Gaulle's judgement and discretion, and this was a major factor in French–American relations right up to the President's death.[27]

So there was no chance of the Americans channelling supplies to North Africa through de Gaulle. But they did want to cultivate the friendship of Pétain and Weygand and to send supplies for this purpose. The British, trying hard to impose an effective blockade, were against this on principle, but both Churchill and Eden felt it necessary in the last resort to yield to Roosevelt's wishes. In September 1941, for instance, when there was argument over the despatch of American fuel oil to North Africa, Eden minuted: 'Dalton [the Minister of Economic Warfare] proposes, and I agree, to accept the situation. . . . The only alternative would be to challenge the U.S. policy of aid for General Weygand and I am sure that it would not be in our interests to do so.' Churchill answered: 'We must submit, after stating our case.' In November Churchill minuted to Eden: 'I think it most important that the U.S. should continue their relations with Vichy and their supplies to North Africa, and any other contact, unostentatiously for the present.'[28]

When at this time Hitler and Mussolini declared war on the U.S. and so brought America into the European war, Roosevelt's personal interest in French North Africa blossomed into the idea of an eventual American military operation there. In January 1942 he told Churchill that he had sent Pétain a statement of American policy through Leahy:

It is most important for the French government and the French people to realise that the President of the U.S. is about the best friend they have; that one of his greatest wishes is to see France reconstituted in the post-war period, in accordance with its splendid position in history. . . . Resistance by the French against German or Italian attack . . . would have not only the moral support of the U.S., but it would also have the physical support of the U.S. by every possible military and naval assistance we could bring to bear.

Pétain's discouraging reply to this was that his government 'would resist any invasion by the Gaullists, the Germans, the British or the Americans'.[29] But this did not dim the enthusiasm of Roosevelt and Leahy for working through Vichy, or their firm belief that the French looked above all to the Americans for their salvation.

Churchill was quite happy with Roosevelt's message to Pétain and minuted to Eden at the end of January:

The President's idea is that we keep the lead as patrons of the Free French while the U.S. try to maintain contacts with Vichy. The Vichy contacts are extremely important at the present time, in view of certain projects which are being considered. . . . It is on the influence of the U.S. on Vichy that I count for the decisive reactions in France.

39

'Certain projects' meant the plan for an operation in North Africa which was to be codenamed *Torch*. Churchill fully shared Roosevelt's enthusiasm for it.

At this point Eden began to rebel, and answered Churchill:

> I am all for the U.S. strengthening their contacts with Vichy, provided the Allied war effort will be helped thereby. I doubt however whether it is wise to count on U.S. influence with Vichy for decisive reactions in France. . . . The Americans have shown themselves all too ready to give in to . . . blackmail. . . . The Americans are in a very strong position in regard to Vichy. They can in my opinion adopt a much firmer attitude.[30]

Churchill went on thinking that the Foreign Office was making mountains out of molehills over the American pro-Vichy policy and practice. At the time of a dispute between the Foreign Office and the State Department in July 1942, he minuted to Eden: 'It is a pity to haggle and bargain over this. So many more important issues are at stake.' That, of course, meant *Torch*. But when Eden replied that there might be criticism in Parliament if he gave way in this matter, so he thought it 'worth while to return to the charge with the State Deparment', Churchill acquiesced.[31]

So the pattern of later Churchill–Eden arguments over American policy towards the French was already set in 1942. The arguments were to sharpen into conflict after *Torch*.

CHAPTER THREE

The End of the Honeymoon

Churchill and Eden fell out not only over American policy to Vichy but also over de Gaulle and Churchill's growing dislike of him. This in turn had causes unconnected with Roosevelt or Vichy.

Although the Churchill–de Gaulle relationship survived the Dakar fiasco more or less intact, British suspicions of bad security and leakages at Free French headquarters had the result that for a time the General was no longer consulted on military matters, and this hurt and annoyed him. But Churchill tried to make friendly gestures. When de Gaulle was in Cairo in the spring of 1941, Churchill sent him a letter thanking him warmly 'for the help which the Free French forces have given us in the victorious African campaign', adding, 'You who have never faltered nor failed in serving the common cause possess the fullest confidence of H.M.G. and you embody the hope of millions of Frenchmen and French-women.' In April he sent a telegram to de Gaulle in Brazzaville: 'I always pay the greatest attention to your telegrams and do my utmost to aid you in every way.'[1]

It was after the Syrian campaign of June–July 1941, planned in co-operation with de Gaulle and with Free French and British troops both engaged, that the first bad trouble with de Gaulle blew up. De Gaulle was disgusted by the terms of the armistice which the local British representatives concluded with the Vichy French in Syria and said he would not accept them – although his own representative had signed them. (The Foreign Office later took the view that the British military authorities had in fact been excessively generous in the armistice talks and made concessions which H.M.G. might not have approved if con-sulted.[2]) In an angry interview with the British Minister of State in Cairo, Oliver Lyttelton, de Gaulle threatened to withdraw Free French troops from the British Middle East Command and to move French parachutists to Syria, and said strong things about the behaviour of the British military men. Lyttelton managed to get him to sign a new agreement on French acceptance of the British Command. But de Gaulle then went to Syria and behaved, according to a British account, 'with extreme arrogance', though the Foreign Office later admitted that there had also been discourteous acts by the local British authorities.[3]

De Gaulle was eventually 'persuaded' to return to England. An incident on his way home made Churchill explode with wrath. He was told on 27 August that in Brazzaville de Gaulle had given an interview to an American journalist who reported that the General had made an offer of bases in French Africa to the U.S. – 'and we shall not ask for any destroyers in return' (a jeer at Britain's destroyers-for-bases agreement with the U.S.). He was also supposed to have said that England was afraid of the French navy and for that reason did not recognise de Gaulle; England was keeping open the Vichy channel with a view to an ultimate deal with Nazi Germany.[4]

This seems to have been an unfair summary of an interview which de Gaulle said he had not intended for publication. Nevertheless, since the failure of his own approach to Weygand earlier in the year, he must have been less tolerant than before towards British and American attitudes to Vichy. In any case, the report stung Churchill to the quick. He telegraphed to Lyttelton at once:

> If de Gaulle interview . . . is authentic he has clearly gone off his head. This would be a very good riddance and will simplify our further course. . . . De Gaulle has put himself entirely out of court. It is a pity you did not warn him as I said. Never mind.[5]

Fuller reports of the interview did not mollify him. He was angered afresh when the British representative in Brazzaville telegraphed that de Gaulle had been warning people there of the dangers of allowing the British to gain a grip on French territory and had told French officials that in one particular instance, had the British not given way, 'we should have been in the unfortunate position of having to fight our allies'. The General was also reported to have said (accurately enough, as things turned out) that not the British but the Americans would win the war. The British representative ended by suggesting that de Gaulle was 'finding the moral responsibility and mental strain of his position more and more exhausting. . . . Probably things might improve if he were able to take a rest.'[6]

Churchill was not so charitable. On 1 September he minuted to Eden that, although all contacts between the Free French in London and British departments should not be ended, certain matters should be 'allowed to rest in deadlock', and 'a generally chilling and dilatory attitude should be adopted towards all requests made by the Free French. No notice will be taken of General de Gaulle's arrival. . . . Should he desire an interview, he will be asked for explanations of his unfriendly conduct and absurd statements.'[7] On the same day the War Cabinet was told of these instructions and agreed that steps should be taken to prevent de Gaulle broadcasting that evening.[8] Morton reported to Churchill that de Gaulle's naval commander, Admiral Muselier, thought the General was suffering from megalomania.[9]

De Gaulle felt the chill as soon as he arrived in London. He wrote at once to Churchill, in his own hand, that he would be happy to be received by him. Churchill answered the next day that he had until recently been looking forward to seeing the General on his return,

> but the evidences I have since received of your unfriendly attitude ...
> towards the British nation have filled me with surprise and sorrow.
> ... Until I am in possession of any explanations you may do me the
> honour to offer, I am unable to judge whether any interviews between
> us would serve a useful purpose.[10]

On the same day de Gaulle saw Morton, and denied that he had spoken to Weller, the journalist, in a way which could be construed into any of the 'unfortunate statements' which had appeared in the American Press. He regretted his threat to move the French parachutists to Syria, saying he was in a violent temper at the time. His one object was to defeat Hitler at Britain's side, but if he honestly thought that the English contemplated doing anything damaging to French interests he must protest with all his might, otherwise Frenchmen would regard him as 'a mere English mercenary' and his value as a symbol of France would disappear. At present – Morton reported him as saying – he was only a small man with a small following, so his protests were louder and more frequent than if he were the recognised head of a great nation. If the situation were reversed, he was sure Churchill would do the same.[11]

De Gaulle followed up this interview with a typewritten letter to Churchill saying that he understood very well why he should want certain explanations: 'Moi-même suis désireux de vous donner ces éclaircissements' – which he then did at some length, concluding that he had come to London to settle things with Churchill with the aim of complete harmony between the two allied peoples.[12]

This letter was as near an apology as de Gaulle was ever likely to make. But if Churchill was inclined to soften, Morton hardened his mood again by reporting on 9 September that some of the Free French were getting 'nearly as tired as we are of their chief's ungovernable temper and lack of balanced judgement'. But, Morton added, there was no one in London to replace him, and it would be hard to bring anyone from

France for the purpose, 'since the name of de Gaulle had become synonymous in France itself with liberation from the German yoke'. Some of the French in London, Morton wrote, were earnestly wondering how they could create a council to control the General's political actions. But, Morton added, 'I fear they will not get far beyond wondering.'[13]

Churchill seized this idea and decided to give it a push. On 12 September he received de Gaulle and they discussed their various differences in conciliatory mood. Churchill then said that it would be in the Free French interest to form an effective council with which H.M.G. could deal; this would give the movement a broader basis and encourage support for it in France and elsewhere. De Gaulle agreed but feared to 'bring into play political factors endangering unanimity'; however, he might call a congress of Free French representatives early in 1942. This was not good enough for Churchill, who said that, while he wished to avoid diminishing de Gaulle's stature as a champion of continued resistance to the enemy, he felt action should be taken now. He warned him that 'already some British figures entertained a suspicion that General de Gaulle had become hostile and had moved towards certain Fascist views'.[14]

Churchill's words must have seemed to de Gaulle both offensive and a piece of meddling in French affairs. Yet he saw a danger signal and decided he must do something, but when it came to forming a council or committee there was turmoil. A number of the French in London were very critical of de Gaulle and made their feelings known with great vehemence to influential British contacts. At this moment they tried to use Admiral Muselier as their mouthpiece and as candidate for the post of head of the proposed committee. In the free-for-all which followed Muselier declared that, whatever happened, he intended that the Free French navy should be entirely at Britain's disposal for the duration of the war. He was reported to have told de Gaulle that, unless some form of democratic control were established in the Free French movement, he would place himself and the navy under the absolute direction of the British Admiralty. De Gaulle then told the Admiralty that he was proposing to dismiss Muselier.[15]

Desmond Morton, in close touch with all sides, telephoned his view to Churchill: Muselier was pro-British, a first-class sailor, a democrat, an adventurer, and quite unsuitable to lead the Free French movement. De Gaulle and his supporters, chiefly army officers, stood for 'an extreme right-wing outlook'. His opponents were liberals and socialists. De Gaulle wanted a committee of devoted yes-men, which would make it useless for the purposes Churchill wanted. Morton added that feeling was particularly high among the 'malcontents' because the General had turned his own secret service into a sort of Gestapo to report to him what his followers said about him; it was in the charge of 'a young man of under thirty called Passy, who . . . holds extreme right political views and is considered dangerously inefficient by Brigadier Menzies and others of our own secret people'.[16] Sir Stewart Menzies was chief of the Secret Intelligence Service, and so a bad enemy for de Gaulle to have made.

In this situation Churchill intervened to prevent an open break between de Gaulle and Muselier, and an open scandal. He saw de Gaulle on 23 September, and rejected the General's request that the British Admiralty should support him if he dismissed the admiral. He said it would be most unfortunate if discouragement set in in France as a result of a breach in the Free French leadership in Britain; and an attempt to 'divert the allegiance of the Free French sailors' in the process could not be tolerated. Churchill said he wanted to think things over and asked de Gaulle not to act against Muselier until they had met again. De Gaulle agreed.[17]

While Churchill was thinking he received a note from the Earl of Bessborough, head of the French Welfare Section of the Foreign Office, and a very strong critic of de Gaulle. Bessborough gave a list of the men de Gaulle wanted on his committee, saying two were abroad and the others yes-men; 'Muselier and his sympathisers hold out for a council not containing de Gaulle'. The General was about to announce his committee.[18] (Bessborough was on Christian-name terms with Churchill.)

At this point – on 23 September – Churchill took the important decision to pass the baby to Eden, who so far – though he had seen the papers – had been outside the turmoil; Churchill seemed to prefer to rely on Morton both for advice on policy and as go-between with de Gaulle. This was damaging to Eden's authority and must have irked him. Along with the baby, Churchill sent Eden a brief. De Gaulle should not be allowed to announce the sort of committee he wanted since it might 'divide Frenchmen and excite ridicule in France'. But, since he had repeatedly expressed very unsuitable anti-British sentiments, he should form a committee by which he should be advised and with whom he should act. De Gaulle should be its accepted head and have definite executive powers, but on fundamental issues and broad policy matters he must be guided by his colleagues. Having invoked the Prime Minister's good offices, he should confer with Muselier and a British representative on the best way of achieving this. Finally, Churchill wrote, control of the Free French secret service must be vested in someone acceptable to the new council and to H.M.G. (This was obviously aimed against Passy.) Churchill concluded: 'The charge of all these matters is committed to the Secretary of State for Foreign Affairs' who should not hesitate to use whatever powers might be needed including 'the forcible restraint of individuals'.[19]

This sounded as though Churchill expected Eden to shut up de Gaulle in the Tower of London, or, anyhow, threaten to do so. But this cannot have been how the War Cabinet interpreted Churchill's brief, otherwise they would not have approved it as they did, including the transfer of responsibility to Eden. But before Eden could take action Churchill sent Morton to de Gaulle at 9.50 a.m. on 24 September, in theory simply to warn him to do nothing and say nothing until he had seen Eden. But Morton soon got involved in discussing the substance of the matter. De Gaulle said he must make an announcement about his committee as soon as he had seen Eden, otherwise he would look a fool. He then, Morton reported, 'launched forth in a tirade, which I stopped by inviting him to calm himself, whereupon he broke into laughter and spoke more moderately'. But he still claimed that Muselier had committed an act of rebellion by threatening to place the Free French navy at British disposal. However, Morton thought that a compromise between de Gaulle and Muselier should be possible. He sent a report of the interview to Churchill and a copy to Bessborough.[20]

As instructed by Churchill, Eden saw de Gaulle that evening along with Muselier and the First Lord of the Admiralty, but without Morton. A settlement was reached and a French National Committee was formed under de Gaulle but containing Muselier. Eden must have felt pleased with the outcome of his skill in conciliation. But the next day Bessborough sent an anguished letter to Churchill:

> I am horrified at the agreement which I understand was made at the F.O. last night when, it is understood, Muselier was obliged, under pressure from the First Lord, to agree to a Committee of Yes-men, which only confirms de Gaulle in his dictatorship. . . . I am convinced that if Morton, with his intimate knowledge of the problems and persons involved, had been present at the Foreign Office last night, no such disastrous agreement could have been made. . . . Yours ever, Vere.[21]

Churchill sent a message thanking Bessborough and saying, 'If the present arrangement does not work the government have power to enforce a better one.'[22]

Bessborough had succeeded in making Churchill feel that Eden had failed him. He sent a copy of his letter to Eden with an ACTION THIS DAY minute:

> This is very unpleasant. Our intention was to compel de Gaulle to accept a suitable council. All we have done is to compel Muselier and Co. to submit themselves to de Gaulle. I understood you were going to make sure that the resulting government represented what we want. . . . Our weight in the immediate future must be thrown more heavily against de Gaulle than I had hoped would be necessary. I am renewing my directions that he is on no account to leave the country.[23]

This stung Eden to anger, but he took it out on Bessborough and Morton, rather than Churchill:

> There are too many cooks stirring this broth. . . . Lord Bessborough like other critics speaks of 'yes-men' but does not tell us where the 'no-men' are to be found. The decision to try to bring Muselier and de Gaulle together was made by the Cabinet. . . . The Free French run round with their quarrels to anybody they can find who will listen to them, at one moment to the Foreign Office, at the next to Morton, at the third to Lord Bessborough. . . . If the task is to be entrusted to the Foreign Office, then instructions must be given to those to whom the various members of the Free French movement are in the habit of running . . . to refer them firmly here.

As a parting shot Eden wrote that the French trade unionist Henri Hauck, in whom Ernest Bevin had confidence as 'representing a sound Labour view', was to join the Committee.[24]

Whether Eden lost his temper spontaneously or by calculation, it worked. The same day he sent de Gaulle a letter according limited recognition. On 10 October there was a meeting between Churchill, de Gaulle and Oliver Lyttelton in an effort to stamp out the smouldering Anglo-French antagonism in Syria; both sides were conciliatory. Churchill then asked whether the new French National Committee had had a satisfactory beginning. De Gaulle said it was functioning smoothly, and he hoped to create an advisory council to include all prominent supporters of the movement throughout the world.[25]

But it soon became clear that the new French National Committee, as sponsored by Eden in September, was not having the effect of taming de Gaulle that Churchill had hoped for. At the end of 1941, in a mood of exasperation with those activities in France conducted by the Special Operations Executive independently of the Free French, de Gaulle proposed that he should take over S.O.E.'s French section. Eden, as the responsible minister, replied on 20 January 1942 that this could not be accepted: 'H.M.G. consider it essential for the proper functioning of the

British Intelligence Service and Mr Dalton's organisation [S.O.E.] that they should continue to maintain contact with any French elements inside or outside French territory through which they find it useful to operate. . . . It would not, we fear, be prudent to rely . . . on the assumption that the National Committee enjoys the adherence, open or secret, of a very large majority of French citizens.'[26]

The sharp tone of this reply may partly have been due to the fact that de Gaulle kept Passy as head of his secret service, in spite of his unpopularity with some British authorities. In spite of this, de Gaulle went on keeping Passy. And in January 1942 he set about getting rid of Muselier once again, and, in spite of urgent pleas from Eden and stern warnings from the War Cabinet,[27] he succeeded this time – without a public breach with the British and without causing any mutiny in the Free French navy. This was a great boost to de Gaulle's authority and control over his movement.

Churchill's decision in September 1941 to bring de Gaulle under some sort of democratic control, to make him more amenable to British wishes, and to entrust the task to Eden, had achieved very little. From then on he was inclined to think Eden soft on de Gaulle and to resent this. He went on believing that de Gaulle's thorny personality could somehow be cushioned and contained within a really effective committee. Eden had probably been sceptical about this from the start, and continued to be so.

But Churchill did not want to get de Gaulle under democratic control purely in order to get him under his own thumb. Perhaps he instinctively felt that de Gaulle's volcanic moods needed the same sort of restraints as those to which he himself submitted. And it is just possible that Churchill's wartime nagging and personal example of going quietly into opposition had a little long-term influence on the General. There was a side of de Gaulle to which military dictatorship must have seemed tempting. But it was a temptation which he just managed to resist.

CHAPTER FOUR

The Impact of Torch

Roosevelt thought of *Torch* – the plan for landings in French North Africa – as his own especial brain-child. Churchill also had a claim to fatherhood but was perfectly happy to yield it to Roosevelt if that would help to get the U.S. Chiefs of Staff to agree. But they disliked the child at the start and never learned to love it, so Churchill wanted to do his utmost to back up Roosevelt in every way.

Torch was therefore bound to have a big impact on British relations with de Gaulle, more particularly since Roosevelt was determined to have nothing whatever to do with him in the planning and execution of the operation. Until *Torch* came in view Churchill had never seriously considered throwing de Gaulle overboard, except in a brief fit of anger. He had taken umbrage at de Gaulle's actions on his own behalf or Britain's. Now he was quick to take umbrage on Roosevelt's behalf. De Gaulle, though he was kept in the dark, gradually became convinced that the Anglo-Americans, behind his back, were planning action in Africa affecting French interests, so he on his side was even more ready than before to take umbrage.

At first, Churchill's idea was not to get rid of de Gaulle but to keep him in play while Roosevelt wooed Vichy through Leahy in Vichy and Murphy in North Africa and their various agents. As Roosevelt's hopes of success in this undertaking soared upwards, the scales were tipped more and more heavily against de Gaulle. Eden stuck by the Foreign Office policy of support for de Gaulle and was more and more impressed by reports from France showing support for de Gaulle among resisters. He tried to right the balance. Morton, still active in Free French affairs in spite of Churchill's transfer of responsibility to Eden, went on playing a curiously ambiguous role. At times he seemed a convinced Gaullist, but he was constantly warning Churchill against the General and particularly against his claims to be undisputed leader of the Resistance forces in France. As a professional intelligence officer, he probably wanted to keep de Gaulle but to get him under firm British control. While Eden, as a politician, quite soon accepted that such control was impossible, Morton did not.

American entry into the war quickly knocked British relations with de Gaulle askew in the mini-crisis over the tiny islands of St Pierre and Miquelon lying close to the Newfoundland coast. They were under Vichy control and there was a wireless station there which worried the Canadians, British and Americans. In mid-October 1941 – well before the U.S. was pulled into the war – de Gaulle had proposed to Eden that Free French corvettes should 'rally' the islands to the Free French. Eden undertook to consult the Canadian and U.S. governments. On 9 December – two days after Pearl Harbor – Muselier said he was ready to move. Churchill told the Chiefs of Staff that he personally liked the idea; the Chiefs of Staff said they were strongly in favour of letting Muselier act 'without his saying anything about it until it had been done'. On 15 December Halifax was instructed to tell the Americans that the British had no objection to the operation but de Gaulle had been asked to wait for thirty-six hours.

The next day Halifax reported that the State Department had referred to Roosevelt who said he strongly opposed any action by the Free French in the islands. Within twenty-four hours William Strang of the Foreign Office told de Gaulle's Commissioner for Foreign Affairs, Maurice Dejean, of Roosevelt's views and said it was vital that any order for the operation should be cancelled; the Americans and Canadians were discussing what should be done with the wireless station. Dejean later telephoned to say that no orders had been given and none would be issued; Strang then wrote Dejean a letter putting all this in writing, and Dejean did not gainsay him. All that happened was that de Gaulle protested to Eden against any plan to take over the wireless station without consulting the Free French.

Without warning, Muselier sent a signal dated 24 December to the Admiralty, saying that on orders from de Gaulle and at the request of the inhabitants he had rallied St Pierre and Miquelon. A British naval liaison officer in the French vessel *Surcouf* reported that during 27 and 28 December the vessel patrolled the entrance to St Pierre harbour; Muselier expected the Americans to allow Vichy ships to intervene and gave orders to fire on any ships that were seen with the exception of British ships. The captain of the *Surcouf* commented: 'And if they are American, it will be just too bad.'[1]

Various things are puzzling about this sequence of events, in particular, perhaps, the British Admiralty's attitude to Muselier's coup. In the U.S. things seemed perfectly clear. Cordell Hull was furious, and the State Department made its displeasure public. They wanted to keep close to

Vichy, and they expected Vichy to be very angry. The U.S. Press, however, was delighted with the Free French exploit and slanged the State Department and Hull.

Just at this time Churchill was staying with Roosevelt at the White House in great friendliness and intimacy. He was bound to feel put out by the unpleasantness that de Gaulle was creating. De Gaulle, however, took the offensive, sending Churchill a message on 27 December complaining that the State Department's favouring of Vichy could do much harm to the spirit of resistance in France: 'It does not seem right to me that in war the prize should go to the apostles of dishonour. I am saying this to you because I know that you feel it and that you are the only one who can explain it in the right way.'[2] Churchill was softened, replying that he had pleaded de Gaulle's case strongly with the Americans; he only complained very mildly of de Gaulle's apparent breach of faith, concluding: 'I am always doing my best in all our interests.'[3] On the same day, visiting Ottawa, he made a speech pouring scorn on Vichy and praising the Free French.

On 4 January 1942 Eden telegraphed to Churchill that it would be extremely hard to get de Gaulle to withdraw from the islands, though he was willing to try. But as the Vichy government had apparently decided to sit back and see what the Americans and British were going to do, 'would it not be well for us all also to sit back and wait?' The next day he and Churchill talked on the telephone; Churchill agreed that the best thing was to keep quiet and do nothing and say nothing (in other words, to leave de Gaulle in possession).[4]

But this did not suit the Americans. At first Roosevelt seemed happy to sit back and watch the State Department getting into trouble; Hull at one time was on the verge of resigning. On 12 January, however, Roosevelt raised the matter urgently with Churchill, pressing him to consider it in connection with *Super-Gymnast* – the operation in north-west Africa later re-christened *Torch*. Because of this project, Roosevelt wanted to keep in with Vichy, so Churchill telegraphed to Eden that he favoured an arrangement – agreed with Roosevelt – by which the islands would 'remain French' (without specifying which France was in question) and would be neutralised and demilitarised (which meant that the Free French would withdraw) while the Americans and Canadians would supervise the wireless station. Eden should tell de Gaulle that this was 'our settled policy' and he must bow to it if he was to retain any measure of recognition. If he refused, the Americans were in a mood to use force – Roosevelt had mentioned the U.S. battleship *Arkansas* – or 'starvation without stint'. Cdurchill would not intervene to save the Free French. Eden was to consult the Cabinet if he wanted, but as Churchill was soon leaving Washington things must be fixed the next day.[5]

Faced with this ultimatum, Eden naturally summoned the Cabinet to his aid. After it had met Attlee, his ally, telegraphed to Churchill that the Cabinet felt British public opinion would not understand why de Gaulle was not allowed to occupy French territory which welcomed him; 'people will not appreciate going easy with Vichy'. Would not American democratic sentiment like the idea of a plebiscite? 'I do not think', Attlee concluded, 'that Cabinet will acquiesce in our compelling de Gaulle though they have agreed to Eden trying persuasion.'[6] Eden also telegraphed saying the Cabinet wanted certain points in Churchill's proposals cleared up. This Churchill did, after seeing Roosevelt, with surprising mildness: in effect, the islands would remain in the hands of those sympathetic to the Free French and the Vichy administrator would be removed.[7]

Urged on by Churchill over the telephone, Eden tackled de Gaulle on 14 January and pleaded with him to yield. De Gaulle said he could not allow the islands to be neutralised and demilitarised; nor could he accept Canadian–American supervision of the wireless station. Eden quoted Churchill as saying there was no other choice. The Americans would certainly act. De Gaulle asked: 'Will they open fire on my ships?' (Eden did not record what he answered; de Gaulle, in his own account, said he would open fire on the Americans.)

After this moment of drama de Gaulle said more calmly that he was anyhow intending to withdraw the Free French ships and might accept Canadian–American 'liaison officers' for the wireless station; but he was not prepared to make any gesture just to please the Americans and it was troublesome for him that the British government were so anxious to give satisfaction to the U.S. If the British showed such 'faiblesse' it would have a very bad effect in France.[8]

After this inconclusive Eden–de Gaulle meeting and a further Churchill telegram waiving the American threat, the Cabinet again met and saw 'strong objection' to U.S. action to enforce a settlement. Eden should try persuasion yet again, but 'it would be wrong to impose a settlement on de Gaulle until everything possible had been done by the method of friendly discussion'. Attlee and Eden were to consult on a reply to Churchill.[9]

So, on the very same day, Eden saw de Gaulle yet again, and a compromise was worked out by which de Gaulle more or less accepted the

Roosevelt–Churchill plan but added three secret clauses to safeguard the Free French position. This news was telephoned to Washington for Churchill. After giving him time to digest it, Eden telephoned him. Churchill was very angry. He did not think Roosevelt would accept the new draft; he would put it to him if Eden advised it but there would be an explosion. Eden had failed lamentably and what made matters worse was that there were a lot of people in the U.S. who would agree with de Gaulle. Eden defended the new draft as 'very fair'; if the Americans did not like it and put out their own statement of the case, de Gaulle would put out his from Radio Brazzaville. At the end of this stormy conversation Churchill agreed to put the revised plan to Roosevelt and ring back.

At 1 a.m. Eden and Churchill talked again on the telephone. Churchill had not yet seen Roosevelt, but now thought the new terms not too bad. Harry Hopkins, however, thought them ludicrous. Churchill thought he might play for time by suggesting to Roosevelt that he should do nothing until he himself had got back to London and talked to de Gaulle.

Churchill then saw Roosevelt, got him to accept this suggestion, and thereafter wrote him a minute recording their talk. In this he said that the proposed draft seemed acceptable, but the secret clauses might be thought objectionable; both Attlee and Eden had telephoned him about the 'very strong feeling there is in England against what is called "appeasing Vichy" '. It would be easy to answer this criticism if 'one could tell them about other things we have in our minds, but these being military secrets cannot be revealed'. (This obviously meant *Super-Gymnast* alias *Torch*.) Churchill concluded that, because of the strong and unanimous objections to a breach with de Gaulle, he ought to try himself to make de Gaulle drop or modify the objectionable secret clauses.

On Churchill's minute Roosevelt wrote: 'O.K. *But* these 2 tiny islands cannot be made an issue in the great effort to save the world. F.D.R.'[10]

So Churchill came home and told the Cabinet that he was going to explain to de Gaulle that it was impossible that there should be a 'formal private agreement'; the Americans would not accept one, though they might perhaps 'acquiesce tacitly in some of his points'. The Cabinet took note.[11]

Eden warned Churchill that de Gaulle saw himself 'in the role of Joan of Arc liberating his country from Vichy; his war is a private war against Vichy'. In the event, when Churchill and Eden met de Gaulle on 22 January, they argued acridly on who represented 'France', with Churchill pointing out that there had been very little rallying to General de Gaulle and he could not claim to monopolise 'France'. However, the meeting ended calmly; de Gaulle finally said the French National Committee might not insist on any formal secret conditions.[12]

Churchill at once reported this satisfactory outcome to the Cabinet and to Roosevelt, to whom he wrote: 'I do hope the solution for which I have worked so hard will be satisfactory to Mr Hull and the State Department. I understood fully the difficulty in which they were placed.'[13]

But the State Department were startled rather than happy. Roosevelt had told them nothing of de Gaulle's three secret conditions or of the compromise statement which had been worked out. Hull was ill. Later Halifax reported that Hull was going away on holiday for some time; he got the impression that the question of St Pierre and Miquelon was 'likely to lie on the table'. On Halifax's telegram Eden wrote: 'Best result? A.E.'[14]

So in practice de Gaulle was left in possession of the islands and may have felt that in the first round he had downed the Americans and kept Churchill more or less in line. Eden, too, could feel satisfaction, for much the same reasons.

In fact, de Gaulle's troubles with Churchill and the Americans were only beginning. In the early part of 1942 both Morton and Bessborough went on stoking up Churchill's suspicions of the General. On 6 January Morton sent to the Foreign Office, with a copy to the Prime Minister, a note on relations with the Free French which prompted Churchill to write to Eden that he thought de Gaulle's 'want of faith for the cause of the United Nations' made it opportune as well as necessary to raise the whole question of his personal power and the composition of his Committee. He added: 'It is better that this should be settled before any developments take place in North Africa.'[15]

So Torch was already casting a long shadow. Bessborough, about this time, wrote that 'de Gaulle as a leader is a liability. His main concern appears to be to fight Vichy rather than the Germans, and to glorify himself. He is anti-British, anti-democratic and vain. He is even disloyal to Winston personally. After an interview with him he boasted openly to his people that he had gained the day and had put Winston on the defensive.'[16]

At this time de Gaulle made a move – which misfired – obviously aimed at strengthening his position against the Anglo-Americans and gaining new friends. The Soviet ambassador, Ivan Maisky, told Eden that de Gaulle had come to him to ask whether the Soviet government would accept a

Free French division in Russia; what did the British think? Eden said the division would probably have to come from Syria where it was under British command, and there might be many practical difficulties. Maisky, however, said he thought the plan would be politically useful. But the British were possessive towards the exiled governments and authorities they had taken under their wing. Churchill backed Eden in putting a stop to the plan: 'I share your objections to this excursion.'[17]

Ever since de Gaulle's return from his disastrous trip to the Middle East and Africa at the end of August 1941, Churchill had been set on stopping him repeating the performance. He laid on Eden the uncomfortable job of preventing de Gaulle leaving Britain while avoiding an open quarrel. In early April 1942 de Gaulle told Charles Peake, now British representative to the French National Committee, that he intended to go to Brazzaville to make a tour of inspection of French Equatorial Africa. Churchill minuted to Eden: 'I have for some months forbidden the use by him of any aircraft to leave this country. Please talk to me.' Eden replied in writing: 'I doubt whether it would be wise for us to stand in the way of his visiting his own territories. It is true that experience shows that he is even less likely to behave well than when he is in England, but this is scarcely sufficient reason to maintain the ban.' Churchill did not yield: 'I think it would be most dangerous to let this man begin again his campaign of Anglophobia in which he indulged when in Central Africa, and which he is now more than ever attracted to.'[18]

Soon afterwards the British carried out an operation in Vichy-held Madagascar without telling de Gaulle, and thereafter kept the Free French away from the island while they conducted abortive negotiations with the Vichy governor. This inevitably reawoke de Gaulle's deepest suspicions of the British. In late May he again told Peake that he wanted to visit Africa and the Middle East 'at the earliest possible date'. On this Churchill's terse comment was, 'Please, "No".' Eden replied, 'I induced him a month ago to postpone his proposed visit to Africa. I fear however that a further attempt on my part would merely increase his suspicions of us . . . and that we should find him even more difficult to deal with than he normally is. . . . I hope you will agree to let him go. He has been rather better lately.' But Churchill would not yield: 'I cannot agree. There is nothing hostile to England this man may not do once he gets off the chain. But bring it up in Cabinet if you want.'[19]

This time Eden did bring it up in the Cabinet, on 2 June. Eden said he would try once again to persuade de Gaulle to postpone his journey, but would deprecate imposing a definite veto. Churchill said there were grave risks in allowing de Gaulle to go to French West Africa 'where he might make statements very unfavourable to this country'. It was much better that he should stay in England until a proper Free French council had been formed; gentle but firm influence should be brought to bear on him to stay, on the ground that he was greatly needed. Eden said he would do his best to persuade the General, but would report back to the Cabinet if he failed.[20]

So Eden tried to exercise 'gentle but firm influence' and saw de Gaulle, saying that the Cabinet had asked him to 'invite the General to consider whether he could not further postpone his visit'. De Gaulle replied that if the British government thought he could really be useful in England and might need to consult him on any subject, it was his duty to remain. He would postpone his journey for about six weeks. But to Charles Peake de Gaulle spoke differently. In the light of this second appeal not to leave England, he said, he could not help wondering whether 'a further project against some part of the French empire' by the British or Americans might not be contemplated, and whether once again it was the intention to keep him in complete ignorance of such plans. In a clear reference to the Madagascar affair, he said he could not endure such a humiliation a second time, and any such action would mean the end of co-operation between the Free French and Britain and the U.S.[21]

However, Eden told Churchill that he had been able to induce the General to agree 'in a friendly spirit' to put off his journey for six weeks; it would help Eden if de Gaulle could be consulted a little in regard to events present and future, though 'there is no need to tell him military secrets'. It would also help if Churchill could 'endure to see him'. This implied that Eden thought Churchill's dislike of de Gaulle was pretty strong. But the exploits of the Free French troops at Bir Hacheim had impressed Churchill who answered that he was quite willing to see de Gaulle, and this would furnish a good occasion. He duly saw de Gaulle on 10 June when, though there was further news from Madagascar of a kind to upset de Gaulle, outward friendliness was displayed; the Press were informed that Churchill had congratulated the General upon his troops' 'brilliant conduct' at Bir Hacheim.[22]

Four days earlier, however, de Gaulle had sent a telegram to his generals in Syria and Africa setting out in some detail his suspicions of the British and Americans. A copy of this telegram fell into British hands in Cairo. It said that he was not disposed to remain associated with the British and Americans, and the Free French should form a united front against all comers and must warn the whole world against Anglo-Saxon imperialist designs. The three Free French generals who received the telegram let the British know that they were badly worried.[23]

This was bound to produce a strong reaction in London. But Eden, when he saw de Gaulle, was relatively mild and smooth in his approach, speaking of 'disturbing reports' and asking for an explanation. De Gaulle replied that he had received information from Catroux in Syria about his bad relations with the British General Edward Spears, from Brazzaville about a possible British threat against the bend of the Niger, and from the U.S. about a possible threat to Dakar, all combining to cause him gravest concern. Since Peake, when he had mentioned his suspicions to him, had offered him no reassurance, it had come into his mind that when he had been going abroad last time Eden had tried to dissuade him and the British had then attacked Madagascar without consulting him; so it was natural for him to think that the British or Americans had some similar plans in mind once again. Eden said the General should at least have told him before telegraphing to his generals; and his suspicions were not justified.

Shifting his ground, de Gaulle said he had really very little suspicion of Britain but deep suspicion of the Americans: was Eden sure they were not planning something against Dakar? Eden tried to dispel de Gaulle's suspicions and admitted that in Syria there might be faults on both sides. De Gaulle then said he would send telegrams to his generals reassuring them, especially in so far as his anxieties concerned the British.[24]

There was yet another cause of trouble which Eden and de Gaulle did not discuss. De Gaulle had tried to veto arrangements made by Catroux in the Middle East with the British naval authorities and Secret Intelligence Service for the training of Free French agents for work in Tripoli, Tunisia and Morocco, areas of first-class importance for *Torch*. The Minister of State in Cairo reported that the S.I.S. representative was much disturbed. Churchill immediately noted this and drew Eden's attention to it.[25]

Towards the end of July de Gaulle told Peake he could no longer defer paying a brief visit of about three weeks to Syria and French West Africa and asked for facilities. Eden saw him on 28 July and reported to Churchill that he found him in a helpful frame of mind; he would not send any more telegrams of the kind recently complained of, and now had no difficulties with the British government. Eden thought de Gaulle would be receptive to any suggestions Churchill might make to him. On 29 July Churchill saw De Gaulle and, to judge by the General's own record which he sent to the Foreign Office, was kind and fatherly, saying there had been faults on both sides and in future they must work together: 'Votre situation a été difficile ces derniers temps. Nos rapports n'ont pas toujours été très bons. Il y a eu des torts de part et d'autre. À l'avenir, il faut nous mettre ensemble et travailler. Faîtes le voyage que vous projetez et revenez rapidement. Si vous avez une difficulté, addressez-vous directement à moi. . . .' Churchill also said that Spears had many enemies but also a friend – the Prime Minister; but he would telegraph to Spears and recommend that he should listen to what de Gaulle had to say, and the General should try to arrange things with him.[26]

So de Gaulle left for the Middle East in August 1942 with at least a show of good will on both sides. But once he got to Cairo and Syria all his anti-British feelings burst out. According to a Foreign Office record written later, 'he adopted an offensive and intransigent attitude over Syrian questions at his first meeting with the Minister of State in Cairo, incited his officers and officials in Syria against the British, complained violently of British methods and imperialist designs to the U.S. Consul-General in Beirut, informed the French National Committee in London that the British were planning to obtain complete domination of Syria and the Lebanon, and demanded that supreme command of Allied forces there should be transferred from the British to the Free French'.[27]

The fat was in the fire again. De Gaulle was 'invited' to return to London but did not do so until the end of September, and then only after the British – who had now completely occupied Madagascar – threatened not to hand it over to the French National Committee so long as de Gaulle went on making trouble for them in Syria.[28]

De Gaulle's fresh outburst of 'Anglophobia', as Churchill liked to call it, raised the question whether Eden had been 'soft' in wanting to let him leave England and persuading Churchill to agree. One reason for his 'softness' was the general belief of Eden and the Foreign Office that exiled governments and authorities should be allowed the maximum of freedom that was convenient, safe and practicable. This saved trouble and argument and was a polite gesture to the principle of non-interference in the affairs of others and respect for national sovereignty even in the cases of those dependent on British hospitality and sometimes on British money. On this issue Eden and the Foreign Office often found themselves at loggerheads with the military and security authorities and with S.I.S. and S.O.E. They seldom won.

A stronger reason for Eden's softness to de Gaulle was the growing evidence in the summer of 1942 of support for the General inside France. This, moreover, he could use in the Cabinet to support his own case for de

Gaulle against Churchill. On 1 June – the day before he put to the Cabinet the case for letting de Gaulle go abroad – he circulated to the Cabinet a memorandum on de Gaulle and French opinion, beginning, 'I have been impressed by recent testimony to the large amount of support which General de Gaulle enjoys in occupied France.' The trade unionists of France, he went on, had sent a May Day message to the workers of the free world proclaiming de Gaulle as the representative of the people of France: 'a huge imprisoned force is behind him in France'. Eden's informants, he said, belonged to left-wing circles in close touch with trade unionists, Christian Syndicalists and the militant section of the Socialist party; they affirmed that resistance to the Germans was synonymous with Gaullism.

There were only two other elements, Pétainism and Communism. Pétainism, the memorandum said, was 'almost finished'. The Communists had grown in strength since Russia had been brought into the war and numbered about 100,000. Eden's informants believed that when the Allies landed in France de Gaulle must come with them and take over Paris at once, as the only means of avoiding civil war and preventing the Communists from seizing power. Eden concluded: 'General de Gaulle has given a declaration to the leaders of the Left organisations in France with which I gather they are satisfied. In view of the oft-repeated allegation that General de Gaulle is a Fascist, my colleagues may be interested to have the above information.'[29]

Eden's memorandum was obviously meant to spike the guns of anti-Gaullists such as Bessborough (and Churchill himself had also used 'Fascist' in relation to de Gaulle), and also to appeal to Labour members of the Cabinet, especially Bevin. He followed it up next day with a memorandum on French–German co-operation in North Africa, just as obviously meant to show that it was wrong to pin faith on Vichy to secure success in *Torch*, as the Americans did. Pétain, he wrote, was a back number; as for the French generals in North Africa, no help could be expected from any of the French fighting services until it was clear that the Allies were winning the war very rapidly; 'meanwhile they will obey orders to resist us'.[30]

Churchill knew what Eden was up to and could not let this oblique attack on Roosevelt pass. Three days later he presented the Cabinet with his own view: 'Whatever our feelings of well-placed scorn and distrust of the Vichy government may be, we ought not to forget that it is the only government which may perhaps give us what we want from France, namely the Toulon fleet and the entry into the French North African provinces. They do not seem to me entirely negligible. . . . I look forward to a time in the war . . . when the great change of heart which has taken place in the French masses and the apparent certainty of an Allied victory will produce a sudden decisive change in the action of the Vichy government.'[31]

These memoranda of Eden and Churchill raised fundamental questions which were to be hotly disputed from *Torch* until the liberation of France. For the moment, they were tactical moves in a duel between the two men.

On 9 June Eden continued his campaign in the Cabinet with a fresh report on opinion in France. A young Frenchman paying a brief secret visit to England had seen Georges Mandel, a member of the Reynaud government much respected by the British. Mandel had said that, though he did not know de Gaulle, he considered that his name had symbolic value and all patriots whatever their opinions must help him unreservedly in his task. Reynaud himself had told the young man that he considered himself 'a simple soldier of General de Gaulle' until victory was achieved.[32]

Early in July Eden put to the Cabinet a more balanced and cautious paper on French resistance, though he reached the same general conclusion as before. Information from 'our secret contacts with the forces of resistance' showed that General de Gaulle was the only leader of French resistance to have emerged since the collapse, but he could not substantiate a claim to be regarded as France or as the head of the government of France.

> We have been largely responsible for building him up in France, and it is clearly impossible for us to drop him now; if we did, most of his chief assistants would follow his orders, and it is most unlikely that any other leader would be forthcoming to take his place. His disappearance would have a bad effect on the forces of resistance in France. . . .

Possibly, Eden added, some other leader such as General Henri Giraud might eventually emerge who would enjoy more support in France than de Gaulle, 'but there is no sign of such a rival at present'. British policy should be 'to support all the forces of French resistance, wherever they may be and whatever their allegiance, without binding ourselves exclusively to any; to continue to support General de Gaulle; and at the same time to encourage him to strengthen his organisation by the enlistment of such representative Frenchmen as he can persuade to come over and join him'. This would best serve the war effort and make provision for Britain's post-war relationship with France.[33]

Apart from safeguarding the right of S.O.E. and S.I.S. to operate independently of de Gaulle, Eden's policy at this point was one of firm if qualified backing for him. He also tried to show him to the Cabinet in a pleasing personal light, as in an account of a small dinner given by Peake in July. Talking of the cleavage between the Right and the Left in France, de Gaulle had said there were two sorts of Right. One was the *petite noblesse de campagne* ('et j'en suis') who were inspired with the highest form of patriotism and were willing to make any sacrifice for the glory of France; many of the clergy belonged to this group. The other was the moneyed classes, the very rich, including the Parisian aristocrats, 'those titled ladies who are the mistresses of Abetz or Darlan or who give receptions to welcome their much-loved conquerors . . . rotten through riches'. As for French views on the Allies, after the Battle of Britain there had been a wave of Anglophilia; with the entry of Russia and America into the war these two now had their share of France's sympathy. De Gaulle, however, did not doubt that England would remain France's favourite ally, 'car les Américains deviendront trop fatigants et les Russes trop inquiétants'.[34]

With this little campaign of memoranda Eden had created an atmosphere in the Cabinet in which it was inevitable that de Gaulle would be allowed to go to Syria in August. But Eden had more far-reaching aims. Just before he left, de Gaulle wrote to Churchill making two requests : that the Free French command should be brought into all planning and decisions on operations in the West; and that this command should be supplied with the necessary material and control for sabotage and intelligence work in France. The British Chiefs of Staff said 'No' to the first and a qualified 'No' to the second of these requests. But Eden challenged the Chiefs of Staff and, cautiously, S.I.S. and S.O.E.

In a memorandum to the Cabinet, Eden wrote :

> The only authority within our reach with which we can work is General de Gaulle. He is, quite rightly in our view, developing his contacts with the organisations of resistance in France. . . . At the outset, at any rate, General de Gaulle would probably be the predominant French authority in metropolitan French territory liberated by the action of the Allied forces. He would indeed probably be put forward as such by the leaders of the resistance movements. . . . There would thus . . . be advantage in discussing with him in advance the administrative problems that would arise in liberated territory. There are strong political grounds for allowing General de Gaulle to participate in major operations undertaken in metropolitan France.

If this recommendation had been followed, many quarrels would have been avoided in 1944.

On de Gaulle's demand to set up his own organisation for special operations and intelligence and to take over 'supreme command of the internal French front', Eden acknowledged that S.O.E. and S.I.S. were insistent that they must go on working independently of de Gaulle and were against an independent Free French organisation working without their knowledge. He did not say in so many words that this attitude was wrong, but he did propose that, 'in view of the growing intimacy of the relations between General de Gaulle's headquarters in London and the resistance movements in France', British policy should at least be 're-examined'.[35]

Given the reports during August of de Gaulle's behaviour in Cairo and Syria, there was little chance of Eden's proposals being adopted, especially so far as S.O.E. and S.I.S. were concerned. Eden also had to reckon with Morton, whom he had left out in the cold in his recent assessments and policy recommendations on France. At the end of August Churchill told Morton to study the first-hand evidence on support for de Gaulle in France and the colonies; it is hard not to assume that he wanted the outcome to be a good deal less favourable to de Gaulle than the picture Eden had been building up.

Morton quickly reported a conversation he had had with Félix Gouin, a prominent Socialist deputy, who said he thought that when the Allies invaded France it would be 'quite unnecessary for General de Gaulle, who has relatively no troops at his disposal, to play a part in the initial operations'. However, the administration of liberated territories should be handed over to him, acting in the name of the French people.[36]

Early in September Morton's full paper was ready, after he had got the approval of every possible organisation : the Directors of Naval, Military and Air Intelligence, S.I.S., S.O.E., the Political Warfare Executive, the Foreign Office – though there it had apparently not been seen by William Strang, the official most closely concerned with de Gaulle.[37] His conclusions were a good deal more cautious about de Gaulle than Eden's. The General, he said, had the support of 'a considerable majority of the French people as a symbol of their desire to see the Axis driven out of French territory', but this, so long as it stopped short of active help to the Free French, was of limited practical value to the Allies. He had so far failed to get substantial support as a military commander or political leader, though it was 'not yet impossible for him to gain political support . . . principally of the Left'. Finally, though at present he carried little weight in France save as a symbol of resistance, any British action interpreted by the French as unjustified betrayal of de Gaulle would 'seriously alienate French sympathy for this country'.[38]

Churchill pronounced Morton's paper 'very good and well-balanced' and suggested that the Foreign Office should circulate it to the War Cabinet. Since nothing happened, a few days later he circulated it himself.[39]

Eden's whole case for de Gaulle had been badly weakened by the General's own actions abroad, or, anyhow, the reports of them; it was difficult for Eden to defend him. In early October he capped Morton's paper with yet another one of his own which reached very much the same conclusions as Morton had. But it was interesting for its emphasis on the French Communist Party as 'the only one of the old political organisations to survive the collapse of France. Its structure and discipline are firmer than those of any other group. . . . It is said to be prepared to co-operate with any genuine elements of resistance.'[40] But on de Gaulle himself Eden had been compelled to make a tactical retreat.

When de Gaulle arrived back in London after his Syrian outbursts he knew there would be what he himself described as 'something of a shock' when he resumed contact with the British government. Moreover, he himself was less willing to show repentance than he had been in similar circumstances a year before.

Churchill and Eden saw him together and, according to de Gaulle's account, each in turn lost his temper, though Churchill was the more emotional, vehemently rejecting the General's claim to be 'France'.[41] In more practical terms it was made clear that the British would not agree to hand over Madagascar to the Free French until matters in Syria had been settled. According to the Foreign Office record, Churchill said the great difficulty lay in working with de Gaulle, who had shown marked hostility to the British. It made him sad, since he admired the General's personality and record. But he could not regard him as a comrade or a friend. Instead of waging war with Germany, he had waged war with England. Eden, seeking compromise, pressed the idea of a deal over Madagascar and Syria. But de Gaulle simply said he would accept the consequences: 'Je tiendrai les conséquences.'[42]

The idea of Eden and the Foreign Office at this moment was to conduct stiff and slow negotiations with de Gaulle first over Syria, then Madagascar; there was no intention to break with him. After de Gaulle had 'recovered his balance', as the Foreign Office put it, the negotiations began.[43] They were deliberately strung out, partly because of real practical difficulties, 'partly because we did not want to have the Free French established in

Madagascar before we knew de Gaulle's reaction to the impending operations in North Africa'.[44]

This was the very big question mark. On the insistence of Roosevelt,
who always quoted the Dakar fiasco to prove his point, de Gaulle was to
be told nothing in advance about *Torch*. Moreover, the Americans hoped
and believed that Vichy officers and officials, trusting in their 'best friend'
Roosevelt, would make the operation a more or less bloodless walk-over.
(For this reason, too, it had to be presented at the start as a purely
American venture, though it was in fact very much a joint Anglo-
American military operation.)

Some sort of explosion from de Gaulle seemed inevitable when *Torch*
actually happened. Churchill may well have been worried about this and
may also have had an uneasy conscience about keeping de Gaulle in the
dark. In any case, at the end of October, without telling Eden, he sent
Morton to see de Gaulle with a friendly message of congratulation from
Churchill about the exploits of a Free French submarine, *Junon*, and of
sorrow about Free French casualties in the fighting in Egypt. Morton
reported to Churchill that after he had given these messages de Gaulle
had 'opened up a little, saying that he knew himself for a man of quick
spirit and temper; had he not been so, he would not have been leader of
the movement'. He firmly believed that he himself represented France,
and that to do so it was essential for him to make himself difficult. De
Gaulle had added that he had given his policy further deep thought and
had always returned to the same conclusion. Morton reported that de
Gaulle felt 'very frustrated and sore' and was especially hurt that he was
given no inside information about Allied operations, even after they had
taken place, and even when some of his own troops were engaged.

On Morton's report Churchill wrote the one word 'Good'.[45] But Eden
was annoyed. He minuted to Churchill that he was glad he had decided
to send Morton to de Gaulle but went on: 'We here have been taking a
stiff line with him, in accordance with what we decided at the Cabinet.
I am only anxious lest the olive branch from No. 10 may appear to
imply that we are speaking with two voices. When you do not want to
see the General personally, might I suggest that you let us convey your
messages? We could . . . thus be sure that action was synchronised.' To
this implied reproach Churchill answered sharply: 'I sent no "olive
branch" but a soldierly compliment about his men.' He also said: 'I
propose to break *Torch* to him on the night before, myself, personally.'[46]

Eden had, however, asserted the Foreign Office's right to handle dealings
with de Gaulle, rather than Morton, with some success. From then on

Churchill used Morton for lower-level contacts with the French, rather than with the General himself. Morton went on sending an enormous number of minutes to Churchill but was consulted less and less; in the latter years of the war he was mainly occupied with the exiled Poles and Czechs.[47]

When Churchill broke the news of *Torch* to de Gaulle in November, the General was deeply resentful but made no public reproaches; instead he made a broadcast welcoming the operation. When, soon after, Eisenhower reported his agreement with Admiral Darlan – detested by the Free French and rabidly anti-British – Eden was at Chequers with Churchill, and recorded in his diary: 'Didn't like it a bit, and said so.'[48] Bracken, as Minister of Information, had warned Eden against any deal with Darlan, 'a fantastic suggestion hatched in Washington': 'There are occasions when it is necessary to be tough with the Americans, who are sometimes capable of doing the maddest things.' Eden agreed.[49]

The British Press and Parliament very much disliked the deal; de Gaulle disliked it even more. Churchill and Eden saw him together. According to Eden's account, although de Gaulle was firm that he could not be a party to any arrangement with Darlan, he 'was unemotional and did not blame us'.[50] According to de Gaulle's account, Eden was 'moved to the point of tears'.[51]

De Gaulle, heartened by the hostile reaction of the British Press to the Darlan affair, felt himself in a strong position. Churchill and Eden allowed him to issue a statement, which was broadcast that night, that he and his Committee took no share in and assumed no responsibility for the negotiations in progress with Darlan.[52]

But trouble was inevitable. On 20 November Eden found himself in a brawl with Churchill over the terms of the Darlan–Eisenhower agreement, which Churchill wanted to accept out of hand. At one moment, Eden recorded in his diary, Churchill said, 'Well, D. is not as bad as de G., anyway.'[53] However, this quarrel did not survive a lunch at Buck's at which, Eden recorded, Churchill 'bore no malice'. The next day government changes were announced and Eden became Leader of the House. He was immediately plunged into a most uncomfortable parliamentary storm over a veto imposed by Churchill on a broadcast which de Gaulle had wanted to make on 21 November. Peake had to inform the General of this veto which, he reported, 'came as a great shock to the General who, however, realised that we had the physical means of preventing him broadcasting'. Peake also noted that the 'mischievous' Soviet ambassador to the exiled governments, Bogomolov, had spent an hour with de Gaulle and had probably been egging him on.[54]

Churchill's motive in suppressing the broadcast, which merely referred in vague and lofty terms to the certainty that the national will could not long be stifled in North Africa, was mainly to please Roosevelt. Also, he was clearly in a state of high excitement over the dangerous and tricky military operation then in progress – an excitement shared in some measure by Eden, which made it easier for him to tolerate Churchill's wilfulness. Churchill sent Roosevelt a personal message on 22 November:

> I felt that in view of impending operations I should not allow anything that might compromise arrangements made by Eisenhower with Darlan or prejudice the military situation. . . . De Gaulle was told that as the operations were under the U.S. Command I felt bound to take your opinion before agreeing to anything which might be detrimental to them. If your view was that broadcasts of this kind were undesirable at the moment, being your ardent and active lieutenant I should bow to your decision without demur.[55]

This sort of language and behaviour were to de Gaulle quite incomprehensible. In his memoirs he wrote that he told Churchill, 'I did not know that on British territory the radio was not at my disposal,' adding that Churchill's action made him realise that it was not at his, either.[56]

Churchill's veto quickly became known. In the House of Commons the Labour M.P., Richard Stokes, after attacking 'the Prime Minister and his red-headed Goebbels [Brendan Bracken]' for preventing the nation from learning the truth about Darlan, said it had come to his knowledge that a de Gaulle broadcast, which had been approved by Eden, had subsequently been suppressed by Churchill. 'There cannot have been anything very bad in the script, otherwise my Right Honourable Friend the Foreign Secretary would not have agreed to it,' Stokes said. This placed Eden in an impossible position. He promised that an answer would be given to the House, and then, pressed by Stokes, said, 'There is no difference between the Prime Minister and myself, none whatever.'[57]

Eden obviously expected that the Prime Minister would himself deal with the storm in the House and give the answer he had promised. Churchill did in fact start drafting one, but in the course of drafting it somehow turned into a statement by Eden himself, with amendments made in the handwriting of both men.[58] So it was Eden who had to tell the House that *he* took full responsibility for the decision to stop the broadcast, which was made in full agreement with the Prime Minister. While he did not want to 'exaggerate' the character of the broadcast, 'we could not take the responsibility for allowing anything to happen . . . which might hamper the responsible commanders or make the task of our own troops and those of our Allies more difficult'. Eden's unhappy statement did not convince the House, and he was attacked from his own side by Robert Boothby and from the left by Aneurin Bevan. It was a tempestuous start to his new job as Leader.[59]

Churchill by this time had the bit between his teeth and proceeded to veto broadcasts which Eden thought inoffensive, desirable or even admirable, and which would also have eased his parliamentary problems.[60] Moreover, Churchill expected Eden to convey his vetoes to de Gaulle. Eden, on occasion, passed the job to Peake. Peake reported on 4 December that when he explained to de Gaulle that a proposed broadcast would have to be changed, 'there was a silence during which the General showed great emotion, but made no comment. The General then said he had no doubt that Mr Eden had more important things to do, and showed Mr Peake out very coldly.'[61]

By this time Roosevelt, relenting a little, had made it known that he was prepared to receive de Gaulle in the U.S. This gave Churchill a fresh argument: 'It would be much better for General de Gaulle not to broadcast before he goes to the U.S. He will only complicate his affairs there.'[62]

Roosevelt's motive for agreeing to receive de Gaulle at this tricky moment was presumably to counter the outcry in the American Press against the Eisenhower–Darlan agreement. The outlook for de Gaulle seemed hopeful: if he could soften Roosevelt, much of his trouble with Churchill would vanish. On Christmas Eve he left for Scotland on his way to the U.S. Before he left he had recorded a broadcast which had been blessed both by Eden and by Morton, and Churchill's approval was sought. Then came the news that Darlan had been murdered, and soon after a most secret telegram from Admiral Leahy in Washington: 'The President desires that the visit of General de Gaulle to America be postponed. This is in view of the unsettled conditions in North Africa following the assassination of Admiral Darlan.'[63] The disappearance of Darlan relieved Roosevelt of the necessity of propitiating his American critics, and Churchill of the need to accept Eden's view and approve de Gaulle's broadcast. A new and stormier phase in the Churchill–Eden dialogue over de Gaulle was beginning.

CHAPTER FIVE

To make or break de Gaulle?

The whole Darlan incident – the public outcry in Britain and the U.S. against the Darlan–Eisenhower agreement, and then Darlan's unexpected disappearance – should in theory have strengthened de Gaulle's position. The name of Vichy had been blackened in the public mind; de Gaulle could and did take up a position of moral indignation, and counted on striking a sympathetic chord. But in time of war moral indignation is not a strong weapon and, as Churchill sometimes tried to explain to de Gaulle, in the U.S. public opinion counted for much less with the President, except in the run-up to an election, than it did with the government in Britain.

With Darlan gone, the Americans reverted to their original candidate for leadership in French North Africa, General Henri Giraud, whom they had brought out of France not long before the landings. He was a simple man, a brave but old-fashioned soldier and quite lacking in political sense. In any struggle for power de Gaulle could easily gobble him up, if he could once cut him off from American support. Since de Gaulle believed that he himself represented 'France' and that 'France' needed 'unanimity', he could well feel that he owed it to France to do this.

Eden and the Foreign Office had a different idea : to get the best of all worlds by arranging a marriage between de Gaulle and Giraud in a broadened French committee, enjoying the blessing of both Britain and the U.S. At the beginning of 1943 they did not realise how firmly de Gaulle was set on 'unanimity', or undisputed control, or how strongly Roosevelt, Hull and Leahy disliked and distrusted de Gaulle; these feelings were intensified by suspicions – for which there was no valid evidence – that Gaullists had something to do with Darlan's murder.

As for Churchill, he was so stung by the British reaction to the Darlan business that he minuted to Eden on 2 January that he should explain to the Americans that it was impossible to muzzle the British Press and Parliament :

There is a deep loathing in this country, particularly strong among the working classes, against what are thought to be intrigues with Darlan and Vichy, which are held to be contrary to the broad, simple loyalties which unite the masses throughout the world against the common foe. . . . You should warn Hull that there is almost a passion on this subject. . . . The remedy is to amend the policy and reach sound ground in the French quagmire.[1]

(Churchill's feeling against Darlan may have been strengthened by a letter from his son, Randolph, from Algiers, warning against the danger of 'sacrificing the future of France to military expediency' and leaving all the official jobs in the hands of 'the old Vichy gang'.[2])

So Eden might well have thought that he had Churchill's backing when he telegraphed to Halifax in Washington on 2 January:

I assume that the U.S. government, no less than H.M.G., wish to see the French empire united as soon as possible under a single authority making its maximum contribution to the war effort. . . . Our experience in dealing with Free French authorities since June 1940 suggests the best solution would be the establishment in Algeria . . . of a single authority in place of the French National Committee in London and Giraud's administration in Algiers. . . . It would not be recognised as the government or even as the provisional government of France. . . . It would be treated as an Allied power and formally admitted to the ranks of the United Nations.[3]

But Eden's policy did not go down well in Washington. On 15 January Eden telegraphed again, saying American suspicions seemed more deep-rooted than he had thought, and he wanted to dispel them. He explained why the British supported de Gaulle and said he thought he deserved it:

Though he depends in part on us for his finances, he has never been subservient to us. He is of autocratic and uncompromising temper (indeed, his personality is a grave impediment to his cause) and is proudly tenacious in defence of French interests as he conceives them. He has small use for the normal processes of international intercourse and has more than once brought our relations near to breaking-point. For all that, we have in the end always had patience with him, for the sake of France whose resistance he worthily represents.

In a side-swipe at Washington's pro-Vichy policy, Eden said Britain had preferred to hand over Syria, Madagascar and Djibouti to de Gaulle's administration 'rather than to take the risk of compounding with a regime whose loyalty must be doubtful'. The Darlan episode had increased de Gaulle's prestige, but 'we are not backing de Gaulle for first place in North Africa. It is for him and Giraud to come to terms if they can. . . . I should hope that the U.S. government will come to look upon him in time with a more understanding and sympathetic eye.'[4]

Eden had put up the best case he honestly could for de Gaulle and for a de Gaulle–Giraud partnership. But at once de Gaulle himself did his best to destroy this case by disdainfully refusing an invitation to come to North Africa, where Churchill and Roosevelt were at that moment discussing war strategy, and to meet Giraud for talks. Eden himself transmitted the invitation and got the rebuff.[5] De Gaulle's own later account suggests that he was holding out for an invitation from Roosevelt; he did not want 'to enter a race wearing the British colours while the Americans back their own entry against me'.[6] In the end he yielded but with the worst possible grace. The Foreign Office interpretation was that, though he was prepared to meet Giraud, he did not want the meeting to take place under Anglo-American auspices, since it was a French internal matter. The subsequent Foreign Office summing-up was: 'He therefore made every sort of difficulty about going. . . . He only undertook the journey after the Prime Minister had threatened to throw him over if he did not. When there his behaviour was arrogant and intractable, contrasting badly with that of Giraud. . . . After his return the Prime Minister gave him to understand that he did not wish to have any more personal dealings with him, although H.M.G. would continue as before to treat with the National Committee.'[7]

So much for Eden's hopes of a marriage of de Gaulle and Giraud and of British and American policies. Roosevelt had been confirmed in his hostility to de Gaulle and Churchill had been made to look silly in Roosevelt's eyes by the defiance of a man dependent on British money – when the British themselves were heavily dependent on American financial support. What was more, Roosevelt obtained a mischievous or malicious pleasure out of rubbing salt in the wound. No wonder Churchill was furious and imposed a personal boycott on de Gaulle.

He was also determined to scale down de Gaulle's pretensions. In March 1943 Morton drew Churchill's attention to a speech made by André Philip, a member of de Gaulle's Committee, saying that, as representative of the French Resistance movement, his mandate was to recognise de Gaulle as leader of resistance and nobody else; 'there was unity among the French people in recognising General de Gaulle as their leader'. Churchill replied to Morton: 'You should tell M. Philip . . . that if this kind of thing goes on, the Prime Minister may be forced to give very direct contradiction to such statements in Parliament.'[8]

Eden, however, had developed a good working relationship with René Massigli, de Gaulle's Commissioner for Foreign Affairs. In April there were complaints from Washington about the activities of de Gaulle's representative there, Adrien Tixier, who was said to have bought a newspaper business and to be conducting anti-American propaganda, which upset Cordell Hull. Roosevelt's close personal friend Harry Hopkins asked if the British could possibly get Tixier removed. Eden replied, 'Please tell Harry that he has indeed landed us with a troublesome baby,' but Massigli readily agreed to recall Tixier on one pretext or another.[9]

Eden's own feelings about de Gaulle and the Americans were strongly reinforced by his visit to Washington in March and his long talks with Roosevelt. The report he gave the Cabinet on 13 April was not flattering to the Americans. There had, he said, been much talk of France. Hull clearly hated de Gaulle, and there had been a good deal of complaint that the British were not doing enough to defend the American case. As for the future, the U.S. did not want to see the establishment of a single French authority, even if that authority was not recognised as a government. Eden had said that Britain would much prefer to deal with one authority, though not necessarily a government like other Allied governments.

The Americans, Eden reported, preferred to deal with individuals. They also wanted to deal separately with the French authorities in the Pacific islands and in Martinique, and Eden wondered whether this was partly due to the U.S. desire to see some of the French Pacific islands 'internationalised' (a polite name for American-controlled). Roosevelt had referred to previous suggestions that Indo-China, Dakar and Bizerta should be 'internationalised'. But at this point, Eden said, the Under-Secretary of State, Sumner Welles, had reminded Roosevelt that he was committed by public statements to restoring the full integrity of the French empire.

Eden added that another point of difference was that the Americans did not want Allied forces landing in France to be accompanied by any French civil authority; they thought liberated territory should be administered by the Allies. Eden had said he thought the British view was different, and would favour having some French civil authority working with the Allied military authorities from an early stage.[10]

Eden, therefore, came away from Washington forewarned and forearmed about certain key issues which were to lead to sharp conflict later. He was also unimpressed by Roosevelt. On his return he tried to impress on de Gaulle the strength of American feeling against him.[11] This probably had the opposite effect from what he had intended.

He also came back to find Churchill urging him to take the job of Viceroy of India, a flattering and alluring offer. Yet, as Eden wrote later, 'I was not sure that it was fair to leave the Foreign Office and the Leadership of the House of Commons at the critical phase of the war.' In any case, King George VI thought Eden should stay. But Churchill's offer must have heightened his self-assurance and his sense of his own political importance.

By this time de Gaulle was involved in bargaining with Giraud for the formation of a joint committee. In late May, when agreement seemed near, a sudden storm blew up. Churchill was in Washington, trying to win Roosevelt's personal backing for his Mediterranean war strategy which the U.S. Chiefs of Staff disliked. Roosevelt gave him a number of memoranda making various charges against de Gaulle. Churchill, his mind less on French affairs than on strategy and the need for pleasing Roosevelt, telegraphed these 'allegations' to London, and told the War Cabinet that 'a very stern situation' was developing about de Gaulle. There should be 'urgent consideration whether de Gaulle should not now be eliminated as a political force, the French National Committee being told that we would have no further relations with them, nor give them any money, so long as de Gaulle was connected with them'.[12]

The War Cabinet met on 23 May to discuss these Churchill telegrams. Attlee was in the chair. According to the minutes, 'The War Cabinet took the view that it was extremely difficult to see how we could break with General de Gaulle at the moment when he was on the point of reaching agreement with General Giraud.' Various ministers joined in the discussion with arguments against a break. Bevin said that opinion among French trade unionists showed considerable fear of growing U.S. influence; they did not altogether like de Gaulle himself, but the Gaullist organisation was looked on as more likely than any other body to stimulate the resistance of the French working classes. (Bevin's trade union informants obviously did not think much of the Communists.) Attlee said that, if the British were to take action against de Gaulle, many Frenchmen now opposed to him would rally to him. It was also pointed out (by whom, was not recorded) that if Britain broke with de Gaulle during or immediately after Churchill's visit to the U.S., people would infer that this had been done under U.S. pressure: 'It must be recognised that U.S. policy towards the French had not met with success, and there was increasing recognition of the fact in the U.S. itself' – and this was probably why pressure was being put on Britain to get rid of de Gaulle.[13]

Three telegrams to Churchill were approved by the War Cabinet and were sent jointly by Attlee and Eden as the Cabinet's unanimous view:

We had no idea that the de Gaulle situation was rankling so much just now. We are fully conscious of the difficulties which de Gaulle has created for us, and of your position under heavy pressure from the Americans. We do not, however, consider that the policy which you so strongly recommend is practicable.

For one thing, they added, union between de Gaulle and Giraud was nearer than ever before. There was much evidence that de Gaulle's personal position in France was strong. There was no likelihood of any of the members of the French National Committee continuing to function if de Gaulle were removed by the British, and the same was probably true of the Free French fighting forces. 'Is there not also a real danger that if we now drove de Gaulle out of public life . . . we would not only make him a national martyr but we would find ourselves accused . . . of interfering improperly in French internal affairs with a view to treating France as an Anglo-American protectorate?'

Attlee and Eden also refuted the American 'allegations' point by point and said, 'The removal of de Gaulle would probably have a disastrous reaction on the whole Resistance movement.' They pointed out that there were 80,000 Free French officers and men manning forty-seven ships including submarines and sixteen corvettes.

> Free French help in the air has also been most effective. . . . Apart from the political objections . . . a precipitate break with de Gaulle would have far-reaching consequences in a number of spheres which the Americans have probably never thought about. Indeed, an impossible situation would be created. . . . We are sorry not to be more helpful, but we are convinced that the Americans are wrong. . . . We do hope that a decision on this question can await your return.

On another issue, which was later to cause so much trouble, they said: 'The President's idea that a proud people like the French will submit to a military occupation run by British and American generals for six months or even a year is surely not practical politics and it is disturbing that his mind should run on these lines.'[14]

This was the first, though not the last, time when Eden rallied the War Cabinet, especially Attlee and Bevin, in resistance to an American-inspired onslaught by Churchill on de Gaulle. As he himself noted in his diary on the Cabinet meeting: 'Everyone against and very brave about it in his absence.'[15] It was, however, a tactic which Eden had tried out earlier in 1943 when Churchill wanted to go to Turkey, with equal success. That time, when Churchill got back to London after his meeting with Roosevelt – so Eden wrote later – 'he immediately set to and said that he had been angry with me for my obstruction of his Turkish plans and had resented my enlisting the War Cabinet against what he wanted to do. He had drafted and cyphered, but not sent, a violent personal telegram.' Roosevelt, he went on, had been much surprised by the difficulty he had with the Cabinet. Eden replied that Churchill's position was not the same as Roosevelt's; it had been his own duty to express a view.[16]

Churchill's angers did not last long. In another case when Eden stopped him interfering in French affairs in North Africa, Churchill was at first angry, then quickly relented. 'This', Eden wrote later, 'was characteristic of Mr Churchill and of something very lovable in him. First the indignation . . . then reflection and a generous acceptance expressed without half-tones or hesitation : these were the successive stages which endeared him to those whom he berated.'[17]

Churchill might have put it differently, as he did when he was forced to yield to American opposition to an operation against Rhodes : 'If one has to submit it is wasteful not to do so with the best grace possible.'[18]

To de Gaulle this would have seemed yet one more trait in Churchill which was incomprehensible, even reprehensible.

At the beginning of June the French Committee for National Liberation (F.C.N.L.) was formed in Algiers with de Gaulle and Giraud as joint leaders, and with apparent Anglo-American blessing. It looked as though Eden's policy, launched in January 1943, had been realised. But for de Gaulle it was only a first step to better things. To Roosevelt it was a mistake which would have to be put right. To Churchill it was a chance to show his loyalty to his friend Roosevelt.

Churchill went straight from his meeting with Roosevelt in the U.S. to Algiers, partly for talks on strategy with Eisenhower, partly to keep an eye on French affairs. He arrived before de Gaulle and, according to the General's account, kept himself informed of the de Gaulle–Giraud negotiations through General Alphonse Georges.[19] Georges had been second-in-command to the French commander-in-chief, Gamelin, until the fall of France; Churchill had cemented a personal friendship with him on a tour of the Maginot Line shortly before the war and thought of him as an old and trusted comrade. Eden, on the other hand, thought him 'a reactionary old defeatist'.[20] The British – after delays because of his high blood-pressure – had smuggled Georges out of France a few weeks earlier. He had then said he was willing to serve under Giraud, but not under de Gaulle unless there was complete Giraud–de Gaulle agreement.[21]

Immediately the F.C.N.L. was formed Roosevelt sent a message to Churchill : 'Even if [events in Algiers] are temporarily settled, you and I will be sitting on top of a probable volcanic explosion.' He was anxious that the Vichy governor, Pierre Boisson, should keep his post at Dakar.

And he disliked the pro-de Gaulle tone of Press reports from Algiers: 'The bride evidently forgets that there is still a war in progress over here. We receive only the bride's publicity. What is the matter with our British–American information services? Best of luck in getting rid of our mutual headache.'[22]

Churchill, eager to show that, even if he had had to bow to the British Cabinet, he could at least influence the British Press, and was also safeguarding Roosevelt's interests, replied optimistically:

> We had the whole Committee to luncheon . . . and everybody seemed most friendly. General Georges, whom I got out of France a month ago and who is a personal friend of mine, is a great support to Giraud. If de Gaulle should prove violent or unreasonable, he will be in a minority of five to two and possibly completely isolated. The Committee is therefore a body with collective authority with which in my opinion we can safely work.

Churchill added that he planned to transfer to the F.C.N.L. the existing British agreements with de Gaulle. He agreed that publicity from Algiers was one-sided: 'This is due to the Press correspondents, most of whom have a de Gaullist bias. I will consult with Anthony about what can be done to correct this. . . . I should have liked to stay another week as the weather was delicious and the bathing was doing me no end of good.'[23]

By this time Churchill was back in London. He may or may not have consulted Anthony, but he immediately telegraphed to Harold Macmillan, now Resident Minister in Algiers, 'Can anything be done to rid the publicity of its de Gaullist bias?'[24] Not content with this, he launched on a venture which showed how little he knew about the Press at working level and how dangerous top-level intervention could be. He personally wrote a paper intended as guidance to the British Press:

> The Prime Minister is somewhat concerned at the bias in favour of de Gaulle in the Press messages from Algiers and their presentation at this end. De Gaulle owes everything to British assistance and support but he cannot be considered as a trustworthy friend of this country. Wherever he has gone he has left a trail of Anglophobia behind him. . . . He has undoubtedly fascist and dictatorial tendencies. . . . We still hope that he will settle down to loyal team-work with the new committee. Up to the present he is struggling for complete mastery. Should he succeed in this, very serious differences will immediately open between him and the U.S. The President, who is the best and truest friend that Britain and Europe ever had, has strong views on the subject.

Churchill's 'guidance' ended with a plea that British newspapers should keep' coolness and impartiality' in these 'French quarrels'. He wanted a copy sent to the U.S. ambassador, John Winant. At this point he wrote to Eden that he proposed to give the guidance to the Minister of Information but before doing so wanted to know what Eden had to say about it. The guidance was read over the telephone to Eden who was in the country; he agreed with it[25] – perhaps the line was bad.

It then went to the Ministry of Information who gave it, as coming from the Prime Minister, to British newspapers and agencies. The British Press – inclined to be Gaullist and presumably unimpressed by Churchill's rhetoric – responded in a very lukewarm way, except for the *Observer*, which went so far as to say that the General might very soon find himself without friends – for which it was attacked hotly by the Communist *Daily Worker* for 'shameless offensiveness'. Churchill was put out by the very half-hearted reaction to his 'guidance'. But the affair might have blown over if the guidance had not been reproduced almost word for word a week or two later by Ernest K. Lindley in the *Washington Post*.

The British ambassador, Halifax, immediately telegraphed:

> This is the most mischievous effort yet in the campaign to involve us in the unpopularity of U.S. policy to de Gaulle . . . and looks like a climax in a series of attempts to divert criticism from the U.S. government to H.M.G. I have of course received no 'statement of British policy towards General de Gaulle' of the kind reported by Lindley. . . . The only natural deduction . . . is that State Department are out to break up the C.N.L. and get rid of de Gaulle. . . .

In a further telegram Halifax said he was sure the Lindley article was based on a secret telegram from Winant to the State Department.[26]

Churchill called this a 'somewhat fussy telegram from ambassador Halifax' and minuted to Eden, 'I propose to send him a cooling message.' Before he could do this another telegram came from Halifax saying yet again that the U.S. government had been 'deliberately feeding to chosen journalists misleading accounts of the British attitude with the object of disarming their own critics. . . . Looked at from here it would seem that early recognition of the Committee [the F.C.N.L.] by the Americans and ourselves is the one good way out.'[27]

This was not Churchill's idea at all. He commented to Eden, 'Edward seems to be working himself up unduly,' and after consulting Eden telegraphed to him: 'We must be careful not to make heavy weather over these French troubles. . . . You must on no account be disturbed by the position over French affairs. "London can take it." I have had long experience of the character and conduct of de Gaulle and it would be an ill day for France, afterwards detrimental to England, if he gained the mastery. Holding this conviction, I must stand with the President, who is our greatest friend, even when I do not entirely share his view on methods.'[28]

One reason for Halifax's 'Gaullism' on this occasion was perhaps his resentment that Churchill had not sent his guidance to him. Although he was a fairly consistent critic of U.S. policy on de Gaulle, he was not always so 'Gaullist' at heart. Roderick Barclay, at that time serving in the Washington embassy and dealing with French affairs, wrote later that Halifax 'was often inclined to share the irritation of Winston and Roosevelt with General de Gaulle and to think that Anthony Eden and the Foreign Office were going too far in their opposition to the State Department'.[29]

Churchill could fairly easily shut up Halifax, but reports of the *Washington Post* article, and eventually Press cuttings, reached London and got into the hands of M.P.s of all parties. Churchill found himself attacked in the House of Commons by his old friend Robert Boothby, who asked 'what steps he is taking to put a stop to the dissemination of misstatements liable to prejudice the relations of this country with the United Nations?'[30] – by which he meant the Free French. This time Churchill did not hand the baby to Eden, but said he took full responsibility since he had personally drafted the text of the guidance to the Press. But since it was a 'confidential document' he was not prepared to discuss it except in secret session, and then only if there were a general desire from the House to have one.[31]

The storm passed. More important things were happening in July 1943, with the assault on Sicily leading to Mussolini's fall. For Churchill it must be said that he was perhaps not just trying to please his friend Roosevelt: he genuinely resented de Gaulle's efforts to dominate the fledgeling F.C.N.L. or to pack it with his own men.

This time Eden did not try to restrain Churchill from rash action. Perhaps, as has been suggested, the telephone line was bad, or Eden was tired and bored.

De Gaulle, with his long memory, did not forget or forgive. When Churchill was convalescing at Marrakesh in January 1944 and asked de Gaulle to visit him, the General treated Macmillan to a list of 'the many indignities that the Prime Minister had heaped upon him', including the Press guidance.[32]

Roosevelt showed no gratitude or sympathy for Churchill in his embarrassment.

CHAPTER SIX

To recognise or not to recognise the F.C.N.L.?

In the summer of 1943 Eden had more important things than Press guidances to argue about with Churchill. He had to get Churchill to resist Roosevelt's mounting pressure for a total break with de Gaulle. An open quarrel between de Gaulle and Giraud sparked off the President. On 17 June a strange outburst from Roosevelt reached Churchill:

> I am fed up with de Gaulle, and the secret, personal and political machinations of that committee in the last few days indicate that there is no possibility of our working with de Gaulle. . . . I agree with you that . . . he would doublecross both of us at the first opportunity. I agree with you that the time has arrived when we must break with him. . . . The war is so urgent and our military operations so serious and fraught with danger that we cannot have them menaced any longer by de Gaulle.

Roosevelt then wrote something that seemed to confirm Halifax's inter-pretation of the *Washington Post* leak: 'Above all I am anxious that the break be made on a basis and for reasons which are identical with both our governments. There are plenty of emotional and dissident people throughout the world who will try to separate England and the U.S. in this matter and we must stand shoulder to shoulder.' He added that he had instructed Eisenhower, as commander-in-chief in North Africa, to keep control of the French forces firmly in Giraud's hands, adding, 'We will not permit de Gaulle to direct himself or to control through partisans on any committee the African French Army. . . .'[1]

But Churchill had learned something from his clash with the War Cabinet in May, and this time he did not dash impetuously to Roosevelt's side. Eden recorded in his diary that Churchill had read him the Roosevelt telegram over the telephone: 'It seemed pretty hysterical to me and Winston didn't really try to defend it. . . . F.D.R.'s mood is now that of a man who persists in error. It has all that special brand of obstinacy, like Hitler at Stalingrad.' Attlee rang up Eden and between them they got Churchill to amend his reply to Roosevelt, though neither liked it much.[2]

After sending it off, Churchill read his reply (and Roosevelt's telegram) to the War Cabinet. In it he welcomed the President's instructions to Eisenhower but did not at the moment favour breaking up the French Committee. The Cabinet discussion swayed to and fro. On one side it was said that it was understandable that the Americans should lose patience with de Gaulle; yet 'he exercised considerable influence in metropolitan France among those in whom the spirit of resistance had not been quenched. To force a break with him now would not restore American prestige in France and might damage ours.' On the other side, 'we could not conscientiously assure the U.S. government that, if General de Gaulle were in control of the French army in North Africa, the Allies could rely confidently upon his loyal co-operation . . . in the Allied military operations now impending'. So the War Cabinet blessed Churchill's reply to Roosevelt, without enthusiasm.[3]

At that time de Gaulle was threatening resignation from the F.C.N.L. Churchill sent off a blast to Algiers: de Gaulle should realise that, if he resigned, he would sever all connection with H.M.G.; journeys by him to Syria, Brazzaville and West Africa would not be permitted; if he stayed in French North-west Africa, 'it seems inevitable that measures should be taken to place him under restraint and so deprive him of the power to stir up trouble'.[4]

But at the Algiers end the U.S. military men were getting worried about Roosevelt's 'autocratic instructions', and Eisenhower's Chief of Staff confided in Macmillan that he would like Churchill to know that a French bust-up would be militarily embarrassing, and that the President seemed inclined to use military security for political purposes when there was no real danger.[5] This bit of back-stairs American military diplomacy helped to keep Churchill on an even keel.

Luckily for the American military men, Giraud and de Gaulle reached a compromise acceptable to Eisenhower if unwelcome to Roosevelt. Giraud was to command the French forces in North and West Africa and de Gaulle the forces in the rest of the French empire. For the moment Churchill was relieved of the painful choice between getting out of step with Roosevelt or having a new row with the War Cabinet over de Gaulle, leading to trouble in Parliament.

Then a new factor was injected into the troubled situation. News came from Moscow that the Free French representative there had asked the Soviet government to recognise the F.C.N.L. and Molotov had declared himself in favour. Churchill minuted to Eden: 'It would be most unfortunate if the Russians were to recognise the Algiers Committee, and they should be warned neither the U.S. nor Great Britain are likely to do so for some time. Moreover, the matter lies in the sphere of the western war, and consideration should be shown to the wishes of the two principal allies of Russia. Pray let me know what you are doing about this.' But before Eden could act Churchill had himself written a message to Stalin that he was concerned to hear he was thinking of recognising the Algiers Committee. De Gaulle, he said, was struggling for control of the French army. 'One cannot be sure of what he will do or of his friendly feelings towards us if he obtained mastery.' He and Roosevelt both felt de Gaulle might endanger the base and communications of the armies about to invade Sicily. Moreover, he wrote, Soviet recognition of the F.C.N.L. would reveal a difference between the Soviet and western Allies which would be most regrettable.[6]

Stalin said 'yes' in an unpleasant way: 'It seemed to us that the British government so far was interested in General de Gaulle. . . . When Giraud and de Gaulle . . . asked the Allies for recognition, the Soviet government thought that French opinion would be unable to understand any refusal. . . . The Soviet government has no information which would confirm the present attitude of the British government to the F.C.N.L. and more particularly to General de Gaulle.' But since the British wanted recognition postponed, the Soviet Union would meet their wish.[7]

The Soviet move reinforced other strictly practical reasons why Eden should press for recognition of the F.C.N.L. On 2 July he circulated a memorandum to the War Cabinet: 'The U.S. government are strongly opposed to General de Gaulle and his followers, and would prefer that he should not be a member of the French Committee. Indeed, they would have preferred . . . to deal with General Giraud alone and to relegate any committee to a purely subordinate role. They have inspired comment in the U.S. Press to the effect that H.M.G. have dropped General de Gaulle and have come round to the American view.' Eden then set out the case for recognition as 'the most effective means of building up the authority of the Committee'. Moreover, it might be difficult to get the Soviet Union to go on delaying recognition. Eden then asked the Cabinet to authorise him to raise the recognition question with the U.S. and Soviet governments, on the basis of a formula which he suggested.[8]

Churchill did not like this and minuted to Eden: 'I did not know you were going to bring this matter before the Cabinet formally. I think what you proposed . . . is altogether premature. . . . The desire to obtain recognition is our most potent lever to ensure the good behaviour of the Committee. . . . I hope that you will not press for a decision . . . at the present time.'[9]

For the moment Eden did not press it. But the next day Churchill heard from Macmillan in Algiers that Eisenhower's deputy was telegraphing to the U.S. Chief of Staff, General George Marshall, strongly urging recognition of the F.C.N.L.: 'He tells me that . . . there are definite military reasons for making this gesture before the date of *Husky*.'[10] (*Husky* was the planned operation against Sicily.)

This seemed to play into Eden's hands and leave Churchill at his mercy. Churchill's immediate reply to Macmillan was, 'We must await the President's reactions.'[11] But Eden was keen to grasp his chance. After a telephone conversation with Churchill he drafted a message for him to send to Roosevelt saying he heard that Eisenhower and his political adviser, Murphy, proposed immediate recognition: 'This is rather sudden. I should like to know your reaction. Our Foreign Office would also like to go ahead and recognise. My chief desire in this business has been to keep in step with you.' In Eden's draft there followed the words, 'and I have no desire to withstand any move to kiss and be friends', which Churchill disliked and cut out. But he left in Eden's conclusion: 'It is however essential that we should act together and that we should agree the extent and moment of our recognition.' Churchill sent the message to Roosevelt together with Eden's formula for recognition.[12]

This alarmed Roosevelt, who took Churchill's message to mean that Eisenhower had decided to act without his permission. (It later emerged that Eisenhower and Murphy had been sending 'a spate of telegrams' to Washington for the past month, urging recognition.[13]) Roosevelt immediately telegraphed to Churchill the text of a message he had sent Eisenhower and Murphy: 'You are not to recognise the Committee under any condition without full consultation and approval of the President. Of course it will be necessary to have joint action by Britain and U.S.'[14]

After issuing this order Roosevelt adopted a policy of masterly inactivity and sent no reply to Churchill's message about recognition. This did not worry Churchill, but it did Eden, who was under strong pressure from the Foreign Office and was growing impatient. Something close to a serious crisis blew up in his relations with Churchill, with talk of resignations in the air. He had drafted, for circulation to the War Cabinet, a detailed paper showing up American policy towards France in a very harsh light. He sent this to Churchill on 13 July asking if he would agree to Eden's sending it to the Cabinet. Churchill then wrote him a letter: 'My dear Anthony, I have just read your paper . . . and it is quite clear that both our points of view may have to be placed before the Cabinet. I am having my own paper printed. . . . If after having read my print you are in the same mind, both papers can be circulated tomorrow.'[15]

According to Eden's diary, late the night before the two had had 'a fierce but friendly argument' about France. Churchill had admitted that 'if we broke on this I should have much popular support, but warned that he would fight vigorously to the death. I told him I wasn't contemplating resignation.' Eden also recorded that, after he got Churchill's 'rather formal' letter, he went over to see him: 'He said he didn't like my paper and thought we might be coming to a break.' Eden added later, in his memoirs: 'This was far from my purpose and was perhaps a sign that the war years could bear even upon him.'[16]

Whatever personal passions it may have unleashed, Eden's paper was in fact a reasoned statement that in post-war Europe Britain might have to work even more closely with France than with the U.S., and that 'Europe expects us to have a European policy of our own and to state it. That policy must aim at the restoration of the independence of the smaller European Allies and of the greatness of France.'

His attack on U.S. policy was based largely on his talks with Roosevelt in March, which he had reported to the Cabinet on his return, but for good measure he threw in Roosevelt's fancy of detaching an area of northeast France, including Alsace–Lorraine, and incorporating it in a new buffer state to be called Wallonia. He added that there was reason to think the Americans were still in touch with Pétain, and seemed to have little sympathy for the more active Resistance movements in France. He asked the Cabinet to agree that he should 'open the ball with the State Department and give them our reasons why we think that recognition soon would benefit us all'.[17]

Churchill's paper, on the other hand, was an impassioned attack on de Gaulle and his well-known trail of Anglophobia, showing many signs of wounded personal pride and hurt feelings:

I have . . . for some time past regarded him as a personage whose arrival at the summit of French affairs would be contrary to the interests of Great Britain. . . . The personality of de Gaulle is no less detrimental to what I believe to be the main interests of France. He is animated by dictatorial instincts and consumed by personal ambition. He shows many of the symptoms of a budding Führer. . . . He would, I have no doubt, make anti-British alliances and combinations at any time when he thought it in his interests . . . and would do this with gusto. . . . I am resolved never to allow de Gaulle . . . to cloud or mar those personal relations of partnership and friendship which I have laboured for nearly four years to develop between me and President Roosevelt. . . .

Churchill then asked his colleagues to realise that this position was fundamental for him, and he believed that, if he explained it fully to Parliament or by broadcasting to the nation, he would be fully supported. After this threat to appeal to the nation over the heads of the War Cabinet – which was perhaps not meant very seriously – he simmered down and wrote that, if de Gaulle 'settled down to honest teamwork' within the F.C.N.L., it might then be possible to get the President to recognise the Committee on the basis of Eden's formula. Even if the Soviet Union recognised de Gaulle 'on account of his recent flirtation with Communist elements', it would still be wise 'to measure our course by the U.S.'[18]

Given the forcefulness of these two conflicting documents, some drama might have been expected when the War Cabinet met on 14 July, if not actual resignations. Instead, there was a slightly grotesque anticlimax. It was on 12 July that Lindley's leak of Churchill's unlucky Press guidance had appeared in the *Washington Post*. News of this had by now arrived in London. This took priority in the Cabinet over the Churchill and Eden papers. According to the minutes, the Cabinet was told that 'the U.S. authorities appeared to have made public use of some parts of a confidential document . . . which the Prime Minister had prepared and sent to [them] for their confidential information only'. Churchill said he would consider sending Roosevelt a personal message about the 'disclosure' and also the general question of the French Committee. At the same time the Cabinet agreed that Eden should speak to the U.S. ambassador about 'a limited degree of recognition' for the French Committee.[19]

So as things turned out Churchill, by the unlucky coincidence of the *Washington Post* leak, had been made to look a little foolish, and so Eden had won the day without a fight.

Awkward side-effects of Churchill's anti-de Gaulle feelings and devotion to Roosevelt were piling up. The British plan had been to transfer the agreements originally made with de Gaulle to the F.C.N.L. Because of the squabbles over de Gaulle, this had not yet been done, and various money problems had been left hanging in mid-air. One of them concerned S.O.E.'s relations with the French Resistance.

In spite of S.O.E.'s determination in principle to remain independent of de Gaulle in its French operations, they had in practice worked more and more closely with his people in London as his influence over the Resistance had grown. On 15 May he had heard from Jean Moulin, a leading member of the French Resistance, later to die at German hands, that a National Council of the Resistance had been formed and had declared that de

Gaulle was 'the sole leader of the French Resistance'; and this had been a useful weapon in de Gaulle's dealings with Giraud.[20]

But in June 1943 there was nearly a crisis in S.O.E.'s dealings with France on purely practical grounds. After the F.C.N.L. was formed Churchill decreed that no further money was to be paid to the old French National Committee in London (which was solidly Gaullist), and further payments were to be made to, or on behalf of, the new F.C.N.L. in Algiers. But this was only to happen after the Algiers Committee had proved itself, and the necessary financial arrangements had been made.

S.O.E. had been in the habit of delivering a monthly sum on behalf of the London Committee to Resistance groups in France. Were these payments now to stop? In mid-June Lord Selborne, the minister in charge of S.O.E., was told that he could send eighty million francs for that month as from the London Committee. But what after that?

On 18 June Selborne wrote to Churchill that, wherever the funds came from, 'for technical reasons the Resistance movements in France must be controlled and supported from London, because the dropping grounds and "reception committees" are out of range of North Africa, and their wireless sets are set up to work to England'. The large sum of eighty million francs was necessary to counter the German removal of Frenchmen of military age for forced labour in Germany – the age-group most likely to be in the Resistance. At the London Committee's request, 20,000 forged ration cards had been made in England and issued to the Committee's key men in France so that they could remain in hiding – but they still needed money for food, so the Committee had applied to the British Treasury for an extra fifty million francs in addition to the normal monthly sum of thirty million francs. 'I hope', Selborne wrote, 'that when we are bringing financial pressure on de Gaulle it will be borne in mind that the element of continuity is indispensable for the maintenance of resistance and that any delay in reaching agreement in Algiers should not be allowed to break continuity.'[21]

Morton, seeing this letter, had the reflex action of the professional intelligence officer, minuting to Churchill: 'I submit that . . . you should insist that direction of the French Resistance movement is to be taken out of the hands of de Gaulle and his satellites here. Otherwise de Gaulle will use this great power, backed by our money, to advance his own political ends in France and not in the interests of the Allied war effort. We should control the French Resistance movement as an integral part of Allied strategy.'[22]

Churchill, in answering Selborne, went even further:

During this period . . . it is imperative to prevent General de Gaulle from having the slightest control over money from the British Exchequer. I was concerned to learn of this greatly increased payment which had been made. I was reassured by the Foreign Secretary, who told me that the money would remain entirely in your hands. We must be careful that the direction of the French Resistance movement does not fall into the control of de Gaulle and his satellites. . . . Let me have your proposals . . . for carrying on the underground work without admitting de Gaulle or his agents to any effective share in it, and without letting any sums of money get into their hands.[23]

Selborne hit back hard. S.O.E., he wrote, were simply carriers; the money was counted and sealed by them and despatched in sealed cases to reception committees of Frenchmen waiting for them on the ground. As for the General, 'organised resistance in France is now almost solid in favour of de Gaulle as the symbol of resistance to the enemy and of democracy. This certainly confers power on de Gaulle, but it also exerts democratic influence upon him. He is well aware that the Resistance groups will follow him only so long as he pursues a policy acceptable to them.' S.O.E., Selborne added, were now working closely, through de Gaulle's London Committee, with the Resistance, on directives from the Chiefs of Staff. There were also 'a score or so' of action groups led by British officers concerned with specific tasks such as sabotage. As for rivals to de Gaulle, 'the name of Giraud counts for very little indeed in France. The name of Georges is mud. The name of anyone else in power in 1940 is manure. The French have their own attitude in the matter and will not accept leadership from Britain or America.'

As for the immediate problem, Selborne suggested that S.O.E. should go on delivering the money to France, but should tell the reception committees that it came on behalf of the Algiers F.C.N.L.[24]

This blast had some effect on Churchill. He replied that he could not agree with Selborne's 'sweeping generalisations' and that the F.C.N.L. could not come into the picture until a financial agreement had been concluded with it. So what did Selborne propose to do about the July payments?[25]

This apparently negative reply must have come as a relief to Selborne. At least Churchill was not going to veto the July payments. Selborne's solution – accepted by Churchill – was that the Treasury should pay the money direct to S.O.E. (instead of to the London Committee, as in the past) and that S.O.E. should tell the Resistance that this was 'an interim payment by S.O.E. pending a new settlement'.[26] The immediate crisis was overcome.

*

The S.O.E. problem was all grist to Eden's mill; here Selborne – by no means always his ally – fought Eden's battle for him. Eden himself tackled Churchill on a much smaller section of the front. He wrote to him on 9 July: 'Madame de Gaulle is shortly leaving for North Africa. I don't know whether you know her, but she has made a consistently good impression on all who have met her here. She is quiet, has avoided expressing partisan opinions, and has set an excellent example in this respect to others in the General's circle. She is also known to have exerted a restraining influence on her husband and to be pro-British. . . . If you agree, I would propose to suggest to the Palace that the Queen should be asked to receive her.'[27]

Churchill did not agree: 'Surely it will look like a demonstration of our de Gaullism to set against the President's Giraudism. Also . . . will it not be held to infer some division between the Court and the Cabinet? I should think it would be sufficient if you entertained her to lunch, or if you like I can do so. . . .'[28] Eden then pointed out that Giraud was coming to London and would no doubt see the king: 'I cannot think that it would look, therefore, as if we were setting de Gaullism against Giraudism. Moreover, this attention is deserved by Madame de Gaulle on her own record. . . . So please help me.' A few days later Eden wrote again: 'I should really like to do something for Madame de Gaulle, who is definitely the better half of General de Gaulle' – and then added in his own hand, 'which you may well say is no great praise!'[29] The eventual compromise was the king for Giraud, the queen for Madame de Gaulle.

Constant if gentle pressure from Eden, the War Cabinet meeting of 14 July, and such practical problems as S.O.E.'s financial arrangements, led Churchill to shift his position and make a new approach to Roosevelt on 21 July:

> It seems to me that something has got to be done about this. I am under considerable pressure from the Foreign Office, from my Cabinet colleagues, and also from the force of circumstances to 'recognise'. . . . What does recognition mean? One can recognise a man as an emperor or a grocer. . . . We submitted to you our formula which would meet our daily practical needs.

Churchill explained that talks were going on with Massigli and General Catroux over Syria, and would soon start with the F.C.N.L.'s financial expert, Maurice Couve de Murville, over financial agreements; there were the questions of powers of discipline over the Free French troops and naval units based in Britain, trade with the French colonies, and so on; Macmillan strongly recommended a measure of recognition.

Churchill ended his message with something almost like a threat to Roosevelt: 'I am therefore reaching the point where it may be necessary for me to take this step so far as Great Britain and the Anglo-French interests set out above are concerned.' Russia would then certainly recognise and this might be embarrassing to Roosevelt: 'I am no more enamoured of [de Gaulle] than you are, but I would rather have him on the Committee than strutting about as a combination of Joan of Arc and Clemenceau. . . . I try above all things to walk in step with you. . . .'[30]

Roosevelt answered immediately and went as far as saying: 'This government is most anxious to join with you and the other United Nations to move along the line of limited acceptance of the Committee, subject always to military requirements, but . . . I do not think we should at any time use the word "recognition" because this would be distorted imply that we recognise the Committee as the government of France as soon as we land on French soil.' Instead he suggested 'acceptance', coupled with a warning to the Committee against 'the promotion of factional interest'.[31]

Roosevelt's reference to 'factions' prompted Attlee to minute to Churchill that, in the light of a current political squabble in the U.S. which he termed 'unedifying', it seemed to invite the retort, 'Physician, heal thyself.' Churchill replied coldly: 'Deputy Prime Minister. Nothing is easier than to find grounds of disagreement with the President, and few things would be more unhelpful.'[32]

Churchill was now willing to sit back and do nothing, and informed the Canadian government, who were anxious to recognise, that if necessary he would leave the matter over for the coming Quebec conference, *Quadrant*. Eden, however, returned to the charge: 'I should dearly like to get this business out of the way before *Quadrant*,' and he proposed a message to Roosevelt including the phrase, 'I am afraid of the consequences of the cold douche which you propose to administer.' To this Churchill answered: 'I cannot feel that the matter is urgent. The Mussolini business holds the field in all minds. I do not want to complicate the day-to-day handling of this major affair by opening up another set of arguments with the President. . . . I should prefer to deal with the matter during *Quadrant*.'

This was reasonable enough, in the light of the great strategic possibilities which Churchill saw opening up for his Mediterranean strategy following Mussolini's fall – possibilities which he knew the American

Chiefs of Staff would find alarming and repellent. However, softening a little, he suggested that Eden should try his hand on a compromise formula, avoiding the word 'recognition' to please the President.[33]

But Eden answered that 'recognition' was needed: 'Unless we use the word the public, and, indeed, the French themselves, may well ask why, having been asked for bread, we give a stone.' So his compromise formula, which Churchill sent Roosevelt on 3 August, did contain the word 'recognition'; and Churchill went so far as to tell Roosevelt that he thought that the American formula 'was rather chilly and would not end the agitation there is for recognition in both our countries'.[34]

Churchill was gradually yielding to Eden. Roosevelt did not yield and asked Churchill to do nothing until they met.[35] Churchill obeyed; but to prevent an explosion in the F.C.N.L. he suggested to Eden that Macmillan should tell 'de Gaulle, Giraud, Catroux, Georges and other friends of mine on the Committee that I shall very shortly meet President Roosevelt and that I am going to try to bring about a satisfactory recognition . . .'.[36] This message was delivered and went down well, though de Gaulle 'seemed apprehensive that the formula of recognition might be unduly restrictive of the Committee's authority'.[37]

On 15 August, after staying privately with Roosevelt in advance of *Quadrant*, Churchill wrote him a personal letter in the train: 'I beg you to go as far as you can in your formula because however justly founded one's misgivings may be there is no use making a gesture of this kind in a grudging form.' He then suggested that, if necessary, there should be two separate but simultaneous British and American documents.[38]

This was what eventually happened: at Quebec Eden tried his hardest to win over Cordell Hull, but Hull would not budge an inch over the word 'recognition' and Roosevelt obviously approved his stand. So the Soviet Union was informed, as Stalin had requested, and separate British and American statements were published on 27 August, as also was a Soviet one.

To the Foreign Office Eden reported on his 'long struggle' with the Americans: 'Mr Hull was obstinate and has left distinctly sour. To bring the Americans so far we had to make it plain that we were determined to recognise whatever their decision.' Churchill's report to Macmillan was rather different: 'In my opinion the President and Mr Hull have gone a long way to meet our desires. You should tell my friends on the Committee that I am sure the right course for them is to welcome the American declaration in most cordial terms and not to draw invidious distinctions.'[39]

Macmillan reported that de Gaulle expressed considerable gratification at the happy solution and did not seem worried by the difference between the British and American formulas. The General then said he was anxious about the growth of the Communist Party in Algeria and in France, though he thought it could be controlled.[40] Perhaps this remark had something to do with the Soviet form of recognition of the F.C.N.L., which was much warmer than the American, or even the British.

After a long struggle and with the Foreign Office constantly urging him on, Eden had won the first round. De Gaulle also had won something and, secure for the moment on the external front, could concentrate on the internal front and on eliminating rivals. Roosevelt, however, had lost nothing of his profound distaste for de Gaulle, and Churchill remained firm and even fierce in his personal loyalty to the President.

CHAPTER SEVEN

After recognition, what next?

One early consequence of Britain's recognition of the F.C.N.L. was that it raised the question of appointing a political representative – he could not yet be an ambassador – to the Committee. Throughout the very wearing months of the summer of 1943, Macmillan – a young, progressive Tory and anti-appeaser – had, as Minister of State, done the job with a skill that at times almost amounted to sleight of hand. Soon becoming an entirely realistic Gaullist, he had worked for compromise solutions in French internal struggles which, as he almost certainly foresaw, would end in de Gaulle's supremacy. At the same time he gave the appearance of carrying out Churchill's somewhat peremptory anti-Gaullist directives, though not always to the extent of pulling the wool over the Prime Minister's eyes. So from time to time he incurred Churchill's anger, all the more because the Prime Minister regarded him as his personal representative. Some rising young politicians might have feared for their future careers, but he seemed quite undaunted by this risk; he probably knew Churchill well enough to guess that the risk was not very real.[1]

Yet in the matter of choosing a representative to the F.C.N.L. Churchill showed that he was very capable of giving political black marks to those who disagreed with him. Macmillan's hands were now fully occupied with Italy and other Mediterranean problems. Early in September 1943 Eden sounded out Duff Cooper to see whether he would like the job with the F.C.N.L., with the prospect of the Paris embassy after liberation. Duff Cooper was an old friend who, after dramatically resigning from the Chamberlain government in protest against the Munich agreement in 1938, had proved a failure as Minister of Information in 1940, and now seemed to be in the doldrums, holding the nebulous post of Chancellor of the Duchy of Lancaster. His wife, Lady Diana, famous for her beauty, was admired and liked by Churchill.

After sleeping on the question, Duff Cooper accepted Eden's offer, believing it a firm one approved by Churchill. But just afterwards, at a dinner-party, he found himself hotly defending de Gaulle against attack and then learned that his remarks had been reported to Churchill who was now having second thoughts, suspecting him of being too Gaullist for the job.[2]

Churchill wrote to Eden, not mentioning the question of Duff Cooper's Gaullism but suggesting that it would be almost an insult to offer the Algiers job to Duff Cooper; in the light of his distinguished political past, the Rome embassy would be more fitting. 'We must not under-rate Duff because he has had bad luck in the war,' he wrote. 'He has great qualities of courage. He is one of the best speakers in the House of Commons. . . . He might easily become a formidable voice and figure in Tory politics in the future. This last is a consideration which should have more weight with you than me.' As an afterthought Churchill, with an eye on planned Cabinet changes, added, 'Coming down to immediate political moves, it would be a convenience to me to have the Duchy at my disposal.'[3]

Rome had not yet been liberated; the post of ambassador did not yet exist, so if Churchill wanted the Duchy he had to get rid of Duff Cooper somehow. So he had second thoughts about sending him to Algiers – on certain conditions. On 14 October he wrote a friendly but demanding private letter:

My dear Duffie, . . . It would be disastrous if one of your high standing and powerful personality were to go to a post in which he would be conscientiously pursuing an absolutely different policy from that which I, as Head of the Government, deem necessary. This would only lead to collision. . . . I should like to feel . . . that you would be doing no violence to your convictions. I am therefore sending you some documents. . . . De Gaulle, I fear, is a man Fascist-minded, opportunist, unscrupulous, ambitious to the last degree. . . . I am sure de Gaulle, having failed to split Britain and the U.S., will try to split them both from Russia. . . . It may well be that after reading the files . . . you will form a different opinion. . . . If so I hope you will say so. This would in no way weaken our friendship. . . .

Churchill then added a postscript: 'P.S. My unchanging goal is a strong France friendly to Britain and the U.S.A.'[4]

Eden, according to Duff Cooper's later account, was more amused than alarmed by Churchill's attitude, 'since his views were in agreement with mine rather than those of the Prime Minister'.[5]

Churchill himself tried to be fair-minded. After having papers containing details of de Gaulle's misdeeds sent to Duff Cooper, he also sent him a long paper by Macmillan on 'The Road to Recognition,' which contained some very damaging charges against Roosevelt and his efforts to break de Gaulle.[6] 'It does not put the emphasis exactly as I should;

nevertheless it is an intelligent and level-headed account,' Churchill wrote in a covering note.[7]

However, Duff Cooper wanted the job. He quickly wrote back to Churchill that the documents had convinced him of the soundness of Churchill's view that de Gaulle was a potential source of mischief and a standing menace to Anglo-French and Anglo-American relations. He explained his pro-Gaullist dinner-table conversation, which had so alarmed Churchill, by ignorance of the facts and argued that 'an individual who had the reputation of being pro-de Gaulle and no longer deserved it, might prove a very suitable British envoy to the French Committee'.[8]

Churchill immediately wrote welcoming Duff Cooper's rapid conversion and felt he could now afford a slightly more generous attitude to de Gaulle, writing that he did not wish to overlook his good qualities or to underrate 'the smouldering and explosive forces in his nature'. Duff Cooper should make every effort to win his confidence and persuade him to work harmoniously with his colleagues and his British and American allies; 'The more the undue prominence of de Gaulle is merged in that of the Committee, the better treatment the Committee will get from the U.S.'[9]

So Duff Cooper got the job. But Churchill still did not entirely trust him to be as stern as he wished. Finding himself, after the Tehran and Cairo conferences, having pneumonia in North Africa, he determined himself to enter the fray and settle fresh crises centring on de Gaulle – and sent a series of messages to London saying that Duff Cooper should not yet come to North Africa. On New Year's Eve 1943 he was still saying: 'I still prefer that Duff should wait in England until I have had a chance to see de Gaulle and other French leaders.'[10]

Eden duly held Duff Cooper back, to his great annoyance and inconvenience. At last Churchill telegraphed that he was inviting de Gaulle to dine and sleep on 3 January 1944, and would be glad if Duff and Lady Diana could join him a few days later: 'I can then explain to him fully the results of my conversation with de Gaulle.'[11]

But Churchill never fully believed in Duff Cooper's conversion. 'I was never able to convince the Prime Minister', Duff Cooper wrote later, 'that I was not influenced by the great admiration and affection that I felt for the General. "You like the man," he would say to me. "I don't." '[12]

The prospective British representative to the newly recognised F.C.N.L. therefore took no part in the Anglo-American arguments, in the closing months of 1943, on the role which the Committee ought to play in France after liberation. During these Churchill seemed at times mentally and emotionally split between practical and political common sense, as expounded by the Foreign Office and the military planners, and his personal loyalty to Roosevelt. The President, during the autumn, became more or less isolated, except for Leahy, in his feud with de Gaulle: Cordell Hull, on his way to Moscow for the Foreign Ministers' conference in October, met de Gaulle in Algiers and got on quite well with him. But Churchill's sense of quixotic protectiveness towards Roosevelt was such that the more he saw him isolated, the more he felt he must stand by him and defend him against attack.

Churchill's personal loyalty was given not only to men of great power such as the U.S. President but also to much smaller men and to men of dubious reputation, if he felt he owed them any debt of gratitude. The results could sometimes be embarrassing or tiresome.

One instance was his attachment to the elderly General Georges, with whom he had fraternised on his pre-war tour of the Maginot Line and whom he had later 'got out of France'. When Churchill was in North Africa when the F.C.N.L. was in its birth throes, he was in close touch with Georges and hoped he would act as a counter-weight to de Gaulle. When he got back to London he sent a 'secret and personal' message to Macmillan in Algiers: 'Shall be glad to be informed of what is going on. Please encourage Georges to send me his own account by letter or telegram.' Eden saw this message before it went and suggested that Churchill should insert the words: 'I do not of course want to prompt Georges to bring all internal French troubles to me, least of all to encourage them.' (Eden did *not* share Churchill's high opinion of Georges, while Macmillan once described him as 'very old-fashioned.'[13]) Churchill refused: 'He is a personal friend and can write privately if he feels inclined.'[14]

At the end of June Georges duly sent a private letter to Churchill – who showed it to Eden – on the conflicts inside the F.C.N.L.: 'The first month has been mediocre.' In the following months Georges backed Giraud in his various struggles with de Gaulle and became more and more gloomy about the prospect of the General's becoming master of France after liberation.[15] In November, when Churchill was on his way to the Tehran conference, he entertained Georges in the *Renown* at Malta; after this Georges – so he told Morton – took steps to let it be known that the interview had occurred and 'for days the whole Committee was buzzing in an endeavour to find out what had passed between the General and the Prime Minister'.[16]

De Gaulle, therefore, had a good idea of what was going on and this must have been one of the reasons why Georges was one of those, among them Giraud, whom he now succeeded in removing from the F.C.N.L. This, of course, upset Churchill who, in spite of the tremendous strategic and political questions he had just been discussing with Stalin and Roosevelt at Tehran, found time to telegraph to Attlee in London : 'I have been chilled . . . by the dismissal of my friend General Georges,' adding that he thought he would not now carry out his plan to visit the French army on his way home.[17]

But he instructed Desmond Morton to go and see Georges on his way back to London, which he did on 19 December. To Morton, Georges 'launched into a very bitter attack' on the F.C.N.L., showing him an article he had written castigating it, which he was arranging to have circulated by hand to the French troops fighting in Italy. Morton suggested this might lead to his arrest. Georges thought the F.C.N.L. would not dare, in view of 'his well-known friendship with the Prime Minister of England'. He was also, by this time, fed up with Giraud, likening him to 'a cooked artichoke whose leaves the Committee were plucking and throwing away one by one, leaving nothing but a sodden core'. Morton left Georges busy writing leaflets attacking the F.C.N.L.[18]

Macmillan, seeing Morton's report on this conversation, perhaps a little mischievously sent a telegram to Eden summarising it and adding, 'I will not conceal from you that this action . . . in pamphleteering in the French army against the Committee causes me concern. I should be glad to know whether you think I ought to give [Georges] a private warning.'[19]

A copy of this telegram went to Churchill in Tunis where he was now laid low with pneumonia. From his sick-bed he telegraphed to Macmillan : 'You may certainly warn General Georges that I could not defend pamphleteering amongst troops contrary to Committee. There was no need to repeat officially to Foreign Office this private information obtained by a member of my personal staff when you are in such direct communication with me.'[20]

Churchill was obviously annoyed with Macmillan but also a little embarrassed by Georges's activities. Yet when he entertained de Gaulle at Marrakesh during his convalescence, on 14 January, he raised the matter : 'I spoke of my regret that General Georges, who was an old friend of mine had been dismissed.' De Gaulle replied that he also respected General Georges but that it was not possible always to find a place in the government for everyone whom one respected.[21] Whatever de Gaulle did or did not know about Georges's activities, he thought it better not to pick this particular bone with Churchill; there were plenty of bigger bones lying around.

In February 1944, in spite of what he knew of Georges's hostility to the F.C.N.L. as it then was, Churchill wanted to suggest to de Gaulle that he should send Georges to London as 'Personal Military Liaison' with the Prime Minister in his capacity of Minister of Defence, in connection with the preparations for *Overlord* (the landings in north-west France). But the idea fell to the ground,[22] perhaps fortunately.

Churchill's devotion to Georges could easily be seen as a means of procuring an ally against de Gaulle, or at least a private source of information about him. Yet there was also a deeper motive. Churchill was convinced that Georges was a true friend of Britain who, by a timely warning of the impending French collapse in 1940, had saved Britain from sending the R.A.F. fighter force to France and to destruction. Churchill wanted to repay this real or imagined debt.

Another instance of Churchill's rather erratic sense of loyalty reveals another of his traits – a refusal to take up an attitude of moral indignation towards men who had erred or strayed politically and a deep-rooted dislike of vengefulness or vindictiveness.

When he was seriously ill in North Africa in December 1943 he was told that the F.C.N.L. had arrested two senior Vichy officials who had come over to the Allied side, Marcel Peyrouton and Pierre Boisson, and also the politician Flandin who had played a brief role in the Vichy regime. (Randolph Churchill had had long talks with Flandin at the end of 1942 and had written warmly to his father about them.[23]) It had been announced that they were to be tried by court martial.

When he had a fever the Prime Minister was even more impetuous than normal. He immediately sent Eden a telegram: 'I am shocked. . . . To Boisson we owe the delivery of Dakar. Peyrouton was invited in by Giraud. . . . I met both these men . . . when in Algiers in February. Both were rendering important services to the Allied cause at a time when the battle for Tunis hung in the balance. I certainly did say to both of them, "March against the Hun and count on me." It will be necessary for me to make this public if de Gaulle proceeds to extremities against them.' There was no specific obligation to Flandin. But, Churchill said:

it does not lie with the present House of Commons to reproach Flandin with his telegram to Hitler after Munich because, as you know, the vast majority of our Party highly approved the act and Mr Chamberlain's action far exceeded that of Flandin.

Churchill then asked Eden to make it clear that 'this kind of persecution' would not improve the F.C.N.L.'s relations with the British, still less the Americans, and that 'we have certain obligations towards the persons involved'. Eden, aware that some bits of this telegram would offend many Tories, gave instructions that it was to be distributed to the War Cabinet *only*.[24]

Churchill telegraphed at the same time to Roosevelt on the same lines, adding: 'I trust . . . you will take what steps you can to impress upon the French Committee the unwisdom of their present proceedings. You no doubt will also be considering the question of offering asylum.'[25]

Roosevelt must have been delighted and immediately instructed Eisenhower to 'direct' the F.C.N.L. to take no action against the arrested men at the present time. He also informed Churchill that he had sent this rather peremptory message: 'It seems to me that this is the time effectively to eliminate the Jeanne d'Arc complex and to return to realism. I too am shocked. . . .'[26] Churchill at once told Roosevelt that he had signalled his colleagues that he was in full agreement, adding, 'To admit that a handful of émigrés are to have the power . . . to carry civil war into France is to lose the future of that unfortunate country. . . .' To London he telegraphed that he felt it essential to support the President.[27]

But in London there was no liking for such direct and authoritarian intervention in the affairs of the F.C.N.L. Eden took a fairly mild line with the Committee's London representative, Maurice Viénot, who said there was no need for immediate alarm. Reporting this to Churchill, Eden quoted back at him his own statement in the House three months earlier, that 'the French people alone must be the judges of the conduct of their fellow Frenchmen in the terrible conditions which followed the military collapse of 1940'.[28] In Algiers Macmillan also made a relatively calm approach to the F.C.N.L., and at the same time recalled to Churchill that Boisson was believed responsible personally for brutalities, even torture, inflicted on British merchant seamen imprisoned in French West Africa[29] – a reminder likely to touch a chord in Churchill's heart.

On Christmas Eve Eden sent Churchill another calming telegram: he could not help feeling that 'literal compliance with the President's message to Eisenhower would land us in a first-class crisis' and might lead to the collective resignation of the F.C.N.L. to which there was no alternative in sight. 'This might bring about immediately in North Africa a situation where British or American troops would have to be diverted from their proper tasks in order to maintain order.' The wise thing would be to try to delay action against the three accused men until after France was liberated. Eden concluded: 'We have not discussed this at all in Cabinet, but I have talked it over with Attlee who agrees.'[30]

Churchill, now less fevered, agreed that literal execution of Roosevelt's order would not have been the best way to handle things, but he was confident that Eisenhower's representatives would 'do all the softening that was necessary'. However, he thought Macmillan had not stated the British case 'with sufficient force or zest'. The greatness of France would not be achieved by the persecution mania of the Committee: 'I want a harder atmosphere established.' Churchill added that he meant to see the members of the Committee and 'possibly de Gaulle himself'.[31]

Roosevelt, too, simmered down and told Eisenhower not to act on his earlier instructions 'in view of developments', but to try to obtain the same ends through informal discussion.[32] Eden went on pleading with Churchill for conciliation:

I hope you will be able to see some of these Frenchmen including de Gaulle. You can do more with them than anyone else, and we have just got to build up a France somehow; though the Bear's manners are steadily improving, I still have no ambition to share the cage alone with him. . . . We have had grand Christmas at home despite local failure of electric light caused by enthusiasm of our American allies, who destroyed cable with their telegraph pole. The first instalment of *Overlord*.[33]

The storm blew over. De Gaulle gave the Americans a promise that Boisson, Peyrouton and Flandin would not be brought to trial till after the war and meanwhile would be kept under surveillance. He gave the same undertaking to Churchill when he saw him on 12 January, after Churchill had first 'remonstrated' with him on the subject. De Gaulle's assurance that the three were not being ill-treated did not satisfy Churchill, who kept nagging Macmillan and the Foreign Office to step up pressure for *better* treatment.[34]

Madame Flandin entered the fray on her husband's behalf. She had been encouraged by Randolph Churchill, who had apparently assured her, during a brief visit to North Africa, that her husband would be restored to her in a few days. Duff Cooper wrote to Eden that he rather resented that, owing to Randolph's admiration for Flandin, he was obliged to plead his cause.[35]

Churchill flung himself into the battle with ardour. As late as 4 March 1944 he minuted to Eden: 'I do not see why [Flandin] should not live under "résidence surveillée" in his own farm. . . . He ought not to be kept for two or three years in bondage. He is no more guilty than N.C. or

E.H.'[36] That, of course, meant Neville Chamberlain and Edward Halifax.

But when after Paris was liberated Flandin and the others were to be sent from Algiers to France and Madame Flandin wanted to come to England, Churchill did not gainsay Eden's view that to agree would be unwise since the French would certainly resent it. 'I will take no responsibility in advising her,' he wrote.[37]

Churchill's personal preoccupation with Boisson, Peyrouton and Flandin may seem eccentric, even frivolous, in a man directing British war strategy at a crucial time. Yet he did still manage to direct his main energies to this vital task, even when seriously ill at Christmas 1943, when he was peppering Eden with telegrams on the need for keeping landing-craft in the Mediterranean, on Tito and the Yugoslav Resistance, and on many lesser subjects. His mental vitality was so overflowing, even when he was weak in body, that he was driven to put a finger in some very small and not very tasty pies. If his energies had been less, Eden's task would have been lighter.

CHAPTER EIGHT

French government or Allied military government, 1944?

In the time between the recognition (or acceptance) of the F.C.N.L. in August 1943 and *Overlord* in June 1944 the pattern of relations between Churchill and Eden and between Roosevelt and Churchill continued much the same so far as France was concerned, though the realities of the situation – the needs of the military leaders and planners – weighed down the scales more and more heavily on Eden's side. But Roosevelt, backed up by Churchill, seemed to become more and more unreasonable and emotional in his judgements. Churchill, in constant contact with the military leaders in London, did see the realities and, but for his loyalty to Roosevelt, would surely have accepted the claims of de Gaulle and the F.C.N.L. to govern France – provisionally – after liberation. But the more he saw his friend Roosevelt isolated from his American subordinates and American opinion on this issue – and the more he felt himself isolated among his Cabinet colleagues and in Parliament in consequence – the more stubbornly he insisted that the President's wishes must be law.

In September 1943, a month after the F.C.N.L. had been recognised, Churchill sent Macmillan a 'personal and most secret' message: 'Our friends on the Committee should realise that anything like the complete subordination of Giraud to de Gaulle and the latter's sole mastery . . . would risk a direct collision with the U.S. and that, while trying to smooth matters as much as possible, I should in the ultimate issue range myself with the President.'[1] After Cordell Hull's meeting with de Gaulle in October, Macmillan's staff reported that Hull's entourage had been saying that 'the real obstacle to a realistic French policy was the President'. Churchill read this report without making any comment.[2] After the Tehran conference in December Churchill telegraphed to Attlee: 'The great obstacle to the rehabilitation of France is the personality of de Gaulle. . . . At Tehran we were all surprised to find how deep was the distrust of Stalin towards France. . . . This does not alter my convictions but it shows how foolish de Gaulle is in thinking he can play Russia off against Britain and the U.S.'[3]

Yet at the Foreign Ministers' conference in Moscow in October it had been agreed that the F.C.N.L. should be invited to join the U.S., Russia and Britain on the Advisory Council for Italy. Churchill liked this, but Roosevelt did not. According to Robert Murphy, who saw Roosevelt on his way to Tehran, the President had forgotten that this invitation had been given, and was not pleased : 'When I went on to say that the Russians were now treating the French Committee as the government of France, Roosevelt was plainly irritated and abruptly changed the subject.'[4]

The Moscow Foreign Ministers' conference had also agreed to set up the European Advisory Commission – without the French, but it was expected to give the Russians a certain say in planning for the post-invasion administration of France, or 'civil affairs'. It was this question which was at the heart of the long-running Anglo-American dispute – or, rather, the dispute between Roosevelt, plus a rather unhappy Churchill, and almost everyone else – that wasted so much time in the months before *Overlord* and even after. The uncertain Soviet attitude was an extra complicating factor.

Eden had foreseen, in the summer of 1943, the damage of trying to impose Anglo-American military government on France (see p. 73 above). This was the firm view of the Foreign Office and of William Strang, who was to become the British representative on the European Advisory Commission, in particular. In October 1943 Macmillan, from Algiers, gave forceful support. In a personal letter to Eden he argued that an Anglo-American occupation, 'though it would not be so oppressive, might be just as offensive to a sensitive people as the Germans'. He went on :

> In my view, all this business . . . is just sheer waste of time. It will break down within three weeks, as it has broken down in Italy and Corsica, and must break down in every self-respecting European country. I should like to see it tried on Tees-side [Macmillan's constituency]! You and I are Tories, and half the strength we have against that form of radical Communism which would like to bully the English people is that they have not forgotten Cromwell and the Major-Generals. I warn you very strongly that if you try any of this nonsense in France there will be a bitter revolt against you. . . .[5]

Eden passed this letter to Churchill saying he was in general agreement with it.[6] He also wrote to him that the original American plan had been to 'hold the ring in France until, by an election, the French people could make a "free and untrammelled choice" of their future government', whereas the British plan had been for an Anglo-American military administration very much more limited in space and time. Now, he added, discussions in Washington had led to a compromise plan providing for a 'French director of civil affairs'. Eden thought this a step in the right direction, but the War Office raised the objection that it would imply recognition of the F.C.N.L. and this the British and U.S. governments would not have. Churchill came down in favour of Eden against the War Office, largely because, as the Foreign Office pointed out, 'The Russians want to go much further in the French direction and this factor makes Anglo-American agreement especially desirable.'[7]

At this point U.S. officials even seemed ready to let the F.C.N.L. play some part in administering France after the Allied landings. But then the blow fell. In November de Gaulle set up a Consultative Assembly which elected him sole president, and he then reshaped the F.C.N.L., inducing Giraud to quit it while remaining commander-in-chief. At the beginning of December the State Department told the British that Roosevelt's attitude had hardened: 'It was no longer possible for any decisions on French affairs to be taken without reference to the President and it could not be foretold what his views would now be.' One by-product of this was that the Americans now insisted that Anglo-American currency should be used in France in the same way as in enemy territory.

From Washington Halifax commented: 'It would seem ... the President, encouraged perhaps by Leahy, is alone responsible for our differences. ... His attitude does not correspond to any current of opinion in Congress or among the American public so that it seems to be a purely personal one.' Halifax recommended that the British should pursue what they themselves thought the wise policy and hope that the Americans would follow – which they might well do if they saw that the Russians agreed with the British: 'After all, the fate of the U.S. is not likely to be so directly affected as our own by the future shape of France.'[8]

Soon after, the British learned that Roosevelt had ordered that *no* further steps should be taken in planning for civil affairs in liberated French territory.[9] The Foreign Office hoped that Churchill would have things out with Roosevelt personally when both were on their way home from the Tehran conference, but this could not be arranged. However, Eden telegraphed to Churchill on 11 December: 'As you will remember, we and State Department were virtually in accord ... but the President vetoed all this. ... Personally I remain of the opinion that we should not attempt to administer France ourselves for a moment longer than the military exigencies of the situation demand.'[10]

In London in January 1944 planning for *Overlord* was gathering momentum. The Chief of Staff to the Supreme Commander, Eisenhower, sent a request to the Combined Chiefs in Washington that de Gaulle should be asked to name representatives with whom negotiations could begin at once: 'The need for prompt action cannot be over-emphasised, since we will desire to turn over to French control at the earliest possible date those areas that are not essential.' Churchill, knowing that this was several jumps ahead of Roosevelt's thinking, minuted: 'We cannot agree to this without more consideration. General Eisenhower should be informed.'[11]

By this time both Eisenhower and his Chief of Staff, General Bedell Smith, had come to the conclusion that for purely practical reasons 'we must be in a position to deal with some sort of government of metropolitan France'. They said that the F.C.N.L., 'whatever its faults might be, represented the beginning of civil government in France'.[12] But when it seemed as though the British and American military men might be finding a way round Roosevelt's veto, Churchill intervened and minuted to Eden: 'I cannot be a party to any manoeuvre to manage the President. Moreover, I am in general agreement with him on this matter.'[13] He also wrote: 'I am not in favour at the present time of making arrangements for the French Committee to take over the civil administration of any part of France we may liberate. We have no guarantee at present that de Gaulle will not hoist the Cross of Lorraine over every town hall and that he and his vindictive crowd will not try to peg out their claims to be the sole judge for the time being of the conduct of all Frenchmen and the sole monopolists of official power. This is what the President dreads, and so do I.' (The shadow of the affair of Boisson, Peyrouton and Flandin was a long one.) Churchill repeated that he would not lend himself to any attempt to prevent Roosevelt 'jibbing'. In reply, Eden could only suggest talking things over.[14]

In the abortive discussions that followed, Eden held his ground. In early March he minuted to Churchill: 'The solution which I would . . . recommend is that we should undertake to facilitate the arrival of the F.C.N.L. in France at the earliest operationally possible moment and thus enable them to discuss with the leaders of the Resistance groups and other representative bodies . . . arrangements for the constitution of a provisional government.'[15]

All this while the European Advisory Commission should, in theory, have been discussing the question of civil administration in France after liberation. Owing to Roosevelt's refusal to sanction any Anglo-American plan, nothing had been done. On 25 March the Soviet ambassador in London, Fyodor Gusev, presented an *aide-mémoire* to the Foreign Office recalling the Moscow conference decision on this point; why then had Eden just said in the House that the British and American governments were examining the matter and that 'whatever we say and do, we shall say and do together' – so ignoring the Soviet Union? Gusev demanded an explanation.[16]

Eden minuted to Churchill that this Soviet intervention made it even more important to agree as soon as possible with the Americans on a directive to Eisenhower. Churchill replied: 'Surely this surly note should give an opportunity to ask the Soviet government whether they will agree to a tripartite commission in respect of the occupied countries in the east of Europe, including particularly the Baltic States, the liberated districts of Poland, and the conquered territories of Romania and Bulgaria as they fall later. . . . I do not think we ought to concede tripartite control of the territories immediately behind our armies unless an equal measure is given out in the east.'[17] This idea revealed the state of Anglo-Soviet relations – the mention of the Baltic States would have been a red rag to the bull (or Bear) – but in the French context was nothing but a red herring.

Early in April 1944 the F.C.N.L. representative in London, Maurice Viénot, told Churchill that the Committee were going to send General Koenig, whom they thought especially acceptable to the British, to London to deal with the British government and with Eisenhower 'for all purposes connected with operations based on the United Kingdom'; and it was of the highest importance that the biggest possible French contingent should take part in these. Churchill said he hoped one French division could take part. Viénot then spoke of reports that Eisenhower was to be allowed to deal with French bodies other than the F.C.N.L.: 'This . . . would involve a foreign general acting as arbitrator between Frenchmen and consequently intervening in French internal affairs.' Churchill replied that the F.C.N.L. 'had failed to obtain the confidence of the President'. He himself, too, had been 'deeply wounded' by their attitude. All his life he had been a friend of France. He was still looking for the France he used to know. In any case, Churchill said, he was unwilling to disturb the President who was resting for two or three weeks. He warned Viénot that in the coming presidential election Roosevelt might be re-elected and then France would have to deal with him for nearly five years more; 'The French must seek to understand the President and to avoid rubbing him up the wrong way.'[18]

By now Churchill was beginning to argue not so much that Roosevelt was right as that he must be humoured. He himself was trying to persuade Roosevelt to accept compromises rather than impose flat vetoes. On 8 April Roosevelt sent him a message saying that the tone of the F.C.N.L.'s requests 'verges on the dictatorial' and that no military information should be given 'to a source which has a bad record in secrecy'. Churchill was willing to accept this so far as *Overlord* was concerned: 'I have tried to further their earnest wish to have the Leclerc armoured division included in the forthcoming battle. But the presence of this single division will not give them any right to be informed of our secrets.' But, he argued, if *Anvil*, the operation in the south of France, were carried out, this would be different. With six or seven French divisions employed, they would be more than half the Allied forces: 'There I think they should be made full partners.' He added that the 74,000 French soldiers in Italy had fought very well with a very small proportion of missing or killed, and this gave them a claim 'to be taken into our confidence in that theatre'. Roosevelt, still away from Washington, said he must consult his advisers before giving an answer, but added: 'In addition to a probability of compromising the security of our plans . . . which might have disastrous effects, it does not appear to me that any military advantage could result from divulging confidential information to the Committee.' However, over a month later Roosevelt did at least agree that the French could be consulted about the battle for Italy.[19]

In his message of 8 April Roosevelt, intentionally or unintentionally, lured Churchill into a trap. He wrote: 'If de Gaulle wants to come over here to visit me I shall be very glad to see him and will adopt a paternal tone, but I think it would be a mistake for me to invite him without an intimation from him that he wants to come.' As Cordell Hull had just said kindly things about the F.C.N.L. in public, Churchill thought this marked the beginning of a thaw, and he leapt on the chance to act as fairy godfather. He replied that he had instructed Duff Cooper in Algiers to give de Gaulle a message that the Prime Minister thought it would be a very good and important thing for the General to pay a short visit to Roosevelt, and this would be helpful to British relations with the F.C.N.L. since, as de Gaulle would understand, 'It is the foundation of our British policy to keep in step with the U.S. with whom we are sharing such great war schemes.' If de Gaulle felt like making the visit, Churchill would suggest to Roosevelt that he should send a formal invitation.[20]

Unfortunately, it was just at this time that de Gaulle, suspecting 'the

Allied missions and general staffs' of still aiming to put Giraud in charge of French affairs, removed him from the post of Commander-in-Chief, a fact of which Roosevelt, away from Washington, was unaware when he sent his message of 8 April. Churchill had long ceased to pin any hopes on Giraud; he had written to Roosevelt in January that de Gaulle was 'a bigger man in his own way than any around him'.[21] But to Roosevelt, publicly committed to Giraud, his removal was both an embarrassment and an insult. And he probably did not want Churchill to win credit as a fairy godfather. He answered him promptly : 'I would be glad to see [de Gaulle], but I will extend no formal or informal invitation.'[22]

But Churchill had instructed Duff Cooper to act at once, and this he had done, getting from de Gaulle the answer that he would be most happy to accept an invitation from Roosevelt at any time; he also expressed gratitude to Churchill. So when Churchill got Roosevelt's second message and sent Duff Cooper 'extreme priority' instructions *not* to take action, these arrived too late.[23]

Nevertheless, Duff Cooper, once launched on the enterprise, was anxious to find ways of saving both Roosevelt's face and de Gaulle's and arranging for the visit to take place. His ingenious suggestions met with a tetchy reaction from Churchill : 'Please do not go apologising to de Gaulle for the President and me.' But he added : 'If de Gaulle can stoop so far as to inquire . . . in Washington whether a visit from him would be agreeable when the President returns from his rest cure, and if he lets me know that he will do this beforehand, I will make sure that a favourable answer will be given, before the *démarche* is made.' Duff Cooper replied quickly : 'General de Gaulle is willing to follow the procedure you indicate.' Churchill then told Roosevelt that de Gaulle would like to inquire whether a visit would be agreeable to Roosevelt after he returned from his holiday, adding : 'I hope . . . you will tell me I may encourage him to take this course. You might do him a great deal of good by paternal treatment.'

But Roosevelt was now on his high horse : 'Owing to accumulation of work here I think it would be much better not to have the inquiry of a visit made at present. It would be much better timing . . . to have the question raised a month from now.'[24]

By this time Churchill's temper was becoming a little short, in spite of his respect for the U.S. President : 'From our previous correspondence . . . I had hoped you would go a little further with this. After all, this man, whom I trust as little as you do, commands considerable naval forces and the *Richelieu*, which are placed most freely at our disposal and are in action or eager for action. He presides over a vast empire, all the strategic points in which are at our disposal.' Churchill then asked if he could encourage de Gaulle to raise the question of a visit in a month's time.[25]

Roosevelt now got even huffier: 'I do not have any information that leads me to believe that de Gaulle and his Committee . . . have as yet given any helpful assistance to our Allied war effort. It seems to me that the forces including naval forces and the *Richelieu* were placed at our disposal before de Gaulle.' De Gaulle could make a request at the end of May, but he would make no promise: 'I will not ever have it said by the French or by American or British commentators that I invited him to visit me in Washington. If he asks whether I will receive him if he comes I will incline my head with complete suavity and with all that is required by the etiquette of the 18th century. This is farther than the Great Duke would have gone. Don't you think so?'[26] (The mention of Churchill's ancestor, the Duke of Marlborough, was presumably meant to add piquancy to Roosevelt's rebuff.)

Fortunately or unfortunately, Churchill was in a good humour when he replied mildly, 'You started me off on this,' then turned to other things and ended: 'I have had a busman's holiday myself, having been Acting Foreign Secretary and Leader of the House as well as my other odd jobs.'[27] (Eden was having a rest under doctor's orders.)

For the time being Churchill gave up his role of fairy godfather. At the end of May he heard from Duff Cooper – not from Roosevelt – that the President had sent a message to de Gaulle through a F.C.N.L. representative that he would be pleased to receive him whenever he cared to come. A few days later he got a letter from Roosevelt making some mention of this. Churchill could not resist trying once again to be helpful. As de Gaulle was by this time in London for crucial talks with the British and with Eisenhower, he rashly said in the course of a long message to Roosevelt, 'I will . . . deliver to him your friendly message to come over to see you.' This provoked Roosevelt into replying: '. . . all good luck in your talks with the Prima Donna. . . . Please for the love of Heaven do not tell de Gaulle that I am sending him a "friendly message to come over to see me". The whole point of it is that I decline absolutely as Head of State to invite him to come over here. . . . The distinction is a very important one.'[28]

All this was at the time of *Overlord*, the grand climax of Anglo-American strategy. De Gaulle was not the only 'Prima Donna'.

*

When D-Day came, because of Roosevelt's vetoes there was still no agreed arrangement on the civil administration of French territory when liberated, or on the position of the F.C.N.L. The military commanders had been left in a vacuum. In mid-May the French Consultative Assembly in Algiers – an advisory body without legislative power – had declared unanimously that the F.C.N.L. was henceforth to be known as the Provisional Government of the French Republic. Eden, back at work, immediately put to Churchill the case for recognising the F.C.N.L. as such: 'The French contribution to the war effort in extent of territory and number and value of its fighting forces is superior to that of any of the Allies with the exception of the Big Three. . . . I have too in mind . . . the desirability of trying to prevent our relations with the French from deteriorating further between now and D-Day.' Churchill answered, 'We ought to find out what the President thinks first. We cannot recognise if U.S. do not.'[29]

Roosevelt's reaction was easy to guess. On 18 May the British Chiefs of Staff were told that he had instructed Eisenhower to have no dealings with any French authority claiming to represent the Provisional Government of France. Eden at this point took the stand that the British and Americans must keep in step. The next day the War Cabinet discussed the matter. Eden suggested a wait-and-see policy – no notice should be taken of the French Consultative Assembly's declaration.[30] Churchill sent a message, approved by the Cabinet, to Roosevelt proposing this. Roosevelt agreed but added: 'I really cannot go back on my oft-repeated statement that the Commitee and de Gaulle have aimed to be recognised as the Provisional Government of France without any expression or choice by the people themselves and that I could not recognise it.'[31] So the President's mind seemed firmly closed.

But it was not altogether certain that Moscow would adopt a wait-and-see tactic, as proposed by Eden. There were reports that it was about to recognise the French Provisional Government. Churchill minuted to Eden: 'I am determined not to sever myself from the President . . . and be found lining up with Russia against him. . . . I would have nothing to do with it. . . . Russia has no right to take this step without consultation with her two allies who are doing all the fighting in the west.'[32] Eden was left with the job of persuading Russia and other Allies not to recognise the F.C.N.L. as a provisional government.

At this crisis both Attlee and Bevin were at Eden's side in fighting Churchill's fixed determination to glue himself to Roosevelt. Attlee wrote Eden a long letter on 31 May:

I agree with you in feeling considerable anxiety over the French situation. We have a much bigger stake in France than the U.S.A. . . . The French are always difficult and never more so when they owe gratitude to others for their deliverance as we saw after the last war. I do not think that the President has any real understanding of the French temperament . . . nor do I think that his attitude is dictated by a zeal for democracy. . . . This did not prevent him from running Darlan and afterwards Giraud. I am very sensible how much we owe to the President but this should not lead us to agree to a mistaken policy. . . . We are the only people in this set-up who can speak as Europeans concerned with the future of Europe. . . .

Eden replied gratefully.[33]

De Gaulle duly arrived in England at Churchill's invitation – approved by Roosevelt – in time for D-Day. Nothing was settled about recognition or about the administration of liberated areas of France. But Eden had succeeded in persuading Churchill that the only thing to do was to try to get de Gaulle to negotiate an agreement on the administration issue with the British, which Roosevelt might then be coaxed into accepting. In the presence of Eden, Bevin and others, Churchill put this plan to de Gaulle on his arrival, only to be met with a haughty rejection; de Gaulle was especially wrathful about the plan to issue Anglo-American military currency in France.

Churchill was furious and said that if he had to choose between de Gaulle and Roosevelt he would always choose Roosevelt. Bevin at first backed Churchill, saying the Labour Party would resent de Gaulle's rejection; the General replied that it was all very well for Bevin to talk, but he himself was in the right and it did not mean anything to say that the Labour Party would be offended. Later, Bevin made it clear that he did not agree with Churchill in choosing the U.S. in preference to France.[34]

The next day Eden wrote to Churchill very much on the lines of Attlee's recent letter to himself: 'I am deeply concerned at the situation which is developing in respect of Anglo-French-American relations. . . . Failure to reach agreement with the French Committee will not be understood in this country. . . . Parliament and public wish to see an arrangement reached with the F.C.N.L.' He proposed one more approach to the U.S. to join in discussions with de Gaulle, coupled with a warning that the British government might have to make their own position public.[35]

The next day was D-Day. Eden again wrote to Churchill. He quoted a recent telegram from Roosevelt saying 'I am absolutely unwilling to police France'; if the President renounced the paternity of France, Eden said, surely he must allow the British to do the schooling in their own way:

'The present position is unfair to H.M.G. and dangerous to Anglo-American relations.'[36] Bevin also wrote to Churchill, pleading the case of his trade union friends in the F.C.N.L. who wanted to work with Britain and knew de Gaulle's weaknesses, but believed there was no alternative to the F.C.N.L.; if they were not given a fair chance, 'France may go completely Communist' and the whole French labour movement might be driven into Russia's hands, with repercussions in Holland and Belgium. So, Bevin wrote, de Gaulle's personality should not be allowed to outweigh the importance of dealing with the Committee.[37]

Churchill, for his part, kept an aircraft standing by to fly de Gaulle back to North Africa 'if necessary'.[38]

Also on D-Day, Churchill and Eden had a midnight row on the telephone. Eden noted in his diary that Churchill was in a rage 'because Bevin and Attlee had taken my view – F.D.R. and he would fight the world'.[39]

On the day after D-Day Eden got the War Cabinet to agree that he should try afresh to get talks going with the French – with the General's representative, if not with the General himself. The Cabinet also agreed that Churchill should advise the king not to receive de Gaulle until discussions had led to a satisfactory outcome.[40]

Eden, however, could make little headway in persuading de Gaulle to allow negotiations. Things were still tense when de Gaulle made his first visit to liberated territory in France in mid-June. Churchill wrote later: 'I had arranged this visit without consulting Roosevelt beforehand.'[41] Perhaps he then got cold feet. At a dinner given by Eden for de Gaulle on the eve of his journey, a letter came from Churchill, who had been upset by de Gaulle's refusal to recognise the Anglo-American military currency for use in France. The General, Churchill wrote, had thereby taken sides against the commander-in-chief: 'This seriously affects the question of de Gaulle going over tomorrow. . . . There is still time to cancel his visit. . . . There is no harm, from our point of view, to the President's taking the lead.'[42] According to both de Gaulle and Eden, the other British ministers present, particularly Attlee, all agreed that de Gaulle should go as planned.[43]

The clear success of de Gaulle's visit to the bridgehead in France mellowed him and also soothed Churchill's anxieties. De Gaulle was now ready for his London representative, Viénot, to start negotiating an agreement on administration with Eden which could then be signed by the British, Americans and French at the same time. Eden believed that de Gaulle's coming visit to Washington would make this possible.

The visit was a public success but the Roosevelt–de Gaulle talks were on such a lofty plane that neither recognition nor the question of administration were discussed. So – without any formal agreement – the second question solved itself in practice on French soil, where de Gaulle's representatives successfully took over administrative control in one area after another, thus relieving Eisenhower of a heavy burden.

On recognition, Eden sent Churchill a long minute on 26 June setting out the reasons in favour once again: 'The French Committee control forces and territories which give them fourth place in the Grand Alliance. Our estimate of General de Gaulle's position in France has been confirmed in Normandy. . . . The effect upon our future relations with France would be good. . . . It is in the interests of the strong France we want to see that we should do all we can to help Frenchmen to recover their self-respect. . . . General de Gaulle told . . . his colleagues that he would prefer us not to recognise the provisional government since he knew that the people of France would choose him and he would then be able to say that he owed us nothing!' Eden added that Roosevelt might change his policy.[44]

Churchill did not reply. On 8 July Eden tried again: 'We ought to get the position tidied up quickly while there is some virtue in recognising the French Committee instead of waiting until we have recognition forced upon us.' Churchill wanted to wait 'until the result of the President's honeymoon with de Gaulle is made known. . . . Should the President make a volte-face and come to terms with de Gaulle, we should have a very good case to present to Parliament showing how foolish it would have been to have had a premature debate which might have spoiled all this happy kissing.'[45] But the happy kissing in Washington did not solve the recognition problem.

There followed a small, unnecessary incident which for the moment made Churchill as personally bitter as he had ever been against de Gaulle. In August 1944 he visited Italy for talks with the military commanders and also with Marshal Tito of Yugoslavia. Before he left he suggested that during a brief stop in Algiers on the way out he should meet de Gaulle. Duff Cooper put this to de Gaulle who said he thought nothing was to be gained by an interview between himself and Churchill at the present time; 'an hour's argument failed to shake him'. De Gaulle then addressed to Churchill a letter of icy courtesy, obviously meant to wound.[46] To Eden Churchill minuted that the letter 'is certainly a good indication of the relations we shall have with this man as he, through our exertion, gains supreme power in France. . . . It was a great mistake to give de Gaulle the opportunity of putting this marked affront on the Head of a Government which has three-quarters of a million soldiers fighting, with heavy losses, to liberate France.'[47] De Gaulle was willing to have some happy kissing with Roosevelt, not with Churchill. He had sensed where the real power lay.

Churchill told his staff that Mrs Churchill was to see de Gaulle's icy letter of refusal to meet him. This she did. Earlier there had been signs that his wife took a kindlier view of de Gaulle and Gaullists than the Prime Minister. On 22 June *The Times* had carried a story from Bayeux on the 'conciliatory declarations' made by François Coulet, de Gaulle's representative, who was reported to have reassured Vichyites that they would be as well treated by him as by the British or Americans, adding that village mayors could obviously not help a certain degree of compliance with Vichy or the Germans. Mrs Churchill stuck the Press cutting on a piece of paper, put a bold line down the side, and wrote on the paper : 'Winston. Please read, and note that M. Coulet, de Gaulle's nominee, does not seem so very intransigent. Clemmie.[48] Perhaps Churchill now felt that de Gaulle's affront would show his wife that her kindly view of Gaullists was wrong.

During the turmoil of the summer of 1944 Cadogan had noted in his diary in a moment of extreme exasperation : 'Roosevelt, P.M. and – it must be admitted – de Gaulle all behave like girls approaching the age of puberty.'[49] In the cooler and calmer days of the autumn all for the moment seemed in better balance. In mid-October, when Churchill and Eden were together in Moscow, Churchill decided to try once again with Roosevelt : 'I understand that Eisenhower is anxious to comply with the request . . . from the French to constitute a large part of France into an interior zone. . . . I suggest therefore that we can now safely recognise General de Gaulle's administration as the provisional government of France. . . . It is important that we should take the same line although we need not necessarily adopt exactly the same wording.'[50]

This was Eden's line; and he told Molotov on 17 October that the British 'felt that the time was near, if our Soviet friends agreed, for us to recognise the French provisional government'. Molotov grumbled as usual : the British and Americans had asked the Soviet Union not to recognise and now the British were making it seem as though the Soviet government had been holding out. In any case he would have to know the American view first.[51]

In Washington there had been a change of mood. Late in September the State Department had asked Leahy to urge Roosevelt to recognise because 'it would be definitely advantageous to the U.S.'; and Leahy, de Gaulle's old enemy, was a realist.[52] Roosevelt's motives at this moment were obscure. On 20 October he answered Churchill's message of the four-teenth saying he thought recognition should be delayed until 'the French set up a real zone of the interior' and the Assembly was made 'more representative'. He also said: 'I am anxious to handle this matter for the present directly between you and me and would prefer ... that the *modus operandi* not become a matter of discussion between the State Department and your Foreign Office.'[53] This tied Eden's hands.

But on 19 October – the day *before* – a telegram had gone from the State Department to the U.S. representative in Paris instructing him to tell the French Foreign Minister 'in strictest confidence for de Gaulle only' that the U.S. would recognise the Provisional Government the moment a decree on the zone of the interior was published. This the U.S. representative immediately did. This news was passed by the Foreign Office to Churchill and Eden as soon as they got to know of it, on 21 October, together with the comment: 'Action of State Department is incompre-hensible in view of President's reply to the Prime Minister. . . . It may already be too late to prevent the Americans getting in first.'[54]

In fact, through the confidential message to de Gaulle, they *had* already got in first, even if the official announcements could subsequently be co-ordinated. The State Department could not have acted without Roosevelt's blessing. Perhaps Roosevelt was determined that this time he himself, not Churchill, should play the role of fairy godfather.

But Churchill had a most forgiving nature where Roosevelt was con-cerned, and he liked happy endings. In November he and Eden had a great public welcome in Paris with de Gaulle at his best as host. Churchill wrote to Roosevelt: 'I certainly had a wonderful reception from about half a million French in the Champs-Elysées and also from the party opposition centre at the Hôtel de Ville. I re-established friendly private relations with de Gaulle, who is better since he has lost a large part of his inferiority complex.' Churchill said he had received most sympatheti-cally the French desire to have a share in the occupation of Germany, on equal terms with the British and Americans. He ended:

What a change of fortune since Casablanca. Generally I felt in the presence of an organised government, broadly based and rapidly grow-ing in strength, and I am certain that we should be most unwise to do anything to weaken it in the eyes of France. . . . I had a considerable feeling of stability in spite of Communist threats, and that we could safely take them more into our confidence. I hope you will not consider that I am putting on French clothes when I say this.[55]

This seemed for the moment to show that the Anglo-French wartime relationship, after many violent storms, had reached a calm and sunlit serenity. France was free and had reasonable hope of a return, if not to greatness, at least to strength and to equality in European affairs with the Big Three; and this was what the British wanted. Eden, in particular, must have heaved a sigh of relief. His policy, it seemed, had been proved right.

CHAPTER NINE

No happy ending

While Churchill was still warm with the after-glow of his Paris visit, de Gaulle set off for Moscow without telling him. He first heard of this from Stalin. He had sent Stalin an account of his talks in Paris and had pressed the French claim for a share in the occupation of Germany. Stalin, replying on 22 November, said in passing: 'General de Gaulle expressed recently his wish to come to Moscow to establish contact with the leaders of the Soviet government. We replied agreeing to this. . . . I will let you know about it.' A few days later Stalin told Churchill there was 'every evidence' that de Gaulle would raise the question of a French–Soviet pact. 'We can hardly object. But I would like to know your view.'[1]

Churchill was quite happy and proposed to reply at once: 'We have no objection whatever to a Franco-Soviet pact . . . similar to the Anglo-Soviet pact. On the contrary, H.M.G. consider it desirable and an additional link between us all.' But Eden was obviously somewhat put out. According to normal diplomatic courtesy, the French could have been expected to inform the British of their intentions. Moreover, the whole business of bilateral treaties in post-war Europe was one which Eden thought should be handled very carefully, so as to avoid a treaty-making race with the Soviet Union. In any case, it would have seemed more natural for France to make a treaty with Britain first. When the matter came up in the War Cabinet on 4 December, Churchill said he was satisfied with Stalin's cordial tone and he wanted to send a cordial reply quickly. But Eden said Stalin's message showed he was in no hurry to conclude a pact with de Gaulle; the reply might be that, though Britain was wholly in favour of a French–Soviet pact, a tripartite pact including Britain would be better. The fact that France had no treaty with Britain might 'create mis-understanding' in the case of a purely French–Soviet pact. Churchill accepted this argument, and a reply went off to Moscow on these lines.[2]

But Eden had counted without Stalin's – or Molotov's – pleasure in mischief-making and de Gaulle's raw nerve on Anglo-Saxon interference. Stalin politely thanked Churchill for his advice and added: 'At the time of receiving your reply we had already begun discussions with the French about the pact. Your proposal in preference for a tripartite Anglo-Franco-

Soviet pact . . . has been approved by myself and my colleagues.' It had been put to de Gaulle who had not yet replied. Three days later Stalin sent another message: 'I communicated to General de Gaulle . . . your preference for an Anglo-French–Soviet pact . . . and spoke in favour of accepting your proposal. However, General de Gaulle insisted on concluding a Franco-Soviet pact, saying that a three-party pact . . . demanded preparation. At the same time a message came from the President, who informed me that he had no objection to a Franco-Soviet pact. In the result, we reached agreement about concluding a pact, and it was signed today.'[3]

Roosevelt, to whom Churchill had also sent his proposal, had answered that he was 'somewhat dubious' about a tripartite pact because it 'might be interpreted by public opinion here as a competitor to a future world organisation, whereas a bilateral arrangement between France and the Soviet Union . . . would be more understandable'. To Stalin Roosevelt had simply said that he had no objection in principle to a Franco-Soviet pact.[4]

From Moscow the British embassy reported that Molotov seemed to have given the French the impression that Churchill was trying to put a stop to the French–Soviet pact, and had remarked at one stage that he hoped the pact would not offend him. It was certain that the Churchill proposal, as presented to the French by Stalin and Molotov, had produced a shock and in de Gaulle at least 'initial resentment'.[5]

Churchill felt that this time it was Eden who had put his foot wrong and had offended de Gaulle. He minuted to him: 'I do not understand why it was that you wished to put this triple pact in my telegram. . . . Neither do I understand why de Gaulle should become so suddenly resentful of the mention of a triple pact, nor why the Russians should like it.'[6] He was in fact baffled by Soviet deviousness and de Gaulle's political psychology, and had apparently not seen that one reason why de Gaulle wanted a pact with Stalin was to strengthen his hand in dealing with the French Communists.

From Washington Halifax telegraphed that U.S. opinion was likely to see a French–Soviet pact, unaccompanied by a French–British pact, 'as a move by France away from Great Britain'. If the French–Soviet pact were followed as soon as possible by a French–British agreement it would have a good effect. But Churchill, obviously chilled by de Gaulle's reaction to the idea of a triple pact, minuted to Eden: 'Surely we should wait till we are asked by the French?'[7]

But on the same day he sent Stalin a letter of fulsome praise for a Soviet film about Kutuzov, the hero of the Russian defence of Moscow against the French in 1812. Churchill went on: 'I like to think we were together in that deadly struggle, as in this. . . . I do not suppose you showed the film to de Gaulle any more than I shall show him "Lady Hamilton" when he comes over here to make a similar treaty to that which you have made with him, and we have made together.' Stalin may or may not have relished the anti-French slant of Churchill's allusions to Napoleon's great defeats but he answered that he would of course welcome an Anglo-French treaty, adding that he highly valued Churchill's praise of the film *Kutuzov*.[8]

One reason why Eden was unhappy about a French–Soviet pact was that it might cut across the plan for a 'western bloc' or west European defence group which the Chiefs of Staff and the Foreign Office had been discussing. Churchill was not keen on it. But once the French–Soviet pact had been signed Eden was eager for a British–French pact to counterbalance it. Churchill – in spite of his message to Stalin – was determined not to hurry. At the end of December he sent Eden a minute warning against haste, either over a treaty or a western bloc:

> You said to me that if de Gaulle attempted to say there could be no Anglo-French treaty until we had settled everything about Syria you would let him wait. It is for him to make the proposal, not us. Meantime we are losing nothing from the point of view of security because the French have practically no army and all the other nations concerned are prostrate or still enslaved. . . . I do not know what our financial position will be after the war, but I am sure we shall not be able to maintain forces sufficient to protect all these helpless nations. . . .[9]

On 5 January 1945 Duff Cooper saw de Gaulle for the first time since his Moscow visit and tried to dispel his suspicions of sinister British motives behind the proposal for a triple pact – without revealing that he thought the General less than truthful in saying that he had gone to Moscow without any intention of signing a pact. (The French embassy in London had said that the French had had a draft ready for some time.) As for an Anglo-French pact, Duff Cooper reported, de Gaulle 'obviously did not wish to give the appearance of desiring one too keenly', and said the two matters in dispute between the two countries were the future of the Rhineland (which the French wanted to sever from Germany) and Syria. Duff Cooper himself was all in favour of a pact, believing that 'the reluctance of General de Gaulle to take the initiative in proposing conversations, a reluctance due probably to personal and temperamental causes, should not be allowed to form an obstacle'.[10]

Churchill was unmoved: 'I hope we shall adhere to our policy of awaiting French initiative. There can be no sort of hurry. France has nothing to give to an alliance at the present time. We should be most unwise to appear as suppliants. This would give de Gaulle every chance of misbehaviour.'[11] He seemed to have adopted de Gaulle's own tactics; above all, he wanted to give the General no chance to inflict a fresh snub, or worse, on Britain.

Eden and Churchill did not see eye to eye over French participation at the Yalta conference, or similar later meetings. Churchill had gone so far as to suggest to Roosevelt that the French should send a representative with a strictly limited role, but had no success. Eden wrote to him: 'I must say that I should myself have liked French participation in some form.' Roosevelt's refusal had settled the question for the moment but Eden still hoped that at Yalta it might be agreed that the French should take part in future meetings; if Churchill pressed Roosevelt, Stalin might well support him. Eden also wrote:

> We have reached the stage now when we must plan for the future. I find it difficult to contemplate a future in which France will not be a factor of considerable importance. She must be interested in almost every European question. If we did not have her co-operation she will be able – not at once perhaps – to make difficult the application of any solution which does not suit her.[12]

Churchill was unmoved and wrote Eden a personal letter. He recognised the force of what Eden said but went on: 'I fear we shall have the greatest trouble with de Gaulle, who will be for ever intriguing and playing off two against the third. . . . I quite agree that France should come in as the Fourth Power, and certainly at any moment when it is proposed to bring in China.' But he did not think they should try for a fixed bargain at Yalta and concluded:

> I cannot think of anything more unpleasant and impossible than having this menacing and hostile man in our midst, always trying to make himself a reputation in France by claiming a position far above what France occupies, and making faces at the Allies who are doing the work. Yours ever, W.

A few days later he again urged Eden not to press the matter.[13]

But at Yalta both Churchill and Eden strongly championed the claim of France not only to share in the occupation of Germany but also in control responsibilities. Roosevelt, though he announced that American occupation would be limited to two years, opposed the idea. Stalin was obstructive. Eden argued that de Gaulle might refuse to accept an occupation zone if he were not treated on the same footing as the three great powers; if so, many people in Britain would think him justified.[14]

From London the Foreign Office told Eden that, if France were excluded from the control of Germany, 'the political consequences in France may be very serious. . . . General de Gaulle's position may be shaken. . . . There are good grounds for thinking that . . . de Gaulle's government, with all his shortcomings, is the only alternative to civil strife and the emergence of a single party government which it would be difficult for us to work with'[15] – a polite way of saying there would be a Communist dictatorship. Churchill and Eden, by their combined obstinacy, were successful, which showed what they could do in the diplomatic field if they fought on the same side. Roosevelt quite suddenly gave way and Stalin then followed him.

But British championship of France at Yalta did not incline de Gaulle to make the first move over an Anglo-French pact. His senior officials, notably René Massigli and Chauvel, were, however, eager to go ahead, and in early April thought they had got de Gaulle in the right mood. When he asked Duff Cooper to call on 5 April he was, in fact, amiable. He began by complaining that it was the Russians who had prevented France from being one of the inviting powers for the San Francisco conference, due to meet shortly to form the United Nations organisation. Duff Cooper then rashly 'mentioned the possibility' of an Anglo-French pact. (Reading the telegram reporting this, Churchill drew a big circle round the word 'mentioned'.) De Gaulle replied there was nothing he desired more, but he wanted something more than the Anglo-Soviet or French–Soviet pacts – an alliance with all outstanding questions definitely settled. Duff Cooper, again rashly, suggested a 'preliminary pact', to be concluded before San Francisco. At this point de Gaulle retreated, saying there was no hurry. Nevertheless, Duff Cooper reported that de Gaulle gave the impression that he was conscious of a new menace looming up from the east which made it necessary for France and Britain to stand together. The next day he said that Chauvel was anxious to come to London to conclude an agreement 'within a week'.[16]

Churchill, in great annoyance, minuted to Eden: 'It crosses my mind that de Gaulle rushed precipitously into the arms of Russia and has been, for the last two years, ready to play Russia off against Great Britain, but that after making an alliance with them he was somewhat disappointed. . . . In trying to sell us across the counter, he has been rebuffed.' He then upbraided Duff Cooper for 'mentioning' an Anglo-French pact and suggesting a 'preliminary pact', so giving de Gaulle a chance to say there was no hurry.

> Why on earth can he not remain passive and be wooed instead of always playing into de Gaulle's hand and leaving him the giver of favours when he has none to give. . . ? He lets the steam out of the boiler every time it begins to gather pressure. . . . If we offer, we shall be snubbed and blackmailed. If we wait, it will be a happy and permanent union.

Churchill then uttered a saying which came strangely from him, though it chimed with what Cadogan had written in his diary of Eden: 'It is a great mistake always to want to do things. Very often they will do themselves much better than anyone could do them.'[17]

Eden stuck to his point in a diplomatic way. He thought the pressure for a pact came from Massigli and from France's point of view Massigli was right. He denied that he ever wished to give the French the impression that the British were suppliants or in a hurry, but he would like to tell Chauvel he could come to London.[18] Churchill replied with another little lecture on the conduct of foreign affairs: 'The essence of diplomacy is the correct timing of the various moves. When you are in the stronger position you can often afford to wait. . . . We must give Time a chance to work for us.'[19] Eden replied that this time the initiative came from the French 'who are now running after us, which is what we desire, and I do not wish to snub them'. He still wanted Chauvel to come. He eventually persuaded Churchill to let him send a telegram to Paris: 'We welcome this French initiative and shall be glad to receive Chauvel here.'[20]

But then came the snub that Churchill had feared. The reply from Paris was that the French Foreign Minister had been thinking of taking a draft pact with him to San Francisco, but might not be able to do this because de Gaulle had not yet made up his mind about an accompanying exchange of notes on the Rhineland and Syria. It was unlikely that Chauvel would go to London.[21]

Churchill could not resist sending a telegram to Eden (now in Washington) saying, more or less, 'I told you so.' To Duff Cooper he sent a sterner message:

> I was sorry that you indulged in a *démarche* to de Gaulle about a Franco-British treaty. . . . The only result of all this has been what I foresaw from the beginning – that this man has another opportunity of inflicting a slight upon the western Allies and of lulling himself with the feeling that they are suitors for his favour. It is neither of interest nor of urgency to us to make a treaty at the present time with

the France of de Gaulle. They will come along in their own time and no one will be more glad to extend the hand of friendship than I.[22]

Duff Cooper thought that de Gaulle had *not* intended to inflict a slight. When he saw him a week later, de Gaulle said that his Foreign Minister *had* taken a draft pact to San Francisco, and then went on to complain – in another context – that the French were left out of everything. On this Churchill commented to Duff Cooper, as often before: 'De Gaulle is the greatest obstacle the Allies have to face in making good relations between France and the western democracies.' Churchill added that he had sent de Gaulle congratulations on the French military achievements in the south of France 'to which surprisingly I received a cordial answer'.[23]

No Anglo-French pact was concluded until after both Churchill and de Gaulle were out of office and Eden had been replaced by Ernest Bevin. Whose diplomatic tactics were at fault in the spring of 1945 – Churchill's or Eden's – can only be a matter of guesswork. Probably, so long as de Gaulle was in power, it made little difference.

There were two more small, sad episodes in relations with France. In the last days of the war French troops moved into north-west Italy, into Cuneo province. Eisenhower ordered that they should withdraw to the frontier so that Allied military government could be set up there under Field-Marshal Alexander, the commander in Italy. The French were, in fact, directly facing U.S. units. The local French commander sent two letters to the American local commander refusing to withdraw. In the second he wrote: 'General de Gaulle has instructed me to make as clear as possible . . . that I have received the order to prevent the setting up of Allied military government in territories occupied by our troops . . . by all necessary means without exception.'

President Truman – still very new in office – asked Churchill to agree to his releasing a statement to the Press disclosing this situation and saying that he had put a stop to the issue of U.S. military equipment and arms to French troops. Truman also asked if he could disclose a message which Churchill had sent him: 'Is it not rather disagreeable for us to be addressed in these terms by General de Gaulle, whom we have reinstated in liberated France at some expense of American and British blood and treasure? Our policy is one of friendship.'

In the end it was not necessary for Truman to publish the statement; the French withdrew. Churchill sent Truman a message: 'I believe that the publication of your message would have led to the overthrow of de Gaulle, who after five long years of experience I am convinced is the worst enemy of France in her troubles. . . . I consider General de Gaulle one of the greatest dangers to European peace. . . . I am sure that in the long run no understanding will be reached with General de Gaulle.'[24]

The Foreign Office – in Eden's absence – challenged Churchill's view that de Gaulle would have fallen. Cadogan wrote to him: 'Certainly it would have come as a bombshell to French opinion. . . . On the other hand . . . there would have been a risk, I think, . . . of the French Press reacting the wrong way and uniting in support of de Gaulle.' If de Gaulle *had* fallen, 'there might well have been very considerable confusion. The difficulty is that in present circumstances in France there is really no one else to take de Gaulle's place. Nor will there be until the elections are held in October or November.' In any case, Cadogan wrote, if and when de Gaulle did go, it would be important that he should go because of French disapproval, not British pressure.[25]

Churchill, in his last weeks of power, had to swallow one final snub from the General. It had been planned that on 18 June 1945 – the fifth anniversary of de Gaulle's first broadcast from London – he would decorate a number of British senior officers. But he then decreed that the ceremonies should be exclusively French, so he would not decorate any Allied officers. Duff Cooper thought this was because of yet another clash with Britain over Syria: he himself intended to go ahead with his own plans to decorate certain French officers on 20 June. Churchill immediately said that arrangements for decorating French officers on 20 June must be cancelled, 'and thus the risk avoided of a refusal for them to attend by General de Gaulle'; as for the 18 June celebrations, it would be 'extremely bad taste' for any British officers to be present. But before his instructions could be conveyed to Paris, Churchill heard that de Gaulle had already given the order that no French officers were to go to the British embassy on 20 June.[26]

So de Gaulle had the last word in the battle of snubs with Churchill. The Foreign Office still counselled restraint. Cadogan wrote to Churchill that it would be wise not to release this news in London: 'French opinion may be forming its own conclusions about de Gaulle's suitability for the future and, if that is so, we must be careful not to appear to be taking a hand in discrediting him.'[27]

This minute was written on 18 June, a sad epitaph on the five-year wartime relationship between de Gaulle and the British.

The records of this relationship show Eden and the Foreign Office at their best, Churchill at his worst. To Eden, it was a first priority that

France should again become strong – quite regardless of de Gaulle. Churchill agreed with the aim but felt, as he wrote in June 1945: 'The personality of de Gaulle stands as a shocking barrier.'[28] Foreign Office policy was remarkably consistent and unusually lacking in opportunism; Strang, the official most responsible, was singularly clear-minded.[29] Eden stood up for this policy firmly, sometimes cajoling Churchill, sometimes answering back when he was in one of his furies. Churchill was swayed this way and that by his emotions – wrath, wounded feelings and hurt pride, unwilling admiration, real love for France and, of course, his personal and political ties with Roosevelt.

Certain questions remain open. Even if Churchill often seemed unreasonable and wrong-headed, were his political instincts and intuitions perhaps sound? If there had been no de Gaulle, would there really have been no one else to lead French resistance to Hitler? How much did de Gaulle's hold on the French depend, in the early years, on British publicity, especially the B.B.C.? (It was largely the B.B.C. which, unwittingly, turned the Yugoslav Colonel Mihailović into a world figure, a symbol of resistance, when really he was no Resistance hero at all.) Again, was de Gaulle really the only bulwark against a Communist takeover in France, as the Foreign Office came to think? In a word, was Churchill entirely wrong in refusing to identify 'France' with 'de Gaulle'?

Finally, was he wrong in thinking that a France headed by de Gaulle would be no friend to Britain? The Foreign Office – and Macmillan – could hardly be expected to foresee the years 1958–69, when de Gaulle kept the British as 'suppliants' at the gate of *his* Europe; but possibly Churchill was not as bad a judge of character as it often seemed. But then, was de Gaulle's unfriendliness Churchill's fault; or did it well up from deeper springs in de Gaulle's strange and complex personality? He clearly envied Churchill's power, despised his apparent subservience to Roosevelt, and perhaps had an inborn tendency towards depression and something like persecution mania. In his memoirs he sets out to show that his angers were carefully calculated; the records – at least, of the earlier war years – suggest that they were very real and almost beyond his control.

If Churchill had left it to Eden to deal with de Gaulle, in a much smoother and more sympathetic way, perhaps the General's emotions and actions would have been different. What is certain is that his relationship with Churchill was made much more difficult by Churchill's relationship with Roosevelt, and that this in turn was the biggest cause of dispute between Churchill and Eden.

PART THREE

Churchill, Eden, Roosevelt

CHAPTER TEN

The Churchill–Roosevelt direct line and its use for Eden

While de Gaulle thought Churchill meek, even servile, in his eagerness to please Roosevelt, a good many Americans, especially those high in the military hierarchy and in the Republican Party, thought he had a dangerously strong influence over Roosevelt, and they worked against it privately or attacked it publicly. Neither view of the Churchill–Roosevelt relationship was true, though neither was entirely false. Both men were many-sided and complex personalities and so their relationship was many-sided and complex.

Each tried to manipulate the other for his own political ends or for his own country's interest. Yet Churchill also came to have a real and strong emotional attachment to Roosevelt, even, in the latter part of the war, a sort of psychological dependence on him. What Roosevelt felt about Churchill is much more difficult to guess; but certainly in the early part of their 'friendship' he found him exciting, amusing and impressive, if also tiring and sometimes boring.

But the underlying reality was that the relationship was unequal because of the great and growing inequality in the strength of Britain and the United States in financial resources, productive capacity and man-power. In a sense the British were the paid mercenaries of the Americans even before the Americans found themselves thrown into the war. The important question is how far Churchill succeeded or failed in offsetting America's weight in the balance by the force of his own personality and his world-wide prestige and by playing such cards as Britain possessed to the best possible advantage, so as to assert some degree of independence both in waging war and in shaping the post-war world.

Eden's attitude to the Churchill–Roosevelt relationship was mixed. He himself was much more cool and critical about Roosevelt than Churchill. Yet both as Foreign Secretary and because of his share in shaping British war strategy Eden saw Churchill's friendly relations with Roosevelt, and in particular their very frequent exchange of personal messages, as a useful way of exerting British influence at the top level, cutting through the chaotic tangle and hang-ups of the Washington bureaucracy, or countering sudden arbitrary moves by one or other American department of state or special pressure group. Because the State Department and its Secretary of State, Cordell Hull, were so often kept in the dark and the cold by Roosevelt, Eden found they could not be satisfactory negotiating partners for the Foreign Office; so a direct line to Roosevelt through Churchill was particularly valuable to the Foreign Secretary.

On the other hand, this 'direct line' enticed Churchill into meddling in even quite minor bits of foreign policy which Eden would much rather have handled on his own. In that way it down-graded his own position and authority. More important was that Eden felt that Churchill's personal affection for Roosevelt could distort his judgement and make him soft in the face of excessive American demands or, at moments, lax in defending British interests. So at times Eden urged Churchill to make use of his 'direct line' to get what the British wanted or to prevent things happening which they did not want; at other times he tried to stop Churchill sending messages, so as to leave the Foreign Office some scope in handling its own business; sometimes he urged Churchill to damp down his more impassioned outbursts, or to harden his protests against high-handed, harmful or even insulting American moves.

When Eden or the Foreign Office wrote draft messages for Churchill to send to Roosevelt – as they often did, either on their own initiative or at Churchill's request – it was rare that he accepted them without at least stylistic changes. Often he rewrote the whole thing in his own way, changing not only the style but also the whole emphasis and approach to fit his sensitive perception of Roosevelt's psychology and the U.S. political scene. But in foreign policy matters he normally wanted Eden to bless the final draft before he sent it off.

The whole exchange of messages, from 11 September 1939 until 12 April 1945, reveals a great deal. The two men, however, also had telephone conversations; Churchill had a special closet in his underground war rooms for the purpose. Some months before they met face to face, Churchill telegraphed to Roosevelt: 'It was very pleasant to hear your voice and receive your encouragement last night.'[1] Then there were their various meetings, from August 1941 to February 1945; and there came to be a web of contacts between the Churchill and Roosevelt families.

When Churchill first met Roosevelt at Argentia two of Roosevelt's sons were there, both in uniform and apparently keen that their father should aid Britain more actively.[2] In 1942 Eleanor Roosevelt came to Britain; Clementine Churchill and one or other of Churchill's daughters visited the U.S. (But it was a long time, in the Roosevelt–Churchill correspondence, before Mrs Roosevelt became 'Eleanor', though Mrs Churchill soon became 'Clemmie' to Roosevelt.) Before the Yalta conference Roosevelt telegraphed to Churchill that he was bringing his daughter Anna. Churchill answered: 'How splendid. Sarah is coming with me.'[3]

The two men also had their little jokes to lighten their relations. In their first exchanges Churchill became 'Naval Person.' Roosevelt's opening message, in September 1939, began: 'My dear Churchill, it is because you and I occupied similar positions in the World War that I want you to know how glad I am that you are back in the Admiralty.' He went on to say how much he had enjoyed Churchill's life of his great ancestor, Marlborough. But what he was really getting at was that he wanted to avoid the British navy tangling with American shipping in the Atlantic, and Churchill saw this clearly, answering: 'We quite understand natural desire of U.S. to keep belligerent acts out of their waters.'[4]

When Churchill became Prime Minister, 'Naval Person' became 'Former Naval Person.' But even then, when actually writing from a warship, he again became 'Naval Person,' and once, when in mid-air, 'Present Aerial Person.'[5]

These little pleasantries obviously gave Churchill childlike pleasure, as did his various cover-names on his trips abroad – Colonel Warden, Colonel Kent, and so forth. When in a good mood Roosevelt, too, enjoyed the game, suggesting that for the Casablanca conference 'the aliases from this end will be a) Don Quixote and b) Sancho Panza'. Churchill replied: 'However did you think of such an impenetrable disguise? In order to make it even harder for the enemy and to discourage irreverent guess-work, propose Admiral Q. and Mr P.N.B. We must mind our Ps and Qs.'[6]

They had, too, during their honeymoon period less pleasant little jokes about de Gaulle and Giraud as 'bride' and 'bridegroom', with Eden on occasion cast as 'best man', and Churchill reporting that the bride and groom had at last 'physically embraced'.[7]

Then from the end of 1941 there were the regular exchanges of birthday greetings or gifts. In 1942 Churchill sent Roosevelt a specially bound collection of his own books; Roosevelt wrote that he was thrilled and would always cherish them.[8] In 1943 Churchill celebrated his birthday at the Tehran conference, perhaps not an altogether happy occasion in spite of all the toasts and heavy bonhomie. On his next birthday Roosevelt, wishing him many happy returns, recalled 'the party with you and U.J. [Stalin] a year ago, and we must have more of them that are even better'. He also sent a framed quotation from Abraham Lincoln with an inscription in his own hand which was given to Churchill when he woke up. Churchill thanked Roosevelt effusively: 'I cannot tell you how much I value your friendship or how much I hope upon it for the future of the world, should we both be spared.'[9] Roosevelt was not spared. There can be no doubt that Churchill's personal sorrow over Roosevelt's death in April 1945 was real and strong.

There was no such emotional content to Eden's relationship with Roosevelt. Roosevelt could treat Churchill as an equal, or, at least, nearly equal; Eden, as Foreign Secretary, was on a lower level. Roosevelt could treat him with gracious friendliness; he could praise his successes or coldly reprove his misdeeds, but never accept him as an equal.

Before the war Churchill and Eden had both believed that it was important for Britain to win Roosevelt's friendship and backing. One reason for Eden's decision to resign as Foreign Secretary in February 1938 was Chamberlain's rather curt and chilly response to Roosevelt's diplomatic initiative for a conference in Washington which would have brought together the Axis powers and the western democracies. Eden did not mention this in his resignation speech in Parliament; nor did Churchill in his speech regretting Eden's departure. But he, too, felt Chamberlain had been wrong in cold-shouldering Roosevelt.

Eden, after his resignation, visited the United States and met Roosevelt. The meeting was agreeable; and three years later, when the U.S. came into the war, Roosevelt sent Eden a message saying he looked forward to seeing him again soon.[10] When Eden finally went to Washington in March 1943 the visit was a public success. But after long talks with Roosevelt on Europe and the future of the colonial powers, Eden formed a rather low opinion of the President's knowledge and judgement. It was perhaps from that time that he was determined that the British should follow a European policy of their own, and if at all possible come to terms with the Soviet Union, so as to be able to act independently of the United States if necessary.

The Foreign Office, too, tended to be critical and rather superior in their attitude to the Americans, suspecting them of ignorance, a somewhat spurious high-mindedness and an over-aggressive defence of their own interests. In all this there was an element of envy and of frustration at Britain's dwindling power to control events. This sort of feeling in the Foreign Office met a sympathetic response from Eden.

The Churchill–Roosevelt relationship was not constant. It waxed and waned. In its early phase Roosevelt wooed Churchill in order to make the British go on fighting (alone); Churchill wooed Roosevelt, partly to get credit and weapons from him but even more to make the Americans fight. Once the U.S. had been pulled into the war relations grew warm and close, and this lasted until the summer of 1943. However, already in January 1943, at the Casablanca conference, Averell Harriman noticed that Roosevelt carefully side-stepped Churchill's effort to get a final private talk with him on their last evening together: 'He always enjoyed other people's discomfort,' Harriman commented later, adding: 'I think it is fair to say that it never bothered him very much when other people were unhappy.'[11]

From mid-1943 on, or perhaps from even earlier, Roosevelt was more interested in wooing Stalin than wooing Churchill. The British had, of course, got a little ahead of him in this field. First Eden went to Moscow in December 1941 and had long and fairly friendly talks with Stalin; then Churchill visited Stalin, at a very bad moment in relations with Russia, in August 1942, and seemed to score a success. This must have been irritating for Roosevelt, who had written to Churchill in March 1942: 'I know you will not mind my being brutally frank when I tell you that I think I can personally handle Stalin better than either your Foreign Office or my State Department. Stalin hates the guts of all your top people. He thinks he likes me better, and I hope he will continue to do so.'[12] Nonetheless, when at this time Roosevelt tried to get Molotov to visit the U.S. before going to London, Stalin did not agree but sent him to London first. And Roosevelt's subsequent efforts to get Stalin to meet him alone without Churchill misfired. This can only have stimulated Roosevelt's eagerness to make Stalin his friend.

A much more serious reason for the cooling of Roosevelt's interest in Churchill must have been a hard-headed assessment of the realities of the future. By the end of the war Britain would be bankrupt and would probably lose the empire – and in any case Roosevelt believed that, on moral grounds, the empire ought to go. On the other hand, the Soviet Union would be the strongest power after the United States. This was stated with brutal clarity in a paper headed 'Russia's Position' said to be from 'a very high-level U.S. military strategic estimate' which the Americans had with them at the first Quebec conference in August 1943: 'Russia's post-war position in Europe will be a dominant one. With Germany crushed, there is no power in Europe to oppose her tremendous military forces. . . . It is . . . essential to develop and maintain the most friendly relations with Russia.' Moreover, in the war against Japan Russia's alliance would be of very great value.[13]

This appreciation – or the thinking which produced it – was obviously a turning-point for the Churchill–Roosevelt relationship, which was thereafter down-graded to second place in Roosevelt's scheme of things. Another sign of the British decline was the transfer of Averell Harriman from his extremely important – for the British – London post as Roosevelt's special envoy to become ambassador in Moscow. This registered a change in the scale of priorities of both Roosevelt and Harriman.[14]

During the autumn of 1943 Churchill must at times have been hurt when he was pressing rather importunately for a meeting with Roosevelt in advance of any three-power conference with Stalin – a proposal which Roosevelt brushed off with occasional shows of coldness or irritation. At the end of October Churchill sent him a message: 'I have a great wish and need to see you. All our troubles and toils are so much easier to face when we are side by side.'[15] But the next day he had to send an apologetic message: 'I was not aware you had been rushed at the last minute on any occasion and I am very sorry . . . if I am to blame.'[16] Roosevelt was not softened.

When in the end the two did meet in Cairo before the Tehran conference Roosevelt's insistence on having a conference with Chiang Kai-shek, the Chinese leader, made it very difficult for Churchill to meet him separately or for lower-level Anglo-American talks to take place. Eden was amazed at Churchill's patience, noting in his diary that when he said they didn't seem to be getting anywhere with their work Churchill agreed: 'F.D.R. was "a charming country gentleman" but business methods were almost non-existent, so W. had to play the role of courtier and seize opportunities as and when they arose.'[17] But all the same Churchill must have missed his long, intimate chats of the past with Roosevelt. And salt must have been rubbed in the wounds at Tehran, when Roosevelt ostentatiously wooed Stalin, avoiding private contact with Churchill, lined up with him in argument and joined him in a rather unkind baiting of Churchill over Stalin's proposal for wiping out the German military élite at one fell swoop; whether this was meant seriously or not, Churchill found it deeply offensive.

Eden, when he got back to London, did not hide his feelings, telling the War Cabinet that from the British point of view the Cairo conference had been unfortunate: Roosevelt had made promises to the Chinese not endorsed by Churchill, and 'the Americans and ourselves had to go to Tehran without having had an opportunity of reaching a decision upon our combined plans for Europe in 1944' – and so the British had to argue them out with the Americans and express dissent from the American overall plan in front of the Russians.[18]

Not long after Tehran a prominent member of the Republican Party, noted for his hatred of Britain (and Roosevelt), declared that Roosevelt was 'double crossing Churchill'. The Foreign Office refused to take this seriously, but admitted there were 'rumours abroad that Roosevelt had not played ball with Churchill at Tehran'. One cryptic comment was: 'The President has retained some faithful friends, but he has certainly lost a good many.'[19]

Nevertheless, Churchill was enormously resilient and used to the rough and tumble of political life. In 1944, especially during the months leading up to *Overlord* – the Normandy landings – his messages to Roosevelt assumed that their relationship was as close as ever. Two days before D-Day he wrote: 'Our friendship is my greatest stand-by amid the ever-increasing complications of this exacting war.' Later in June – at the end of a message of sharp protest at Roosevelt's attitude to Anglo-Soviet relations – he wrote: 'I cannot think of any moment when the burden of the war has laid more heavily upon me or when I have felt so unequal to its ever more entangled problems. I greatly admire the strength and courage with which you face your difficulties.'[20]

In November 1944, after Roosevelt had again won the presidential election, Churchill wrote to him: 'It is an indescribable relief to me that our comradeship will continue and will help to bring the world out of misery.'[21] A few weeks before Roosevelt's death Churchill wrote:

I hope that the rather numerous telegrams I have to send you on so many of our difficult and intertwined affairs are not becoming a bore to you. Our friendship is the rock on which I build for the future of the world so long as I am one of the builders. I always think of those tremendous days when you devised Lend-Lease, when we met at Argentia, when you decided with my heartfelt agreement to launch the invasion of Africa, and when you comforted me for the loss of Tobruk by giving me 300 Shermans [tanks]....[22]

It was one of Churchill's big disappointments that Roosevelt never fulfilled his promise to visit Britain – one day. It seems that Roosevelt's advisers thought the visit would be unpopular in America. In a message sent not long before Roosevelt's death Churchill wrote: 'All the time I shall be looking forward to your long-promised visit. Clemmie is off to Russia next week . . . but she will be back in time to meet you and Eleanor. . . . Peace . . . will not bring much rest to you and me (if I am still responsible). . . . There will be a torn, ragged and hungry world to help to its feet; and what will U.J. or his successors say to the way in which we should both like to do it?' Twelve days later he asked Roosevelt whether he had ever got this: 'It required no answer, but I should like to know that you received it.' Roosevelt then acknowledged it briefly, but said nothing about visiting Britain.[23]

From 1943 onwards Churchill was certainly the wooer, forgiving and swallowing Roosevelt's inconstancies. The other side of the picture is that at the same time Churchill sent Roosevelt a volley of telegrams, often several a day, standing up for British wartime policies and post-war interests, barbed with some fairly sharp if courteous criticisms of American actions or intentions, if not of Roosevelt himself. In this he was often egged on by Eden or Beaverbrook or other responsible ministers; but he obviously did it with some relish.

It can be argued that he sacrificed de Gaulle to Roosevelt. But even if he did not always go as far as Eden and others wanted, he did not sacrifice what he saw as serious British interests.

What Roosevelt thought about his personal relations with Churchill can only be a matter of guesswork. There were good reasons why Roosevelt should tire of him. There was Churchill's unquenchable physical and mental energy which, in an older man, contrasted all too sharply with Roosevelt's drawbacks as a cripple, bravely as he overcame them. Churchill would fly anywhere at a moment's notice, with zest. He wrote to Roosevelt on 1 April 1942: 'I am personally extremely well. . . . Perhaps when the weather gets better I may propose myself for a weekend with you and flip over.' In October 1944 he wrote to Roosevelt: 'We reached Moscow from London in 36 hours, 23 hours in flight, and on the whole I feel better for the voyage.'[24] (Stalin once called Churchill a 'desperate fellow', forever flying around the world, and compared him to the Holy Ghost.[25]) Roosevelt could not move so freely.

There were also limitations on Roosevelt's physical stamina; he had bouts of what was called 'influenza', which forced him to go away and recuperate. He wrote to Churchill in March 1944 that his old attack of 'grippe' had hung on: 'It is necessary for me to take a complete rest of about two or three weeks.' Churchill replied that he himself was having 'a busman's holiday', acting as Foreign Secretary while Eden was on sick leave.[26] Churchill had the power of recovering from his bouts of pneumonia or sudden fevers with extraordinary speed, retaining his mental energy however weak he was physically for the time being. But if Churchill's drive and energy were demonic, Roosevelt's were not. Early in the war he once wrote to Churchill that once a month he went to his country house, Hyde Park, for four days, and would 'crawl into a hole and pull the hole in after me'.[27] Churchill's weekends at Chequers, however, were simply a continuation of work.

If Churchill's energy could be tiring, so too could his passionate interest in war and making war; on this he was happy to discourse endlessly. Roosevelt at times wanted to switch off the subject and was, anyhow, more interested in American politics or the future world order. According to Beaverbrook – an old friend – there were moments when he wanted to get away from Churchill and turn to the delights of his beloved stamp collection.[28]

The difference in vitality and temperament showed, too, in their attitudes to their political problems at home. Churchill, a natural fighter, enjoyed going into the lion's den and facing a critical or even hostile House of Commons and winning it over to his side – or at least getting a respectable majority. He wanted to lead and mould political opinion, not follow it. This did not mean that he did not have great respect for Parliament – especially when it supported him. He wrote to Roosevelt in April 1944: 'The House of Commons . . . showed itself steadfast in the cause and put all malignants in their place. It is an immense comfort to me to feel this mighty body behind me.'[29]

Roosevelt had a different idea. He had – at least in outward show – to follow American opinion and respond to it, rather than move ahead and lead it after him. This he made very plain to Churchill over the whole question of American entry into the war and his differences with Churchill over Italy, Greece and Spain. One consequence was that Churchill was far readier to defend Roosevelt against British attack than Roosevelt was to defend Churchill against American attack.

When Churchill told Roosevelt that he must oppose him because of the views of the War Cabinet or Parliament, the Americans did not believe him, thinking this was just a device for getting his own way; Harry Hopkins teased Churchill about this, in front of Stalin, at Tehran.[30] But the records suggest that his respect for Parliament and the War Cabinet was real, not feigned.

One outcome of the American system was that Roosevelt relied heavily for advice on his closest friends and advisers, and most of them were not very friendly towards Churchill. Hopkins was perhaps an exception; he showed great friendship for Britain in the hardest days and often helped both Churchill and Eden in a most valuable way. But his simple idealism was shocked by Churchill's – and Eden's – reactionary imperialism, as he saw it; and when in 1943 he became devoted to the idea of cultivating Soviet friendship, his feelings for the British became rather uncertain.

Admiral Leahy, Roosevelt's 'Chief of Staff' from the time he left his job in Vichy, knew very little about the British and suspected them deeply in a rather naïve way. Cordell Hull, though he apparently came to like and respect Eden, was very sensitive to the anti-British strains in American opinion. General George Marshall and the U.S. Chiefs of Staff were deeply suspicious of Churchill's apparent switches and swerves in strategic thinking, and also his influence over Roosevelt in strategic matters. So Roosevelt lived and moved in an atmosphere which was not very favourable to Churchill.

The biggest benefit that Churchill got from his friendship with Roosevelt, in practical terms, was the power it gave him, at least until July 1943, to get his own – or British – strategic ideas accepted by the U.S. Chiefs of Staff. They distrusted him as a man who liked 'exotic' operations and who also went back on agreements he had accepted. The cause for this suspicion lay in the enthusiastic welcome which the British, above all Churchill, gave to Marshall when he came to London in April 1942 and proposed a massive Anglo-American invasion of Europe – by which he meant France – at the earliest possible date. Churchill had feared that after the disaster of Pearl Harbor the American military chiefs would turn away from their earlier decision to give priority to the war in Europe and switch American resources to the Pacific. So he was immensely relieved to find this was not so. General Hastings Ismay, who was present, wrote later: 'Everyone was enthusiastic . . . everyone seemed to agree with the American proposals in their entirety. No doubts were expressed . . . Perhaps it would have obviated future misunderstandings if the British had expressed their views more frankly. . . . Our American friends went happily homeward under the mistaken impression that we had committed ourselves.'[31]

When the Americans discovered that the British had grave misgivings about any operations in France in 1942, they felt there had been broken faith; and they continued to suspect Churchill of faithlessness from then on.

Churchill was able, however, to get Roosevelt to overrule his Chiefs of Staff over early landings in France and make them accept the idea of landings in French North Africa (which they did not like, though the President did). Thereafter, by the same method, Churchill got unwilling American agreement to the invasion of Sicily and then the Italian mainland.

Churchill's 'Mediterranean strategy' was never liked by the American military leaders. Nor was his Middle East strategy. In May 1941 Roosevelt sent Churchill a message taking quite lightly the prospect of a British withdrawal from the Middle East, provided the Iraq oil wells were destroyed first. Churchill consulted Eden before replying and the answer was a joint effort: it would make all the difference in the Near East if the U.S. were 'immediately to range herself with us as a belligerent' and Roosevelt should not 'underrate the gravity of the consequences which may follow from a Middle East collapse: in this war every post is a winning post and how many more are we going to lose?'[32] Five months later – with the U.S. still neutral – Churchill wrote to Roosevelt that he hoped to 'allay the doubts and anxieties of some of your generals about the wisdom of our trying to hold the Middle East and . . . the Nile Valley'.[33]

Eden, both as Secretary of State for War and as Foreign Secretary, was strongly behind Churchill's determination to hold the Middle East and, later, his Mediterranean strategy.

Roosevelt's own attitude was not quite clear. Both because of the views of his Chiefs of Staff and for reasons of home politics he wanted to keep clear – publicly – of military entanglements in the eastern Mediterranean or the Balkans; these could and should be left to the imperialist British. Churchill, aware of American sensitivity on this point, pulled up Eden when, during the Anglo-American talks at Algiers in May 1943, he indiscreetly used a phrase suggesting that Anglo-American troops might be used in the Balkans. 'Eden and I were in full agreement on the war policy,' Churchill wrote later, 'but I feared that the turn of his phrase might mislead our American friends.'[34]

On the other hand, Roosevelt seems at times to have felt he could have it both ways: keep clear of all above-ground military involvement in the taboo area, but exercise power there by underground means, through General William Donovan's Office of Strategic Services (O.S.S.). At the beginning of 1941 Donovan had made a lightning tour of the Balkans as Roosevelt's special representative, much to Churchill's satisfaction. By 1942 Donovan had a representative in Cairo. That summer Roosevelt is reported to have asked the exiled King Peter of Yugoslavia what he would say to the Americans' taking control of the organisation of aid to the underground movements of the Balkans and central Europe.[35] Perhaps he did not mean this altogether seriously; but in October 1943 he sent Churchill a message proposing that Donovan should take over the direction of all British or American agencies in the Balkans. Churchill turned this down firmly, even brusquely;[36] O.S.S. went on operating in the area, sometimes in co-operation with the British and sometimes in conflict.

Above ground, the Balkans and the eastern Mediterranean remained a taboo area for the Americans, and Roosevelt felt free to disclaim all responsibility and to criticise the British.

The setback to Churchill's Mediterranean strategy which hurt him most was the failure of his plans to take key islands in the Aegean, caused by lack of the necessary landing craft. After the loss of Cos and the decision to evacuate Leros he wrote to Roosevelt: 'I will not waste words in explaining how painful this decision is to me.'[37] Roosevelt did not waste sympathy on him. From this time Churchill's power to influence the decision of the Anglo-American Combined Chiefs of Staff, through Roosevelt, steadily dwindled. He fought back, with a certain limited success, over the retention of landing craft in the Mediterranean for the Italian campaign, and over a modest postponement of Overlord. (He remained at times, and privately, gloomy and sceptical about the Overlord strategy, and wrote to Cadogan as late as mid-April 1944, 'this battle has been forced upon us by the Russians and by the U.S. military authorities' – but was not going to raise any 'timorous cry' about it.[38])

At Tehran and again in the summer of 1944 Churchill lost out over the plan for an operation through Istria and the Ljubljana Gap to Vienna; Roosevelt had first mooted the idea at Tehran, much to the alarm of his military advisers, but later disowned it.[39] In June 1944, with General Harold Alexander, Harold Macmillan and Field-Marshal Smuts all pressing strongly for it and Eden very much in favour for political reasons, Churchill championed the cause with the Americans as more worth while than landings in the south of France. He got a very sharp 'No' from the U.S. military chiefs which stung him into writing the draft of an impassioned message to Roosevelt, saying there was very grave dissatisfaction at the way in which the control of events was now being assumed one-sidedly by the U.S. Chiefs of Staff, and the opinions of the British Supreme Commander in the Mediterranean were completely brushed aside:

This obviously cannot continue, and, with the very greatest respect, I must request a further and formal discussion upon the matter. . . . We are entitled to press for better and more equal treatment. We have as many troops and forces engaged on the whole in Europe, including both theatres, as you have yet brought into action. . . . It is, I am sure, the duty of those who bear our responsibilities and of the high commands to place themselves in reasonable and equal relationship. Otherwise it would be necessary, in particular, to devise some other machinery for conducting the war. . . .

This threat to break up the Combined Chiefs of Staff and the joint command structures in the field was a very grave one; perhaps Churchill never meant it seriously but was simply letting off steam. In any case, he sent his draft to Eden, who may well have smoothed him down. A fortnight later Churchill let Eden know that he had decided not to send it.[40] But he did not accept final defeat and managed to keep the project alive on paper – though not in reality, since his own Chiefs of Staff had serious doubts about it – until a much later stage in the war.

In the last months of war in Europe Churchill failed in his impassioned opposition to Eisenhower's one-man decision not to drive for Berlin but to let the Russians capture Germany's capital city. He forgave Eisenhower for his strange (and politically harmful) change of plan, and Roosevelt for his rather weak defence of it, but continued to fight against Eisenhower's decision, after the German surrender, to withdraw to the agreed dividing line in Europe so that the Russian armies could advance westwards. But by then Roosevelt was dead and their personal friendship, for what it was worth, no longer counted in the balance.

In one special field the Churchill–Roosevelt direct line won what looked like an extremely important gain for Britain. This was their agreement on Anglo-U.S. partnership in developing atomic energy, both for military and civilian purposes, first set out in their agreement at Quebec in August 1943 and reaffirmed by them privately in September 1944. This partnership included an undertaking that neither country would use the atom bomb without the other's consent. And, mainly on Churchill's insistence, it excluded the Soviet Union, as also, to Eden's regret, France. Churchill saw this nuclear partnership as most valuable not only in the war but also as a key factor in a post-war Anglo-American special relationship. But the 1944 agreement led to difficulties because Roosevelt told no one about it, so that after his death the British had to tell the Americans. (In Britain, Eden was one of the very small number of people who knew about it; Attlee and Bevin were not among them.) Nevertheless, the 1944 understanding had long-term as well as short-term importance, and it would certainly never have been accepted by the U.S. side but for Churchill's power to persuade Roosevelt.[41]

Eden, who sat in on many of the discussions on war strategy, could see clearly enough the importance of the Churchill–Roosevelt relationship in influencing the decisions of the Anglo-American Combined Chiefs of Staff in Washington, at least until the last phase of the war. But he would have hated the idea of any equivalent to the Combined Chiefs in the foreign policy field. His Washington visit in March 1943 was a seeming triumph. Halifax reported to Churchill: 'From the first he clicked with everyone from the President downwards, both in private and in public. He has never put a foot wrong.'[42] (Eden had his own American ancestor, though a much more remote one than Churchill's.) But he never got on easy and intimate terms with the State Department, such as it was at that time. As early as January 1942 he wrote: 'U.S. policy is exaggeratedly moral, at least where non-American interests are concerned.'[43] He seems to have gone on thinking this.

Above all, he wanted to be able to carry out an independent policy of his own. In the foreign policy field he wanted to use the Churchill–Roosevelt direct line for this purpose. This he did with some success for wartime ends. In the long term, both Eden's idea of an independent British policy and Churchill's idea of a lasting Anglo-American partnership ended in the dustbin of history.

CHAPTER ELEVEN

Whose finest hour?

In the first political crisis of Churchill's career as war leader Eden could give him very little help. Although as Secretary of State for War he had Cabinet rank, he was not a member of the War Cabinet of five which Churchill formed on 11 May 1940. In this Churchill had included two Conservatives, Chamberlain and Halifax, known as the architects of the appeasement policy, and two Labour Party men, the quiet but rock-like leader Clement Attlee, and the less respected but popular Anthony Greenwood. The Liberal Party leader, Sir Archibald Sinclair, as Secretary of State for Air was, like Eden, outside the War Cabinet and did not even have Cabinet rank; but since his party belonged to the new national coalition he often attended War Cabinet meetings, especially when political issues were at stake.

In this War Cabinet of five Churchill did not at the start have the authority and control which he later won for himself. What he had most to fear was the opposition of his fellow Conservatives. In the beginning Chamberlain and Halifax sometimes seemed to play the chief role in War Cabinet discussions where foreign relations were at issue. Up to a point this left Churchill free to put all his strength into the immediate urgent problems of waging war against great odds. But it could also be dangerous.

The Conservatives had a vast majority in the House of Commons and a good many were still devoted to Chamberlain; if they could not have him as Prime Minister, they would rather have had the sober and civilised Halifax than Churchill, the wild man and rebel. After a speech by Churchill in the House that summer Chips Channon, a reliable weather-vane, wrote in his diary : 'He leaves me unmoved. There is always the quite inescapable suspicion that he loves war, war which broke Neville Chamberlain's better heart.'[1]

In the event of a military disaster, such Conservatives could be expected to welcome Halifax the peace-maker in place of Churchill the war-monger. If Halifax's peace-making could be conducted under the highly respectable umbrella of the patronage of the U.S. President and aimed at preserving all that was best in European civilisation, so much the better. Churchill and the policy he stood for – no surrender, fight to the end – would be doomed.

Probably neither Halifax nor Churchill ever thought of their relations in such harsh, crude terms, but both must have known in their bones that this was the underlying political reality. Later, in his war history, Churchill wrote that the possibility of coming to terms with Hitler was never on the Cabinet agenda, or even mentioned 'in our most secret conclaves'.[2] Perhaps by then he had forgotten some of the discussions of late May 1940.

At this time the French government of Paul Reynaud, as the British–French military position in Belgium crumbled to bits, turned more and more to the idea of mediation – mediation by Roosevelt to stop Mussolini declaring war, mediation by Mussolini to win 'reasonable' peace terms from Hitler, mediation by Roosevelt to soften Hitler's demands on a beaten France. Reynaud was, too, desperately anxious that Britain should go along with France in seeking mediation and peace negotiations. Roosevelt had kindly and comforting words for the French and British and obviously hoped to keep them fighting; but the words came from a great distance and a great height.

Churchill was at first willing to make an effort to keep Mussolini out of the war. At the Cabinet's behest he wrote to him on 16 May: 'Is it too late to stop a river of blood from flowing between the British and Italian peoples?' But he added: 'Whatever may happen on the Continent, England will go on to the end, even quite alone . . . and I believe with some assurance that we shall be aided . . . by the United States.'[3] But on 22 May the British ambassador at Rome reported that Mussolini was only awaiting the establishment of the Germans in the Channel ports to declare war.[4] Nevertheless, when the French then proposed that Roosevelt should be asked to make a new approach to Mussolini, saying that France and Britain might be willing to remedy Mussolini's 'grievances', Halifax proposed that the answer should be that 'we fully endorsed the suggestion'. Churchill did not object. And when Halifax reported to the War Cabinet that an Italian diplomat in London had suggested a British approach, Churchill again said he saw no objection to pursuing the matter, but there must be no publicity, since it would amount to a confession of weakness.[5]

While Churchill was willing to go a long way to keep Italy out of the war at that particular moment, he must soon have seen where this line of thought might lead. Probably on 25 May, Halifax drafted a message for

Churchill to send to Roosevelt 'concerning American action in the event of Hitler trying to impose peace terms on us after the collapse of France' (as the Foreign Office later described it). In this suggested message Churchill was to say to Roosevelt:

> If you felt it within your power at the chosen moment to say to Hitler that, while you recognise his right to obtain terms that must necessarily be difficult and distasteful to those whom he had defeated, nevertheless terms that were intended to destroy the independence of Great Britain or France would at once touch the vital interests of the U.S. . . . the effect might well be to make him think again. If you felt it possible . . . to go further and say that, if he insisted on terms destructive of British independence and therefore prejudicial to the position of the U.S., U.S.A. would at once give full support to Great Britain, effect would be all the more valuable. . . . Undoubtedly the ancient civilisation and culture of this Continent is today in greater danger than it has ever been.[6]

This message drafted by Halifax – a somewhat tortuous appeal to Roosevelt to intercede with Hitler to get good peace terms for Britain – was never sent or, so far as is recorded, discussed by the War Cabinet. But it must have been in Churchill's thoughts during two stormy War Cabinet meetings on 27 and 28 May. These took place in the knowledge of an assessment made by the Chiefs of Staff on 26 May of Britain's chances of survival if France collapsed. They said that air superiority was the crux; to achieve superiority over Britain, the Germans would have to knock out the R.A.F. and also the aircraft factories, especially in Coventry and Birmingham; their success would depend partly on the 'moral effect on the workpeople and their determination to carry on in the face of wholesale havoc and destruction'. Germany, they concluded, had most of the cards; but this might be counterbalanced by 'the morale of our fighting personnel and civil population'; they believed it would.[7]

In the discussions that followed in the War Cabinet the morale factor was uppermost in the arguments of Churchill and the Labour leaders; Halifax was more concerned with the probable destruction of the aircraft factories. Churchill wrote later that the War Cabinet were all of one mind: 'There was no discussion. Heart and soul we were together.'[8] This is not borne out by the War Cabinet minutes of 27 and 28 May.

The immediate subject of the meetings was a plea from Reynaud for a fresh appeal to Mussolini, both through Roosevelt and directly by Britain and France, this time using as bait specific territorial concessions in the Mediterranean (which for Britain would have meant the offer of Malta and Gibraltar). Chamberlain, though doubtful of success, wanted to send Reynaud a soft answer, not a blank refusal, so as to keep the French in a good mood. But the Liberal leader, Sinclair, thought such an approach would show weakness, and any weakness on our part would encourage the enemy and undermine morale in Britain; the suggestion that the government were prepared to barter away pieces of British territory would have a deplorable effect. Attlee said the suggested approach would be 'very damaging to us'. He was backed by Greenwood: 'If it got out that we had sued for terms at the cost of ceding British territory, the consequences would be terrible.'

Churchill himself was sure fresh approaches to Mussolini would be futile and would be regarded with contempt and would, moreover, 'ruin the integrity of our fighting position in this country'. He went on:

> Anyway, let us not be dragged down with France. . . . If this country was beaten, France [would] become a vassal state; but if we won, we might save France. . . . Even if we were beaten, we should be no worse off than we should have been if we were now to abandon the struggle. . . . If the worse came to the worst, it would not be a bad thing for this country to go down fighting for the other countries that had been overcome by the Nazi tyranny.

This was altogether too much for Halifax, who said he was conscious of 'certain rather profound differences of points of view', and he challenged Churchill to say whether he really meant that under no conditions would he contemplate any course except fighting to a finish. The previous day, he said, Churchill seemed to agree that, if 'matters vital to the independence of this country were unaffected', he would be willing to discuss terms. Now he spoke of nothing but a fight to the finish. He, Halifax, 'doubted if he would be able to accept the view now put forward by the Prime Minister'. Churchill, he went on, had said that two or three months would show whether Britain could stand up to air attack. This meant that the country's future turned on whether the enemy's bombs happened to hit our aircraft factories. He, Halifax, was prepared to take that risk if Britain's independence was at stake; but if it was not, he would think it right to accept an offer which would save the country from avoidable disaster.

Churchill, trying to avert a clash and keep the Cabinet together, replied that the question before the Cabinet was difficult enough without getting involved in an issue which was quite unreal and most unlikely to arise. But Chamberlain then challenged Churchill to say what he would do if

Hitler, 'being anxious to end the war through knowledge of his own internal weaknesses', were to offer terms to both France and England. Churchill, again trying to avoid a collision, replied that he would not join France in asking for terms; but if he were told what the terms offered were, he would be prepared to consider them.[9]

After the meeting Halifax said to Cadogan, who had been present: 'I can't work with Winston any longer.' Cadogan replied: 'Nonsense, his rhodomontades probably bore you as much as they do me, but don't do anything silly under the stress of that.'[10]

In his own diary Halifax recorded: 'We had a long and rather confused discussion. . . . I thought Winston talked the most awful rot, also Greenwood, and after hearing it for some time I said exactly what I thought of them, adding that if that was really their view, and if it came to the point (i.e. over an approach to Italy) our ways must separate. Winston was surprised and mellowed, and, when I repeated the same thing in the garden, was full of apologies and affection. But it does drive me to despair when he works himself up into a passion of emotion when he ought to make his brain think and reason.'[11]

So it would seem that during the Cabinet Halifax threatened to resign – though from the Cabinet minutes over the question of peace terms with Germany rather than the approach to Mussolini. At such a moment Halifax's resignation could have had a very serious effect, not just on Churchill's position as Prime Minister, but on British morale and unity at a moment when the British expeditionary force had not yet been saved through Dunkirk. If Churchill did his best to coax Halifax round, that was not surprising.

But the next day the War Cabinet fought over the same ground yet again. Halifax and Chamberlain again argued for an approach to Mussolini. Halifax said that in the unlikely event that Mussolini could get out of Hitler 'terms which would not affect our independence', we ought to consider them; we might get better terms before our aircraft factories were bombed than we might in three months' time. Churchill said that to him the essential point was that the French wanted to get the British to the conference table with Hitler: 'we should then find that the terms offered us touched our independence and integrity. When at this point we got up to leave the conference table, we should find that all the forces of resolution which were now at our disposal would have vanished.'

The Labour ministers gave Churchill support as before. Attlee said there was grave danger that if Britain did what France wanted it would be impossible to rally the people. Greenwood added that in the industrial centres anything like weakening on the government's part would be a disaster.

Halifax said he could not see what there was in the French suggestion about mediation that Churchill thought so wrong. Churchill said the chances of decent terms being offered at that time were a thousand to one against. Moreover, nations which went down fighting rose again, but those who surrendered tamely were finished.

The meeting broke off for forty-five minutes, leaving Chamberlain and Halifax to draft a reply to Reynaud. Churchill used this respite to meet all the ministers who were not members of the War Cabinet. It is not recorded if Eden was among them. For Churchill, this meeting was probably the turning-point. When the War Cabinet met again at 7 p.m. he told them that the other ministers 'had expressed the greatest satisfaction when he had told them that there was no chance of our giving up the struggle'. He did not remember having ever before heard a gathering of persons occupying high places in political life express themselves so emphatically.[12] In his war history Churchill wrote that he was surprised by the demonstration: 'Quite a number seemed to jump up from the table and come running to my chair, shouting and patting me on the back. I was sure that every minister was ready to be killed quite soon, and have all his family and possessions destroyed, rather than give in. In this they represented the House of Commons and almost all the people.'[13]

The reply that went to Reynaud that night was, according to Churchill, for the greater part in his own words; he had, however, accepted Chamberlain's idea that the stress should be on timing rather than a flat rejection of any approach to Mussolini. It concluded: 'Our success must depend first on our unity, then on our courage and endurance.' A few days later the French government made an approach to Italy on their own; it was futile.[14]

What was strange about the whole long argument over mediation and peace terms was not that Halifax and Chamberlain were peace-mongers in any discreditable sense of the word; they undoubtedly believed that they were standing up for Britain's best interests and the values of civilisation. It was that they were so blind to the hard fact that an appeal for mediation or for peace terms, at a moment when Britain was down and very nearly out, could not possibly persuade men like Hitler and Mussolini to be generous and 'decent'; or that it could not fail to have a disastrous effect on the ordinary people of Britain.

In Churchill's view it would also have destroyed all hope of getting solid material aid out of Roosevelt, as he badly wanted, instead of inviting him to play the peace-maker, as Halifax wanted.

How to get help from Roosevelt had been in the forefront of Churchill's mind since he became Prime Minister. On 15 May he wrote to him asking for 'the loan of 40 or 50 of your oldest destroyers'. Roosevelt replied that he could not do this except with the specific authorisation of Congress, and it might be unwise to ask Congress at that moment. On 20 May Churchill wrote to say he was very sorry about the destroyers. He then made a thinly veiled threat:

> Our intention is whatever happens to fight on to the end in this island. . . . In no conceivable circumstances will we consent to surrender. . . . If . . . others came to parley amid the ruins, you must not be blind to the fact that the sole remaining bargaining counter with Germany would be the fleet, and if this country was left by the U.S. to its fate, no one would have the right to blame those then responsible if they made the best terms they could get for the surviving inhabitants.

After writing this Churchill wondered if he had gone too far. He noted to Ismay: 'I fetched this back during the night for a final view; but decided not to alter anything. Now despatch.'[15]

Roosevelt brooded for a few days and then suggested to the British ambassador that if things came to the worst the British navy, aircraft and merchant vessels should be transferred to Canada or Australia before they could be captured or surrendered; it would be better if the king and government moved to Bermuda rather than Canada since the American republics might be 'restless' at monarchy being based on the American continent.[16]

All this did not go down well in the War Cabinet. It was said that 'President Roosevelt seemed to be taking the view that it would be very nice of him to pick up the bits of the British empire if this country was overrun. It was as well that he should realise that there was another aspect of the question.' Sinclair thought it important to get the U.S. to realise that the British meant to fight on. As for the British ambassador's own suggestion that Trinidad, Newfoundland and Bermuda should be leased to the U.S., Churchill said that 'the U.S. had given us practically no help in the war, and now that they saw how great was the danger, . . . they wanted to keep everything which would help us for their own defence'.

Churchill was also all against any appeal to the U.S. for mediation: 'A grovelling appeal, if made now, would have the worst possible effect.'[17] Whether he had in mind the message drafted by Halifax a few days earlier, or was thinking only of Reynaud's proposals, he certainly put paid to the idea of calling in Roosevelt as peace-maker. When on 16 June the War Cabinet met to consider Reynaud's request for British agreement to France's enquiring through the U.S. government what armistice terms Germany would offer France, Churchill insisted that one danger of invoking Roosevelt was that 'he might give advice which was of application to the United Kingdom as well as to France. He might, for example, issue an appeal to all the belligerent governments to call the war off. This might to some extent shake some sections of British public opinion, the whole of which was at present united and inflexible.' All thought of coming to terms with the enemy must be dismissed so far as Britain was concerned: 'We were fighting for our lives and it was vital that we should allow no chink to appear in our armour.'

Churchill then called on the service ministers to give their views. Eden could at last give him support, saying he entirely concurred in the course proposed by the Prime Minister; the British reply to the French 'should contain no hint or suggestion of the likelihood of peace negotiations'. All that Halifax said was that if Roosevelt were asked to take part in peace negotiations on behalf of France it would be useful for him to have Britain's views. Churchill said the essential point was that Germany should not get the French fleet; Roosevelt should play the trump card of threatening to declare war to prevent this. There was no talk of peace moves by, or on behalf of, Britain.[18]

The Battle of Britain and Hitler's failure to carry out his invasion threat made Churchill's position in the War Cabinet almost impregnable, and also removed the danger of any damaging mediation offer by Roosevelt. In September Chamberlain was forced by cancer to resign, and he died in November. The clash of temperament and political strategy and tactics between Churchill and Halifax during the crucial days at the end of May 1940 had its sequel, even though the outward show of War Cabinet unity was preserved. At the end of 1940 Churchill sent the reluctant Halifax to Washington with the job of getting as much aid as he could out of Roosevelt and if possible pulling him into the war. Churchill could then bring Eden into the War Cabinet as Foreign Secretary, friend and ally.

One important, if unintended, side-effect of Churchill's 'fight to the death' stand and his blocking of Halifax's hankering for peace moves was to make Roosevelt go against all precedent and his wife's wishes by standing for a third term as president. Robert Sherwood wrote later that, if the British had told the White House that they must sue for peace in the event of the fall of France, 'nothing but over-inflated personal vanity could have induced Roosevelt to seek a third term. . . . So long as Britain held out . . . Roosevelt wanted to stay in the fight.'[19]

But over a year passed after Roosevelt's re-election before he got into the fight, in Churchill's sense of the word. Meanwhile, the Lend-Lease agreement required tedious and frustrating negotiation. By the end of 1940 most of Britain's disposable foreign assets had been sold to pay for U.S. war equipment, and Churchill wrote to Roosevelt that it would be wrong and mutually disadvantageous if, after victory was won and civilisation saved, 'we should stand stripped to the bone'.[20] In May 1941 Eden and Churchill argued about the best way to get active American help in the Battle of the Atlantic. Eden wrote that the Americans did not realise how serious things were; so there should be a statement in Parliament disclosing the full extent of British shipping losses, even though this might have a bad effect elsewhere. Churchill, writing just after Hitler's deputy, Rudolf Hess, had landed in Scotland, wrote back: 'The master key to American action would be the knowledge that the British Empire could at this time get out of the war intact, leaving the future struggle with a Germanised Europe to the U.S. But this you did not want me to say.'[21] He did not say it.

In the end the Americans did help with Atlantic convoys; and when Churchill went to meet Roosevelt at Argentia he had great hopes – partly raised by Harry Hopkins[22] – that the President was now ready to go to war. He was disappointed; all that Roosevelt said was that he 'would wage war, but not declare it, and . . . become more and more provocative'. Churchill told him that he would not answer for the consequences if Russia had to sue for peace and 'hope died in Britain that the U.S. were coming into the war'. Roosevelt made no promises;[23] and Halifax told the War Cabinet a few days later that he thought the President was 'perhaps unnecessarily prudent about not putting too great a strain on public opinion'.[24] In November Smuts described Roosevelt as 'Hamlet-like'.[25]

So when the Japanese attacked Pearl Harbor and Hitler and Mussolini declared war on the U.S., both Churchill and Eden felt enormous relief.[26] Roosevelt's Hamlet-like hesitations were at an end. He was no longer a potential peace-maker or rich and benevolent well-wisher, but an ally.

CHAPTER TWELVE

Franco and Salazar: diplomacy or force?

Even while Roosevelt was still playing Hamlet and the U.S. was still firmly neutral there was one place where he seriously thought of a joint military operation with the British. This was the Spanish and Portuguese Atlantic islands. In German hands they could be a serious threat to the shipping routes not only of Britain but also of the United States. Both Spain and Portugal were neutral, both were dictatorships. In Spain General Franco had established himself in power with Axis help and might wish to repay his debt. Portugal had a 600-year-old treaty with Britain but Dr Salazar was a difficult, touchy and ultra-cautious man. The problem was how to make sure that the Atlantic islands did not fall under enemy control.

The strategic importance of the islands, and even more of the Iberian peninsula itself, was painfully clear to the British from the very beginning. If a hostile Spain made Gibraltar unusable, what would happen to Britain's Mediterranean life-line? In the Atlantic, the Azores were nearly as great a potential danger. The question was whether to use diplomacy to keep Franco genuinely neutral and to persuade Salazar to be benevolent, or whether to use force, at least to take the Atlantic islands.

From 1940 on this question led to arguments between Churchill and the Foreign Office. Just after the fall of France the British ambassador in Lisbon was arguing against any plan for using force to take over the Portuguese islands: 'We shall be charged with a breach of alliance and of dragging Portugal into the war. . . . We ought, I submit, to lay our need before Dr Salazar.' But the Chiefs of Staff thought the denial of the Azores and the Spanish Cape Verde Islands to the enemy essential; they wanted to send in the Rifle Brigade and a battalion of infantry.[1]

Churchill sympathised with them. He minuted to Halifax: 'Must we always wait until a disaster has occurred? . . . I am increasingly attracted by the idea of simply taking the Azores one fine morning out of the blue, and explaining everything to Portugal afterwards. She would certainly have every right to complain. . . .'[2] Churchill's buccaneering mood was deplored in the Foreign Office. They argued that 'if we take what will be regarded as the first act of aggression we shall most probably swing the whole peninsula against us'.[3] No action was taken.

One powerful champion of diplomacy was the ambassador in Madrid, Sir Samuel Hoare, a senior Conservative politician. He had blotted his copybook by his pact with the French Foreign Minister, Pierre Laval, condoning Mussolini's Abyssinian aggression, but then became one of the inner group of four in the Chamberlain government – the others being Chamberlain himself, Halifax and Sir John Simon – who privately discussed foreign policy and came to be regarded as the men of Munich. So he was not loved either by Churchill or by Eden, who had clashed with him directly when Foreign Secretary; but his influence in the upper reaches of the Conservative Party was considerable. In May 1940 Churchill did not want him in his government and disposed of him by sending him to Madrid.

The choice turned out to be brilliant. Hoare took his job extremely seriously, established good relations with two Spanish Foreign Ministers out of three who held office between 1940 and 1945, and even acquired a certain limited influence on Franco. His combination of flexibility, patience and stubborn tenacity, his prestige as former holder of 'most of the great offices of state', as he himself once wrote,[4] his keen sense of his own dignity and importance, all gave him much more weight both in Spanish affairs and in his dealings with his own government than any ordinary ambassador could have had.

Hoare naturally threw this weight on the side of diplomacy rather than force (though in October 1940, when he reported that there was a fifty-fifty chance of a German drive into Spain, he recommended preparations for supporting anti-German resistance based on the Spanish army).[5] When in December 1940 Eden became Foreign Secretary, Hoare was obviously worried. During the Spanish Civil War, when both were in the government, Hoare had thought that Eden had felt almost passionately, seeing the conflict 'as one between absolute right and absolute wrong, in which the dictators should at all costs be totally defeated and democracy totally defended'.[6] If Eden was going to take a passionately moral stand now, Hoare was going to be in difficulties. So he wrote him a personal letter of congratulation of which the real point was to find out whether Eden stood by the existing Cabinet policy of keeping Spain neutral or wanted to switch to an anti-Franco line.[7]

Eden cannot have relished making this choice, or have liked the idea of buttering up Franco. But there were very strong practical arguments for keeping Spain out of the war. Moreover, if the decision was in favour of diplomacy, not force, policy-making in the Iberian peninsula would be in his own hands, even if this landed him in tussles with Churchill – and, as things turned out, with the Americans. Churchill once wrote to him : 'I very often back you up when the United States are foolish about your countries, Spain, Portugal, etc.'[8] It must have been pleasant for Eden to reckon Spain and Portugal among 'his' countries; in any case, he reassured Hoare and thereafter argued hard for diplomacy.

This was not always easy. In March 1941 the Chiefs of Staff reported that the Germans seemed active in the Cape Verde Islands, but did not recommend immediate counter-action. In April, however, Churchill was all for making necessary preparations; Eden agreed 'in principle'.[9]

At the beginning of May Roosevelt stepped into the discussion. Stung by a strong Portuguese protest about a proposed U.S. 'friendly naval visit' to the Azores and reported Spanish nervousness about a similar visit to the Spanish Atlantic islands, Roosevelt sent Churchill a message warning him rather peremptorily off any British expedition to the islands except in the case of German attack on Portugal itself or on the islands. He went on :

> I know you will not mind my saying that in the event of a British expeditionary force you make it very clear to the American people that in case of Azores it is for purpose of British defense and . . . that Britain will restore islands to Portuguese sovereignty at close of war. . . . The reason I suggest this is that as you know most of Azores are in Western Hemisphere under my longitudinal map reading. . . .

After consulting Eden, Churchill sent a sharp answer : Roosevelt's conditions would make it almost certain that the British would be fore-stalled by the Germans in the islands. If the British moved, they would certainly promise to restore the islands after the war : 'We are far from wishing to add to our territory, but only to preserve our life and perhaps yours.'[10]

By the end of May Roosevelt had switched to a different line : that there should be a joint U.S.–British plan, which could 'function at the pressing of a button', for taking over the Azores and Cape Verde Islands if the Germans moved into Spain or Portugal; he himself was preparing an expeditionary force of 25,000 men; Salazar might be 'induced' to invite American–British protection of the islands. Churchill's answer was that the British had expeditions long prepared and waiting by their ships : 'We should welcome collaboration with an American token force before, during or after occupation of Atlantic islands and if you wish would turn them over to you as a matter of mutual war convenience.' Churchill pointed out that the British were already having talks with the Portuguese on British aid and were hoping that Salazar would accept British protection in the islands.[11]

So for the British diplomacy was still the first choice; and since Hitler did not move against the Iberian peninsula but against Russia, diplomacy held the field during the summer. But when Roosevelt met Churchill at Argentia in August 1941 he was still eager to find a way of getting U.S. forces into the Azores, suggesting that Churchill should arrange for Salazar to ask for American help there, on the grounds that the British were too busy elsewhere; U.S. forces would be ready to move to the islands in mid-September.

Churchill was happy but Cadogan, at a meeting in the Prime Minister's cabin in the *Prince of Wales*, argued against any British or U.S. action unless the Germans actually made a move first; otherwise they might merely provoke the Germans into action or alternatively might find it hard to justify their own action. Luckily, the argument became unreal when General Marshall revealed that it might be very difficult for the U.S. army to provide the forces needed to occupy the Azores.[12] So neutral America did not undertake the venture – which in any case Salazar would have bitterly opposed.

The next moment of serious tension was on the eve of *Torch*. The preparations for the North African landings involved a great deal of activity at Gibraltar, and Gibraltar's security was essential to their success, especially since the British had insisted on landings inside the Mediterranean as well as on the Atlantic coast. Franco was bound to be extremely touchy about the whole thing; there was no knowing whether in a fit of anger he might not throw himself into Hitler's arms. Hoare used all his diplomatic skills to make sure that Franco turned a benevolently blind eye to what was going on at Gibraltar; and, when the moment came, he transmitted to Franco a formal message from the British government that the operations were directed solely to removing the Axis threat to North Africa and that there was full sympathy with Spain's desire to keep the evils of war from the Iberian peninsula. (Hoare also had the agreeable job of conveying to the U.S. ambassador Roosevelt's parallel message to Franco, since the American diplomatic cyphers were thought insecure.[13])

All went well, and Hoare wrote to Churchill: 'I can claim that at this corner of the front we have held the position.' In the Foreign Office Cadogan minuted: 'Sir S. Hoare has done very well, and is of course not the last to say so.' Eden replied: 'By all means let us administer the congratulatory syrup if this is the moment for another dose.' The dose was duly given.[14]

As for Portugal, there was an understanding between Churchill and Roosevelt that Britain should do the job. Salazar, like Franco, was an uncertain quantity, though better disposed towards Britain. The normally cheerful and self-confident British ambassador, Sir Ronald Campbell, had written in April 1942 that, though he would not go so far, yet, as to say that Salazar was becoming unbalanced, his suspiciousness, pride and obstinacy seemed to be getting the upper hand. A few months later he wrote that Salazar was becoming, if not crazy, at any rate abnormal; the 'jesuitical strain in him' seemed to be coming out more and more. The U.S. ambassador in London, Winant, told Eden that he knew Salazar: he was half peasant, half priest; Eden said he preferred the former.[15]

However, Salazar swallowed *Torch* without much trouble. Churchill sent a personal message of assurance that the British and Americans had no evil intentions towards either Portugal or Spain and were contemplating no action involving any Portuguese territory; they desired to spare the Iberian peninsula the horrors of war. Salazar was satisfied.

This assurance, at least in theory, tied Britain's hands and meant that it was no longer possible to take the Azores by force, unless the Germans attacked first. But Roosevelt's restless mind, once *Torch's* success was certain, flitted again to the Portuguese islands. Early in 1943, without telling Churchill, he asked President Vargas of Brazil – with which Portugal had special ties of language and blood – to suggest to Salazar that Brazil should take on the defence of the islands. The Brazilians – not the Americans – told the British of Roosevelt's move.[16] From Lisbon Campbell commented that Salazar would go down fighting sooner than do anything which he considered inconsistent with the honour and dignity of Portugal; he would not allow himself to be jockeyed into the war by the back door; he would either refuse to come in and take the consequences, or he would come in voluntarily and honourably. Campbell added that Salazar 'is not liked by the mass of the people but they stick to him because . . . they have a mystical belief in his wisdom'.

Campbell pointed out that neither Britain nor the U.S. could use force against Portugal without violating promises given to Salazar, and if Brazil acted the world would assume that she had been put up to it by the Americans or British. He then suggested: 'Would it not be better for us to invoke the alliance?'[17] (The alliance concluded by King Edward III and King Ferdinand and Queen Eleanor of Portugal in 1373 was a very remarkable historical survival.)

Eden's first reaction was to warn the U.S. and Brazil off the grass. He telegraphed to Halifax: 'I am surprised that the President should have raised this very delicate question with the Brazilian government without prior consultation with H.M.G. and without even mentioning his intentions to the Prime Minister at Casablanca.' He thought nothing should be done until the success of Torch was clear; and then it should be the British who made the first move.[18]

However, the British Chiefs of Staff wanted something done about the Azores. The U-boat war in the Atlantic was going badly and air facilities on the islands might make all the difference. They wanted Eden to put up a plan to the War Cabinet.[19] Before anything had been worked out Eden went to Washington, where Roosevelt assured him that he was fully content to leave the handling of the Portuguese business to the British; he had no idea of using force. He explained his interest in the Azores (not very convincingly) by saying that what he had in mind was their use in the post-war period for four-power meetings.[20]

Yet when Churchill went to Washington not long after Eden's return Roosevelt talked differently: the stress was on force rather than diplomacy. The President wanted joint plans to be prepared for 'capturing' the Azores. Churchill, eager to win over the American Chiefs of Staff to his Mediterranean strategy, found it easy to yield a point over the Azores – particularly as the idea of such an operation had appealed to him since 1940.

But the cause of diplomacy was not lost. Salazar himself took a hand in the game. Encouraged by the Allied successes in North Africa, he himself proposed to Campbell that in the light of the changed military situation the two governments should review the conclusions reached in their earlier staff talks. This, the Foreign Office thought, gave an excellent opening for the British to invoke the Anglo-Portuguese treaty and ask for air facilities in the Azores; and they put this to Churchill on 10 June. On the same day Eden raised the matter in the War Cabinet. Churchill said he was sceptical about a diplomatic approach if not backed by force; nevertheless, it was worth trying and he would send a message to Roosevelt at once. At this stage our policy should be 'all inducements and no threats'. All the same, preparations to use force should go ahead, with 20 August as the target date.[21]

The War Cabinet was content. Churchill rewrote the message which the Foreign Office had prepared for him to send to Roosevelt, so as to lay the stress on contingency planning for capturing the Azores, as he had agreed in Washington. Since plans could not be put into operation before the end of August there was in the meanwhile a good opportunity to ask for facilities immediately. If Salazar agreed, 'we shall . . . be saved all the trouble and expense of mounting a considerable expedition and any stigma that may be attached to threatening or using force against our oldest ally'. If Salazar refused, the War Cabinet agreed that 'we should not hesitate in August to use all necessary force'.[22] By this formulation Churchill warded off any accusation that he had gone back on the Washington agreement; Roosevelt raised no objection.

So the British started negotiating with Salazar. Frank Roberts of the Foreign Office and staff officers went out to Lisbon. At one point Eden suggested that he himself should go out to help matters forward. But Salazar politely said 'Later.' Campbell thought he feared an attempt to rush him and force his hand: 'Portugal is every bit as mulish as Spain'.[23] Eden was perhaps chagrined but complied with Campbell's suggestion that his visit should be 'held in abeyance'.

There was one particularly awkward point. Early on, Salazar made it plain that he wanted only British troops in the islands. This, Eden minuted to Churchill, 'might be awkward *vis-à-vis* the Americans, but his wish is not unnatural. . . . I think we should be wise to gloss this over for the present. Once we have fixed matters up it should not be too difficult to extend the facilities . . . e.g. by the operation of American aircraft from the islands.' Churchill approved this tactic: 'The great thing is to worm our way in and then, without raising any question of principle, swell ourselves out. We should use cash locally to make ourselves popular and smooth the way. The only thing that matters is getting a couple of squadrons at work in a month from now.'[24]

Churchill sensed from Roosevelt's messages that the President was finding it hard to keep his fingers out of the pie. In early July he sent him a report on the negotiations, adding: 'The enemy already know something is afoot and we are making all possible haste.'[25]

It was not clear why the need for haste was so great. There had been a startling improvement in the war against the U-boats in the Atlantic (owing to *Ultra*'s achievements). On 14 July Churchill telegraphed to Roosevelt that the bag of U-boats was seven in thirty-six hours; he wanted to release a joint statement on this 'record killing'. Roosevelt answered that, though an announcement would discourage the Axis, particularly Italy, this advantage would be more than outweighed by its effects in the U.S., where the wave of optimism that had followed recent successes in the anti-submarine war was 'definitely slowing down production'. So, said Roosevelt, 'I doubt the wisdom . . . of giving the cat another canary to swallow.'

Churchill answered: 'My cat likes canaries and her appetite grows with eating. However, news is now out-dated as we have altogether 18 canaries this month.' A fortnight later he telegraphed: 'The July canaries to date number 35, making a total of 85 in the 91 days since May 1st. Good hunting. . . . Let us settle together on the 12th what food our cats are to have.'[26]

But in spite of the big July bag of canaries Churchill felt the negotiations with Salazar must be hurried. On 14 July he wrote to Roosevelt: 'You will see we have decided to insert the thin end of the wedge. I am more than pleased with the way in which the Portuguese have responded to the invocation of our ancient alliance.' But ten days later he wrote to Eden complaining of Portuguese procrastination, of 'this vast verbiage and haggling': 'The time has come to let them know that this nonsense must cease. Every form of ceremony and civility has been exhausted. We must have the facilities in these islands by August 15. They ought to be told this, and the expedition should be prepared in accordance with what was agreed at Washington. We cannot go on fooling any longer.' The next day he wrote to Eden: 'I should very much like to see you bring this off. But August 20 seems a fateful date to me. WSC.'[27]

Eden withstood this battering. He wrote that he agreed that the time had come to force a decision with Salazar. But as for dates, the Chiefs of Staff would be content with 15 September for arrival in the Azores. If Salazar refused this date, Campbell should say the negotiations were at an end. He should not threaten the use of force – if only because it would take a certain time to organise an operation on this basis. Churchill, checked again, could only agree.[28]

On 31 July Roosevelt sent Churchill a brief reminder that, in spite of success against U-boats, the Azores were still needed.[29] But Salazar would not accept 15 September and suggested 15 October as the target date. Campbell thought it would be a grave mistake to break over a matter of a month.[30] In London there was a stormy meeting of the Defence Committee on 2 August, at which Churchill blew up, accusing the Portuguese of inventing imaginary dangers to spin out the discussions. He was unwilling to tolerate these delays and the Portuguese should be told that 15 September was the latest acceptable date. Eden argued back: if Churchill insisted on 15 September, it would be necessary to seize the islands by force – and this would take so long that the facilities would not be obtained until some time *after* 15 October. Eden suggested 1 October as a compromise. Churchill refused. The meeting broke up. Later, however, Churchill, Eden and one or two others agreed on 1 October.[31]

Of this meeting Eden wrote in his diary: 'Something of a shouting match going on for an hour or more. . . . No result at the meeting but we reached agreement . . . after the meeting. . . . As I said good-night he said he was sorry if he had been obstreperous at meeting, but he felt S. was intolerable. I replied that I feared that I had been obstreperous too. "Oh you, you were bloody!" On which note we said good-night.'[32]

In the end Salazar insisted on 8 October, and Churchill gave in. Eden had planned to announce the agreement – which he could have done with some pride – in the House of Commons on 12 October. But by then he was off to Moscow for the Foreign Ministers' conference. So it was Churchill himself who did the job with suitable pomp and ceremony, proclaiming that the Anglo-Portuguese treaty was without parallel in world history. His Right Honourable Friend the Foreign Secretary, he said, had conducted the negotiations with the very greatest skill and patience.

Perhaps Eden's greatest skill had been in keeping Churchill's impatience – fuelled by his eagerness to keep a promise to Roosevelt – within manageable bounds.

Churchill had good reason to be worried about this promise. The U.S. Chiefs of Staff were annoyed at having been kept out of the negotiations and obviously suspected that Churchill was double-crossing them and going back on the Washington agreement. Churchill was aware of this and on 20 September he telegraphed to the British representative on the Combined Chiefs of Staff: 'Do tell [Admiral] King that he must have confidence in my resolve and undertaking to bring the U.S. fully into these islands for all purposes of the war. Everything is moving in our favour. . . . He should remember that the reason why the Portuguese are more frightened of the Americans than of the English is because they think the Americans want the Azores, whereas the English in this respect at least are innocent lambs.'[33]

On 7 October, however, Roosevelt, at the direct request of his Chiefs of Staff, turned on the heat: the British, as soon as they were installed, should immediately provide facilities for the Americans in the Azores. The Americans also wanted to negotiate with the Portuguese themselves. Churchill, in line with Eden, pleaded that Salazar should be given a little time to see how the Germans reacted – or failed to react – to British entry into the islands. After that the question of U.S. entry could be tackled: 'Supposing that Salazar refuses, being afraid that you will stay there after the war and of the ambitions of Pan-American Airways, I will immediately report to you.' Then would be the moment for the Americans to make a direct approach to Salazar.[34]

Impatient at further delay, the Americans started putting pressure on Salazar. He became very touchy. By January the argument turned on whether an American air squadron could be stationed in the Azores – Salazar was by this time ready to give the Americans naval facilities and air ferry facilities. The Americans were talking about gate-crashing – sending a squadron without Salazar's blessing. Eden was scathing, minuting that the American approach had been clumsy and inept. There was no reason why a British air squadron should not go instead of an American squadron, so he hoped Roosevelt would drop this demand. If he did not, Salazar was quite capable of threatening to oppose American landings by force.[35] The British Chiefs of Staff suggested that an American squadron should operate with British markings as a British unit.[36]

Churchill stood by Eden and the Chiefs of Staff. Scrapping a more diplomatic draft prepared for him by Eden, he sent Roosevelt a message in his own words. He admitted that for a long time he had been sceptical of the Foreign Office view that Salazar could be brought to meet Anglo-American needs by invoking the old treaty, but to a very large extent he had done so; 'although we possess overwhelming strength, it would be . . . rather inconsistent with our general attitude towards small powers to override them roughly in matters of neutrality'. (That bit sounded more like Eden than Churchill.) He suggested an American squadron with British markings: 'Please remember that we were quite ready to put large numbers of troops into American uniforms at the time of Torch.'[37]

Roosevelt agreed not to try to gate-crash; the British could have one more chance to bring Salazar round. Campbell tried; Salazar said he did not mind American pilots but they must be incorporated in the R.A.F.; the demand for a separate squadron was 'simply a matter of American pride or prestige'. Campbell thought that Salazar 'did not intend to be bounced'.[38]

It still took time before Salazar's touchiness and American self-esteem could be salved and a satisfactory arrangement made; and it is fairly clear that both Eden and the Foreign Office got some fun out of American discomfiture and annoyance. But they would never have had this childish pleasure if Churchill had not used his direct link with Roosevelt to damp down the irritation of the U.S. Chiefs of Staff and restrain their impatience and even anger at what they saw as a humiliating and unnecessary delay and a British breach of faith.

During 1943 the limelight was on Lisbon. In Madrid Hoare was getting restive, feeling that he had spent long enough in political exile. Neither Churchill nor Eden could think what other job to give him if he came home; they wondered whether a decoration – a G.C.B. – would keep him happy.[39] He was also upset, when he came to London on leave, to find that there were rumours that he was at odds with the Foreign Office and was pursuing a personal policy of his own in Spain. He asked Churchill to clarify the position publicly. Eden reacted sourly to these worries of Hoare's, writing in January 1944: 'It is a further tribute to Sir S. Hoare that is required, not a statement that my foreign policy is my own.'[40]

Hoare was therefore in a mood to get on his high horse when a long, frustrating Anglo-American dispute started over Spanish deliveries to Germany of wolfram (essential to arms manufacture). Towards the end of 1943 the State Department launched out on a campaign of getting tough with the neutrals and bringing them into line by the most forceful economic or other means. They were particularly stern towards Spain; pressure on the dictator Franco was bound to be popular at home. So without telling the British in advance they stopped U.S. oil deliveries to Spain to force Franco to put a total stop on all wolfram deliveries to Germany.

Hoare and the Foreign Office did not agree with this method, holding that Franco's face must be saved; he could not be seen to yield to direct threat or blackmail. They preferred to get him to whittle down deliveries to an insignificant total; and they thought it was more important to get Franco to break German spy rings on Spanish territory and to recall the Spanish 'volunteers' – the Blue Division – from the Russian front. In February 1944 Hoare reported that the cutting off of oil had caused the tide to turn against the Allies: 'The Spaniards are getting into their martyrdom mood, the results of which history shows to be thoroughly dangerous and irresponsible.'[41]

Eden was for backing Hoare's line, saving Franco's face and going for practical results. Churchill was hesitant, writing to Eden: 'It is natural that Ambassador Hoare should be greatly concerned with the maintenance of agreeable relations. At the same time it is not an unreasonable position for the U.S. to take that if the Dons want American oil they should stop sending wolfram to Germany.' But after talking to Eden he came down more or less on his side, sending a message to Roosevelt that Hoare would back up the American ambassador, but then adding: 'When a large, strong, healthy elephant (no reference to the G.O.P.) comes into a garden and tramples on the flower-beds some perturbation is natural among the local gardeners. As you know, we have had our own point of view about this. . . . It will be tiresome if Germany gives the gasoline and Spain becomes even more definitely associated with the Nazis.'[42] (The G.O.P. was, of course, Roosevelt's political enemy the Republican Party, whose symbol was an elephant.)

Roosevelt, declaring that Spanish wolfram could be 'directly translated into terms of British and American casualties', insisted on a total embargo and was against the sort of compromise the British wanted. Hoare reported that the Spaniards rejected a total embargo but would reduce their exports to a purely symbolic amount and fulfil his other requests – stopping German spying and sabotage and recalling the Blue Division. Eden thought it right to settle on this basis, but the State Department had the bit between its teeth and delivered a virtual ultimatum. Hoare sent a message of alarm about the possible consequences, which was scrambled to Churchill at Chequers in the early hours of the morning. Eden suggested that the best thing to do was for Churchill to send Roosevelt a message pretending the ultimatum had never happened but recommending acceptance of the terms which Hoare had obtained from Franco. Churchill agreed to send a message on these lines, adding for good measure: 'We have just had a stick of bombs around 10 Downing Street and there are no more windows. Clemmie and I were at Chequers. Luckily all the servants were in the shelter. Four persons killed.'[43]

Perhaps Roosevelt was more interested in the stick of bombs than in wolfram. He replied that he was pleased that the Spanish problem was to be settled quickly, and happy that Churchill and Clemmie had escaped the bombing.[44] There must have been at this time a serious lack of communication between the President and the State Department, who continued obdurate and self-righteous. A month later there was still no agreement between British and Americans, and Hoare, thoroughly fed up, was determined to come to London – and Churchill and Eden knew that if he came he would make his discontent well known.

So Eden drafted a message for Churchill to send to Roosevelt urging a rapid settlement of the wolfram question on a compromise basis. Churchill added something of his own: '. . . I earnestly hope that you will give your consideration to our appeal without which we shall be in very serious difficulties as among other things Ambassador Hoare, who has held most of our great offices of state and is a Member of Parliament, now evidently wishes to resign. I could not support in future the policy which is now being enforced upon us.'[45]

In writing this Churchill was reacting to a very stiff telegram from Hoare: 'I cannot stand by and see all our work end in futility;' it would not be fair to ask him to remain week after week 'waiting upon ignorant dictates of the State Department'. But Eden did not want Hoare in London until a settlement had been reached, and with Churchill's agreement asked him to stay on – for a week at most.[46]

But Hoare had to stay on much longer than a week. There was a long haggle over exactly how many tons the Spaniards could be allowed to send to Germany. Churchill pointed out to Roosevelt that only nine tons were at issue; Roosevelt replied pompously that the American public attached 'the greatest importance' to Spanish wolfram shipments: 'They are most insistent upon a policy of firmness . . . and a contrary course on the eve of military operations would, I believe, have the most serious consequences.[47]

The deadlock was broken almost accidentally. Hull suggested that if Britain, not the U.S., supplied oil to Spain, it would be easier to accept a compromise over wolfram; he could then make a better case for the deal. Churchill immediately seized on this and telegraphed to Roosevelt that he was ready to take upon himself the entire responsibility for the settlement. Roosevelt perhaps did not want Churchill to take all the credit for the deal and authorised Hull to accept the British proposal on the restriction of Spanish wolfram shipments.[48] On 2 May an agreement was reached covering the points originally put forward by Hoare; but for the Anglo-American wrangle, it could have been made four months earlier.

It may be doubted whether the slightly ridiculous squabble was worth while. Perhaps Eden would not have stuck to his guns so tenaciously if he had not feared the political mischief that Hoare could make at home; Churchill, too, was very aware of this. Equally, Roosevelt's stiff-necked attitude was perhaps due to fear that Hull might yet again threaten to resign. Sherwood wrote later that this threat was for Hull a secret weapon the President could seldom ignore.[49]

At one point in the wrangle Hoare told Eden that he wondered whether the Americans were really aiming at the fall of the Franco regime.[50] In June 1944 Churchill made it quite clear to Roosevelt that this was not his aim: 'I do not care about Franco but I do not wish to have the Iberian peninsula hostile to the British after the war. We should not be able to agree here in attacking countries which have not molested us because we disliked their totalitarian form of government. I do not know whether there is more freedom in Stalin's Russia than in Franco's Spain. I have no intention to seek a quarrel with either.'[51]

But towards the end of 1944 there began to be pressure from the Left for action to get rid of Franco. Attlee put to the War Cabinet a paper saying all Britain's allies would like to see the regime destroyed and Britain was in danger of appearing to be Franco's only external support. In view of 'Spanish xenophobia', it would be useless to take overt action to change the regime, but 'we should use whatever methods are available to assist in bringing about the downfall of General Franco', especially in the economic field.[52] Selborne, the Minister of Economic Warfare, put in a rival paper deprecating Attlee's view: there was no reason to believe that Franco was any worse than 'our allies Stalin and Salazar'.[53]

Spain was discussed in the War Cabinet on 27 November. Eden leaned towards Attlee's side; he said most Spaniards thought that, if the Franco regime persisted, there was bound to be an explosion before long. Churchill said there was great danger in interfering in the internal affairs of other countries; he would send Franco a 'rough' letter, but thought he should then be left to stew in his own juice. This satisfied Attlee. It was agreed that Eden should draft a letter for Churchill.[54]

The idea was that Hoare – who had become Viscount Templewood and stayed on in Madrid – should deliver Churchill's letter when he took his final leave of Franco. Churchill had no taste for the letter and refused to be hurried by the fact that Hoare had fixed his departure date, writing to Eden: 'The relations between England and Spain have gone through many vicissitudes . . . since the destruction of the Spanish Armada, and I cannot feel that a few hours' more consideration on my part of the letter for which I am to be responsible are likely markedly to affect the scroll of history. . . . His Lordship's and Lady Maud's luggage will have to put up with whatever delays are necessary.'[55]

In the end Hoare had to make his farewells to Franco without any letter from Churchill to deliver. After a long delay Churchill put his name to the 'insulting' letter drafted by Eden, which he described as setting out Eden's policy, but he did it with bad grace, writing that: 'I have not the slightest intention of starting an anti-Franco crusade, any more than I wish to walk down the street with him arm in arm.'[56]

Both Franco and Salazar outlived both Churchill and Eden and remained in power till they died. But that was hardly Churchill's fault.

CHAPTER THIRTEEN

The Italian imbroglio

In the Anglo-American drama over the politics of Italy – comedy rather than tragedy – Churchill, Eden and Roosevelt took different roles from those they played in the French drama. Churchill and Roosevelt were often at loggerheads, Eden and Churchill were usually allies. Churchill, instead of insisting that the British should meekly follow Roosevelt's wishes, was defiantly claiming Britain's right to take the lead. Eden therefore was at one with him, except when he felt he was pushing things altogether too far.

British and American feelings about Italy were very different. Italian aggression in Abyssinia and Mussolini's intervention on Franco's side in the Spanish Civil War had been unpopular in Britain. The British found it cheap and easy to feel contempt for the Italians, and this was encouraged by Churchill in his earliest wartime broadcasts. Then, as Churchill told Stalin and Roosevelt at Yalta, 'the British people would not easily forget that Italy declared war on the Commonwealth in the hour of her greatest peril, when French resistance was on the point of collapse, nor could they overlook the long struggle against her in North Africa before America came into the war'.[1]

Abyssinia and Spain were remote to most Americans, but there were about six million Italian-Americans, many of them very vocal and many in New York; this was bound to incline both the State Department and Roosevelt towards displays of friendliness to Italy, especially when an election was in the offing. So while Churchill found it easy to win applause at home by being tough on Italians without much distinction between the 'good' and the 'bad', Roosevelt found it profitable to be 'soft' and give every encouragement to 'good' Italians.

Eden was perhaps more liable than Churchill to take a moral and 'anti-Fascist' view of Italian politics; in 1938 he had bitterly resented Chamberlain's efforts to butter up Mussolini behind his back. But when it came to asserting British leadership in Italian affairs, he was close to Churchill.

However, Churchill's overriding interest in Italy was strategic, and his foibles and prejudices in political matters were – usually – prompted by, or subordinated to, his conception of the best way of waging war against Germany on Italian soil.

In the *Torch* operation he had been willing to let the Americans take command and even, at the start, to disguise British participation. But once he had won over the Americans to his Mediterranean strategy – the invasion of Italy – he felt that the balance should change. British or 'British-controlled' troops in Italy always outnumbered the Americans considerably; the overall Mediterranean command, at the end of 1943, passed to the British general Sir Henry Maitland Wilson. Anglo-American integration remained, but the weight of responsibility – at least in Churchill's view – lay with the British. And this, he took it, held good in the political field as well as the military.

This was not altogether Roosevelt's idea. He was sure that the Italians (like the French) loved the Americans and disliked the British, so that it would be of military advantage for the Americans to show the flag. On the eve of the assault on Sicily he proposed to broadcast a message to the Italian people 'as President of the U.S.A. against whom on December 11th 1941 your government declared war'. Since the British had been fighting Italy since June 1940, this was too much for Churchill, who sent a message that the War Cabinet had thought of a joint Anglo-American declaration; he had been prepared to act as the President's 'lieutenant' in *Torch*, but in Sicily the British expected to be 'equal partners', and this would certainly seem justified by the proportion of troops, naval forces and aircraft involved. He would, however, accept Roosevelt's proposed broadcast, provided he made certain changes, without which 'untoward reactions might grow among the British people and their forces that their contribution had not received equal or sufficient recognition'.

Roosevelt gracefully yielded, and suggested a joint declaration. Churchill replied: 'It is lovely working with you. Everyone here would like a joint message.'[2]

The next problem – which Italians to do a deal with – was also settled amicably. For the British it was no surprise when Marshal Pietro Badoglio came forward. He had played a notable military role in the Italian war against Abyssinia but knew that world war was quite another matter, and had made contact through an intermediary with S.O.E., letting them know that he was prepared, at the right moment, to establish a military government – in other words, to get rid of Mussolini. He wanted to co-ordinate action with the British. The War Cabinet was told this in mid-March 1943, and approved the contact, provided no commitments were made. S.O.E. also had contacts with anti-Fascist groups in Italy, but this was the first time they had been in touch with 'influential circles'.[3]

When, in July, Badoglio resurfaced, Roosevelt raised no objection, sending a message to Churchill: 'There are some contentious people here who are getting ready to make a row if we seem to recognise the House of Savoy or Badoglio. They are the same element which made such a fuss over North Africa' (by which he meant Darlan). Roosevelt added that he had told the American Press that he would deal with anyone who could best give, first, disarmament, and second, assurance against chaos. He and Churchill could say something about self-determination in Italy at the proper time. Churchill replied that he, too, would deal with 'any Italian authority who could deliver the goods', and was not in the least afraid of seeming to recognise the Italian royal house and Badoglio. He thought it too early to talk of self-determination.[4]

So far, so good. Mussolini fell, the British and Americans dealt with King Victor Emmanuel and his new head of government, Badoglio. Badoglio brought over the Italian fleet; and Churchill, remembering the tragic fate of the French fleet, was grateful to him. Macmillan described Badoglio at this time as 'honest, broad-minded, humorous . . . with the horse common sense and natural shrewdness of the peasant, a loyal servant of his king and country, without ambition . . . a little like General Georges but with more restraint and dignity'.[5] This was, of course, calculated to recommend him to Churchill.

The king was a more shadowy figure. In 1940 the British ambassador had reported that he was contemplating abdication and taking himself off to America; with advancing age his mental energy was declining and he had become cynical and indifferent. Macmillan's description was much the same: '74 years old, physically infirm, nervous, shaky, but . . . with a certain modesty and simplicity of character. . . . I do not think he would be capable of initiating any policy except under extreme pressure.'[6]

Churchill did not want the king to take initiatives; he wanted docile Italians who would do what the Allied commanders wanted. There is no sign that his belief in the monarchic principle was uppermost in his mind at this time. But he thought that the Italian navy in particular would feel personal loyalty to the king.

However, neither the king nor Badoglio could be called anti-Fascist. It was not long before the U.S. State Department, still smarting under the brickbats thrown at them over the Darlan affair, wanted to put anti-Fascist Italians in the forefront. They did it without asking the British.

On 4 September the British embassy were told that Hull and Adolph Berle, of the State Department, had already agreed that Count Carlo Sforza should be allowed to go to North Africa on his way to Italy. Sforza, who had briefly been Foreign Minister before Mussolini took power, had lived for many years in the United States as a notable anti-Fascist and enemy of the king. When the British queried this decision, Berle said that about half the six million Italian-Americans had been anti-Fascist and the rest pro-Fascist; now the second half wanted to rehabilitate themselves, so they all now looked on Sforza as their leader. The State Department would not be able to justify a refusal to let him go to Italy in the eyes of the Italian-Americans. Halifax commented: 'Italo-Americans are a pretty important voting element concentrated in blocs at important centres and the elections are clearly in the Secretary of State's mind.'

The British thought Sforza had little influence in Italy. The scene was set for a long British–American wrangle. Churchill was at that moment in Washington. Eden telegraphed to him from London that if Sforza arrived in Italy the Italians would think the Allies were backing him against Badoglio; it would be better to wait and see how loyally Badoglio tried to deliver the goods. Churchill had a talk with Roosevelt over lunch, and Roosevelt agreed that nothing should be done for a few days.[7]

But then the Foreign Office changed their minds. S.O.E. had been in touch not only with Badoglio but also with the 'six parties', or, rather, self-appointed representatives of the Liberal, Christian Democrat, Socialist and Communist parties and two other groups, and they were against Badoglio and the king. Moreover, Mussolini, now under German control, had formed what he called a republican government. The Foreign Office, with their usual habit of trying to couple the most unlikely bedfellows, thought the right thing would be to prop up the monarchy and build up Badoglio as a rallying point for resistance to the Germans, while at the same time trying to get the six parties to collaborate with Badoglio and the king. To achieve this feat they now suggested that Sforza should be 'brought into the fold'; 'it may be that . . . Badoglio would be glad of his support'.[8]

This pleased Churchill, since he thought it would please Roosevelt: 'This might well suit you,' he telegraphed to him. A day or two later Sforza sent a letter to Berle which was to become the tablet of the law for Churchill, who assumed that it pledged Sforza to loyal and lasting support not only for the Badoglio government but also for the king. In fact, Sforza said all Italians should sink political differences in the struggle against the Germans, so he would support Badoglio for this purpose; he said nothing about the king. Shortly after, in a public speech before leaving the U.S., he spoke against the king.

This stung Churchill into sending a message to Roosevelt: 'According to reports here Sforza has been abusing and deriding the king of Italy ... surely he should be cautioned that he must play with the team. We don't want him to do a Balaam on us.' Roosevelt made light of the matter, so Churchill returned to the charge: 'I don't see much use in having him go to Italy merely to undermine whatever small fighting head against Fascism and the Germans Eisenhower has been able to produce out of the Italians.' He then suggested that Sforza should stop off in London 'and let us give him further friendly treatment'. Roosevelt agreed: 'I hope you can effectively indoctrinate him.' At the same time he sent Eisenhower instructions that only 'men of unequivocal liberal and democratic principles' should be brought into the Badoglio government; 'it is only through the use of such men . . . that this government can feel justified in supporting the present Italian government'.[9] In other words, there was to be no Darlan in Italy.

By this time Churchill was beginning to look on Italy as a sort of British preserve. He wrote to Eden, in another context, that the whole Italian people would 'undoubtedly be brought into the British (and American) system in Europe'. They would lose the empire and 'all lodgements on the eastern side of the Adriatic' and might have to surrender Trieste to become an open port, but they could be reconciled to these forfeits.[10]

He was in this mood when Sforza arrived in London. Eden saw him first and asked if he stood by his letter to Berle. Sforza said he stood by the principles contained in it, but added that Badoglio had no psychological or moral sense and the royal family was doomed; however, he would collaborate with those who were in favour of waging war against Germany. Eden again asked if he stood by the letter to Berle; Sforza said he did. On 12 October Churchill put the same question and Sforza gave the same answer (repeating it in a letter written in his own hand from Claridges); but he again complained of Badoglio's inadequacy and again declared the monarchy doomed. Churchill argued that the monarchy was the only thing that represented any continuity in the Italian state and the only remaining symbol of Italy; and Sforza, according to Cadogan's record, 'in the end gave . . . explicit assurances that he would do his best to support the king and Badoglio . . . with the proviso . . . that the Italian people should ultimately be free to choose their regime'.[11]

Churchill may have thought that he had now got Sforza pinned down, but he clearly took a dislike to him and somehow got hold of the idea that his opposition to the king stemmed from a remote feud between the House of Savoy and the House of Milan, from which Sforza could be expected to claim descent. He minuted Cadogan: 'It is quite evident to me that the old fool wants to be king himself, hence his republicanism.'[12] The old fool, Sforza, was born in 1873, Churchill in 1874.

Cadogan cannot have taken as low a view of Sforza as Churchill. On 19 October Macmillan telegraphed that the time had come to bring some representative civilian ministers into the Italian government; if they refused to serve under Badoglio, what about Sforza as prime minister? Cadogan, in Eden's absence in Moscow, suggested answering that, provided the king's abdication was not raised, there would be no objection to Sforza as head of government. Churchill would not have this: 'I regard Sforza as a useless gaga conceited politician. . . . It is far better to wait until Rome is taken. A much stronger government can be formed in this world city where lie the title deeds of Italy and Catholicism. Meanwhile Badoglio is the only solid peg.' Silly and irresponsible questions in the House of Commons should be ignored.[13]

The tough reply which Churchill sent Macmillan did not prevent a minor political crisis in Italy. Sforza said the king had offered him the premiership but he had refused out of loyalty to Badoglio. Churchill, receiving a letter from Sforza, wanted to send a reply saying, 'I am sorry to see how much trouble you are making,' but was dissuaded by Eden. The situation became easier when Eisenhower, then still holding the Allied command in the area, came down in favour of letting the king and Badoglio carry on (though, according to Macmillan, the U.S. political representative, Robert Murphy, obsessed by the Darlan complex, wanted to see the king go). Heartened by this news, Churchill telegraphed to Roosevelt on 6 November: 'We should lose a lot in breaking up the present king–Badoglio show. Victor Emmanuel is nothing to us but his combination with Badoglio did in fact deliver the Italian fleet . . . and . . . is at this moment holding the loyalties of a very large part of the unhappy army and people. . . . I do not believe that Sforza counts for anything that will make men kill or die.' (He struck out of his first draft the phrase, 'I thought Sforza a very vain and foolish old man.'[14])

Roosevelt sent a noncommittal reply: the king, he had been told, only clicked before lunch; so perhaps his grandson could succeed him; all the parties should soon be brought into the government.[15]

Churchill was helped at this point by the arrival of a secret message from the Rome representatives of the six parties through Ivanoe Bonomi, a former prime minister, which had the effect of making the king tell Badoglio to carry on until Rome was freed. This gave Badoglio confidence that, even if the liberation of Rome was delayed, he could keep Sforza at bay.[16]

So far, so good. British policy in backing the king and Badoglio could be defended on military grounds, and so long as Eisenhower was commander Roosevelt and the State Department had to listen; and so long as the British and Americans were more or less united there was little Sforza could do. But Eisenhower left to take charge of the preparations for *Overlord*; his successor, the British general Maitland Wilson, carried less weight in Washington. The liberation of Rome was long delayed. And 1944 was the year of the U.S. presidential election. There was more or less bound to be trouble.

Eden, left to himself, would probably have been a good deal more flexible over Italian politics than Churchill, who became more and more stubborn in defending his 'wait until Rome' policy. Eden might be irritated by the State Department but he tried to avoid unnecessary friction and was sensitive to parliamentary opinion at home. Also, since the Foreign Ministers' meeting in Moscow, he was making a special effort to work with the Russians on European questions. On the other hand, when it came to standing up to the Americans he was with Churchill; and he seems to have liked Sforza almost as little as Churchill did.

In January 1944 – to Churchill's displeasure – there was a meeting in Bari of Italian politicians including Sforza and his friend, the philosopher, Benedetto Croce. This had perhaps more impact in the U.S. than in Italy itself, and Halifax reported that the State Department now wanted the king removed quickly. In February he said that it was publicly known in the U.S. that the State Department was against the king and Badoglio; if they survived, American opinion – possibly with the State Department's help – would conclude that this was because the British opposed the State Department.[17]

Churchill, with Eden's agreement, asked Roosevelt to make sure that no decision was taken in Washington without consulting the British: he was much concerned at any attempt at working with Sforza and the Italian politicians at that critical juncture. Roosevelt replied that he had given the necessary directions to the State Deparment, but added: 'I think . . . that you and I should regard this only as a temporary reprieve for the two old gentlemen.'[18]

*

Churchill, rather rashly, took Roosevelt's message to mean that he could count on his firm backing for his own Italian policy. So he set about trying to get the Italian political situation under control. One difficulty was that, because of the integrated Anglo-American command structure, he had to find a way of getting his orders to British officers without advertising them to their American colleagues, some of whom were in strong sympathy with the State Department. So he started using a 'special channel' – the Secret Intelligence Service – to send messages to General Wilson and to General Mason-Macfarlane, the British Deputy High Commissioner, who was in close touch with the Italian politicians. He told them both that he and Roosevelt had agreed to support the king and Badoglio until 'we get to Rome' so the Italian government should not be broadened for the time being: 'We have surely got enough troubles on our hands.'[19]

General Wilson, most irritatingly, replied through normal channels – so that his telegrams went to Roosevelt and the State Department – that the king should be told to abdicate at once in favour of Crown Prince Umberto, who should then call on the six parties to form a fresh government. This was embarrassing for Churchill, but he refused to budge, insisting to Wilson that British policy had Roosevelt's agreement: 'If you cannot control the Italian politicians now, when they are weak and out of office, what will your position be when flushed with success they are formed into a government whose first need it must be to make capital with the Italian people by standing up to the British and Americans?' The next day Churchill sought – and got – the War Cabinet's backing for his stand; the day after, he told the House of Commons that he would be sorry to see an unsettling change in the Italian government when the battle was at its climax: 'When you have to hold a hot coffee-pot it is better not to break off the handle before you are sure that you will get another equally convenient and serviceable.' He claimed that his policy of winning the battle of Rome before changing the government had been 'agreed provisionally' with the U.S.[20] With this statement he had 'publicly committed' himself, as he told Roosevelt,[21] which, from one politician to another, meant that he could not eat his words before a respectable time had passed.

Washington had different ideas. The State Department had got Roosevelt to approve a telegram agreeing to General Wilson's proposals for the king's abdication and a government of the six parties. Eden, in a remarkable understatement, wrote to Churchill on 24 February: 'There seems to be a divergence . . . between us and the Americans which may lead to a muddle.' He suggested trying to straighten things out by getting the Americans to agree to a joint warning to the Italian politicians to keep quiet; the Russians could be drawn in through the Advisory Council for Italy created by the Moscow conference.[22]

Eden's hopes were quickly dashed. General Wilson reported that the king had agreed with the politicians that he should now announce his intention to abdicate when Rome fell. This seemed to cut the ground from under Churchill's feet. He wrote to Eden: 'It is very embarrassing that General Wilson should continually be pouring out statements to the President and State Department which are contrary to or critical of the policy which he has been instructed to pursue. He could no doubt reply that he is an Allied commander. . . . At the same time . . . we might have some sort of conversation with our man before he sends out his information messages.' Eden replied, 'I could not agree with you more.'[23]

But before Wilson could be shut up Roosevelt told Churchill that he wanted to approve the six parties' plan for the king's abdication: 'We should assure at the earliest opportunity the active co-operation of the liberal political groups.' Churchill replied unrepentantly that he had no confidence in either Croce or in Sforza, who had definitely broken his undertakings.[24] Nevertheless, with both General Wilson and Roosevelt against him he was hard pressed.

At this moment he got relief from an unexpected ally, or so he thought. The Soviet political representative, Alexander Bogomolov, suddenly told Badoglio that the Soviet Union wanted to establish diplomatic 'arrangements' with the Italian government and exchange representatives. Badoglio accepted.

Churchill was delighted. Feeling that his Italian policy was vindicated, he wrote to Eden: 'I am glad the Soviet government are to establish diplomatic relationship with Badoglio. It is a sensible step for them to take.' But Eden took a gloomy view: the Russians had done all this without telling the British anything, and they might be trying to undermine the position of the Allied Control Council and pursue an independent policy of their own. He wanted to ask the Soviet government for an explanation. But after talking to Churchill he sent instructions to Moscow conveying much less shocked surprise than he had originally intended.[25]

To Roosevelt Churchill telegraphed with some glee: 'I do not believe the ambitious wind-bags now agitating behind our front that they may themselves become the government of Italy have any representative footing. . . . I see that this is also the Soviet view. They are certainly realistic.' He added, however: 'Of course their aim may be a Communist Italy. . . . I can assure you that this danger is also in my mind.' His idea was, as before, to try to form a broadly based government 'taking into account the opinion of the Democratic North of Italy'.

This crossed a message from Roosevelt showing that the Soviet move had in no way influenced him: 'I did not at any time intend to convey to you agreement that we postpone all political decisions until after Rome had been taken.' As for the six parties' programme for the king's abdication, 'I cannot for the life of me understand why we should hesitate any longer in supporting a policy so admirably suited to our common military and political aims. American public opinion would never understand our . . . apparent support of Victor Emmanuel.'[26]

So much for Churchill's 'provisional agreement' with the U.S., of which he had told the House. He called the War Cabinet to his aid, and again they cheered him on. If anything, they stiffened Churchill's proposed reply to Roosevelt, saying there should be a proviso that even a settlement reached in Rome could not be final because it would have to be reviewed when the great industrial centres in the north, like Milan and Turin, were liberated; they were essential to a democratic solution. Reporting this to Roosevelt, Churchill said the Cabinet asked him to stress the great importance of not exposing to the world any British–U.S. divergence: 'It would be a great pity if our respective viewpoints had to be argued out in Parliament and the Press.'[27]

This plea – or threat – seemed to work. Roosevelt softened, answering that he fully agreed that 'we should not permit our divergent views to become known publicly'. The time might come when pressures built up and the six parties' plan should be adopted; meanwhile, the situation should be carefully watched.[28]

So, with the Cabinet's help, Churchill had won a tactical success. To Macmillan he telegraphed (through 'special channels'): 'We certainly do not intend to give way to pressure by the Croces and Sforzas,' and he advised him to get any help he could from his Russian colleague 'who also takes a sensible view'.[29]

While Churchill was fighting his little political battle with Roosevelt he was also fighting him on a quite different Italian problem. This showed that, even if he sometimes seemed pig-headed and short-sighted on the king–Badoglio question, he was quite sincere in putting the campaign in Italy first and in fearing that a political upheaval might cause trouble in the Italian armed forces, especially the fleet, now helping the Allies.

This other battle with Roosevelt was over the fleet. If Roosevelt wanted to please his Italian friends and the Italian-Americans, he wanted even more to please Stalin. At the Moscow conference in October 1943 Stalin had demanded certain Italian naval vessels as his rightful share of the booty. Eden, advised by the ambassador in Moscow that agreement to this would have a 'stupendous psychological effect' (and perhaps carried away by the rather spurious atmosphere of good will) said he thought the demand 'moderate and reasonable'.[30] At Tehran Stalin raised his demand again and Churchill and Roosevelt agreed. Churchill assumed that no ships would actually be handed over until the fighting in Italy was ended.

But in January Stalin pressed for the ships immediately. The British Chiefs of Staff and Churchill were very worried about the reactions in the Italian fleet if it became known that some of their ships were going to Russia. So he proposed to Roosevelt that he should offer Stalin, instead of the Italian ships, a British battleship and cruiser on temporary loan. Roosevelt agreed but wanted to make Stalin a considerably bigger offer, to include eight Italian destroyers and four Italian submarines 'as soon as they can be made available'. He did not believe the Italian navy would seriously object. In any case, the promise made to Stalin at Tehran must be fulfilled quickly.[31]

Churchill insisted that no demand should be made on the Italians. A kind of unpleasant triangular haggling between Churchill, Roosevelt and Stalin followed, with Churchill trying to save the Italian fleet from any immediate loss. In the middle of it all Roosevelt told American journalists that one-third of the Italian fleet had been promised to Russia at Tehran and transfer was being discussed. Churchill burst out: 'I have never agreed nor have you ever asked me to agree to a division of the Italian fleet into three shares.' The British government would not agree to it: 'We hold very strongly that losses entailed in the Italian war must be considered. We bore the whole weight of that war from 1940 onwards until British and American troops entered Tunisia as the result of *Torch*.' About 100 Italian warships were now doing important work for the Allies; 'a relationship has been established between the Italian fleet and the British and American fleets. . . . Once you accept a man's services and he fights at your side . . . a different status and relationship are established.'[32]

The haggling was concluded at considerable sacrifice to the British but without any mutiny in the Italian fleet. Perhaps Churchill had exaggerated the danger, but he certainly took it very seriously. So it is fair to say that his support for the king and Badoglio stemmed far less from devotion to monarchy than from his conception of strategic requirements and the need for order and calm behind the front.

Churchill's simple glee at the sudden Soviet wooing of Badoglio did not last long. The Foreign Office were worried over the success of the Russians and Italian Communists in getting all the Italian limelight. Eden minuted: 'The Russians are getting away with it in Italy. We shall have a Badoglio government of all the talents, including Communists. The latter will swallow up the other Left parties, and perhaps in due course Badoglio also.'[33]

But at this moment it was not the Soviet tactic to cause a political split in Italy, just the opposite. In March they had sent home the exiled Italian Communist leader Palmiro Togliatti (known in Moscow as Ercoli). On a stop-off in Algiers he was seen by a member of Macmillan's staff, who reported: 'He is a weedy little man with no obvious fire-ball characteristics. His line was generally that Italy must unite, sinking all political differences, in order to drive out the German invader.' The question of the monarchy could be left over until after the war. Togliatti was surprised to hear that the acting party leader in Italy was conducting a struggle against Badoglio.[34]

Togliatti quickly switched the party line to 'unity under Badoglio'. But this did not mean keeping the Badoglio government exactly as it was; it meant that the six parties should enter it, the Communists included. There was similar pressure from the American side. Macmillan reported that his colleague, Murphy, had just been in the U.S. where he had had long talks with Roosevelt, who was 'very keen to have something to show politically before the presidential election', and had only agreed very reluctantly to Churchill's 'wait until Rome' formula. Macmillan recommended to Churchill that it would help Anglo-American relations if some forward move were made, and if the six parties now wanted to enter a Badoglio government this chance should not be missed. Churchill, with an unwonted docility which showed his trust in Macmillan's good sense (Eden was on sick leave), said he did not mind provided Badoglio remained head of the government.[35]

So after heated haggling and with a good deal of help from Togliatti a broad-based Badoglio government was formed on 21 April. Churchill sent congratulations both to Macmillan and to the newly appointed political representative in Italy, Sir Noel Charles, who replied that he was sure the new Badoglio government had the Russians' support: 'It looks as though with luck Badoglio and Togliatti may be able to keep ultimate control even after arrival in Rome.' On 17 April Churchill told the War Cabinet that the Italian position was very satisfactory and even mentioned Sforza without saying anything rude about him.[36] His complacent mood about Italy can perhaps only be explained by the fact that at that moment he was grappling with a major Greek crisis including military mutiny, which may have diverted his energies.

But at the beginning of May he had time to worry about Italy again, minuting to Eden that there might have to be a showdown with the Russians about 'their Communist intrigues in Italy, Yugoslavia and Greece'. Eden replied that the Russians were playing a more subtle game in Italy than in the Balkans. He was sure it wanted careful watching; one of the members of the new government was 'a Russian-trained Communist in whose mouth butter is not melting at present'.[37]

But in Italy Sir Noel Charles went on thinking Togliatti helpful. Towards the end of May he reported that Togliatti hoped that Badoglio would remain prime minister until the north was liberated; Badoglio then might have trouble in Rome but Togliatti hoped to be able to control the situation if he could go there. This roused Churchill to sudden wrath. He drafted a telegram to Charles:

I do not like Togliatti's attitude. Having boosted the king and Badoglio into a certain position he now wants to ruin them. . . . If the whole manoeuvre of the Communists has been to get Italy in their hands by breaking down every alternative structure, you should not hesitate to use language suitable to the rights and dignity of Britain which has done four-fifths of the fighting against Italy from the day she entered the war. Do not take it all lying down. A good row with the Russians is sometimes a very healthy episode.

After writing this blast he told Eden he did not want the telegram to go off, but it conveyed his views on the subject. Eden telegraphed less pugnaciously to Charles: 'Togliatti's attitude is disquieting. . . .'[38]

So Churchill had now put a black mark against Togliatti as well as Sforza. That left Badoglio. But when the new Badoglio government asked whether the Italians could be accepted as allies, Churchill rejected the plea harshly, minuting to Eden: 'No one has pressed more than I have for the Badoglio–Victor Emmanuel combination, but one does not always want to be changing every day just to meet Italian whims and "try-ons". Badoglio is very lucky to be where he is now, the king will be very lucky if he gets away to retirement and untroubled demise, and we shall be very lucky if we never have anything worse than the present Italian government to deal with.' This did not please Eden, who wanted to build up Badoglio by giving him some encouragement.[39] He got none from Churchill.

Nevertheless, when the Allies reached Rome Churchill expected Badoglio to stick firmly to his job while broadening his government. He was furious when things went wrong.

The plan was that General Mason-Macfarlane, when Rome fell, should get from the king a document transferring power to his son Umberto, who was to become Lieutenant of the Realm, and then take Badoglio and other ministers to Rome for one day to contact the politicians there and bring some of them into his government. Macmillan expressed doubts about the plan; it would be awkward to have a political crisis in Rome. But since Eden's own man, Charles, backed the plan, Eden overruled Macmillan.[40]

Rome fell on 4 June. The plan went ahead. The king was persuaded with some difficulty to sign the necessary document, Macfarlane took Badoglio and his party to Rome. There they met the elderly former prime minister, Ivanoe Bonomi, and other party politicians; there was agreement all round that the politicians would no longer serve under Badoglio, but would under Bonomi. Badoglio resigned willingly enough, refusing to take any other government post. Macfarlane allowed his party to stay in Rome longer than the allotted twenty-four hours, and a Bonomi government was formed with Togliatti, Sforza, Croce, the Socialist Saragat and the future Christian Democrat prime minister, Alcide de Gasperi, among seven ministers without portfolio.

During the process of government-making, Bonomi asked Macfarlane if he thought Sforza would be a good choice for Foreign Minister. The latter said rashly that he thought 'the appointment would not meet much approval on the part of the Allied governments'.[41] He had no right to say this on behalf of the Americans or Russians, who would have objected strongly.

In the Foreign Office the reaction to Badoglio's exit and Bonomi's entrance was surprise, some gloom and acquiescence. Cadogan minuted that the affair had been bungled and Macfarlane ought to have prevented any announcement until London had been consulted. But it would be impossible to withhold recognition from Bonomi; Churchill had said in the House on 22 February: 'It is from Rome that a more broadly based Italian government can best be formed.' Eden told the War Cabinet that 'our position was weak' since the Italians had not been told to consult the British in advance and Macfarlane had acquiesced. All that remained was to make sure that the Bonomi government accepted the obligations undertaken by Badoglio. The War Cabinet took note.[42]

Churchill, on the other hand, was very angry both with Macfarlane and with Charles and was at first determined to keep Badoglio in power, come what may. He telephoned a message to Eden : 'I am surprised and shocked about Badoglio being replaced by this wretched old Bonomi. We have lost the only competent Italian with whom we could deal.' Furious telegrams went to Charles and Macfarlane. However, Churchill also decided to ask Moscow and Washington their views, and Eden, probably with some relief, agreed with this. To Roosevelt Churchill telegraphed : 'I think it is a great disaster that Badoglio should be replaced by this group of aged and hungry politicians. . . . I thought it was understood that he was to go on at any rate till we could bring the democratic north in. Instead we are confronted with this absolutely unrepresentative collection. . . . I have had no opportunity of bringing the matter before the Cabinet.'[43] To Stalin he wrote in much the same strain. (The 'aged and hungry' Bonomi was born just a year before Churchill himself.)

Attlee, with some courage, chose this moment to stand up for the rights of the Cabinet, writing to Churchill about the 'strong view' expressed in his telegrams to Roosevelt and Stalin : 'I think that it is unfortunate that a line should have been taken with our Allies on a matter of this kind on which there may well be differences of opinion before it has been discussed in Cabinet.'[44]

This was a warning signal to Churchill that he had gone too far and might lose the Cabinet support which he had so far had. He sent Attlee a frosty answer but showed the first signs of climbing down; he claimed that it would have caused great inconvenience to have convened the Cabinet on a Sunday afternoon; he had now had friendly replies from Stalin and Roosevelt and on this basis the matter could be discussed in Cabinet. He himself had not reached any final conclusion, and in any case Badoglio might refuse to return. The Cabinet met that day; according to the discreet record, 'the view was expressed that there might be something to be said for a change at this stage, and that in any event Marshal Badoglio might insist on resigning'.[45]

Stalin's reply was curious : he, too, had been surprised, he said, thinking Badoglio could not be replaced without Anglo-American consent; he would have no objections if they now suggested another government instead of Bonomi's. Roosevelt agreed with Churchill's suggestion – prompted by Eden – that the matter should be dealt with by the Allied Advisory Council. For this Churchill thanked him, adding that he saw great difficulties in persuading Badoglio to resume his thankless task 'at his great age'. Vaunting his own youthfulness, Churchill added: 'I had a jolly day on Monday on the beaches and inland. . . . We went and had a plug at the Hun from our destroyer, but although the range was 6,000 yards he did not honour us with a reply. . . . How I wish you were here.'[46]

Macmillan could not resist saying 'I told you so,' which implied a criticism of Eden that Eden did not like. He also pointed out that Macfarlane had committed a blunder in saying that 'the Allied governments' would not like Sforza as Foreign Minister, and the State Department had immediately sent a protest, since it had no objection to Sforza and also – Macmillan pointed out – because Sforza had a strong following in the vital state of New York where there was a large Italian vote. As for the future, Macmillan did not think it possible 'to put Humpty Dumpty in place again after our own officers . . . have allowed him to tumble off'.[47]

On 16 June Churchill was coming to the same conclusion, writing to Eden: 'I fear we shall have to accept the results of the intrigue against Badoglio,' and again later that day, after getting a message from Roosevelt, 'it is not worth while putting Badoglio up again'. Also that day he told the War Cabinet that he and Eden felt it wise to accept Bonomi, and it was agreed that he should tell Stalin this. He did so in the course of a long and chatty message which ended: 'Hitler has started his secret weapon upon London. We had a noisy night. We believe we have it under control. All good wishes in these stirring times.'[48]

With the formality of a resolution passed by the Allied Advisory Council the crisis was ended. Churchill's face was saved but he was still sore, writing to Eden on 20 June: 'We have had to accept this extremely untrustworthy band of non-elected come-backs.' And when he heard that the Bonomi government had taken the oath to 'the country' and not to the Crown, he minuted to Eden: 'This is very unpleasant, and shows the class of people we now have to deal with.'[49]

It was not until Churchill visited Italy in August 1944 and got the welcoming cheers that always warmed the cockles of his heart that he began to thaw out in his feelings for Italians in general and the existing Italian government. (Some weeks later he blandly admitted to Stalin that his attitude had been changed by the cheering crowds; Stalin replied that the crowds had supported Mussolini too.[50]) He declined to see the Crown Prince, now Lieutenant of the Realm. When he left he issued a message of 'encouragement and hope for the Italian people', advising them to stand by the principles of democracy.[51]

In the same mellow mood, and also because he wanted to help Roosevelt pull in the Italian-American vote, he agreed with him, at Roosevelt's country home in September, to issue a joint declaration promising to hand over an increasing measure of responsibility to the Italian people. The War Cabinet, meeting with Attlee presiding, did not much like this and wanted to make a number of changes and to delay publication. Urged by Attlee and Eden, Churchill, on his way home, sent a message to Roosevelt saying 'Anthony has made some valid comments' and asking for delay. But Roosevelt was in a hurry. Eden, however, held out, pleading Churchill's absence: 'In view of the strong feelings in the War Cabinet, I feel that only the Prime Minister can give the answer.' The declaration was finally issued on 26 September.[52]

For this timely help in the presidential election campaign Churchill perhaps thought Roosevelt owed him a certain debt. Eden wrote a few weeks later to Washington of 'the trouble which the Prime Minister himself personally took to support the President in his declaration about Italy. . . . This declaration was far from popular here and would certainly never have been joined in by us except that the Prime Minister was anxious to show his loyalty to the President.'[53]

Roosevelt does not seem to have reciprocated this feeling. There was still the Sforza problem. Macmillan wrote later: 'Sforza was like a red rag to a bull to Churchill, and I sometimes felt that Roosevelt, who had a great sense of fun, used this Italian politician like a matador's cloak to infuriate his colleague and friend.'[54]

In November 1944 the Bonomi government was having a minor crisis. One factor was said to have been Sforza's constant interference in foreign policy. Sir Noel Charles reported that Sforza – who had just been appointed ambassador in Washington, which would have happily removed him from the range of Churchill's wrath – was now hoping that he could get the post either of Foreign Minister or of deputy prime minister. Churchill wrote to Eden saying Charles should oppose Sforza's appointment to either post: 'He is a vain and intriguing person.' Before Eden could act, a British official had told the Foreign Under-Secretary in the Bonomi government that Sforza was not acceptable to the British. Eden, who seems to have had no thought of pointing out the dangers to Churchill, sent instructions to Charles in the same sense.[55]

Inevitably, the British intervention against Sforza became known. From Washington Halifax reported that the State Department felt somewhat resentful at not having been informed of British objections and believed these could only build Sforza up as a martyr. He added that there was mounting criticism of the British in the American Press and radio. This inspired Churchill to dictate a long and furious telegram to Halifax: 'We felt ourselves fully entitled to make the Italian government aware of our view. . . . We have been accorded the command in the Mediterranean as the Americans have the command in France, and as our troops engaged in Italy are four times those of the United States [these last words were struck out], therefore we have a certain position and responsibility.' If necessary, Churchill wrote, he would disclose the fact that he considered Sforza an intriguer and mischief-maker of the first order.

But having let off steam by dictating this blast Churchill said he wanted to talk to Eden about it; the next day, in calmer mood, he asked his private office what had happened to 'the tirade I wrote to Halifax about Sforza'. It turned out that Eden had been quite happy that the tirade should be loosed off, and it was.[56]

Almost immediately there was more serious cause for wrath. Edward Stettinius, who had just succeeded Hull as Secretary of State, put out a statement pointedly dissociating the Americans from the British over Sforza: 'This government has not in any way intimated to the Italian government that there would be opposition on its part to Count Sforza.' Italy was an area of combined responsibility, and the U.S. expected Italians to work out their problems on democratic lines without outside interference.

This rebuke to the British – reasonable enough in normal circumstances, but particularly wounding when the British were already under fire over the civil strife in Greece – enraged Eden as much as it did Churchill, and he immediately wrote – for Churchill's approval – an angry telegram to Washington. Churchill himself sent a message of protest to Roosevelt, later described by Sherwood as perhaps the most violent in all their correspondence.[57]

I was much astonished at the acerbity of the State Department's communiqué . . . and I shall do my best . . . to avoid imitating it. I feel however entitled to remind you that on every single occasion in the course of this war I have loyally tried to support any statements to which you were personally committed. For instance in the Darlan affair I made the greatest possible exertions. . . . Also in the matter of the division of the Italian fleet I not only did all in my power to avoid the slightest appearance of difference between us, though the difference was considerable, but H.M.G. actually supplied 14 out of the 15 warships to the Russians to make up for their one third share of the Italian fleet to which you had referred.

Churchill also recalled that he himself had proposed to Roosevelt the bulk of the 'mitigations' in relations with Italy, agreed in September 1944. Therefore, he said, 'I was much hurt that a difference about Count Sforza should have been made the occasion for an attempt on the part of the State Department to administer a public rebuke to H.M.G.', and he did not remember that the State Department had ever said anything comparable about Russia or other Allied states.[58]

This came as near to an accusation of disloyalty and ingratitude as Churchill was ever likely to get. But Roosevelt gave very little ground: he deplored any offence given by the statement to Churchill personally, but it was necessary to make the American position clear, and the British had not consulted the U.S. over Sforza. Stettinius was much more friendly and said he would try to make a helpful statement on Greece which would be useful in the coming debate in the House of Commons.[59]

The War Cabinet, when it met on the eve of the debate, was told by Churchill that the British had every justification for their attitude to Sforza and he was going to make this clear in his speech. No dissent by other ministers was recorded. Nor, in the Commons, was this part of his speech a cause of dispute: the Italian squabble was swamped by the Greek civil war. Churchill's majority was comfortable if not over-whelming. Much of his success was undoubtedly due to a certain anti-American flavour in some of his words.

Churchill quickly forgave Roosevelt, but he was getting a little tired of Italy. In January 1945 Eden was afraid of the Communist menace in northern Italy, thinking there might be civil war, as in Greece. Churchill wrote to Eden: 'Can't we get the Americans to take charge? It would be very wise to hand it over. What interests have we there that would suffer? I will certainly put it across the President.'[60] But perhaps Churchill did not mean Eden to take this seriously; he certainly did not.

The ghost of Sforza went on haunting Churchill. In June 1945 there was fresh trouble in the Bonomi government and reports that Sforza might become prime minister. The ambassador, Charles, asked for advice. Churchill was reluctant to eat his own words, but he finally minuted: 'It is no part of our policy to interfere with the turmoil of Italian politics.

The ambassador's attitude should be one of mild disdain, but there should be no veto. If the foolish and crooked old man becomes prime minister, I shall have the pleasure of having as little to do with him as possible.'[61] If Churchill had taken this line a year earlier he would have saved himself a great deal of needless trouble.

In pursuing his personal vendetta against Sforza Churchill probably did himself more harm than he did to Italy. Very probably, too, he greatly overestimated Sforza's power to do evil things and perhaps underestimated his good will. As for Anglo-American relations, Sforza was not a fitting or worthwhile subject for a public quarrel. What is strange is that Eden did so little to restrain Churchill either over his open attempt to interfere in Italian politics or his unilateral moves made without consulting the Americans or Russians, as he was theoretically obliged to do. And – apart from Attlee's personal note of warning during the June crisis – the same could be said of the War Cabinet.

There were perhaps three reasons. There was in the British a strain of dislike and contempt for the Italians, a hangover from the Mussolini years: to see Churchill browbeating Italians gave a little low-grade pleasure. Then, too, for Eden, Attlee and others it must have been heart-warming to see Churchill standing up to Roosevelt and the State Department over Italy, as he so often refused to do over France. Finally, they were so busy fighting Churchill over de Gaulle that it would have been unwise to tackle him on a second front, over Italy.

CHAPTER FOURTEEN

Greece: the President, the King and the Communists

Greece was a country where Churchill and Eden felt the British had special responsibilities and also, after they fought there in 1941, special rights. Militarily it came under the British Middle East Command and was never under joint Anglo-American command. For the Americans it lay in the taboo area of the Balkans and east Mediterranean, where military and political entanglements were to be avoided except for underground work by the O.S.S.; the British could be left to carry on their imperialist and somewhat shady machinations there if they wished.

This, at least, was the theory. In practice Churchill and Eden both wanted U.S. moral support when they were in political difficulties over Greece. But they wanted support for their own policies, not American initiatives or interference, still less American policies that conflicted with their own.

Roosevelt was only sporadically interested in Greece. When in a good mood he was quite happy to give Churchill a helping hand. In a bad mood he was capable of minor political sabotage. And if the British did things that offended the moral sense of the State Department and the American public, he washed his hands of them.

If Roosevelt was an uncertain factor, so also was the relationship between Churchill and Eden over Greece at any given moment. Broadly speaking, both felt a sense of personal loyalty and obligation to King George II. In 1940-1 the king had been largely responsible for asking the British to help Greece first against Mussolini and then against Hitler, and at one crisis he overruled his own commander-in-chief to secure agreement on an Anglo-Greek operational plan. Since Eden, carrying out his first big mission as Churchill's special envoy, was himself deeply involved in the plan-making, this affected him closely. Both Churchill and Eden were also touched by George II's unflinching loyalty to Britain in spite of the painfully quick collapse of the British campaign in Greece.

But though both Churchill and Eden felt an obligation to try to help George II return to his country as king, they differed about means to this end, also about how far the case should be pressed. Since the king, publicly identified with the pre-1941 dictatorship of General Ioannis

Metaxas, had never been popular, and since after 1940 there was a powerful wave of republican feeling among Greeks both inside and outside the country, there were very awkward political and propaganda problems for the British. Would it be right to try to impose the king on an unwilling country, or could the Greeks somehow be persuaded to love him? If so, how could the policy of H.M.G. – and the personality of the king – best be presented to the Greeks in general and the Resistance groups inside Greece in particular?

During 1943 and 1944 Churchill and Eden gave rather different answers to these questions. So did they, too, to the even more difficult problem of how to deal with the strongest Resistance group, the Communist-led 'liberation movement', EAM, with its military wing, ELAS. (These acronyms always confused and annoyed Churchill.) Both he and Eden were violent in their detestation of the misdeeds of EAM/ELAS (which made a much stronger impression on them than its achievements, such as they were). But Eden, swayed by the practical arguments of the military experts and the propagandists, and aware of the danger of possible Soviet intervention, could see the disadvantages of a head-on clash or total break with EAM/ELAS and the Greek Communist Party. Churchill, at times, seemed blind to all such dangers. He utterly condemned EAM/ELAS (when he could remember what the initials stood for), wanted nothing to do with them and would have liked to destroy the leadership.

Since one of the strongest political weapons of EAM/ELAS was outright opposition to the king's return and any British attempt to impose him by force, the problems of the king and of EAM/ELAS became closely intertwined. It was almost inevitable that there should be wrangling between Churchill and Eden over tactics, if not over strategy.

One added problem was George II's personality. He was a reserved, suspicious and stubborn man, inclined to gloom. The British ambassador to the exiled government, Reginald Leeper, wrote to Eden: 'He is not a happy man'; in co-operation with the king's friend Mrs Brittan-Jones, Leeper was trying to give him more confidence in himself.[1] But the king always resented and suspected Eden's efforts to persuade him to present himself to his people in a more favourable light.

The first major crisis came in August 1943 with the arrival in Egypt of six delegates from inside Greece, three of them representing EAM/ELAS, conducted by Brigadier Eddie Myers of S.O.E. The king and his government-in-exile, headed by the moderate Emmanuel Tsouderos, were in Egypt; Eden had persuaded them to move there from London on the grounds that they would be nearer the Greek armed forces in the Middle East and to Greece itself; perhaps he was also finding that in London they took up far too much of his time and patience.

George II was extremely annoyed at the arrival of the delegates; there were no royalists among them and they were demanding participation in the government and a pledge from the king that he would not return until after a plebiscite. S.O.E. argued that, if the delegates went home empty-handed, British relations with the Resistance would be made very difficult; the British military were interested in fostering Greek resistance; the ambassador, Leeper, was distracted and unwell.

When the crisis in Cairo was at its hottest, Churchill and Eden were in Quebec meeting Roosevelt, Hull and the Chiefs of Staff. George II sent identical messages to Churchill and Roosevelt saying he did not want to make any promises: 'I feel very strongly that I should return to Greece with my troops even if I left my country after a short period to work for its national interests amongst our allies.'[2] Churchill wrote to Eden: 'If substantial British forces take part in the liberation of Greece, the king should go back with the Anglo-Greek army. This is much the more probable alternative. If however the Greeks are strong enough to drive out the Germans themselves, we shall have a good deal less to say in the matter. . . . In any case he would make a great mistake to agree in any way to remain outside Greece while the fighting for liberation . . . is going on.'[3]

In London the Foreign Office view was set down by Sir Orme Sargent, a Deputy Under-Secretary: it was important that the British and U.S. governments should speak with one voice, but the Americans were much less convinced than the British of the desirability of supporting the king and Roosevelt might not want to promise him such support. On the other hand, it was to be hoped that Roosevelt would recognise that 'Greece is and always has been a vital British interest and the king is entitled to look to us for support, in return for the valiant role he played in the early part of the war.' Eden took this line in advising Churchill. Simultaneously, Smuts weighed in with advice to Churchill to make British support of the king quite clear, otherwise there might be chaos in Greece and other Balkan countries: 'We may have a wave of disorder and wholesale Communism set going all over those parts of Europe.' Eden endorsed this view, too.[4]

So Churchill sent George II a message: 'We are all looking forward to your returning to Greece at the head of your armies and remaining there until the will of Greek people is expressed under conditions of tranquillity.'

Roosevelt, persuaded by Churchill, undertook to send a 'similar' message. This was in fact a lot vaguer than Churchill's categorical pledge: he hoped all Greeks would accept the king's promise of constitutional government as a guarantee that they would be able to express their political will freely; meanwhile, they should subordinate other considerations to the urgent need to win the war. Churchill explained to Eden that Roosevelt's angle as head of a republican state was not necessarily identical with the British, but he was 'highly favourable' and there was no difference of aim.[5]

So in September 1943 there was a show of British–American unity over Greece. This did little if anything to solve Greek problems. The return of the six delegates from Cairo empty-handed had, as S.O.E. had predicted, led to a virtual civil war when EAM/ELAS, fearing that the British were about to land with the king in their pockets, set about trying to eliminate rival Resistance groups while the going was good. Brigadier Myers had not been allowed to go back but was sent to London to report. Eden, after seeing him, asked Churchill to impress on him that 'the policy enunciated by H.M.G. is the one he must follow'.[6] That meant full support of George II, which Myers thought contrary to what most Greeks wanted.

Churchill had Myers to lunch at Chequers, and obviously liked him. Myers showed him a broadcast he wanted to make to the Greek guerrillas, and asked if he could include a message from Churchill. Churchill, his romantic vein kindled for a moment, wrote in his own hand:

> The Greek people must be masters of their destinies. . . . England, always their friend, will never interfere in their politics and will always champion their sovereign rights. We have obligations of honour to King George because he fought for the Allied cause. These we must discharge. They do not in any way affect the full freedom of the Greek people to settle their own affairs once conditions of tranquillity . . . are re-established. . . . We will help you all we can and more and more.

But almost at once Churchill had second thoughts, telling Myers it was too risky: the Americans were very interested, and he did not want to go over the heads of his colleagues.[7] So the broadcast went without a message from Churchill.

In October Churchill read reports of ELAS attacks on other groups and of the killing of a British officer. Angered, he wrote to Selborne, the minister in charge of S.O.E., and to the Foreign Office: 'EAM and ELAS should be starved and struck at by every means in our power. But I

fear these means are small. . . . We must know which side we are on.'
Selborne, though he liked the king and detested Communists, argued
against a break with ELAS; the only way to force them into submission
would be to bomb them and that could never be done in wartime. The
only solution, he thought, was to guarantee a free post-war plebiscite
on the monarchy.[8]

It was left to Eden, in Cairo on his way home from the Moscow
Foreign Ministers' conference, to try to reach an agreement with the
British military, S.O.E. and Leeper. He had as little love for EAM/ELAS
as Churchill, saying they were 'a gang of extremists whose aim is to seize
control of Greece against the wishes of the majority' and that under EAM
rule 'Greece would look to Russia and not to ourselves for support'. The
agreement worked out in Cairo was, however, a compromise: to break
with EAM/ELAS by stages, trying to discredit the Communist leaders
and winning over the rank and file. To achieve this, something must be
done about the king. The solution would be to ask the king to declare
that a regency council would be set up in Athens and he himself would
not return until the question of the monarchy had been settled; the
Archbishop of Athens, Damaskinos, who had been in contact with the
British and had suggested ways of stopping EAM seizing power, should
be secretly authorised by the king to appoint the regency council.[9]

Eden put this compromise plan, when he got back to London, to the
War Cabinet who, meeting in Churchill's absence with Attlee in the
chair, showed little enthusiasm. On one side the Chiefs of Staff thought
a break with EAM/ELAS would be against British military interests; on
the other Smuts, who was there, feared the plan would lead to the king's
abdicating and blaming the British for the consequences. No decision
was taken. Cadogan noted in his diary: 'A. didn't get it all his own way,
and I think that's right. I'm doubtful about a complete and sudden break
with EAM and holding a pistol to the head of the king.' The War Cabinet
met again six days later and decided to leave it to Churchill and Eden to
deal with the matter in Cairo, on the general basis of the compromise
plan.[10]

Eden reported to Churchill, then on his way to the Tehran conference,
how things were going. Churchill sent him a 'most secret and personal'
telegram: 'I grieve deeply at this and prefer to wait till you come out
before approaching the king.' It was not until after Tehran that the Greek
problem was tackled. Churchill, Eden, Roosevelt, George II, Harry Hopkins
and Smuts were all in Cairo. Eden's staff prepared a brief for him to use
in persuading George II to appoint a regency council in Athens under

Damaskinos and to announce that he himself would not return until there were 'stable conditions'. Desmond Morton, also in Cairo, saw this brief and put it before Churchill, writing that he had shown it to Harry Hopkins 'who thinks this is the right policy and has promised to recommend it to the President'. Churchill noted: 'I approve tho' with regret.'[11]

So, with Churchill's unhappy blessing, Eden saw George II, and reported back that the king had taken it quietly; he had then seen Tsouderos, the Greek prime minister, who had said the plan was in the king's best interest but was sure he would not make up his mind until Churchill had urged him to accept. Eden concluded: 'A word from you will satisfy the king that he is doing the right thing.'[12]

On the same day the U.S. ambassador to the Greek government, Lincoln McVeagh, saw Roosevelt and told him he thought British policy was right, and left a memorandum setting out the British case. Eden could reasonably hope that the whole plan was sewn up and all that remained was for Churchill to say the final word. On 6 December George II wrote to Churchill asking for a private talk before making up his mind. Churchill invited him to lunch next day.[13]

But before then all Eden's hopes had been dashed. George II saw Roosevelt who said it would be a great mistake for him to accept the British plan; or, as Lincoln McVeagh put it, the President had 'turned him down with the king without any warning'. The king also saw Smuts and told him Roosevelt had complained to him that he had not been consulted by the British on 'this change of policy'. Smuts said afterwards that the king now felt that the Americans were his friends and the British were trying to get rid of him; having got this into his head, there was a danger that he might abdicate.[14]

So this was the position when George II lunched with Churchill and Eden next day. Exactly what Churchill said is not in the public records; but clearly he did not want to go flatly against what Roosevelt had said, or to risk the king's abdication; perhaps, too, he was not sorry to be spared the disagreeable task of browbeating the king into accepting a plan which he himself did not like.

In his memoirs Eden wrote that, when he went to the final Cairo meeting with Roosevelt, George II was again with the President, and 'when the President emerged, he was cold towards me and complained of the way I had been treating the king. . . . I pointed out that I had kept the U.S. government informed at every stage.' The next morning, driving to the airport with Churchill, Roosevelt had 'complained bitterly' of Eden's conduct and, according to Churchill, had been 'much wrought up on the subject'.[15]

In August 1944, again arguing with Churchill that it would be in the king's own interest to declare he would not return until his people had expressed their will, Eden recalled this incident: 'As you know, I have always held this view and pressed it strongly last December when my attempts were frustrated by the President's explosion to you on the way to the aerodrome.'[16] Roosevelt's strange behaviour had left a lasting mark.

It can only be a matter of guesswork why Roosevelt, who in September had seemed very willing to help out Churchill but cautious about committing himself over the king's return, should in December have sabotaged a British plan which provided a satisfactorily 'democratic' solution for this problem. He was probably exhausted after the Tehran conference and perhaps did not take in what McVeagh said to him. He was in a bad mood with Churchill who had been notably stubborn and pugnacious on various other issues. It was one of his hobbies to collect foreign kings, just as he collected foreign stamps. Smuts, who liked to have a finger in every pie, may have put him up to it. One or other or all these things may explain an otherwise inexplicable act.

After the Cairo fiasco Eden's energies turned to plans for bringing the warring Resistance groups in Greece together or, at least, stopping them fighting. These were backed by the Chiefs of Staff for military reasons and were put into effect by the skill and firmness of Myers's successor, Colonel Christopher Woodhouse. But Churchill remained bitterly hostile to EAM/ELAS, minuting in January: 'There seems to be no limit to the baseness and treachery of ELAS and we ought not to touch them with a barge pole;' and in February, 'They are more hated by the countryside even than the Germans. Obviously giving them weapons will . . . only secure the domination of these base and treacherous people after the war.'[17] Nevertheless, arms supplies were resumed at the beginning of March.

At this point the question of the king became acute. Damaskinos was still urging that George II should sign a secret act appointing a regent (himself), and all political parties and Resistance groups were said to back this. But the king, in Cairo, told his prime minister that he would not accept it. Eden wrote to Churchill that he did not find it easy to decide what advice to give; perhaps it would be best to tell the king that this was something he should settle in consultation with his government. The ubiquitous Smuts was far more downright, advising George II strongly against the Damaskinos plan on the grounds that it would be almost equivalent of abdication and desertion of his people. This pleased the king who replied to Smuts insinuating that Damaskinos had been put up to proposing the plan by the British; he recalled that in Cairo in December much the same proposal had been put to him by the British, but had, thanks to Smuts's kind intervention, been averted.

George II then sent copies of Smuts's message and his own reply to Churchill, who passed them to Eden. Eden wrote from his home in the country, where he was having an enforced rest: 'I am sorry that the king still harbours suspicions of our services. We have been at immense pains to meet him. . . . I continue to think that the king would have been in a stronger position today had he made the declaration we advised him to make last December in Cairo. I think it now most unlikely he will reign in Greece . . . but I regret it very much.'[18]

Eden was out of London for most of April, and Churchill determined to run Greek affairs in his own way. George II was by this time visiting London, staying at Claridges, and Churchill had no intention of urging him to appoint a regent. But in Egypt the situation in the Greek armed forces was getting out of hand. EAM/ELAS had formed a political committee, with some claim to be a provisional government, in north-west Greece, but had proposed collaboration with the Athens politicians and the exiled government. Owing to the king's attitude, this had met with no response. Agitation, assumed to be instigated by EAM or its sympathisers, then started in the Greek army and naval units in Egypt. Leeper telegraphed on 3 April: 'The king of Greece is playing with fire. . . .'[19] On the same day Tsouderos telegraphed his resignation to the king in London.

Churchill intervened strongly, telling the king to go to Egypt and deal with matters, and telegraphing to Tsouderos that he was much shocked at his resignation; it was his duty to remain at his post. The next day he sent Leeper a message: 'Do not let all these excitable quarrelsome Greeks upset your calm . . . it will do no harm for them to have two or three days to cool their heels and their heads.' Hearing that George II had decided after all to accept Tsouderos's resignation, he saw him and told him yet again to go to Cairo and keep Tsouderos in office. The king seemed to agree but then, receiving an offer from the son of the great Eleftherios Venizelos, Sophocles, to take the job of prime minister, he changed his mind. Sargent of the Foreign Office advised the king that he would be wise to accept Venizelos's offer so as to end the crisis in the Greek forces. Churchill overrruled Sargent and again told the king he must stick to Tsouderos.[20]

During the political vacuum which Churchill himself had helped to create the trouble in the Greek armed forces had developed into mutiny. So he, having given his orders to the king, Tsouderos, Leeper and Sargent, now turned to the military commanders. He telegraphed to Cairo: 'A mutinous brigade murdering its officers should certainly be surrounded and forced to surrender by stoppage of all supplies. . . . We cannot tolerate political revolutions carried out by foreign military formations. . . . Large numbers of British troops should be used so as to overawe and minimise bloodshed.' To Leeper he telegraphed: 'You should stick to the line I have marked out. . . . You speak of living on a volcano. Wherever else do you expect to live in times like these?' He then bade him 'celebrate Easter Sunday in a manner pious and becoming'. Next day he sent him another telegram telling him 'to rise to the occasion'.[21]

On 11 April, for the first time, Churchill reported briefly to the War Cabinet, saying that all food supplies had been cut off from the mutineers, but they had access to water; there were adequate British forces to control the situation. It was another six days[22] before he again reported to the Cabinet, who seem to have been surprisingly passive – perhaps partly because there was no Eden to argue with Churchill.

George II arrived in Cairo and on 12 April issued a statement that the whole nation would be called on to decide by free vote on the future regime; but he said nothing about staying out of Greece until the people had decided. The next day he appointed Venizelos prime minister (as he would have done a week earlier if Churchill had not stopped him). Venizelos then announced that the delegates of the Resistance organisations and the Athens politicians were to come to Cairo for discussions. This should in theory have satisfied the mutineers and restored order, but by then things were out of hand and the mutiny went on.

Churchill then reconsidered a suggestion which Leeper had made on 12 April, that it would help if it could be stated that the U.S. and Soviet governments were in agreement with British action over the mutinies, so as to put a stop to criticism in the U.S. and the Soviet Union. Churchill replied sternly: 'On no account accept any assistance from American or Russian sources, otherwise than as specially enjoined by me.' But on 16 April he sent Roosevelt a message beginning blandly, 'You will be aware of the disturbances which have broken out among the Greek armed forces.' Restating his general policy, he wrote that Greece could be a republic or a monarchy, entirely as the people wished; the British sought no advantage for themselves and only wanted to uphold Greek independence and freedom.[23]

Roosevelt responded warmly : he hoped Churchill would succeed 'in bringing the Greeks back into the Allied camp and to a participation against the barbarians that will be worthy of the traditions established by the heroes of Greek history'. He went on : 'As one whose family and who personally have contributed by personal help to Greek Independence for over a century', [sic] he hoped Greeks everywhere would set aside pettiness and regain their sense of proportion : 'let every Greek think of their glorious past'. Having thus put a rather strange spotlight on the Roosevelt family, he said Churchill could quote him if he wanted.

Churchill was delighted and told Roosevelt that his message would go to the king and his ministers and be read to the mutineers. Six days later he told Roosevelt that the mutineers had surrendered with no Greek casualties. Roosevelt said he was very pleased indeed by Churchill's success.[24] During this crisis, therefore, Roosevelt had been ungrudging in his support for Churchill, never querying his handling of the mutiny or his backing for George II.

Churchill, for his part, had clearly enjoyed himself running Greek affairs without Eden's restraining hand. He had directed a king's actions and quelled a mutiny at long range with considerable gusto, never asking himself whether the mutiny might not have been curbed much more quickly by an earlier political compromise.

It was left to Eden, when he came back to work, to tackle the tedious and complex task of bringing about the political compromises which could make it possible for the British and the exiled government – with or without the king – to re-enter Greece without bloodshed. At the same time he tried to secure a Soviet promise of benevolent non-interference in Greek affairs in return for a smiliar British promise over Romania.

During the summer these things were gradually and painfully achieved. Things looked up when a new man stepped to the front of the stage, a politician from Athens, George Papandreou, who seemed to have some of the strength of personality and colourfulness which Churchill admired. His admiration grew when Papandreou succeeded in getting EAM representatives to agree to enter a broad-based government, without extracting any clear promise from the king about his return.

But when the EAM leaders then seemed set on wrecking the arrangement and George II urged him to denounce them publicly and cut off supplies, Churchill became warlike. Eden pointed out that such action would provoke a lot of criticism from the left wing in Parliament, and it would be necessary to convince the Chiefs of Staff and 'our Socialist colleagues in the War Cabinet also' – and the Americans, too, all the more since by that time there were O.S.S. officers in Greece. Churchill, in spite of this, said he would fight hard. Luckily, Colonel Woodhouse had come to London from Greece, and succeeded in persuading first Eden and later Churchill that a break with EAM – still more, a withdrawal of British officers – would be a bad mistake.[25] The crisis passed and in August the EAM representatives finally took their places in the Papandreou government.

The next job was to get agreement all round on sending British troops into Greece as the Germans withdrew, as a counter-weight to the armed forces of EAM/ELAS who might attempt a *coup d'état*. Eden put this to the War Cabinet on 9 August, saying that if there were a civil war it would be very injurious to British prestige and 'might add Greece to the post-war Balkan Slav bloc which now showed signs of forming under Russian influence and from which we were anxious to keep Greece detached'. There was no question of forcing any particular form of government on Greece, nor, Eden said, not quite accurately, 'were we in any way committed as regards the position of the king'. The Dominions Secretary, Lord Cranborne, an old friend and colleague of Eden's, then put in his oar: 'there was much to be said for the king standing aside and not returning to Greece until the plebiscite had taken place'.[26]

Eden then resorted to a curious ruse. The War Cabinet was recorded in the minutes as having reached four decisions, including the despatch of 10,000 troops to Greece. But a few days later a 'corrigendum' was circulated recording a fifth decision: 'There would be advantage . . . in the king not returning to Greece until after the plebiscite. . . . The Secretary of State for Foreign Affairs should advise him that this is the wisest course. . . .'[27]

Churchill had been present at the Cabinet meeting though not for the whole time. He then left for Italy where, among other things, he was to meet Papandreou. Eden sent a telegram to Churchill from London on Greek affairs and mentioned in passing 'the Cabinet decision that the king of Greece should be advised not to return to Greece until after the plebiscite, but to come to London'.[28]

Churchill's reaction was quick and sharp: 'I know of no British Cabinet decision that the king of Greece should be advised not to return. . . . I certainly never consciously agreed to any such decision. . . . The expression of opinion of a single Cabinet Minister is not a decision of the Cabinet. . . . The matter is serious because it is quite possible that if the king believed such a decision represented our policy he would abdicate.' He also telegraphed to the Secretary to the Cabinet, demanding who had suggested the 'corrigendum'. The answer came that it had been requested by Eden.

Having caught Eden out in what he might well have seen as a bit of sharp practice, Churchill was then quite ready to forgive him – partly perhaps because Papandreou had put him in a position to crow over Eden. He telegraphed to him that he liked Papandreou and wanted him and his government to move to Italy: 'As to the Greek king and the corrigendum, they none of them want him to make a fresh declaration now.'[29] So that cut the ground from under Eden's feet.

George II was, in any case, in a particularly stubborn mood. He told Leeper on 30 August that he had no intention of making any further statement and disliked intensely the idea of staying in London for months awaiting a plebiscite. A few days later he dismayed Eden by telling him that he was intending to go to western Greece with his troops. Eden tried hard to persuade him to wait until the Papandreou government was established in Athens and had invited him to come, but got the definite impression that the king thought otherwise.[30]

Churchill took good care to square Roosevelt over the despatch of British troops to Greece, writing to him on 17 August: 'We have always marched together about Greek policy, and I refer to you on every important point. The War Cabinet and Foreign Secretary are much concerned about what will happen in Athens. . . . I do not expect you will relish more than I do the prospect either of chaos and street fighting or of a tyrannical Communist government being set up.' In this context, he proposed the sending of 10,000 British troops, including parachute troops, for which the help of the U.S. Air Force would be needed. Nine days later Roosevelt replied that he had no objection, provided the U.S. aircraft could be spared.[31]

Churchill could therefore assume he had Roosevelt's personal blessing in Greece, and no reason to think that he disapproved of his attitude to George II. But Eden went on worrying about the king, and not long before the troops landed he again raised the question with Churchill. If the king tried to go to Athens, he wrote, the government would break up: 'We shall then be left with 10,000 men in Greece, no government and maybe a civil war.' There would probably for a time have to be a regency council. (This prediction turned out accurate in almost every point.) Churchill by this time was willing to put military needs first, answering Eden that it would be impossible even to consider the king's return until

Papandreou's government was firmly established and ready for it. But he still disliked the idea of a regency council.[32]

Early in October Churchill saw George II and told him that he could not let him go to Greece, since it would prejudice his chances with his own people if it were thought he were being put back by the British. The king – so Churchill told Eden – 'accepted my views as he knows I am his friend and work constantly for his return if that can be done in accordance with the wishes of his people'. The king obviously no longer thought Eden a friend.

But Eden stuck to his point, answering Churchill: 'I fear there may be no alternative to a regency council, though I understand your reasons for disliking the idea.' Churchill would not budge, replying that as soon as Papandreou was established in Greece he should bring the king back; 'in fact I shall lose interest in the Greek situation if Papandreou turns traitor to the king'.[33]

Churchill's mood by this time was one of mixed pig-headedness and quixotry over the king and the regency, and he was becoming more and more isolated from his colleagues and officials. But the mood persisted even when, some weeks after the British landings and the return of the Papandreou government, fighting broke out in Athens. Press reports of the firing which began it on 3 December, appearing both in the U.S. and Britain, usually presented it as having been started by the police against harmless EAM demonstrators. And these set the tone. The cause of the civil war was not the question of the king – or only indirectly. It was the attempt of the British and the Papandreou government to get EAM/ ELAS to lay down their arms. On the other side, EAM could use the argument that if they disarmed they would be the defenceless victims of ruthless 'monarcho-Fascist' – and British – armed forces trying to impose the king; and this was an effective weapon in their struggle to turn American and British public opinion against Churchill and his policy.

The Press reports had repercussions inside the War Cabinet. Attlee, normally most level-headed, wrote to Eden questioning Leeper's view of things in Athens: 'His suggestion . . . that the journalists who were eye-witnesses of the events in Athens must all be wrong seems hard to swallow.' Eden wrote back defending Leeper against any charge of bias against the Left, using the rather odd argument that he happened to know that Leeper strongly shared his own view at the time of his resignation in 1938.[34]

Press criticism in the U.S. of the British was emotional and indignant, and on 5 December the State Department, on Stettinius's authority, issued a statement expressing more measured criticism (as also of British policy in Italy). The Foreign Office found this all the more wounding because the Soviet government had scrupulously refrained from comment.[35]

But worst of all was Admiral King's action in banning the use of U.S. naval vessels for carrying supplies and men to the British in Greece, an order given without reference to the Combined Chiefs of Staff or the Mediterranean Supreme Commander, General Wilson. This so infuriated Churchill that he rang up Harry Hopkins on an open telephone line to protest. In justification of this insecure method of communication, he noted on paper: 'It is very unlikely that we shall be listened in to, but even if we are, what can they do that would be worse than the American ships being cut out of the traffic and an open breach between Britain and the U.S. becoming known?' Hopkins recorded that the line was so bad that he could not tell what the Prime Minister was saying. But he understood enough to go to Leahy next morning and get him to persuade King to withdraw the order.[36]

The next day Churchill wrote to Hopkins: 'The President might be reminded of our very close agreement on so many occasions about the Greek situation. . . . I certainly do not want to fight another war against ELAS. If . . . you can get any word of approval spoken by the U.S. in favour of the Allied intervention in Athens, you may save many British and Greek lives and set free soldiers who are needed elsewhere.'[37]

But Roosevelt had no intention of giving any public word of approval. He wrote to Churchill on 13 December that he had been as deeply concerned as Churchill himself over 'the tragic difficulties you have encountered in Greece'. He would like to help, but limits were set by 'the traditional policies of the U.S.' and the mounting adverse public reaction:

> No one will understand better than yourself that I, both personally and as Head of State, am necessarily responsive to the state of public feeling. It is for these reasons that it has not been possible . . . to take a stand along with you. . . . I don't need to tell you how much I dislike this state of affairs as between you and me. . . .

Roosevelt then suggested exactly the solution which he had personally sabotaged just a year before: British efforts might be 'greatly facilitated if the king himself would approve the establishment of a regency in Greece and would make a public declaration of his intention not to return'.[38]

By coincidence, on the same day Macmillan, then in Athens, telegraphed: 'Could the President be got to join with us in advising the king to appoint the Archbishop as regent?' Churchill rebuked Macmillan for proposing this.[39] To Roosevelt he sent thanks for 'the kindly tone' of his message, but added that he and Eden had suggested a regency to George II who had 'refused to allow this'. He also wrote:

> You will realise how very serious it would be if we withdrew, as we easily could, and the result was a frightful massacre and an extreme left wing regime under Communist inspiration installed itself, as it would, in Athens. My Cabinet colleagues here of all parties are not prepared to act in a manner so dishonourable to our record and name.

He added that Ernest Bevin, who had valiantly defended British action in Greece at the Labour Party conference, had won universal respect.[40]

Three days later he wrote again to Roosevelt: 'I am sure you would not wish us to cast down our painful and thankless task. . . . I have felt it much that you were unable to give a word of explanation for our action but I understand your difficulties.'[41]

By now Churchill was being pressed by Eden in London and by Field-Marshal Alexander, Macmillan and Leeper in Athens to cut short the civil war (and so save Alexander having to withdraw a further division from Italy, with serious results on the battle there), whether or not George II agreed. But the king, perpetually shifting his ground, played for time with some skill. (It would be interesting to know whether he was once again egged on by Smuts, who had always been against Damaskinos and who now telegraphed to the War Cabinet that, when the EAM revolt had been suppressed, the king should return to Greece to discharge his proper constitutional functions.[42]) On 16 December Eden told the War Cabinet that, if George II persisted, the only course open would be to tell him that the British would be forced to recognise a regent and withdraw recognition from the king.[43]

But Churchill obviously found it very hard to climb down and yield. He voiced dark forebodings that Damaskinos might turn out to be a left-wing dictator and it might be impossible to get rid of him. Eden took the opposite view. On 16, 18 and 21 December there were long and rambling War Cabinet meetings; each time an excuse was found for delaying a decision which Churchill could not bring himself to take.[44]

Perhaps it was in part a need to save face that made him set out on his Christmas flight to Athens, taking along a rather reluctant Eden, who could think of better ways of spending Christmas. Then, too, he always wanted to be at the scene of action and see things for himself, especially if there was fighting, as there was in Athens. At this point he asked Roosevelt to get the U.S. ambassador – who was being so neutral that he would not let British troops draw water from his well – to be helpful. On 27 December Roosevelt agreed.[45]

In Athens Churchill decided he liked and respected Damaskinos and would accept him as regent; and the U.S. ambassador was present as observer at the first meeting between Damaskinos, Papandreou and EAM delegates, over which Churchill presided. A Soviet observer, Colonel Popov, was also there. After personally launching the peace-making, Churchill could return home with Eden with a sense that honour had been saved and his policy vindicated.

There was still the job of selling the regency to the king. At last Roosevelt did something to help, by sending the king a message. On 29 December Churchill thanked him for this, saying the War Cabinet had now authorised him and Eden to urge the king to appoint Damaskinos; if the king refused, he would advise Damaskinos to assume office and Britain would then recognise him. The next day he wrote to Roosevelt: 'Anthony and I sat up with the King of Greece till 4.30 this morning at the end of which time H.M. agreed.' George II, he later wrote, 'behaved like a gentleman and with the utmost dignity'; but a message from Roosevelt would give him comfort.[46]

Churchill's passionate interest in Greece then flagged. He wrote to Eden on 7 January 1945: 'We do not wish to mix ourselves up too closely in the dramatic affairs of Greece, but rather to get our troops out of the place as soon as we can. . . . It is the Greek government which has to keep order. We must avoid having the air of keeping them under tutelage and above all of patronising them. Then indeed we should gain the hatred of the whole Greek people. . . .' In April he again wrote to Eden: 'We are still aiming steadily at the old bull's eye, viz., a free unfettered plebiscite as between monarchy and republic. . . . After this is over, our responsibility towards Greece will have been largely discharged. Their fate will be broadly put in their own hands.' Eden agreed,[47] but things did not turn out that way.

Roosevelt's impact on Anglo-Greek relations was at times mildly helpful, at others negative and once, in December 1943, harmful. At no time did he put himself out to help Churchill, who was rash to imagine that his own support of Roosevelt over French affairs would be repaid.

As between Churchill and Eden, both tended to be strangely emotional and excitable in their dealings with Greek affairs. But from November 1943 Eden did his best, in spite of Churchill's fixed ideas, to work for a regency under Damaskinos as the only practicable solution. Of Churchill it is fair to ask whether the April mutinies and the civil war of December

1944 could not have been ended a good deal more quickly and quietly if he had been willing to allow a political compromise at an earlier stage. He once wrote to Eden, 'the Greek position has got to get worse before it gets better',[48] and perhaps he felt that in Greek matters high drama was needed before a crisis could be resolved.

The two men spent a great deal of time wrangling over Greece. But perhaps each contributed something useful. Churchill showed the bulldog tenacity and forcefulness, Eden the flexibility and readiness for ingenious compromises, which were both needed if order was to be made in the chaos of Greek wartime politics. In the long term the British got very little for themselves or for their supposed imperial interests. But the Greeks gained something. They would never have been happy inside the Soviet empire.

CHAPTER FIFTEEN

A Special Relationship?

In September 1943 Churchill, writing to Attlee and Eden about planning for the post-war world, said that nothing should prejudice 'the natural Anglo-American special relationship'.[1] This dream of a special relationship was the most powerful of the various dreams of the future which fired him at various times, and helped to explain his readiness to make sacrifices for the sake of friendship with Roosevelt. Attlee, Eden and the Foreign Office thought otherwise, fearing that in practice a 'special relationship' could only mean American domination of Britain.

In the last year and a half of the war there was some evidence for their view. Churchill's correspondence with Roosevelt was much more concerned with Anglo-American wrangles than with planning for a post-war world. In so far as these became known to him, they must have delighted Stalin, as typical of the internal contradictions destined ultimately to destroy capitalism. For Churchill they must have been a cause for grief but, spurred on by Beaverbrook, Eden and other colleagues, he stood up stoutly for British post-war interests.

Overshadowing these disputes was anxiety about the vast scale of Britain's wartime debts to the U.S., dating back to 1940 and Lend-Lease, and the effect these might have on Britain's post-war standing in the world. In February 1944 Roosevelt, in an offhand way and seemingly out of the blue, asked Churchill if he could reduce Britain's gold and dollar holdings in the U.S. to about one billion dollars. This caused some alarm and indignation in London and Churchill replied that the dollar balances were Britain's total reserves, while in the common cause Britain had incurred liabilities of at least ten billion dollars. Roosevelt's request, he wrote, would not be consistent with any conception of equal sacrifice: 'We have not shirked our duty or indulged in an easy way of living. We have already spent practically all our convertible foreign investments in the struggle.' He did not know how he could put to Parliament the case for dispersing the last liquid reserves. Roosevelt replied soothingly that he was sorry if he had caused anxiety but the question was troublesome.[2] It was temporarily shelved but there remained an uneasy feeling that Britain's debts gave the U.S. a whip hand in negotiations on other matters.

It was at this time that Eden sent a secret and personal telegram to Halifax about current discussions with the U.S. of certain post-war questions, saying that in some quarters in London the Americans, including the government, were regarded as predatory and as bound to become more so under the influence of the coming election, so that the discussions could only do Britain injury or end in deadlock.[3]

Eden particularly mentioned oil as one of the most sensitive issues. The Americans were pressing for an international conference on Middle East oil, and Hull was to lead the U.S. delegation. Beaverbrook, with special responsibility for oil matters, was deeply suspicious of U.S. plots to take over Britain's Middle East oil interests.[4]

He communicated them to the War Cabinet. Churchill wrote to Roosevelt on 20 February: 'There is apprehension ... that the U.S. has a desire to deprive us of our oil assets ... on which among other things the whole supply of our navy depends.' If a high-level oil conference were announced it might become a question of first magnitude, and he would not be able to give an assurance that there would be no demand for 'transfer of property'. Roosevelt hit back by saying that he was disturbed by the rumour that the British wanted to 'horn in on Saudi Arabian oil reserves', and in view of the great long-range importance of oil to the post-war world he himself intended to preside at the first meeting of the oil conference in the White House.

To this Churchill replied: 'When I read the telegrams to the Cabinet this evening, I found them ... very much disturbed at the apparent possibility of a wide difference opening up between the British and U.S. governments on such a subject and at such a time.' Roosevelt then climbed a little way down and assured Churchill that 'we are not making sheep's eyes at your oil-fields in Iran or Iraq'. Churchill reciprocated by saying that the British had no thought of trying to horn in on U.S. interests in Saudi Arabia; Britain sought no advantage as a result of the war, but would not be deprived of anything which rightly belonged to her.[5] With that the matter was allowed to pass to a lower level and to Beaverbrook's negotiating talents.

An even more acid argument was over civil aviation and the Chicago conference laid on by the U.S. to plan the post-war set-up. In this field Britain had an advantage in the airfields at various points in the Commonwealth and empire important for world air routes. But there were suspicions of American intentions: just before the war, in August 1939, with an eye, so the British believed, on American civil aviation interests, the U.S. had laid claim to sixteen islands in the south Pacific owned by Britain and New Zealand.

When Eden visited Washington in March 1943 Roosevelt told him that there should be liberty for aircraft to use airfields of other countries, but not for passengers or goods to be transported by foreign airlines from one airfield in a foreign country to another.[6] This the British could accept. But in 1944 the Americans put forward what Beaverbrook called new and quite unacceptable demands, personally backed by Roosevelt. The War Cabinet discussed the matter on 22 November; Churchill said there would be no justification for accepting the new U.S. proposals, and he then told Roosevelt so.[7]

In reply Roosevelt brandished the big stick, telling Churchill that Congress would not be in a 'generous mood' when it next discussed Britain's Lend-Lease needs (further dollar credits) if it and the people felt that the U.K. had not agreed to a 'generally beneficial air agreement':

> They will wonder about the chances of our two countries, let alone any other, working together to keep the peace if we cannot even get together on an aviation agreement. I hope you will review the situation once more.

In spite of this threat to the 'special relationship', Churchill stood fast. Three days later he sent Roosevelt the unanimous view of the War Cabinet, pointing out that by wartime agreement the U.S. had been specialising in building transport planes, while the British concentrated on combat aircraft; in consequence, after the war the U.S. would be in an 'incomparably better position' than Britain to build up a post-war civil aviation industry. What was needed was an agreement to make sure that Britain and many other countries were not 'run out of the air altogether as a result of your flying start'. He hoped Roosevelt would not bring the threat of less generous Lend-Lease treatment into the discussion, and concluded:

> You will have the greatest navy in the world. You will have I hope the greatest air force. You will have the greatest trade. You have all the gold. But these things do not oppress my mind with fear because I am sure the American people . . . will not give themselves over to vainglorious ambitions.[8]

By this appeal to his better feelings Roosevelt was slightly softened, but not much. In the end the Americans did not get all they wanted. But they got some of their own back by negotiating a separate civil aviation agreement with the Irish Republic without telling the British. Churchill thought Roosevelt had undertaken not to do such a thing, and told him so. Roosevelt would not have this and hit back: 'Aviation circles in this country are becoming increasingly suspicious that certain elements in England intend to try to block the development of international flying . . . until the British aviation industry is further developed.'[9] This was Roosevelt's last word on the matter.

There was a minor but unpleasant dispute about Argentine beef. The State Department wanted to bring down the dictatorial regime of the colonels in Argentina. Although the British had not been consulted, they complied with Roosevelt's wish that they should join in, and Eden, after talking with Churchill, recalled the British ambassador from Buenos Aires. But when it came to an American demand that the British should not make a new meat contract with Argentina the matter became serious. Churchill wrote to Roosevelt about Britain's meat difficulties: 'Please remember that this community of 46 m. imported 66 m. tons a year before the war and is now managing on less than 25 m. The stamina of the workman cannot be maintained on a lesser diet in meat. You would not send your soldiers into battle on the British service meat ration, which is far above what is given to workmen.'

But Roosevelt wanted to talk on a much higher level than meat rations, appealing to Churchill to support 'the whole Allied stand in this hemisphere against this broad Fascist movement', and later, 'I know that we can continue to count on your help to liquidate this dangerous Nazi threat.' Churchill went on talking about beef and mutton, and resented what he called a 'threat of indirect blockade' by the State Department if Britain did not cut down its meat purchases from Argentina. (They had threatened to stop supplies to Argentina of tin-plate for packing meat.[10]) The wrangle had not been finally settled when Roosevelt died.

Over oil and civil aviation Beaverbrook took the lead in championing British interests; Eden sympathised but sometimes thought Beaverbrook made tactical mistakes by over-dramatising things, and would have liked to use more diplomatic methods, working through friendly members of the State Department. But one argument with the Americans, in the spring of 1944, did concern Eden closely.

This was the plan, blessed by Eisenhower as Supreme Allied Commander, for intensive day and night bombing on French railway centres as a preparation for the Normandy landings. The War Cabinet discussed it on 3 April, and were told that casualties among French civilians might be between 80,000 and 160,000, of whom perhaps one fourth would be killed. Churchill said he felt some doubts. Eden spoke more strongly, saying the R.A.F.'s 'very high prestige' would be lost if the plan was carried out – they would have to do the night bombing – and French railwaymen would stop helping with railway sabotage. Above all, Eden said, 'he feared that these attacks would affect our position in France and Belgium *vis-à-vis* Russia, whose reputation in these countries now stood very high, and might be a handicap to our relations with these two countries after the war'. The War Cabinet decided to ask for restrictions on the bombing.[11]

Nevertheless, the programme went ahead. On 27 April the War Cabinet discussed it again. By this time the R.A.F. had dropped twelve times the weight of bombs dropped by the Americans; earlier estimates of casualties had, however, been very greatly reduced. But Churchill said that there was a danger that the British might later be told that the great loss of French life was entirely due to the blind night bombing by the British. The plan was certainly wrong on humanitarian grounds. Eden again said the attacks would gradually alienate the mass of French opinion, and he did not believe them essential to the success of the battle. Churchill consulted Eisenhower; he replied that emasculation of the plan would make *Overlord* much more dangerous. Churchill turned again to the War Cabinet. Eden once more spoke against the bombings because of the reaction on European opinion :

> After the war, Eastern Europe and the Balkans would be largely dominated by the Russians, whereas the people of Western Europe would look to us. If the recent attacks were continued we might well find that they regarded us with hatred.[12]

On 7 May Churchill wrote to Roosevelt that the War Cabinet were much concerned about the number of French killed in the attacks, fearing that they might leave a legacy of hate; they wanted Roosevelt to look at the matter 'from the highest political standpoint'. But Roosevelt replied that, however regrettable the loss of life might be, he was not prepared to place any restrictions on the military commanders that might cause 'additional loss of life to our allied forces of invasion'. Roosevelt's word prevailed. When the War Cabinet discussed the bombing at the end of May, Eden said yet again he was anxious over reports that opinion in France, 'even among our supporters', was being turned against us. But by that time the R.A.F.'s share of the bombing was about 95% completed; British leverage was therefore small.[13]

Roosevelt's response to Churchill showed that he could not accept anything that risked avoidable American casualties. His attitude to British casualties was not quite the same. In the last weeks of the war the U.S. Chiefs of Staff hatched a plan for launching pilotless 'war-weary U.S. bombers' loaded with some 20,000 pounds of high explosive at industrial targets in Germany. The British Chiefs of Staff at first agreed to the plan, but the War Cabinet opposed it because the Germans might retaliate against London. Roosevelt wrote to Churchill that his Chiefs of Staff thought the plan most valuable in the all-out offensive against Germany; the Germans were unlikely to retaliate, and it would be useful experience for the war against Japan. He requested the British to think again.

Before Churchill had answered, Roosevelt died. Churchill sent a message to the new President, Harry S. Truman, that if the Americans really thought the war-weary bombers necessary to end the war, 'we will not dissent'. But he pointed out that 30,000 Londoners had been killed by air attack and even a few big explosions in London would be a very great disappointment to people who had hoped their long ordeal was nearly over. The ultimate decision must rest with the American military advisers : 'We shall make no complaint if misfortune comes to us in consequence.' Truman, with sound common sense, answered that the project should not be pressed further in Europe.[14]

When Japan's turn came, it was the atom bomb, not war-weary bombers, that the Americans used, so it did not matter that they had lost the chance of trying them out in Europe.

While all these unpleasant conflicts and arguments were going on, the Americans and British jointly carried out military operations which were remarkably successful, with a degree of co-operation never seen in the First Word War – even if there was later much questioning whether the war could not have been ended more quickly, and whether more of Europe could not have been kept free of Soviet control. Also, at many lower levels there was plenty of Anglo-American good will and friendship. The fact, or myth, of the Churchill–Roosevelt special relationship fostered the right climate of feeling for all this.

When it came to planning for the post-war world, both Churchill and Roosevelt liked to have broad, hazy visions of the future but found detailed blue-prints cramping or a bore. Both liked keeping open as many options as possible. They differed in one very important respect. Churchill always thought of the U.S. as Britain's chosen partner for the future; it might or might not be possible to bring the Soviet Union into the partnership. Roosevelt turned to Stalin as his equal, whose friendship and co-operation were essential to the new world order. A lesser role was left for Churchill: Stalin was the man of the future, Churchill a man of the past.

In aiming at an equal partnership with the U.S., both Churchill and Eden – and, with certain doubts, Attlee – seemed to take it for granted that the British Commonwealth and empire would survive the war. Roosevelt, however, thought that the British, French and Dutch empires would and should melt away; the Japanese had started the work, and it would be morally right to help in completing it. But the British refused to recognise that their empire was doomed. Unrest in India was a very serious problem during most of the war. Roosevelt once tackled Churchill, in the early part of 1942, offering well-meant but tactless advice. Churchill's reaction was so sharp that Roosevelt refrained from pressing him thereafter – but felt perfectly free to discuss the independence of India with Stalin at Tehran,[15] as also the removal of Indo-China from French colonial rule.

In Britain some people were always very suspicious of American intentions towards the empire. When in August 1941 Roosevelt and Churchill jointly issued the Atlantic Charter, which stated the right of all men to choose the form of government under which they would live, the British government felt it necessary to state that they did not regard their colonies as being covered by this. The Americans no doubt saw this as typical reactionary imperialism but refrained from open combat.

In November 1942 the War Office wrote a paper on Anglo-American relations which Churchill had printed and circulated. According to the War Office, the U.S. War Department was planning to build an army of ten million men; one motive was 'the need for the U.S. to be militarily strong in order to dominate the policy of the United Nations, both during the war and in the making of the subsequent peace'.

This attitude takes various forms, ranging from the establishment of a 'Pax Americana', in substitution for the 'Pax Britannica' (now regarded by many Americans as having finished its useful life), to a definite American imperialistic policy which aims at the building up of American power and prestige in various parts of the world. It is difficult to ignore the fact that, under the guise of the war effort, this is already being attempted or achieved, at Britain's expense, in the Argentine, New Zealand, Persia, Australia, India, Egypt, Turkey, to mention only a few places.[16]

This was an extreme view, but suspicion lived on. The Americans were equally suspicious of Britain's determination to pursue its supposed imperial interests in Greece, the Balkans and elsewhere.

Churchill was certainly not immune to such suspicions. But, whether from deep conviction or wishful thinking, he nevertheless had strong faith in Anglo-American partnership as the key to world peace. He carried this idea to lengths which Eden and other Cabinet colleagues, above all the Foreign Office, found foolish or dangerous. When he visited Washington in May 1943 Churchill launched the idea at a lunch with Vice-President Henry Wallace, the Secretary for War Henry Stimson, Harold Ickes and others. He told them that the proposed world organisation did not exclude a special friendship: he could see small hope for the world unless the U.S. and the British Commonwealth worked together in fraternal association. The citizens of each, without losing their existing nationality, should be free to settle and trade with equal rights in the other's territory. There might be a common passport, even some common form of citizenship. He would be in favour of the Americans using British bases for defence purposes.

In particular, Churchill made two suggestions – which apparently were well received at the lunch party but went down badly in the Foreign Office – first, that after the war there should continue to be an Anglo-American Combined Staff; second, that there should be constant contact to make sure that 'the main lines of our foreign policy ran closely together'.

The next day Churchill saw both Roosevelt and Wallace who seemed 'a little anxious lest other countries should think that Britain and U.S. were trying to boss the world'. Churchill said it would be wrong 'to be put off the necessary and rightful action by such considerations'. Wallace was also worried by the citizenship proposal. Roosevelt, however, liked the military side of Churchill's plan, agreeing that it was essential that the Anglo-American staff institutions should be continued 'for a good long time after the war'.[17]

Halifax, who had been there, had his doubts and wrote privately to Eden that, if there were to be a 'fraternal association', it was important that the Dominions should be brought in:

> It was certainly not in Winston's mind that it should be an affair between the U.S. and the U.K. only. . . . If it were, the U.K. would of course be in a secondary position, and the suggestion in this form might start undesirable ideas in American minds. As a U.S.–U.K. system, the British outlook . . . might easily be swamped.[18]

Undeterred by such dark thoughts, and with Roosevelt's blessing, Churchill propounded his ideas publicly in his Harvard speech on 6 September 1943, mentioning both the Anglo-American Combined Chiefs of Staff and possible common citizenship.[19] To post-war planners in the Foreign Office, this just meant that Britain would be for ever subservient to the U.S. Gladwyn Jebb satirised the whole idea savagely in a document which he circulated to friends, proposing a merger or fusion of the U.S., Britain and the Commonwealth, the union of the whole vast 'Free World' in the interests of Anglo-America, and a Council of Europe as a sort of dependency of the Combined Chiefs of Staff in Washington.[20]

Attlee, like Halifax (and Jebb), was troubled over the problem of inequality. In April 1944 he told the War Cabinet that he thought it important to make sure that the British Commonwealth should speak as a single unit. If that could be done, the empire would be in as strong a position in the post-war world as the U.S.A. and the Soviet Union. But if the Dominions insisted on being dealt with individually, as separate nations, the empire as a whole would be in a much less satisfactory position.[21] (It was strange that Attlee, who three years later was to grant India independence, should then have talked as though Canada and Australia could be kept in apron-strings.)

Churchill's other pet project – though a secondary one – was for a Council of Europe. He had written an article on 'the United States of Europe' as early as 1930; he was partly inspired by the half-Austrian, half-Japanese Count Richard Coudenhove-Kalergi, the prophet of the European idea, who peppered him with letters and publications during the war years.[22]

The exact shape of the project varied a little according to circumstances. When in January 1943 he made an impromptu dash to Turkey to persuade the Turkish leaders to think hard about entering the war, and wanted to overcome their fears of the Russians' overrunning the Balkans, he was inspired to set down his 'Morning Thoughts' and to communicate them to the Turks. He wrote that, within a future world organisation for preserving peace, there should be 'an instrument of European government' to be formed not only by the 'great nations of Europe and Asia Minor' – that is, including Turkey – but also by a number of confederations – a Scandinavian bloc, a Danubian bloc, and a Balkan bloc. He then said that no one could be certain that the victors would never quarrel among themselves or that the U.S. might not once again retire from Europe, but Britain would do its utmost to organise resistance to any act of aggression committed by any power, and believed that the U.S. would co-operate and even possibly 'take the lead in the world'. In this context, Turkey's highest security lay in becoming a 'victorious belligerent'.[23]

This vision of Europe – even though Churchill had a very practical aim in unfolding it to the Turks – aroused little enthusiasm in Eden; and when he visited Washington the following March he reported to Churchill that Harry Hopkins said it was important that 'there should be no attempt to set up a European Council, for this would give free ammunition to the isolationists who would jump at the chance of sitting back in a similar regional council for the American continent'.[24] From then on Eden gave first priority to getting U.S. involvement in a future world organisation, leaving planning for Europe to follow after.

But Churchill remained in love with his idea and when, soon after Eden, he, too, was in Washington and lunched with Wallace, Stimson and Ickes, he talked to them not only about the need for an Anglo-American 'fraternal association' but also about the need for three regional councils subordinate to a 'World Council' – one for Europe, one for the American hemisphere, one for the Pacific. Some twelve states or confederations would form the regional European Council. None of the Americans present was recorded by Halifax as having raised any doubts or objections.[25] Nevertheless, Hull and the State Department, like Eden, went on focusing all energies on the creation of the new world organisation, and thought the idea of a Council of Europe a distraction, perhaps harmful.

In April 1944 Churchill was still loyal to the idea, telling the War Cabinet that under the world organisation, where three or four great powers would be responsible for keeping the peace of the world, there would be regional councils for Europe, America, Asia and, if necessary, Africa. The British would in one way or another belong to them all : 'The special position of the U.K. in relation to Europe; the position of authority of Canada in the American continent; our position and responsibilities in Asia and our African commitments would establish the British empire in the various councils.'

It was left to Eden to ask how, in this scheme of things, the U.S. was to be associated with the solution of European difficulties, which would be important. Churchill replied that he did not feel there need be any insuperable difficulties in associating the U.S. with 'regional arrangements for Europe' – but he did not say exactly how.[26] The Commonwealth leaders met in London shortly after, and Churchill and Eden presented them with rival papers on post-war organisation. According to Eden they preferred his, but he produced a compromise document which preserved Churchill's Council of Europe – this to include the U.S., the Soviet Union and Britain[27] – which to many Europeans at that time would not have seemed a very European body.

Six months later, when the birth pangs of the world organisation were proving difficult and the Soviet armies had swept a long way westwards in Europe, Churchill's vision had begun to wilt badly. He told the War Cabinet on 27 November that he had at one time hoped that a European regional arrangement might be possible, but now felt doubtful whether it could ever be realised – though perhaps once the world organisation had been set up, 'there was nothing against a special European group'.[28]

By this time Churchill – just back from Moscow – was pinning his faith, with alternating hope and despair, on a triumvirate of the Big Three – Roosevelt, Stalin and himself – to organise post-war Europe.

In the closing months of the war in Europe, the problem of what to do with Germany should in theory have been in the forefront of Churchill's thoughts. In practice it was not.

His feelings towards the Germans were at times harsh, at others humane, according to circumstances. At Casablanca Roosevelt, wanting to wipe out all memories of the Darlan affair, announced that Germany must surrender unconditionally. Churchill, who had not expected this public statement, acquiesced (as did the War Cabinet, though they would have preferred to have been consulted in advance). But he was never entirely happy about it. Not long before *Overlord*, the British Chiefs of Staff questioned whether the unvarnished 'unconditional surrender' formula might not stiffen German resistance. Churchill told Cadogan he thought it useless to refer the question to Roosevelt, who was 'very much disinclined to re-model his statements', and added: 'He announced it at Casablanca without any consultation. I backed him up in general terms.'[29]

As for splitting up Germany, Churchill was in favour of cutting off Prussia and forming a south German federation, but not much more. In January 1944 Attlee asked him just what had happened in Tehran: in a Cabinet paper, Churchill had written that Britain, the U.S. and Russia had agreed that Germany was to be decisively broken up into a number of separate states. Attlee commented: 'I do not recall that we have ever taken so definite a decision. For myself, while desiring the decentralisation of Germany and the severance of certain areas, I am sceptical as to the efficacy of partition enforced by the victors.' Churchill replied: 'This was certainly the President's view and that of Stalin. I did not commit H.M.G. beyond "the isolation of Prussia".' Three months later Churchill told the Foreign Office that at Tehran both Roosevelt and Stalin had 'wished to cut Germany into smaller pieces than I had in mind'.[30]

At Yalta in 1945 Stalin wanted a firm decision to dismember Germany; Roosevelt was agreeable, Churchill was not, the decision was referred to Foreign Ministers and was still open at the Potsdam meeting, where dismemberment was for varying reasons dropped by all the Big Three. The feelings of the War Cabinet had their influence on this outcome.

What touched Churchill more closely was the human problem of Stalin's intentions towards the Germans. When at Tehran, over dinner, Stalin proposed that 50,000 German officers and technicians should be shot, Churchill was deeply shocked: 'The British Parliament and public will never tolerate mass executions,' he said. Roosevelt's rather clumsy effort to pass the whole thing off as a joke did not convince him, though Eden seems to have thought Stalin did not mean it seriously. Harriman, who was there, wrote later that Churchill had been 'horrified' at Stalin's suggestion.[31]

A month later, in a message to Roosevelt, Churchill made light of his own indignant reaction, calling it 'my high falutin'. But in February 1944 he said in a speech, 'unconditional surrender means that the victors have a free hand. It does not mean that they are entitled to behave in a barbarous manner.' In April he wrote to Cadogan that at Tehran it had not been possible to ascertain whether Stalin was joking or not: 'The atmosphere was jovial but also grim. He certainly said he would require 4 million German males to work for an indefinite period to rebuild Russia.' And when Churchill and Eden were in Moscow in October and Churchill was doing his best to create an atmosphere of cosy intimacy with Stalin, he none the less said that Britain would not agree to mass execution of Germans, because one day British public opinion would cry out. But it was necessary to kill as many as possible in the field and the others should be made to repair the damage done to other countries.[32]

Roosevelt's attitude to Germany wavered. At Casablanca he had launched 'unconditional surrender'. On the eve of the Normandy landings he seemed to have switched to a soft line, proposing that he, alone, should give a somewhat mushy message of friendly reassurance to the German people after D-Day. Churchill told the War Cabinet he doubted the timeliness of such a message, but for his own part would be ready for Roosevelt to 'act as spokesman'. The Australian Prime Minister, John Curtin, joined Smuts – both were present – in objecting, saying he disliked both the tone and idea of the message; he supposed that because of the feelings of the German-Americans, Roosevelt now wanted to move away from unconditional surrender. Eden insisted that any statement to the Germans must be made by the three leaders jointly. The War Cabinet asked Churchill to head Roosevelt off the idea, which he tactfully and successfully did.[33]

But five months later, at the second Quebec conference, Roosevelt backed the plan of his Secretary of the Treasury, Henry Morgenthau, for the 'pastoralisation' of Germany – the wholesale destruction of its heavy industry; Morgenthau was desperately keen to convince the Russians of American good will and sincerity.[34] Churchill's scientific wise man, Lord Cherwell, fell for the plan and joined forces with Morgenthau and Roosevelt to get Churchill to agree. Then Eden, who had known nothing about it, arrived in Quebec, was horrified and said sc at the conference. Churchill, having pledged himself to Roosevelt, tried to squash him. 'This', Eden wrote later, 'was the only occasion I can remember when the Prime Minister showed impatience with my view before foreign representatives. He resented my criticism of something which he and the President had approved, not, I am sure, on his account, but on the President's.'

Fortunately for Eden, Hull also was horrified, and the two of them managed to get the plan shelved. On the journey home, it seems, Churchill was never heard to mention it.[35] But Stalin must have found the Morgenthau project very much to his taste. When Churchill and Eden went to Moscow in the following October, Stalin said German heavy industry would have to be destroyed, and Molotov asked Churchill what he thought of the plan. Churchill side-stepped the question by saying that Roosevelt and Morgenthau were not very happy about its reception.[36]

In the event, the fundamental decisions about Germany were not settled until after Churchill and Eden had left office.

For Eden, the job of post-war planning brought a series of frustrations caused by Churchill or at certain times by Roosevelt. It was a field in which he could reasonably have hoped to shine and to take the lead. He had had first-hand experience of the virtues and vices of the pre-war League of Nations, to which the U.S. had never belonged, and of the practice of traditional European diplomacy. He was young and aimed to be forward-looking.

Yet Churchill was always discouraging or thwarting him. In the autumn of 1942 Eden put forward what he called the Four Power Plan for joint responsibility by the U.S., Britain, the Soviet Union and China in keeping the peace. Churchill wrote to him:

Any conclusions drawn now are sure to have little relation to what will happen. It is even dangerous to discuss some aspects . . . for instance the position of Russia. . . . I hope that these speculative studies will be entrusted mainly to those on whose hands time hangs heavy, and that we shall not overlook Mrs Glass's Cookery Book recipe for Jugged Hare – 'First catch your hare'.

At that early stage in their wartime relations, Eden was not willing to take this lying down, writing that he was most disappointed at Churchill's minute; his plan was not a vague project for an indefinite future:

My design is to have a basis of a foreign policy now, which policy, if the basis is sound today, should carry us over into the peace. It is from every point of view bad policy to live from hand to mouth when we can avoid it, and the only consequence of doing so is that the U.S. makes a policy and we follow, which I do not regard as a satisfactory role for the British empire.[37]

Although Churchill was so sceptical, the four-power concept survived and was merged in planning for the post-war world organisation, the United Nations. When Eden went to Washington in March 1943 Roosevelt held forth on this theme, saying that the organisation should have an executive committee of four powers, in which it was essential to include China – though not France, who, in his view, could be induced to give up certain parts of the French empire and put certain territories at the U.N.'s disposal; Europe, including France, should be disarmed.

This was not at all to Churchill's taste and he telegraphed to Eden that it showed 'the dangers which will attend any attempt to decide these matters while the war is raging'. He added that any proposal to rank France lower than China even in matters affecting Europe and to sub-jugate all Europe, after disarmament, to the four powers 'would certainly cause lively discussion'. Eden had been quite right to protest about France.[38] (It was always when Roosevelt was most actively pushing Nationalist China's claims to greatness that Churchill became most keen to champion France; he refused to accept Roosevelt's rating of China as a great power and said more than once that China would be just a 'faggot vote' for the U.S.)

In spite of these early stumbling blocks, planning for a United Nations organisation went ahead, and Churchill interfered little with Eden when he tried to work closely with Hull and the State Department in this field. Yet he constantly threw cold water on post-war planning. On the future of Germany, he wrote to Eden as late as January 1945:

I think it is much too soon for us to try to decide. . . . It is a mistake to try to write out on little pieces of paper what the vast emotions of an outraged and quivering world will be after the struggle is over. . . . Guidance in these mundane matters is granted us only step by step. . . . There is therefore wisdom in reserving one's decisions as long as possible.[39]

Perhaps Eden's most solid achievement, and one that he saw as his personal triumph at the Moscow Foreign Ministers' conference in 1943, was one in which Churchill took little interest. This was the creation of the European Advisory Commission, bringing Britain, the U.S. and the Soviet Union together in planning the post-war organisation of Germany and, in theory at least, the treatment of a restored Austria and other ex-enemy countries.

Eden felt it was a major success that the E.A.C. was to be based in London and so, because of the efficiency of the Foreign Office in handling this sort of job, gave a chance for Britain to play a leading role in the shaping of post-war Europe. He had always felt this was what ought to happen, writing to Churchill in July 1942 : 'We should always consult U.S. government, but our object should be to bring them along with us. They know very little of Europe and it would be unfortunate for the future of the world if U.S. uninstructed views were to decide the future of the European continent. Our diplomacy should be equal to this task.'[40]

Eden appointed as British representative on the E.A.C. one of the most respected senior officials of the Foreign Office, Sir William Strang, and for a short time Eden's dream came true. Strang certainly did play the leading role and, very slowly and with much difficulty, the necessary work on Germany – in particular the drawing of the occupation zones – was carried forward. But on occupation zones for Austria or armistice terms for Romania, Hungary and Bulgaria very little could be achieved.

One reason for Strang's difficulties was the Soviet delegate's lack of the necessary instructions; another was that the U.S. delegate was accorded very little help or authority by his government. Strang wrote later : 'So exasperating did Soviet dilatoriness become that Mr Eden made sharp remonstrance to Mr Molotov. What the Soviet government felt, I think, was that time was on their side : as their military advance into Central Europe proceeded, their bargaining position would improve.'[41]

On the Americans Strang commented, 'there were people in Washington who did not like the Commission. The military authorities . . . were displeased by the invasion of what they regarded as their preserves by the

State Department. . . . There were others, including (it would appear) President Roosevelt himself, who saw it as a threat to U.S. leadership, since here was a body where the British delegation could and would use its tactical and other advantages to seize the initiative.'[42]

Strang was putting it mildly. Halifax wrote to Eden in May 1944 about a talk he had had with Stettinius, who had said that the position over the E.A.C. was 'bad' : the reason for the President's attitude was probably the fear that, since the U.S. could only be represented by a more or less scratch team far from their own goverment, 'it would mean too much of a lead would be taken by the United Kingdom who would be able to get through solutions which the President might not particularly like and generally organise Europe on lines of U.K. policy. The U.K. might thus figure in the eyes of the European countries . . . as leaders in Europe . . . something which he supposed the President might not wholly relish.'

Eden sent a copy of this letter to Churchill, who ticked it without comment. Strang minuted on it : 'I am, on instructions, firmly taking the lead in the E.A.C. on the question of consultation with the European Allies about surrender terms for Germany, and . . . the participation of their forces in the occupation. . . . The Americans cannot take any effective lead in Europe.' Against this, in the margin, Cadogan wrote : 'But – if we are subservient – they can stand in the way of our doing so.' Strang also argued that the sooner the joint Anglo-American command ceased to be, once the war was over, the better : 'We cannot have a free foreign policy in Europe so long as there is an American Supreme Allied Commander responsible to the Combined Chiefs of Staff. . . .' (So much for Churchill's Harvard speech.)

Gladwyn Jebb, prominent in Foreign Office post-war planning, commented even more sharply : 'I have no doubt that the President's attitude is as described by Stettinius. It is nevertheless a deplorable attitude and I feel that the Secretary of State is absolutely right in holding that we *should* take the lead in Europe, whatever the President may want or not want. . . .' He added that in any case the President was being a dog in the manger, since the American Chiefs of Staff had already said that American troops were not to stay long in Europe.[43]

But apart from the solid but limited work done by the E.A.C. Eden and the Foreign Office could not get very far in 'taking the lead' in Europe. In 1944, however, the smaller west European Allies, through their exiled governments in London, gave Eden an opening for a new initiative. Paul-Henri Spaak, in particular, pressed for action; as early as 1941 he had written to a Conservative M.P. : 'After the war Europe will be glad to unite behind Britain's victorious leadership. . . . If Britain fails to recognise her duty to Europe, if she does not pursue a continental policy which makes her a strong leader of Europe, she must expect to be rapidly deprived of the fruits of her present efforts.'[44] By the summer of 1944 his idea was more modest, of a group of the west European Allies and Britain. The Dutch and Norwegian exiled governments also favoured the idea, and suggested to the Foreign Office that there should be discussions about ways of aligning foreign policies, possibly also getting arms from Britain.

Unfortunately, that summer Eden felt inhibited by the need to get agreement with the Americans and Russians on the main lines of the future United Nations organisation, thinking this must be done first, before undertaking any joint talks with the smaller west Europeans; and as Spaak in particular was getting restive because there was no British response, Eden saw the Belgian, Dutch and Norwegian Foreign Ministers one after the other during July. According to Spaak, he said that Roosevelt and Hull might have been embarrassed if attempts to organise Europe had begun without them, since the isolationists in the U.S. might have used them as an excuse for claiming that Europe had no need of the U.S.A. But he added that the Russians had approved the idea of a west European organisation, basing himself (rather rashly) on the remarks made to him by Stalin in 1941. Eden's general tone was encouraging.[45]

At this time the 'post-hostilities planners' working under the auspices of the Chiefs of Staff were also beginning to advocate a west European defence group – but as a necessary element in Britain's defence against a potentially hostile Soviet Union. Some Foreign Office officials were shocked by any assumption that Britain might within a decade find itself at war with Russia, but towards the end of 1944 Eden gave instructions for a study of what came to be called a 'western bloc'. When Eden put it to Churchill the latter was extremely sceptical, thinking the west European Allies would be too weak to be of any use to Britain and Britain would be too poor to arm them. Eden argued back, saying that the proposed group would be organised under the aegis of the United Nations; it would be essential to build up France; the danger was that, if the west Europeans, especially the French, thought the British were not going to accept *any* commitments on the Continent, they might make defence arrangements with the Russians.[46]

But on 20 November Stalin told Churchill that de Gaulle was going to Moscow; since Press reports had appeared about a possible western bloc, Churchill was afraid de Gaulle would make trouble with Stalin on the subject and sent Stalin a message mentioning it and saying he had 'not yet considered this'; he trusted first in the Anglo-Soviet alliance and close collaboration with the U.S. to form the mainstays of a world organisation : 'It is only after and subordinate to any such world structure that European arrangements for better comradeship should be set on foot, and . . . we shall have no secrets from you.' A few days later, after discussion in the War Cabinet, and on Eden's advice, he made the ill-fated proposal for an Anglo-French-Soviet treaty, which de Gaulle rejected.[47]

So both Churchill's 'special relationship' with the U.S. and Eden's 'western bloc' were left as unfinished business, to be carried further by the Labour government after both men were out of power.

The post-war 'special relationship' lasted for a decade and in tenuous form even longer; it was neither as equal nor as important as Churchill had hoped, nor as humiliating and harmful for Britain as the Foreign Office had feared. The 'western bloc' was realised in the Brussels treaty organisation of 1948, then merged in the Atlantic alliance of 1949, both seen as defensive measures against Stalin's Russia. Germany was dis-membered, not on the lines wanted by Churchill but along the border between the Soviet and Western occupation zones. As Strang himself wrote later, if there had been no agreement in the European Advisory Commission on the zonal frontiers, when the Russian and Anglo-American armies met, the British and Americans might have negotiated a boundary over a hundred miles further east, though Berlin would not then have come under four-power administration.[48] So perhaps there may have been some virtue in the great reluctance of Churchill – also Roosevelt – to take firm decisions before the fighting stopped.

The problem of Britain's wartime indebtedness caused a minor crisis in Anglo-American relations under the Attlee government, but in the end the U.S. did not carry out Roosevelt's vague threats in practice. Nevertheless, Churchill's lively awareness of Britain's overall debt to the U.S. lay at the heart of his relationship with Roosevelt, to whom he once wrote (in the middle of a bitter argument) of 'our financial relationship and the scale on which you are helping us to play our part in the common war effort and . . . many other kindly and friendly acts'.[49] It was part of his code of personal and public behaviour – perhaps the code of an aristocrat – that debts should be fully and freely acknowledged and gratitude ungrudgingly given.

Unfortunately, Roosevelt was insensitive to the finer points of Churchill's code, which was perhaps rather extravagant and high-flown for a poor relation like Britain. More realistic was Churchill's firm perception of the present and future facts of world power : his keen sense of the inevitability of U.S. leadership was more acute than the wishful thinking of Eden and the Foreign Office about an independent British policy in Europe and beyond.

PART FOUR

Churchill, Eden, Stalin

CHAPTER SIXTEEN

Churchill, Eden, Stalin: Unaccountable Joe

To both Churchill and Eden, working with Roosevelt brought frustrations and sometimes humiliations, but also, to Britain essential material aid, and to Churchill personally a lot of pleasure. Above all, though the twists and turns of Roosevelt's mind and mood were sometimes hidden, they worked in broad daylight. They were well informed about the inner tensions and feuds inside the U.S. administration and about the political atmosphere in Washington and public opinion throughout the country.

Trying to work with Stalin was very different. Churchill and Eden seemed like men trying to find their way along a winding underground tunnel with a treacherous surface underfoot and sharp jutting rocks on each side. In the blackness they lurched and stumbled, and though they were trying to go in the same direction they sometimes collided.

Whistling in the dark to keep up their spirits, they, Roosevelt and others came to speak of Stalin as Uncle Joe, U.J. or simply Joe. In fairy tales, as also in *Hamlet*, uncles are wicked, but 'Uncle Joe' seemed to suggest something homelier. Stalin might be curmudgeonly, cantankerous and crusty, the Bear who could only be expected to growl, as Churchill once wrote,[1] but perhaps there was a kindly streak in him, though hardly a heart of gold. It also implied that he was in some way different from his colleagues and underlings. No one ever thought of calling Molotov Uncle Vyacheslav or Vyshinsky Uncle Andy.

Most attempts to pierce the Soviet gloom were based on the idea that Stalin was readier to be friendly than the rest of the Moscow leadership. Churchill wrote to Eden in 1943 that there were two forces in Russia : '(a) Stalin himself, personally cordial to me, (b) Stalin in Council, a grim thing behind him, which we and he have to reckon with.'[2] Eden tried to take a sceptical view, saying in 1942 that Stalin was 'oriental' and practised hard bargaining, mistrusting anyone who failed to use the same method.[3] But generally he believed Stalin more reasonable than Molotov, who was the rigid, difficult one of the pair. Ernest Bevin, too, at times thought this.[4] There was thought to be a 'hard' group, or, as George Kennan (later the leading U.S. kremlinologist) expressed it in a paper which was given to the British, there was a 'xenophobic group'

who controlled the information which reached Stalin and so misled him.[5]
In 1945 a senior official in the Foreign Office speculated that it was the
'victorious Soviet Marshals' who were being hard and aggressive, whereas
Stalin himself could be 'statesmanlike'.[6]

Everyone agreed that the Soviet leaders were pathologically suspicious
of the British and non-Communists in general; some thought this must be
treated as a malady to be healed by firmness, patience and understanding,
or what was sometimes called therapeutic trust. One commonly held
theory was that they suffered from an inferiority complex. This was
often used by the Soviet ambassador Ivan Maisky to explain any piece of
rude or offensive behaviour. It was accepted by Sir Archibald Clark Kerr,
when ambassador in Moscow, and by other British officials. One
independent-minded wartime official in the Foreign Office thought the
Russians wanted to be 'members of the club', even though they thought
some of its rules 'damn silly'; he commented ironically : 'It's too sad that
Stalin and Molotov were not at Eton and Harrow, but what can we do
about it?'[7]

The intelligence service does not seem to have given very much help
in analysing Soviet motives and actions. When in 1920 the British government was making its first serious effort to negotiate an agreement with
the Soviet Union, the Prime Minister, David Lloyd George, had the advantage of seeing the deciphered intercepts of the messages exchanged
between the Soviet negotiator in London and his government in Moscow.[8]
The relevant British services must have been trying to do the same thing
in the Second World War. If they succeeded, the Soviet government must
have been very efficient in keeping anything of interest out of its
diplomatic messages to its representatives in London and elsewhere.
(References to diplomatic intercepts have in theory been weeded out of
the British Foreign Office documents now open to inspection, but one or
two oddments have escaped the weeders. In the case of documents dealing
with the Soviet Union, only one, of very small importance, has been
spotted by the present author.[9])

Perhaps the secret of the Soviet leaders' success in baffling the British –
and Americans – as to their short-term and long-term aims lay in the
absoluteness and arbitrariness of Stalin's power and his dictation of policy
according to his mood, fears or hopes of the moment. Also, his one
constant aim was probably much simpler and cruder than the British
ever brought themselves to imagine – to get out of his Allies, no less than
his enemies, as much as he possibly could in the circumstances by
whatever means were open to him at that moment. The British, trying to

read much more complex and long-range planning and motives into Soviet actions and words, only succeeded in bewildering and muddling themselves. So they were left, after all the theorising, with the conclusion that, as Eden wrote to Churchill in 1943, 'Joe is unaccountable'.[10]

Stalin may or may not have been better informed about the British than they were about him. Talking about the British to the Yugoslav Communist Milovan Djilas in June 1944, Stalin said: 'They steal our dispatches, we steal theirs.'[11] Soviet 'stealing', by whatever technical means, may have been efficient. Churchill, after explaining *Torch* to Stalin for the first time, was 'deeply impressed' by Stalin's 'swift and complete mastery of a problem hitherto novel to him'.[12] Possibly it was not quite so novel as all that.

Perhaps, too, after the spring of 1944 one source of information was cut off from Stalin. According to a telegram from Churchill, in April the British authorities were 'weeding out remorselessly every single known Communist from all our secret operations'. This followed the sentencing of 'two quite high-grade people to long terms of penal servitude for their betrayal, in accordance with the Communist faith, of important military secrets'.[13] Not all such men, however, were known.

Faced with such an unfamiliar, wary and devious partner – or antagonist – Churchill, with his openness, his childlike spontaneity and easily stirred feelings of admiration, gratitude, anger or wounded pride, seemed highly vulnerable. Eden, basing himself on long British experience of diplomatic dealing with a wide range of countries and types of government in all continents, and on the Foreign Office tradition of cool, dispassionate reasoning, seemed likely to have the better chance of handling Stalin successfully. But he, too, was often impulsive and swayed by the emotion of the moment, by psychological pressures from friends or rivals, from Allied leaders or from Stalin himself; also by a natural desire for personal success. His officials could, on demand, present his policies towards the Soviet Union – or their own – as logical and consistent, yet in reality they often veered to and fro, and chopped and changed between 'toughness' and 'softness'.

So Eden was changeable in his attitude to Stalin, even if his changes were less violent than Churchill's. Churchill swung between his hankering for a sort of personal comradeship-in-arms with Stalin, a deep respect for Soviet military achievements and the Russian people's capacity for human endurance, and, on the other hand, revulsion from Soviet ruthlessness or brutality, particularly towards small nations, and, in the closing phase of the war, fear of Soviet domination of post-war Europe, coupled with an almost panic feeling of helplessness.

In April 1944, for instance, he wrote to Eden: 'Although I have tried in every way to put myself in sympathy with these Communist leaders, I cannot feel the slightest trust or confidence in them.' Yet six months later he told the War Cabinet that he himself felt that Russia was ready and anxious to work with Britain. And after the Yalta conference he told them that he felt no doubt whatever that Stalin was sincere; he was a man of great power and Churchill had great confidence in him, but 'much rested on Premier Stalin's life'.[14] In June 1945, appalled by reports of the torture of a Bulgarian woman, secretary to a non-Communist politician, he wrote to Eden: 'Whenever these Bolsheviks think you are afraid of them, they will do whatever suits their lust and cruelty.' Eden replied that in this case the Soviet Union could hardly be held directly responsible.[15]

Yet if Churchill seemed more changeable, more easily swayed by his moods, than Eden was in relation to Stalin, nevertheless his openness and forthright speaking, his declarations of friendship alternating with outbursts of indignation or wrath or with stubborn obstinacy, may have puzzled Stalin and thrown him off balance more than Eden's more conventional diplomacy could do. After Churchill paid his first difficult visit to Moscow in August 1942 to break to Stalin the bad news of the delay of the second front, Molotov told the British ambassador – who had said that Churchill had 'taken a liking' to Stalin – that this had been fully reciprocated; Stalin had been impressed by the Prime Minister's spirit and dynamic qualities. To the Communist Djilas, Stalin put things differently, letting it be seen that he thought Churchill a far-sighted and dangerous 'bourgeois statesman'.[16]

On one occasion, at least, Churchill's openness got a response from Stalin. General John Deane, head of the U.S. military mission in Moscow who complained bitterly of Soviet unwillingness to give any information on military plans, described a meeting between Stalin and Churchill in October 1944. When the British military representative was giving an excellent explanation of Allied plans in western Europe, Churchill kept on interrupting him, jumping up to demonstrate certain details on the map. Then, when Soviet plans were being presented by a Red Army general, Stalin interrupted him, took over the pointer, and outlined Soviet plans on the map in considerable detail.[17]

*

For Churchill, the idea of alliance with the Soviet Union required a much bigger emotional upheaval than for Eden. After the Bolshevik revolution he had strongly backed military intervention in Russia. When this failed, he still felt strongly against the Bolshevik regime. When in 1920 Lloyd George proposed to the Cabinet conclusion of a trade agreement with the Soviet Union, Churchill voted against it and was quite pale and extremely upset at the moment of decision, insisting that he must stay free to denounce the 'odious character' of the Bolsheviks. Earlier he had spoken of the regime as 'foul baboonery' and later wrote of the leaders as 'crocodiles with master-minds'.[18]

In time, Churchill simmered down. With the rise of Hitler his attitude changed, partly under the influence of the Soviet ambassador, Maisky, who visited him at Chartwell. He criticised the Chamberlain government for half-heartedness in their talks with the Soviet government about mutual aid against Hitler in the summer of 1939. But then came the Ribbentrop–Molotov pact and later the Soviet attack on Finland; Churchill swung back again and urged that submarines should be sent into the Black Sea to stop Soviet oil supplies to Germany and was in favour of other warlike action.

Then in June 1940 came the fall of France, and Churchill – though he very much disliked Soviet annexation of the Baltic States at this time – saw the need to look for support against Germany wherever he could find it, and agreed to a Foreign Office proposal that he should send a conciliatory message to Stalin – his first – suggesting Anglo-Soviet consultation in face of the threat of German 'hegemony over the continent'. With Britain alone and threatened by invasion, Stalin was cold to any such approach, except in so far as he could use it to strengthen his bargaining position with Hitler. But Churchill and the Foreign Office went on looking for common ground with the Soviet Union, especially over German military moves in the Balkans; and in the spring of 1941 Churchill made a point of trying to give Stalin advance warning of Hitler's intention to invade the Soviet Union. His warnings, like those of others, fell on deaf ears. Stalin did his best to propitiate Hitler as before. At the moment of Hitler's attack, therefore, Churchill had no cause to love the Soviet government, but had reached a hard-headed assessment of the value to Britain of Soviet involvement in the war against Hitler.

Eden had had no violent feelings about the Bolsheviks or the Soviet Union to overcome. In the 1930s his dealings with the Russians, as Minister of State for League of Nations affairs or as Foreign Secretary, had been at a time when the Russians seemed to want to play a constructive role in European affairs. In 1935 he had been sent by the Baldwin government to Moscow and had met Stalin. In the summer of 1939, when out of office, he suggested to Halifax that he should go to Moscow to help on the Anglo-Soviet talks; Halifax himself was unwilling to go, and Eden was the only British minister to have visited Stalin. Chamberlain did not agree and Churchill, when Eden told him what he had done, thought he had been unwise, since he would have been in a very difficult position as Chamberlain's emissary.[19]

So Eden had some reason, though not a strong one, for believing that he was well fitted to cultivate good relations with the Soviet leaders. He had in fact a certain reputation in Moscow, and was described at a public lecture there in 1944 as leader of the 'Young Conservatives' who advocated a progressive policy at home and international collaboration abroad; his 1935 visit was recalled and also his resignation of 1938 'when the adherents of the appeasement policy triumphed'.[20]

When Eden again became Foreign Secretary and was sent by Churchill to the Middle East and the Balkans at the beginning of 1941, Sir Stafford Cripps, then ambassador in Moscow, telegraphed to him: 'Is there any chance of your sparing a few days to come here on condition that I could arrange an interview for you with Stalin. . . ? I most strongly urge you to let me try and arrange such a meeting.' The idea must have appealed to Eden, but Churchill vetoed it with a 'most immediate' telegram: 'Do not act on Cripps's suggestion . . . without further reference here. . . . A mere visit would do no good. They might simply trade it off to Germany. I would hardly trust them for your personal safety or liberty.'[21] So Eden did not go.

Cripps went on trying to woo the Russians by hints that Britain might go some way towards recognising Soviet annexation of the Baltic States. Churchill wrote to Eden in April: 'None of this seems worth the trouble. . . . Now is the moment for a sombre restraint on our part, and let them do the worrying.' Eden replied that he had already made up his mind that nothing was to be gained from further attempts with Russia. On 8 May Eden told the War Cabinet that it would be a mistake to think Russia would resist any German demands unless they affected Stalin's position at home.[22]

By mid-June there seemed no doubt that Hitler was about to attack. On 19 June the War Cabinet discussed the line to be taken publicly if a Soviet–German war broke out. Churchill said that Germany should be presented as an insatiable tyrant that had attacked in order to obtain material for carrying on the war; the War Cabinet 'took note'. In the minutes there was no suggestion that he or Eden mooted the idea of going beyond this cool and noncommittal statement – perhaps not surprisingly, since three days earlier the Cabinet had been told that diplomats in Moscow believed that Russia could not hold out for more than three or four weeks.[23]

Yet when, on Sunday, 22 June, the Germans invaded Russia, both Churchill and Eden – together at Chequers – were carried away by a surge of excitement and hope which took them far beyond such aloof detachment. Churchill told Eden that he would broadcast to the nation that night saying that the Russians would be treated as Britain's partners in the struggle against Hitler; Eden, in accord, summoned the Soviet ambassador, Maisky, and assured him that Britain would intensify its war effort so as to help Russia,[24] and discussed an exchange of military missions.

So Churchill and Eden acted together, but on their own. The next day, Monday, Churchill told the War Cabinet that he had had to 'act quickly' and hoped they would approve the line he had taken in his broadcast; Eden was to make a statement in the House.[25] The War Cabinet raised no dissenting voice, and so Britain was launched impulsively, even enthusiastically, on a policy of open-hearted partnership with the Soviet Union.

It was a novel and daring policy. If Russia went under in a few weeks, as most though not all the military experts forecast, little would be lost. If the Russians survived and conquered, there were bound to be many political pitfalls and a vast strategic problem. Churchill and Eden were up against something very much bigger than they seem to have bargained for on 22 June. To cope with Stalin and a militarily successful Soviet Union, they needed firm, consistent co-operation with the U.S. and a united front at home.

It soon turned out that Roosevelt was an uncertain quantity where the Soviet Union was concerned. He was more unrealistic than the British ever were about Soviet aims and capabilities. On 26 June he wrote to his old friend, Leahy: 'Dear Bill, . . . Now comes this Russian diversion. If it is more than just that it will mean the liberation of Europe from Nazi domination. . . . I do not think we need worry about any possibility of Russian domination.'[26] In 1942 he wrote to the U.S. ambassador in Moscow: 'I have just a hunch that Stalin doesn't want anything but security for his country, and I think that if I give him everything I possibly can and ask nothing from him in return, *noblesse oblige*, he won't try to annex anything and will work for a world of democracy and peace.'[27] Roosevelt's carefree optimism made things difficult for Churchill and Eden. Though they could sometimes induce him to take a relatively stern line towards Stalin over Poland, they could never count on him for backing, let alone leadership, in firm dealing with the Soviet Union.

At home, too, they had problems. Inside their own party some Conservatives, especially the older men who had backed Chamberlain on appeasement, and also some younger men who had belonged to Eden's group and opposed appeasement, such as Duff Cooper or Selborne, put up strong resistance to concessions or conciliatory gestures towards Russia. Early in 1944 Eden wrote of the easily roused suspicion of Russia, 'never very far away in some sections of the Conservative Party'.[28] Moreover, Churchill himself was very sensitive to the feelings of Conservatives of this sort. Eden felt this factor to be a hindrance rather than a help.

Inside the War Cabinet Eden could not count on Attlee or Bevin to support him if he wanted to conciliate Stalin; both were sceptical and hard-headed in their view of the Soviet Union, Attlee on grounds of moral principle, both on the basis of their experience of dealing with Communists at home. On the day after Hitler invaded Russia Churchill suggested that Labour ministers should in their speeches go on drawing a 'line of demarcation' between Labour Party tenets and those of Communists. The Labour ministers agreed, and Attlee said he was going to stress this in a broadcast the next evening. The Home Secretary, Herbert Morrison, said he did not propose to withdraw the existing ban on the Communist *Daily Worker*. Two years later, when Stalin abolished the Comintern, the War Cabinet, with Attlee presiding and Bevin and Morrison taking part, decided it was 'undesirable' that the government should make known its views on this event; if Eden had to make a statement in the House, it should be purely factual.[29]

Yet if Attlee and Bevin were tough and realistic about the Soviet Union, Morrison, under the influence of Beaverbrook, who at one time wooed him and tried to set him up against Bevin, was later apt to be 'softer' than the other two Labour leaders. A fair number of the rank and file of the Labour Party were pro-Russian in a simple, high-minded way. Churchill wrote to Eden in 1944: 'I am getting a little tired of being told by the left wing that we have fallen behind their altruistic standards.'[30]

But much the strongest and most powerful champion of all-out aid and alliance with Russia was Beaverbrook, who at times had a certain influence over Churchill – according to his own account, even on Sunday, 22 June 1941, when Churchill was pondering on his broadcast.[31] Through his ownership of the *Daily Express*, his contacts with British factory-workers as Minister of Aircraft Production and his personal friendship with Roosevelt and other prominent Americans, he was in a position to embarrass Churchill considerably, at least during 1942 and the early months of 1943, especially by his intensive campaign for an early second front in the west to help Russia.

Eden, however, found Beaverbrook a useful ally in his effort to persuade Churchill and the Cabinet, in the early months of 1942, to recognise Stalin's territorial claims in the west. He wrote to him warmly and gratefully in February that he had counted on him much 'especially in our Russian affairs'.[32]

Yet Beaverbrook's enthusiasms were apt to be self-defeating. Politically he was too erratic, too much of an eccentric and a lone wolf, to carry great weight in Cabinet discussions. On the other hand, his influence on public opinion, both directly through his newspapers and by other means, was probably important. In the latter part of the war he formed a sort of private alliance with Brendan Bracken, originally the devoted personal follower of Churchill. Bracken, from the summer of 1941, was Minister of Information and could, up to a point, influence the Press and radio which, whether for this reason or from independent conviction, generally presented the British public with a picture of unclouded happy comradeship with Russia; there might be small squabbles here and there, but hopes for lasting friendship and co-operation were rosy. (Bracken had no need to exert influence in this direction on *The Times* which, guided on Soviet affairs by Professor E. H. Carr, argued at a high level of discourse for giving top long-term priority to the alliance with Russia.)

The Foreign Office took varying views at different times over the silence about the problems of relations with the Soviet Union. The head of the Northern Department, dealing with Russia, wrote in January 1944: 'We have suffered much from the suppression of all public criticism of the Russians, and if it went on it would surely lead to disaster. For it would mislead the Russians . . . and lead straight to a policy of appeasement.'[33] Yet a year later, when Churchill and Eden were seriously worried over Soviet actions in Poland and the Balkans, Sir Orme Sargent, arguing for a policy of abandoning at least part of this area to the Russians, found public ignorance a considerable advantage: 'The British public are not likely to know what is going on in countries in Russian occupation, for the censorship will prevent correspondents from reporting the true facts. For instance, the Press has not explained the true inwardness of the recent changes of government in Romania; nor has it reported on the blood bath in Bulgaria. . . .'[34] (These facts, which were well known to the Foreign Office, could of course have been released to the Press in London.)

The climate of opinion created by public ignorance of Soviet actions and the British government's fears for the future made it very difficult for Churchill and Eden to use publicity as a weapon against Stalin, as they sometimes thought of doing during the crucial months when the shape of post-war Europe was being moulded by force of arms. The facts, if revealed, would either have been disbelieved – and Churchill and Eden thereby discredited – or else the shock would have undermined people's readiness to carry on a long and weary war. At best it would have been a weak, uncertain weapon, but there were one or two occasions when Churchill or Eden threatened to use it, and it did in fact soften or sweeten Stalin, at least for the time being. Even after the fighting in Europe ended Churchill still had some faith in it. Writing to Eden over a torture case in Bulgaria for which he held the Russians responsible, he proposed threatening them with publication of the facts: 'The Soviet government has no wish to come out into the world smeared with such tales. Let them then behave and obey the ordinary decencies of civilisation.'[35]

But by that time Anglo-American military strategy and tactics had put the Soviet armies in a position where Stalin had no need to worry seriously about a little adverse publicity in the West.

Differences between Churchill and Eden over Stalin were tactical, or the product of momentary moods or circumstances, rather than matters of fundamental strategy. Eden liked it to be known in the Foreign Office that he sometimes thought differently from Churchill. In a personal letter to Clark Kerr in Moscow he wrote: 'As regards the Prime Minister and myself, personal relations have never been better. Of course we do not always see eye to eye on everything but you are already aware of that.'[36]

In the Northern Department of the Foreign Office there was some criticism of both Churchill and Eden for being over-excitable in their dealings with Stalin. Christopher Warner wrote in January 1944: 'It is very important . . . to try to get the great ones out of their habit of "extremes" about Russia. They must take things in their stride . . . the attitude of mind which throws the hat high in the air when Molotov and Joe turn on their kindly and responsive mood for the benefit of the Prime Minister and the Secretary of State, and gets in a flap whenever the Soviet Press is a bit naughty, is most prejudicial to a sound conduct of policy.' Another member of the department, Geoffrey Wilson, wrote that it was no use trying to deal with Russian affairs in a mood of high elation at one moment and black depression at another. He also wrote that at the top level there was little or no understanding of the problems or personalities concerned: 'The Prime Minister thought he could conduct a personal correspondence with Stalin on the same sort of family basis as that on which he conducts his personal correspondence with the President. Owing mainly to Stalin's failure to respond, it didn't come off. . . . Our hopes were pitched too high.'[37]

This judgement of Churchill's exchange of messages with Stalin was perhaps too harsh. But it is hard to guess what Stalin made of the stream of personal missives he got from Churchill from 1941 to 1945. Usually they were discussed in advance with Eden, sometimes actually prompted by Eden or the Foreign Office, who submitted their own drafts, which were redrafted by Churchill and often read to the War Cabinet before they were sent. In the early days Churchill tried to make Stalin feel that he was treating him with the same sort of openness and intimacy as he did Roosevelt. Unlike Roosevelt, he believed in telling Stalin bad news straight away, as over the delay of the second front or suspension of convoys to Russia, instead of beating about the bush and postponing the day of reckoning. He wrote to Eden in March 1943: 'My own instinct has always been to tell him the whole truth at once. . . . We might just as well be hanged for a sheep as a lamb.'[38] At the same time he believed in keeping Stalin well informed on the military actions of the western Allies, sending almost weekly reports, so as to get him to show some respect, and making a point of detailing British, as distinct from American, achievement. He also went out of his way to congratulate Stalin, in most flowery terms, on every Soviet military success; he also on occasion withheld such congratulation as a token of displeasure, as over the capture of Orel in 1943.

In all this he tried to fathom what sort of a man Stalin really was and how he could best influence him. He believed Stalin respected force of arms: before *Overlord* he felt in a weak position to exert pressure on him; after the victories in France he felt stronger, and was readier to take a strong line.[39] He tried to work towards some sort of personal friendship with Stalin, and this myth may for brief moments have had a fleeting reality. But Stalin was not the man to let himself yield to any such feeling and he could see clearly Britain's diminishing weight in the world power balance. It was pleasanter and more profitable to let himself be wooed by Roosevelt than to argue things out with Churchill.

Eden undoubtedly thought himself more level-headed in his approach to Stalin than Churchill was, and, so long as his senior officials were there to restrain him, this was true; when he was on his own in Moscow it was far from true. Until the very end both men swung between fear and hope, uncertain whether the Russians were predatory and greedy or simply uncouth and unpolished in their diplomatic manners. If in 1945 Churchill was the gloomier, this was because he was the war leader preoccupied with the military carve-up in Europe, while Eden was busy building a world organisation to keep the peace and thought Russia an essential pillar. Churchill thought the Iron Curtain more important than the U.N. Perhaps he was right.

CHAPTER SEVENTEEN

Stalin's acid test: the Soviet frontiers

Of the many hard problems of dealing with Stalin, Churchill and Eden were most at odds over recognition of Russia's western frontiers as established with Hitler's blessing after September 1939. On this Eden felt himself to be the hard-headed, far-sighted realist, who had somehow to persuade Churchill to face the distasteful and amoral facts of life with Stalin. Churchill especially disliked the idea of leaving the three tiny Baltic States to Stalin's mercies. Even more important was his partnership with Roosevelt, publicly celebrated in the Atlantic Charter, which in its ringing phrases set out to safeguard the weak and rule out territorial grabbing. Churchill gave more weight than Eden to partnership with America, Eden more weight than Churchill to partnership with Russia. Both were changeable, but this difference between them was constant.

What Stalin wanted from Britain, in 1941 and later, was first, military action to draw off German troops, and next, political recognition of Soviet territorial gains. Even when Russia was still neutral, Molotov had put pressure on Cripps over the Baltic States, at one moment turning on the heat by refusing to see him.[1]

For Eden, once Russia was in the war, there was a strong temptation to yield. He was personally under heavy pressure from Maisky for British military action, and Beaverbrook was egging Maisky on by suggesting that such action was possible. When a Soviet military mission arrived in London in July 1941 they brought a message from Stalin to Eden urging that Britain should draw some of the weight off Russia.[2]

Since all the British could do was to carry out heavier air attacks in the west, Stalin became more and more pressing. In early September Churchill told the War Cabinet that 'the possibility of a separate peace could not altogether be excluded', and he said the same thing to Roosevelt.[3] Beaverbrook – recommended to Stalin by Churchill as 'one of my oldest and most intimate friends' – and Averell Harriman went to Moscow to offer Anglo-U.S. supplies of war materials. Beaverbrook quickly reported that he had signed an agreement which had effected 'an immense strengthening of the morale of Moscow', and urged good coverage in the British Press. He also reported that Stalin had said he would like to see

Anglo-Soviet relations 'placed on a more permanent and satisfactory basis'.[4]

This was Eden's cue to move to the front of the stage. Something clearly was needed. In spite of the Beaverbrook–Harriman visit, the Soviet government was still dissatisfied and suspicious. Already in September Bevin had complained to the War Cabinet about Maisky running his own propaganda campaign to British workers to get them to work harder for Russia; Morrison said 'various bodies' seemed to be stirring up trouble against the government on the issue of help to Russia.[5]

From Moscow Cripps telegraphed in October: 'They [the Soviet leaders] are now obsessed with the idea that we are prepared to fight to the last drop of Russian blood as Germans suggest in their propaganda.' Churchill replied angrily to Cripps: 'They certainly have no right to reproach us. . . . If we had been invaded and destroyed in July or August 1940 . . . they would have remained entirely indifferent'; the Soviet accusation left him 'quite cold'.[6]

After some unpleasant Anglo-Soviet exchanges in November, Churchill sent Stalin a warm message: 'At the very beginning of the war I began a personal correspondence with President Roosevelt which has led to a very solid understanding. . . . My only desire is to work on equal terms of comradeship and confidence with you.' He suggested that, since Stalin wanted to discuss the post-war organisation of peace, Eden, whom he knew, should go to Moscow. He concluded:

> We expect that Soviet Russia, Great Britain and the U.S. will meet at council table of the victors as the three principal partners. . . . The fact that Russia is a Communist state and Britain and the U.S. are not and do not intend to be is not any obstacle to our making a good plan for our mutual safety and rightful interests.

Stalin, mollified, agreed to Eden's visit.[7]

So Eden was launched on his first big diplomatic mission of the war – and one which gave him a chance to wipe out the bad repute of his Balkan mission some nine months earlier. He told the War Cabinet that the important task would be to exorcise suspicion from Stalin's mind that Russia was to be excluded from 'an Anglo-American scheme for peace'. This could be done by a joint Anglo-Soviet declaration pledging collaboration in the peace settlement and making suitable allusions to the Atlantic Charter, which could be used to side-step the awkward question of Soviet territorial demands. The War Cabinet approved this plan as a basis for Eden's talks in Moscow, on the understanding that he would refer back if any changes were mooted and that he was to 'avoid being drawn into any precise discussions as regards territorial changes'.[8]

This left Eden with very little scope to sweeten Stalin's humour; so he eventually got Churchill to agree that he might offer the prospect of ten R.A.F. squadrons to fight in Russia. But then, just as he had set off for Moscow, the Japanese attacked the U.S. at Pearl Harbor; Churchill had to telegraph to Eden that this meant that ten squadrons could *not* be offered.[9] Soon after, he himself set off for the U.S. to co-ordinate strategy with Roosevelt.

So Eden met Stalin empty-handed. Nevertheless, his first message to Churchill was most hopeful: 'I believe that I have established friendly relations with Stalin. I am sure that he is entirely with us against Hitler. Our first day has been definitely good.'[10]

But Stalin was applying his usual treatment: first, a pleasing warmth (so thawing his visitor's defences); next, a piercing, icy blast; finally, a moderate glow, so that the visitor left grateful for small mercies. At their next meeting he told Eden that he was willing to leave Poland aside for separate Soviet–Polish negotiations, but he wanted clear commitments on the Baltic States, Finland and Romania, not any vague declarations. He also proposed a 'secret protocol' on the future shape of Europe, on which he had fairly precise ideas.

Attlee reported this to the War Cabinet on 19 December, adding that Eden had offered to discuss the proposals with his colleagues and the Americans on his return home; this, however, had not satisfied the Russians who said that, unless the British recognised the Soviet frontiers, they would not sign any joint declaration. Eden had asked urgently for the view of the Cabinet and, if possible, Churchill too.

All members of the War Cabinet present – that included Bevin – agreed that no such commitment could be given to the Russians; there was the Atlantic Charter and the British promise to the U.S. at that time that they would make no secret commitments. The Cabinet sent Eden a telegram saying this and adding that Eden could go no further than he had already done; but this did not mean that Britain would necessarily oppose Soviet claims at the peace.[11]

Churchill, on his way to the U.S., sent Eden a telegram saying the same thing more forcibly: to approach Roosevelt with such proposals would be 'to court a blank refusal and might experience lasting trouble'. But he advised Eden not to be 'rough' with Stalin, and threw in some fatherly comfort: 'Do not be disappointed if you are not able to bring home a joint public declaration. . . . I am sure your visit has done utmost good and your attitude will win general approval. This voyage seems very long.'[12]

So Eden left Moscow with nothing but a rather nebulous communiqué to show for his pains. But at their last meeting he also left Stalin with the impression that within two or three weeks he, Eden, would be able to clear matters up and then an Anglo-Soviet treaty – covering frontier questions – could be signed.

This, however, was quite out of the question, as Eden found when he got home. With baseless optimism he telegraphed to Churchill urging him to take up with the Americans the case for 'immediate recognition' of the Soviet 1941 frontiers, on the basis of 'stark realism'. This was needed to get really close and intimate collaboration with Russia; in any case, nothing the British or Americans could do would stop the Russians from getting what they wanted at the end of the war.

Churchill sent a snorting reply. The 1941 frontiers had been acquired by acts of aggression in shameful collusion with Hitler. Eden had said that recognition was for Stalin 'the acid test of our sincerity'; 'I on the contrary regard our sincerity involved in the maintenance of the principles of the Atlantic Charter . . . on this also we depend for our association with the U.S.A.' At the end of the war Britain and the U.S. might be the most powerfully armed economic bloc the world had ever seen and Russia would need their aid. Any government which he, Churchill, headed would stand by the principles of freedom and democracy in the Atlantic Charter.[13]

Eden did not give up hope; Maisky prodded him with hints that Stalin was getting impatient and the two or three weeks' time limit was long past. When Churchill was back home Eden put a paper to the War Cabinet arguing that it would be wise to get on good terms with the Soviet Union quickly since at the end of the war Russian prestige would be so great that 'the establishment of Communist governments in the majority of European countries will be greatly facilitated'. It would be difficult to harmonise Anglo-Russian co-operation with Anglo-American co-operation and, if forced to choose, the British would no doubt choose the U.S.; but Stalin's demands were not unreasonable and the arguments for accepting them were overwhelming – but for the Atlantic Charter and U.S. opposition.[14]

Churchill did not like this, writing to Eden, 'Would it not be wise for you to discuss the matter with me first?' But when the War Cabinet discussed Eden's paper Beaverbrook flung himself into the fray saying that, subject to U.S. views, Stalin's request should be accepted; no time should be lost in holding out a hand of friendship. Moreover, Beaverbrook said, Russia had so far contributed far more to the war effort than the U.S.

Eden argued the same case less dramatically. Attlee took flatly the opposite view: Eden's proposal was dangerous and might 'stultify the causes for which we were fighting'. As soon as one claim had been agreed there would be others, and pressure for concessions right and left; this might have a serious effect on British morale. Bevin, too, wanted to know whether Stalin's claim could be regarded as his ultimate aim. Eden said yes, Stalin had been quite specific. Morrison took a line rather nearer to Beaverbrook's than to his Labour colleagues'. The debate ended in a draw: Eden was told to send Washington a 'balanced statement' giving the reasons for and against accepting the Soviet demands.[15]

This was not good enough for Beaverbrook, who immediately put in a paper to the Cabinet saying it was 'flinching from our clear responsibility' to avoid making a clear recommendation to the U.S. that Stalin's demands should be met. If the Cabinet could not agree, 'may we not appeal to public opinion, so that the people may settle the deliberation on our behalf?' (Beaverbrook would, of course, have been well placed to influence opinion through his papers.) According to his own account, 'this plan was resented by Mr Bevin and denounced by the P.M.', and there were threats of resignation by Attlee on one side and Beaverbrook himself on the other.[16]

Nobody resigned, but Beaverbrook returned yet again to the charge on 19 February with a memorandum arguing that Britain was bound by Churchill's broadcast of 22 June 1941 to concede Stalin's 'rightful frontier claims'. But by this time Churchill had had enough and gave instructions that this paper was not to be circulated to the War Cabinet but 'put by'.[17]

Perhaps Churchill had at first hoped that Roosevelt would put a quick end to Eden's proposal for recognising the 1941 frontiers. But if the British approach to the Americans was cautious and oblique, the American response was also oblique. On 19 February Halifax reported that he had at last had a chance of discussing the matter with Roosevelt, who thought it was 'largely a question of presentation'; it would be desirable not to get into too much detail since this would involve a secret treaty. The next day, however, he had to report that Roosevelt, now mildly indisposed, seemed to have gone back on what he had said: he was now confident that he himself could reach agreement direct with Stalin, and proposed to do so through the Soviet ambassador in Washington, Maxim Litvinov.

This at least was what the Under-Secretary of State, Sumner Welles, told Halifax. Halifax commented to Welles that this put Eden in a difficult position since it was with Britain, not America, that Stalin wanted to sign a treaty. Welles replied that the American people were going through an 'emotional cycle': they were ready to make any sacrifice for principles which would mean a better world, but any departure from these would be disastrous.[18]

Churchill took this quite cheerfully, telling the War Cabinet that he thought it would be of advantage to Britain that Roosevelt should handle the matter. The opposite view was also expressed – that Russia wanted agreement with Britain, not with the U.S. Eden proposed a compromise: that he should propose to the U.S. ambassador in London, Winant, that there should be three-power talks in London. This Churchill accepted.[19] But there was no immediate American response.

Eden then won over Churchill to the final step – a direct appeal to Roosevelt – persuading him to send him a message on 7 March. In this Churchill still referred in an aloof way to 'the Foreign Office view about Russia', but went on:

> The increasing gravity of the war has led me to feel that the principles of the Atlantic Charter ought not to be constructed so as to deny Russia the frontiers she occupied when Germany attacked her. . . . I hope therefore that you will be able to give us a free hand to sign the treaty which Stalin desires as soon as possible. . . . The weight of the war is very heavy now, and I must expect it to get steadily worse for some time to come.[20]

A few days later Halifax learned from Welles that Roosevelt was going ahead with his idea of talking to the Soviet ambassador; he commented that this was 'in the highest degree embarrassing' since the British were the people principally concerned. Roosevelt in effect told Litvinov that Stalin should trust him to safeguard Soviet interests at the end of the war; Litvinov then asked what would happen if Roosevelt were then no longer President.[21]

Here Beaverbrook took a hand in the game once again. After a number of threats – not seriously meant – he had actually resigned from the government, mainly to be free to pursue his campaign for a second front. Now, with Churchill's private blessing, he set out for Washington to try to persuade Roosevelt to give way over Russia's 1941 frontiers. Or so, at least, he informed Stalin personally in a message sent from his home in Surrey on 19 March; he also asked Stalin to arrange for Litvinov to pass messages between them secretly. Churchill also sent a message to

Stalin saying that Beaverbrook had gone to 'help smooth out the treaty question'.[22]

But Beaverbrook failed. He told Churchill that Roosevelt was afraid of difficult and even dangerous political repercussions at home if he could be accused of 'selling Balts down river'. In early April the situation took a new turn with the arrival of General Marshall and Harry Hopkins in London to press for British agreement to an early second front, or assault on the Continent. The British embassy in Washington thought one reason why Roosevelt was so keen on this was to give Stalin satisfaction without conceding the 1941 frontiers.[23]

Stalin cut through the Anglo-American tangle by proposing that Molotov should visit London to negotiate a treaty, thereafter accepting Roosevelt's invitation to Washington to discuss the second front. Roosevelt chipped in with a message to Stalin that Molotov should go to the U.S. first. When Churchill was told this the worm turned; he wrote to Roosevelt that he could not now suggest to Molotov a change in the order of his visits; he would, however, suggest that Molotov should go on to Washington before anything was finally settled.[24]

Stalin and Molotov must have been puzzled by seeming British subservience to American wishes. Perhaps they thought that the clever Churchill was using Roosevelt's feelings as an excuse for getting out of the promise that Eden seemed to have made.

The reality was different. By the time Molotov arrived in London the British had reached the point of being willing to face Roosevelt's displeasure and public criticism in the U.S. If Molotov, trying to strike too hard a bargain, had not raised his price too high, he might have got a treaty recognising the 1941 frontiers.

For Churchill, however, it would have been a hard decision. At this point he seemed even more influenced by signs of revolt at home than by Roosevelt's disapproval. At the end of April Churchill sent Eden a report from his Parliamentary Private Secretary that there had been leaks about the proposed treaty, especially in so far as this concerned the Baltic States, and there were hostile comments inside the Conservative Party that 'this is Munich over again but worse'; the foreign affairs committee were planning to tackle Eden; the matter could become a major crisis. Eden thought the report exaggerated. But a few days later John Simon, now Lord Chancellor, wrote a long and lofty letter to Churchill saying he was deeply disturbed, particularly since he understood that the Americans refused to be parties to any such bargain. He ended with a warning that, if the matter were debated in the House of Lords, he might not defend the treaty.

This, too, Churchill sent to Eden, saying it was a serious letter. Eden, perhaps indignant at such an attack from a 'man of Munich', replied that he would rather talk to Churchill privately than write. But then he got a further note from Churchill: 'I do not want to face a bunch of resignations. The Lord Chancellor and Mr Duff Cooper from very different angles have expressed strongest objections.'[25]

The next attack came from the Conservatives' foreign affairs committee, who sent a 'deputation' to Eden demanding an explanation; although he put up a strong case, the deputation was not satisfied. At a subsequent meeting the committee said the government should have got the consent of the House of Commons before agreeing to any recognition of the Soviet frontiers, and they thought the result in the country would be disastrous. Eden told Churchill he thought reports of the committee's feelings were exaggerated.[26]

A further warning was shot across Eden's bows by Cardinal Hinsley, the Catholic Archbishop of Westminster, through Desmond Morton, who told Churchill that the Cardinal wanted him to know of his 'profound apprehensions' about 'a treaty of a certain kind' with Moscow. He would keep silent if he possibly could, even if he felt the treaty to be very wrong, but he would 'almost certainly' be forced into the open and compelled to denounce it in strong terms. It would, moreover, produce a wave of anti-British feeling in Catholic circles in Spain, France and America. This, too, Churchill passed to Eden.[27]

Yet another warning came from James Stuart, the Conservative Chief Whip, who told Churchill on 22 May that, though Eden might be able to show that the treaty was essential for the prosecution of the war, he was disturbed about its possible political repercussions; 'the impression may be given that our pro-Russian sympathies have carried us away to an extent which will disturb American and Polish opinion'.[28] (Eden himself believed that it was the Polish exiled government, working through a close friend of General Sikorski, Victor Cazalet, who were responsible for much of the agitation inside the Conservative Party.[29])

A year and a half later Churchill wrote to Eden that it should be remembered that the reason why they had sheered off agreeing to Stalin's territorial demands had been 'the perfectly clear menace of very considerable division of opinion in the House of Commons'.[30] Just how serious this division really was, was never put to the test. But it must have taken Eden a good deal of political courage to face Molotov, when he at last arrived, and try to negotiate a treaty including recognition of the 1941 frontiers, apart from Poland. He was perhaps considerably relieved when Molotov raised new demands – for British agreement to Soviet bases in Romania and Finland, and for tacit British withdrawal of its public non-recognition of the 1941 Soviet–Polish frontier.

This gave Eden an opening to put forward an alternative proposal – which was Cadogan's invention – for a twenty-year treaty of mutual assistance which contained no mention of frontiers but promised post-war co-operation. He can have had little hope that Molotov would accept it. In the event he – or, rather, Stalin – did. During the talks Molotov had asserted that there was no foundation for saying that U.S. opinion was against recognition of the 1941 frontiers: 'There were friendly elements in America who would certainly not raise any objections.'[31] But the U.S. ambassador, Winant, with whom Eden was in close touch, convinced Molotov – as Eden could not – that there really were strong American objections. This – no doubt coupled with Soviet expectation that Roosevelt would give a firm promise of a second front, which Churchill had not – decided the day. Stalin authorised Molotov to drop the 1941 frontiers and sign the twenty-year treaty before going to Washington.

Everyone was happy. Eden had the personal triumph of which he had been robbed on his Moscow visit; Churchill told the War Cabinet – with Simon present – that they were greatly indebted to the Foreign Secretary for the successful upshot.[32] All danger of a parliamentary revolt vanished.

Eden, in the glow of success, told the War Cabinet that relations with the Soviet Union were now on an entirely different and far more satisfactory footing. In fact, they were just entering a particularly difficult phase. Roosevelt, assuming (with some justification) that when Marshall and Hopkins had visited London in the spring the British had been firmly committed to a second front in the west in 1942, gave Molotov the firm pledge on this point which Churchill had carefully not given. What was more, Roosevelt made the pledge public, without warning Churchill. Churchill then had to tell Molotov, on his way home from Washington, that as far as the British were concerned no large-scale operation in the West was possible before April 1943.[33]

This was enough to sharpen Stalin's suspicions. In July came the Anglo-American decision to carry out *Torch* and to drop the idea of even a minor operation in the west in 1942, such as Churchill had still thought possible when he talked to Molotov in June. Churchill, after asking Roosevelt to let Harriman come with him, went to Moscow himself to break the news to Stalin. When he got back he told the War Cabinet that he thought he had established relations with Stalin which would make Anglo-Soviet co-operation easier. To Roosevelt he wrote: 'I am sure the disappointing news I brought could not have been imparted except by me personally without leading to really serious drifting apart.'[34] This must have been very irritating for Roosevelt: in April, without telling Churchill, he had proposed that he and Stalin should meet, but Stalin had said he could not. Roosevelt was to make two more unsuccessful efforts to arrange a meeting with Stalin before the three-power conference at Tehran.

In the winter of 1942–3 Anglo-Soviet relations got into difficulties – not over the general question of Russia's western frontiers, but over the specific question of Poland, and the exiled government's total refusal to recognise the 1941 frontiers. When Eden visited Washington in March 1943 he talked about this and also the wider frontier question with Roosevelt, who led off by asking if Eden thought Russia would want to Communise all Europe after the war. Eden answered that he did not think so and, anyhow, the best way to avoid it was to keep on good terms with Russia. Roosevelt, so Eden told the War Cabinet, seemed to have reconciled himself to the Russians getting the Baltic States. He also thought Soviet terms for Finland reasonable. As for Poland, Roosevelt thought the Big Three should unite in settling fair terms and then persuade the exiled government to accept them.[35]

It seems clear that from the time of his talks with Litvinov in April 1942 Roosevelt had felt that he could deal easily enough with all awkward frontier questions if he could only talk to Stalin face to face. He could then explain, as one politician to another, that Stalin could count on him not to make any trouble about the 1941 frontiers, but could not expect him to say so publicly until the war's end because of the political problems it would stir up inside the U.S. (or the votes it might lose him in the 1944 presidential election).

However, in the sumer of 1943 Stalin went on blocking Roosevelt's suggestions for a private meeting. But he eventually agreed to a meeting of the three Foreign Ministers – Eden, Molotov, Hull – in Moscow in October.

For this Eden prepared with the utmost diligence. (General Ismay, who went with him to Moscow, wrote later that he had earlier thought Eden one of fortune's darlings, attributing his meteoric success to charm and a lucky flair; Moscow proved him wrong, since Eden was extremely thorough and had every aspect of a problem at his fingertips.[36]) As part of his preparations, Eden got the Foreign Office to write for him a detailed paper on Russia's western frontiers to go before the Cabinet.

In this Eden recalled that in December 1941 Stalin had told him that he regarded the frontier question as the main question in the war for the Soviet Union; he believed this was still the Soviet view. On the Baltic States, Eden said that in the negotiations with Molotov in 1942 the British had already committed themselves to accepting the Soviet claim. He suggested that in Moscow he should have 'exploratory' talks and tell Molotov that, while Britain did not propose to recognise territorial changes, they would, when the right moment came, raise no objection to the Soviet claim to the 1941 frontiers in the Baltic States, Finland and Romania. Poland was a special case, but on this, too, Eden thought he should 'explore' the position in Moscow, in preparation for the coming Big Three meeting to which Stalin had now agreed. There, Eden thought Roosevelt would be more forthcoming than Hull.[37]

Churchill was taken aback by Eden's paper, and reminded him of the division in parliamentary opinion at the time of the 1942 treaty negotiations: 'I know of no reason for supposing that this same opposition might not manifest itself again, perhaps in an even stronger form. The opponents would have the advantage of invoking very large principles against us.' At a peace conference things would look different. Also, it was important to get the American attitude clear before going beyond the 1942 Anglo-Soviet treaty. Churchill also produced his own 'notes' for Eden (and the Cabinet), declaring that all territorial transfers must be settled at the peace table. But he then added a broad hint to the Russians that all would be well when the time came: Britain reaffirmed the Atlantic Charter, 'noting that Russia's accession thereto is based upon the frontiers of 22 June 1941'. The War Cabinet had a long and rather rambling discussion, concentrating mainly on the special Polish problem.[38] But the Polish exiled government begged Eden not to discuss this at Moscow; and, in the event, the frontier question did not come up there at all, so Eden's preparatory work was wasted.

At Tehran Eden tried to do some hard bargaining with Stalin over the future Soviet–Polish frontier; but Churchill, when it came to the point, let him down over the disputed city of Lwów.[39] As for Russia's other western frontiers, the progress of the war and the strategic decisions reached at Tehran – not all pleasing to Churchill – made it certain that, whatever the British thought, the Russians would – as Eden had forecast in January 1942 – get what they wanted and perhaps a good deal more.

Perhaps this was in Churchill's mind when, after his convalescence at Marrakesh, he wrote to Eden on 16 January 1944 on the frontier question:

> I ask myself, how do all these matters stand now? Undoubtedly my own feelings have changed in the two years that have passed since the topic was first raised during your first visit to Moscow. The tremendous victories of the Russian armies, the deep-seated changes which have taken place in the character of the Russian state and government, the new confidence which has grown in our hearts towards Stalin – these have all had their effects.

The question of the Baltic States and the disputed territories in Romania had 'very largely settled themselves through the victories of the Russian armies; there remained the Polish frontier, which now had to be tackled for urgent practical reasons. It would be far better to shelve it all until after the defeat of Hitler, but this might well not be possible. What did Eden think?'[40]

Eden replied that all the areas in question were part of the former Tsarist Russia, except for northern Bukovina (in Romania). Eden went on: 'I am convinced . . . that we should agree to all these claims.' Nobody would mind about Romania or Finland; as for the Baltic States, it would be better not to recognise formally before a peace settlement, 'otherwise we should certainly have a clamour here and abroad'. He suggested telling Stalin that the British would not dispute Soviet claims, but warning him that they would go on saying that all territorial matters would have to be finally settled at the peace settlement.[41]

No action was taken. In late March Churchill, in a different mood, wrote to Eden in a different spirit: 'What are we to say to our Parliaments and nations about modifications in the Atlantic Charter? We are being blamed today for departing from idealistic principles. Actually all this is done for the sake of Russia, who is resolved to seize the Baltic States and take what she wishes from Poland and Romania. Nor do we know that a second series of demands may not follow her further military victories.' The next day he wrote again: 'This question is of the greatest importance. At present H.M.G., and in particular you and I, are being abused for weak departures from the Atlantic Charter. The left wing are taking a prominent part in this.'

Eden replied: 'Our powers of leverage are, I am afraid, much weakened by the fact that we have, either in public or in private, already acquiesced in the strength of their claims to the Baltic States and Bessarabia. . . .'[42] By this time, because of the Red Army's advance westwards, the problem was quickly becoming academic.

*

Perhaps it had always been academic. Eden had argued that early recognition of the 1941 frontiers would purchase Stalin's good will, which would be valuable in a post-war Europe wholly or partly dominated by Russia. But it can easily be argued (as Churchill sometimes did) that Stalin would merely have swallowed the recognition, remained deeply suspicious of Britain, and asked for more. On the other side it can, less easily, be argued that in 1942 Stalin still had a slightly open mind and a real interest in coming to terms with Britain, and that recognition might have inclined him to choose Churchill as his chief partner. Roosevelt, however, was determined that he himself should be Stalin's chosen partner and that he, not Churchill, should be the one to purchase Stalin's good will. In this Anglo-American tangle Eden had no chance to prove his theory right or wrong.

CHAPTER EIGHTEEN

Churchill's touchstone: Poland

The frontier question may or may not have been for Stalin the acid test of British sincerity. For Churchill, as he once wrote, Russian treatment of Poland was a touchstone of Anglo-Soviet relations.[1] As such, it absorbed a great deal of the time, trouble and energy of both Churchill and Eden.

Britain's strategic or economic interests in Poland were very small. Churchill once wrote to Stalin that Britain had no 'sordid or material interests' there.[2] Stalin probably did not believe him and may have thought that Britain was hoping to use Poland as a jumping-off ground in a future war against the Soviet Union, but there is no evidence that any such idea ever occurred to Churchill or Eden. The commitment to Poland was a matter of political honour and human feeling, which had its origin in Chamberlain's sudden impulse, in April 1939, to give Poland a guarantee which Britain was totally unable to fulfil. When Hitler attacked Poland all Britain could do was to declare war on Germany – which did nothing to stop Hitler overrunning the larger part of Poland and handing over the rest to the Soviet Union. The unfulfilled guarantee left the British with a sense of obligation to see an independent Poland restored, if not necessarily with the pre-1939 frontiers.

Britain did not, like the U.S., have seven million people of Polish origin whose votes could sway election results. But during the war there were up to 40,000 Polish soldiers, airmen and others in Britain who made many friends. The exiled government in London energetically cultivated good contacts in high places. If Churchill or Eden had wanted to 'betray' the Poles, they would have had to face a strong backlash in Parliament and in their own Conservative Party.

Pro-Polish feelings existed in the Labour Party too, although not far to the Left. Of those who were against the 'London Poles', the best placed were Churchill's friends Beaverbrook and, at least in 1944, Bracken, who at the time of the Warsaw rising in 1944 wrote of the Poles as 'a feckless race', while Beaverbrook wrote to Eden: 'The Poles have always been unsatisfactory . . . their war effort has been consistently over-valued . . . they have exhibited anti-semitism in a virulent form.' He added that friendship with Russia was far more important than Anglo-Polish relations.[3]

Both Churchill and Eden were personally sympathetic to the Poles, even though they found individual members of the London government infuriating and destructive, not only of Anglo-Soviet relations but also of Poland's hopes for the future. Eden, rather earlier than Churchill, concluded that the exiled government must give way over the frontier with the Soviet Union; but once Churchill became convinced that this must be done he was ready to bully the London Poles more fiercely than Eden could ever do.

Churchill did this, however, not to please Stalin but because he thought it the only way to save any chance of an independent Poland – also to get a seemingly decent solution to put to Parliament. At moments, Churchill seemed ready to risk an open quarrel with Stalin; Eden would go some way in this direction, but would then pull Churchill back from the brink. For both men, what clinched the matter was British helplessness, in military terms, to do anything to stop Stalin getting what he wanted in Poland. Publicity was the only weapon, and it was an uncertain and double-edged one.

In spite of – or because of – Roosevelt's seven million voters, Britain had to take the lead and carry the baby in the Polish–Soviet problem. Roosevelt, though he wanted a power of veto over British action, was well content not to carry the public responsibility. Whoever carried that was bound to be unpopular all round.

The moment Churchill welcomed the Soviet Union as a war partner in June 1941, Eden started trying to bring the Polish exiled government and the Russians together. A special problem – in addition to the frontier question – was the many thousands of Poles inside Russia, in prison camps or suffering other unpleasant fates. Because of the (comparative) realism of the prime minister, General Wladyslaw Sikorski, and at the cost of several resignations from his government, a Polish–Soviet agreement was signed at the end of July. This covered the problem of the Poles in the Soviet Union but left the frontier question open; however, Eden had to get the War Cabinet's approval for a written assurance that the British government did not recognise territorial changes made since August 1931.[4] This embarrassed the British when they later strove to get the Poles to agree to the Curzon line (laid down by the Lloyd George government in the Polish–Soviet conflict of 1920).

A much more important factor in the frontier question was the powerful and highly organised underground movement inside Poland, in close contact with the London government, from 1940 through S.O.E., with the unique privilege (until early 1944) of independent cyphers. The underground was dead against any frontier concession at all, and this tied the hands of the London government and blocked all British efforts for a Polish–Soviet compromise on the frontier.

From July 1941 on Eden felt a personal responsibility for trying to make the Polish–Soviet agreement work. The problem of the Poles in Russia was partly solved by getting Stalin to let some of them leave for the Middle East, where the British eventually equipped about 80,000 Poles who later fought with distinction in Italy and elsewhere. But because the London government felt obliged from time to time to assert their claim to the pre-1939 frontier, Stalin's hostility revived and in late 1942 he took retaliatory measures against the Poles still in Russia; his aim, so the Foreign Office thought, was to force the London government to accept the Curzon line.

During the early months of 1943 tension between the Russians and the London Poles grew unpleasantly, though Eden tried to smooth things down. In February Sikorski wrote to Churchill asking him to help in getting better treatment for the Poles in Russia. Churchill liked Sikorski and thought him the best of the exiled Poles, but hesitated to intervene personally. He wrote to Cadogan in early April: 'At the present time my influence is not supported by a sufficient military contribution to the common cause to make my representations effective.'[5]

Meanwhile, Eden, visiting Washington, was told by Roosevelt that, if the Poles got East Prussia and perhaps 'some concessions' in Silesia, they would gain rather than lose by accepting the Curzon line; the Big Three should agree on a just solution at the appropriate time and this the Poles would have to accept. Rather unwisely, Cadogan passed on these 'stray thoughts' of Roosevelt's to the Soviet ambassador.[6]

But the immediate problem was the Poles in Russia. When Eden got home he urged Churchill to send Stalin a message asking him to let another 50,000 leave. It was at this moment that the Katyn time-bomb exploded.

On 15 April Churchill had Sikorski to lunch. Sikorski told him that German propaganda was making great play with the alleged discovery near Smolensk of a common grave containing the corpses of large numbers of Polish officers. He also gave Churchill a paper setting out facts about Polish officers missing in Russia.

So the riddle of Katyn was set: had the Poles in the mass grave been killed by the Russians while they occupied the area between late 1939 and the summer of 1941, or by the Germans after they overran it in their invasion of Russia? Churchill's immediate response was to say that this was an obvious German propaganda move to sow discord between the

Allies; he had fullest sympathy with Poland, but the Poles should give no 'unnecessary provocation'. Yet there seems small doubt that from the start he believed the Russians responsible for Katyn. He inserted in the record of his talk with Sikorski, after his remark about German propaganda: 'I may observe however that the facts are pretty grim.'[7]

From Moscow, Clark Kerr commented: 'In a horrible way it seems to fit in with the Poles' story of the disappearance of 8,300 officers. . . . Anger and unconvincing terms of Russian denials suggest a sense of guilt. . . . It is uncomfortable to reflect upon the consequences of an enquiry which might show the guilt was there.'[8] It does not seem from the available British records that either Churchill or Eden ever said they disbelieved the German story.

But equally, neither ever thought of allowing the Katyn tragedy to upset Anglo-Soviet relations or to destroy the chances of Soviet–Polish reconciliation. They persuaded the London Poles to tone down their public statements and withdraw their request to the International Red Cross to investigate Katyn, which had infuriated Stalin who, in a message to Churchill, accused the Sikorski government of having 'contact and understanding' with Hitler in an anti-Soviet campaign, so delivering a treacherous blow to the Soviet Union.[9]

Churchill's one idea was to persuade both Poles and Russians to forget the past and look to the future. Eden told the War Cabinet on 19 April that the Poles were 'greatly upset' but that he, like Churchill, was trying to persuade them to treat it as a German propaganda move (which was different from saying it was untrue). The Cabinet's view was that the Poles should not let this 'incident' divert them from efforts to get the Russians to let the remaining Polish troops and their families go to the Middle East.[10]

A week later Churchill told the Cabinet that the Soviet Union had decided to break off relations with the London government. He and Eden, he said, had just seen Sikorski and urged him 'to ignore what had happened or might have happened before the Russo-Polish treaty', and to concentrate on improving future relations and getting the Poles out of the Soviet Union. (This way of dating the Katyn 'incident' was weighted on the side of belief, rather than disbelief, in the German version.) Eden said that Stalin might refuse to restore relations with the London Poles until they had accepted Soviet frontier demands; possibly he might set up an alternative Polish government under 'Soviet influence'.[11]

Churchill begged Stalin to stay his hand about breaking relations with the London Poles; Stalin refused, saying he was 'obliged to take into account the public opinion of the Soviet Union which is deeply indignant at the ingratitude and treachery of the Polish government'.[12]

Churchill also saw Maisky and said: 'Grim things happen in war; this affair of the missing Polish officers was indeed grim.' But if they were dead they could not be resurrected; it was the living Poles in Russia that mattered. Maisky, in Churchill's view, 'felt acutely the Russian position and his attitude was one of appeal alternating with bluster'. He harped on the fecklessness of the Polish government who 'could not understand the folly of a nation of 20 million provoking one of nearly 200 m.', and (with an unconscious echo of Hitler) added that Russia's patience was not inexhaustible.[13]

Churchill's feelings about Katyn were perhaps most clearly revealed in a minute to Eden of 28 April: 'There is no use prowling morbidly round the three-year-old graves of Smolensk.'[14] So in his own mind he accepted that the killing dated back to 1940, when the Russians were in possession of the area, not to a later date when the Germans had overrun it.

Nevertheless, after a great deal of discussion with Eden and drafting and re-drafting, he sent Stalin a message on 28 April which contained no hint of this belief: 'Eden and I have pointed out to the Polish government that no resumption of friendly or working relations with Soviet Russia is possible while they make charges of an insulting character against the Soviet government and thus seem to countenance the atrocious Nazi propaganda.' He appealed for 'patient discussion' about the release of the remaining Poles in Russia, and also fired a carefully calculated and discreet warning shot about any idea of forming a Moscow-based Polish government, also expressing an equally discreet hope for a restoration of relations with the London government.[15]

This inspired Molotov to tell Clark Kerr that the idea of a Soviet-based Polish government was a libel put out by German propaganda and fostered by pro-Hitler elements among the Poles.[16] So the warning shot had worked for the time being. But Stalin obviously had no intention of restoring relations with the London Poles until they had recognised the Curzon line.

Whatever Churchill or Eden felt about Katyn, they were not going to let it wreck relations with Stalin. At the beginning of May Churchill telegraphed to Clark Kerr: 'I think it would be a pity that our Polish discussions with Stalin should interrupt the more or less weekly flow of friendly messages I have been sending him about operations. I am sure these give him pleasure and maintain our indispensable contact.' He also suggested that Clark Kerr should try a joke on Stalin: 'I should like him to give me a fighting Pole for every German I catch in Tunisia . . . and a Polish dependent, woman or child, for every Italian.' Churchill added that such jokes were in questionable taste but had their uses. (However, he got Eden's approval before sending off the telegram.)

Clark Kerr tried the questionable joke on Stalin; Molotov had to explain it to him, but he then 'got a good laugh' and said that no Italian was worth a Polish woman, so the deal would not be fair on him.[17]

With that Churchill put Katyn behind him, until a greater Polish tragedy exploded – the Warsaw rising, which put his would-be friendship with Stalin at serious risk.

The rising was launched at the end of July 1944 by the Polish underground army just when the Red Army seemed about to reach the city. For a long time past Eden had feared a clash between the underground army and the Russians. As early as October 1943 he put a paper to the Cabinet stating that there was a 'secret army' of about 65,000 men in close contact with the London government. The British had not armed it adequately except for sabotage purposes. Both the London government and the British had advised against premature revolt, seeing the secret army's role as keeping order and discipline during and after liberation. But the Moscow-controlled Polish Communist Party, working with Soviet paratroops and partisans, was inciting immediate action. When the Soviet army reached the pre-1939 Polish frontier they might try to break up the underground organisation, if it came into the open and offered collaboration, 'thus facilitating any designs they may have of running Poland in their own way'. Eden's solution was to try to resolve the frontier question before the Russians entered Poland.[18]

The Tehran conference blighted Eden's hopes. On the frontier, Churchill and Roosevelt both let Stalin understand that they had no objection to the Curzon line – when Eden tried to argue that the Poles should have Lwów, Churchill said he was not going to 'make a great squawk about Lwów' – and Churchill also made it clear that he was going to bully the London Poles into accepting it, which was much easier said than done. Stalin for his part launched a bitter attack on the underground army, declaring they were in contact with the Germans and killing partisans. Neither Roosevelt nor Churchill could have any idea what was going on in Poland. Stalin wanted a guarantee that the Polish government would urge the Poles to fight the Germans instead of 'indulging in machinations'.[19]

So Stalin had thrown down the gauntlet both to the London government and to the underground movement. Throughout the first half of 1944 both Churchill and Eden tried very hard both to get the London government to accept the Curzon line and so restore relations with the Soviet Union, and also – which was even more urgent – to get some sort of co-operation established between the underground army and the advancing Red Army, as it crossed first the pre-1939 and then the 1941 frontiers. The task had been made all the more difficult by Sikorski's death in an air crash in July 1943. His successor, Stanislaw Mikolajczyk, the Peasant Party leader, found it harder to influence the extreme anti-Soviet members of his government, still more the underground army, which saw itself as controlling the London government, not the reverse.[20] In April there was, briefly, successful co-operation between the underground and the Red Army in one area of eastern Poland, but a German counter-attack soon stopped it.[21]

In early May Moscow was denouncing the Polish underground as traitors who were torturing and shooting Polish patriots. This provoked Churchill to an outburst to Eden: 'I fear that very great evil may come upon the world. . . . The Russians are drunk with victory and there is no length they may not go.' He also wanted to send Molotov a warning:

> One of the greatest obstacles to Anglo-Soviet friendship and collaboration is the Soviet opinion that we will put up with anything. I have the honour to assure you this is not the case. If you want wordy warfare to begin between our two countries on the subject of Poland, you have only to continue the present declarations of the Moscow radio. . . . We shall start telling our own people and the world, which will listen, not only on the broadcast but in Parliament.[22]

But this did not suit Eden who was just then trying to arrange a deal with Russia over Greece and Romania. Churchill's warning was not delivered.

So when the Warsaw rising started, the Soviet–Polish breach had not been healed, and the British public knew little of the tension behind the scenes.

The first news of the rising reached London in a message to the London government from the commander of the underground army: 'We have started fighting in Warsaw at 1700 hours. . . . Send urgently ammunition and anti-tank weapons.' The second message requested assistance from the Russians 'through their immediate attack from outside'. The British Chiefs of Staff at once passed this request to Moscow, and the request about supply dropping to the Mediterranean Command;[23] this job could only be done from air bases in Italy. From then on, efforts which because of the distance and the dangers, were inevitably small-scale, very costly and largely ineffective, were made to carry supplies to Warsaw in R.A.F. aircraft flown by Polish volunteer pilots. On the Russian side, the requested 'immediate attack from outside' did not come.

From the start both Churchill and Eden wanted to give all-out support to the rising. Eden wrote to Churchill on 2 August asking him to impress on the Chiefs of Staff the 'vital necessity of making a maximum effort for the next few days'. They had known that the Polish underground planned a rising, but had refused its request that the British should decide the timing, saying they were too far away and advising co-operation with the Russians. In late July the London Poles told the British that everything was ready for the rising, and on the 26th they requested active assistance for it. The British told the Poles this was not practically possible, and left the timing to the underground command in Poland.[24]

The British also understood, even if they did not spell it out, that one of the motives of the leaders of the rising was to prevent the Russians setting up a puppet government of their own in Warsaw, and to vindicate the right of non-Communist Poles to have a truly Polish government. They certainly knew that the leaders wanted to strengthen the hand of Mikolajczyk, who had just arrived in Moscow in the hope of getting some sort of agreement with Stalin.[25] According to one Polish account given to the British, Mikolajczyk told Molotov in 31 July of plans for a general rising in Warsaw; Molotov's reply was that 'our troops are 10 km. from Warsaw'; on 3 August Mikolajczyk spoke about the rising with Stalin, who said he would order help to be given; and on 9 August Stalin told Mikolajczyk that he had counted on Soviet troops entering Warsaw on the 6th, but on the 4th the Germans had brought up four Panzer divisions, so that the Red Army had had to make a 'wide encircling movement' requiring time.[26] For the first ten days, therefore, Stalin seemed friendly.

But by mid-August he had become bitter and hostile about the rising, its leaders and the British. He wrote to Churchill that he was now convinced that the 'Warsaw affair' was a reckless and terrible adventure costing the population great sacrifices: this would not have happened if the Poles had maintained contact with the Soviet command. Molotov said that 'the crime' of the Polish leaders was that they did not want to collaborate.[27] Stalin's suspicions of the British were most forcibly stated in a Soviet note of early September :

There can be no doubt that if the British government had taken steps to see that the Soviet Command had been warned of the proposed Warsaw rising in good time, then events . . . would have taken a totally different turn. Why did the British government not find it necessary to warn the Soviet government of this? Was it not a repetition of what happened in April 1943, when the Polish émigré government, in the absence of resistance on the part of the British government, came out with their slanderous statement hostile to U.S.S.R. about Katyn?[28]

Perhaps Churchill, too, was haunted by the ghost of Katyn. In August he was in Italy, and on the 14th he telegraphed to Eden: 'It certainly is very curious that the Russian armies should have ceased their attack on Warsaw and withdrawn some distance at the moment when the underground army revolted.' But Eden replied that he understood that the Russian armies had suffered a definite setback and that was why they had failed to advance on Warsaw as the underground had expected.[29]

Up to this point Eden had tried hard, in spite of very heavy pressure from the London Poles, amounting at times to emotional blackmail, to keep some balance and be fair to the Russians. But then his temper snapped. It had been agreed with the Americans that only U.S. long-range aircraft, flying from bases in England, could carry out effective supply dropping, and then only if they could land on Soviet airfields afterwards. A request to use the airfields had gone to Moscow but Vyshinsky rejected it, tersely and rudely. On 16 August Eden turned to the War Cabinet, who approved and even hardened the instructions he wanted to send to Clark Kerr: the ambassador was to say that, if the Soviet negative attitude continued, 'suspicions concerning Soviet good faith and future Soviet intentions' would be confirmed, and might well 'receive public expression' which would be highly damaging to Anglo-Soviet relations.[30]

The War Cabinet also agreed with Eden that in a matter of such gravity Churchill (still in Italy) should send a message to Stalin. Churchill said he would, provided Roosevelt would do the same. He asked Roosevelt to do this, saying that, if the Germans triumphed in Warsaw, 'no measure can be put upon the full consequences that will arise'. But Roosevelt responded with the text of a very brief, mild and friendly message to Stalin, 'hoping' he would approve supply dropping by U.S. planes on Warsaw. Churchill accepted Roosevelt's text, saying 'our thoughts are as one'; however, he also pointed out how unyielding the Soviet attitude seemed to be.[31] But Roosevelt had already gone as far as he was willing to go in risking his relationship with Stalin.

Eden was pressed by the London government to recognise the underground army formally as a combatant force. There were fears of a German wholesale massacre; also reports had come in that the Russians were carrying out mass arrests of the underground army all over Poland. Mikolajczyk was being urged to resign his post. When Eden put the question of recognition of the underground army to the War Cabinet on 24 August, he had a difficult time – probably because Beaverbrook and Bracken were there. According to the minutes, ministers (unnamed) argued against recognition: should not an effort be made to 'take the Russians with us'? Was it not of great importance to concentrate on bringing the Russians and Poles together? The compromise solution was to ask the Americans to act with Britain, and to consider a fresh approach to the Russians.[32]

But the reply which Stalin sent to the joint Roosevelt–Churchill message, denouncing the leaders of the rising as criminals and evading the question of aid, appeared to rule out any useful new approach. Roosevelt seemed content to let things lie, writing to Churchill, 'I do not see that we can take any additional steps at the present time.' But to Eden Churchill suggested asking Roosevelt to agree to another joint message to Stalin, this time proposing that he should turn a blind eye if U.S. aircraft landed on Soviet airfields, 'without enquiry as to what they have done on the way'. Eden agreed wholeheartedly, telling Churchill that he had already suggested to Winant that the U.S. planes should 'gate-crash'. But Roosevelt fought shy of this idea, telling Churchill that, in view of Stalin's attitude about the use of Soviet bases, it would not be 'advantageous to the long-range general war prospect' to send another joint message – though Churchill could send one alone if he wanted.[33]

This was how things stood when, on 28 August, in the absence of both Churchill and Attlee, Eden took the chair at the War Cabinet, with Beaverbrook and Bracken present. There was a discussion both of supply dropping and of recognition of the underground army as combatants. Bracken said that, if it got out – as it was sure to do – that the Russians were not allowing U.S. aircraft to use Soviet airfields, the result would be 'prejudicial to unity between the United Nations' (the implication being that it should not be allowed to get out). Beaverbrook proposed negotiation with the Russians 'with a view to trying to get an accommodation'. The conclusion was to refer to Churchill.[34]

But by this time opinion in Parliament was beginning to be restive. On 30 August Victor Raikes, M.P., wrote to Eden asking for Parliament to be recalled to discuss Poland: 'If those responsible for British foreign policy at this critical time can show the world that Parliament is determined to support the principles underlying the Atlantic Charter, it would clear the air and encourage some hope of a just and peaceful European settlement.'[35]

By this time Churchill was back in London and, in spite of a temperature of 103 degrees, flung himself into the Warsaw problem. He told Mikolajczyk he should not resign but go on trying for a solution of Polish–Soviet difficulties, but added, 'our great military victories in France put us in a stronger position *vis-à-vis* the Russians'. He also told Eden he wanted to get Roosevelt to send a new joint message to Stalin: 'We regret to inform you that owing to your refusal to receive American or British planes carrying aid to Warsaw the September convoy [of British–U.S. supplies to Russia] will not sail.' This, he thought, would be the only thing that would make Stalin realise 'the gulf he is opening between himself and the civilised world'. But Eden persuaded him to stay his hand.[36] (Roosevelt would never have agreed.) Churchill then left for Quebec.

The War Cabinet met on 4 September, with Eden in the chair, and without Beaverbrook and Bracken. They agreed – apparently with very little discussion – that, since Stalin might not realise how deeply British opinion was stirred about the sufferings of Warsaw and what a shock it would be if the Poles were overwhelmed without help from outside, a telegram should be sent in the name of the War Cabinet, giving warning of 'the probable effect of all this on future Anglo-Russian relations'. Eden was to draft it. The same day, without any consultation with Roosevelt, a telegram went to Moscow:

> The War Cabinet wish the Soviet government to know that public opinion in this country is deeply moved. . . . Whatever the rights and wrongs about the beginnings of the Warsaw rising, the people of Warsaw themselves cannot be held responsible. . . . The War Cabinet themselves find it hard to understand your government's refusal to take account of the obligations of the British and American governments to help the Poles in Warsaw. Your government's action in preventing . . . help being sent seems to us at variance with the spirit of Allied co-operation. . . . Out of regard for Marshal Stalin and for the Soviet peoples, with whom it is our earnest desire to work in future years, the War Cabinet . . . make this further appeal to the Soviet government . . . to provide facilities for U.S. aircraft to land on your airfields.[37]

To this formal appeal there was no immediate response. Churchill again urged Roosevelt to gate-crash – without Stalin's consent. Roosevelt refused, saying he was informed that the fighting Poles had left Warsaw and the Germans were in full control, so the problem had 'unfortunately' been solved and there seemed nothing to be done.[38]

Roosevelt spoke too soon. On 9 September Clark Kerr telegraphed the

Soviet reply to the War Cabinet's collective telegram; and though unpleasant about the failure of the Poles and the British to consult the Russians in advance about the rising, it agreed that, since the British were so insistent, the Soviet command would organise aid to Warsaw jointly with the British and Americans.[39]

Clark Kerr commented: 'This is an unexpected and remarkable climb down.' Eden telegraphed the news to Churchill, now in Quebec: 'This is really a great triumph for our persistence in hammering at the Russians where we had a good case. . . . Your judgement was correct when you said that Stalin had not understood the significance of his refusal on world opinion. The violence of our representations has made him understand it and he has now come round.'[40]

If Churchill and Eden felt they had won a joint moral victory over Stalin, it came too late for Warsaw. The long and costly and largely ineffective efforts of Polish volunteer pilots and the R.A.F. to fly supplies from Italy were followed up by one major operation from England by U.S. heavy bombers, on 18 September; the Russians, too, dropped supplies. But the one thing which could by then have saved Warsaw – the arrival of the Red Army – was long delayed. In the first half of September there was a Russian offensive north of Warsaw; the Red Army occupied most of Romania and pushed into Bulgaria and reached the Yugoslav frontier. They had also reached the Czechoslovak frontier. But the Russians could not or did not cross the Vistula to reach Warsaw.[41] On 5 October the news reached London that the commander in Warsaw, General Bor, and his staff were surrendering to the Germans. The German ring had closed round the city and the rising was ended.

A few days later, when Churchill and Eden were in Moscow, Stalin told them that the failure to relieve Warsaw had not been due to any lack of effort by the Red Army, but entirely to the enemy's strength and difficulties of terrain; he could not, however, admit this failure before the world. Churchill replied that he accepted this absolutely; criticism had only been directed at the 'apparent unwillingness of the Soviet government to send aeroplanes'.[42] But a question-mark must still hang over the Red Army's role – and Stalin's inner thoughts – in the Warsaw tragedy.

It was a tragedy which had brought Britain and the Soviet Union closer to an open quarrel than any other event in the war. Nevertheless, at his moment of triumph over the Soviet 'climb-down' of September, Eden immediately turned to the job of trying to bring the London Poles and the 'Moscow Poles' together. Bevin did what he could to help him through his friends among the Polish Socialists in London, notably Jan Stanczyk.[43] While Churchill and Eden were in Moscow in October they got Stalin to agree to see Mikolajczyk and then brought him to Moscow, where Churchill bullied him (as he believed, for Poland's good) into accepting the Curzon line in return for the dubious prospect of heading a government formed fifty-fifty of London Poles and Moscow Poles. Mikolajczyk had pleaded hard for Lwów as the one thing that could conceivably make this deal acceptable to the London government. Eden had also tried to mediate personally with Stalin, pleading for Lwów for the Poles; but Stalin said pathetically that he was an old man and could not be expected to go to his grave under the stigma of having betrayed the Ukrainians – and they insisted on Lwów.[44]

Since Mikolajczyk had not even Lwów to offer, he lost the confidence of most of the London government and had to resign, being replaced by an elderly hard-line Socialist, Tomasz Arciszewski, who was against all compromise with the Russians. Churchill, worried about the 80,000 Poles fighting with the western Allies in Italy or France, continued to recognise the Arciszewski government.

Nevertheless, Churchill and Eden were both determined to stand up for the Poles at Yalta. Before they left London Churchill told the War Cabinet that recognition was the one counter which remained in Britain's hands; the British position should be to remain adamant on ensuring a free, sovereign and independent Poland, and on getting free elections. Eden agreed. Bevin thought Stalin might yet make a dramatic gesture and cede Lwów to Poland. Morrison said the Poles were very popular in Britain and there was a good deal of feeling that the Russians had been 'very harsh and imperialistic'.[45]

At Yalta Churchill and Eden fought hard to get a formula providing for a mixed government of London and Moscow Poles and for free elections. At the War Cabinet meeting on 19 February 1945 Attlee welcomed them back and congratulated them. Churchill said he was quite sure Stalin 'meant well to the world and to Poland'. Stalin had said that Russia had committed many sins against Poland and had joined in cruel oppression of the country; the Soviet government would not repeat that policy. Churchill said he felt no doubt Stalin had been sincere. Two days later Churchill seemed more doubtful: if the Yalta terms were carried out in good faith, all would be well, but if not, 'our engagement would be altered'.[46]

There were already rumblings inside the Conservative Party. The Chief

Whip wrote to Eden that the Poles had been active in lobbying, and he advised against calling for a confidence motion on Poland in the House, so as to avoid an open split: a display of disunity among Conservatives would be deplorable. Eden replied that he and Churchill had nothing to fear either from the Right or from the Left; he was sure the country approved their work.[47]

It was not only among Conservatives that there was strong feeling. When on 3 March Eden had to tell the War Cabinet that the three-power talks in Moscow about forming a mixed Polish government were going badly, Bevin said there was 'much feeling in Labour circles' over Poland. Churchill defended what had been done at Yalta: 'We were bound to assume the good faith of an ally.' But if the Russians did not carry out the Yalta terms 'it would be necessary to give the full story to Parliament' and there must be no risk of Parliament feeling they had been deceived.[48]

From then on Churchill was eager to take a strong line with Stalin over Poland – but to do it jointly with Roosevelt; Roosevelt wanted a softer, more roundabout approach. Their messages to one another showed the difference clearly. Finally, on 13 March Churchill threatened to use the publicity weapon, writing to Roosevelt:

> We can of course make no progress at Moscow without your aid, and if we get out of step the doom of Poland is sealed. . . . Soon I shall be questioned in Parliament . . . and I shall be forced to tell them the truth. . . . I do not wish to reveal a divergence between the British and the U.S. governments but it would certainly be necessary for me to make it clear that we are in presence of a great failure and utter breakdown of what was settled at Yalta, but that we British have not the necessary strength to carry the matter further. . . . Combined dogged pressure and persistence would very likely succeed.

To this Roosevelt replied: 'I do not understand what you mean by a divergence between our governments on the Polish negotiations;' he could not agree that there had been a breakdown of the Yalta agreement.[49]

In the end Roosevelt sent a very mild message to Stalin. Churchill sent a message of his own: 'If our efforts to reach an agreement about Poland are to be doomed to failure, I shall be bound to confess the fact to Parliament. . . . It is as a sincere friend of Russia that I make my personal appeal to you . . . not to smite down the hands of comradeship in the future guidance of the world.'

Some days later Churchill got from Stalin a 'personal and secret' message saying that, if Mikolajczyk would accept the Yalta decisions and say he stood for Polish–Soviet friendship, he might 'use his influence' to get the ban of Mikolajczyk's participation in a mixed Polish government lifted. Churchill wrote to Roosevelt that this concession, if seriously meant, would be important. Roosevelt, a dying man, replied: 'I would minimize the general Soviet problem as much as possible.'[50]

Mikolajczyk and five other London Poles eventually joined the Polish provisional government in Warsaw, and this was recognised by Britain and the U.S. at Potsdam. But Poland could not be called truly independent or sovereign and the elections held in 1947 were not free. Both Churchill and Eden had fought hard and long, with very weak weapons, to fulfil an obligation. It was not their fault that they failed.

CHAPTER NINETEEN

Czechoslovakia: Beneš the tight-rope walker

President Eduard Beneš of Czechoslovakia was unique among the exiled leaders from central and eastern Europe in that he was the only one who tried to do a balancing act between Britain and Russia. Churchill and Eden did not know whether to cheer or groan, whether to let him fall on the Russian side or to give him a helping hand.

Britain was not bound to Czechoslovakia by any guarantee or treaty, as she was to Poland, but by the feeling of shame which many people felt over the Munich agreement of 1938, through which Chamberlain had compelled Beneš to cede large strips of territory and strong defence positions to Hitler. Neither Churchill nor Eden needed to feel any personal guilt, since both had been public critics of Munich (Eden with tact and discretion). Both – unlike Chamberlain and Halifax – were thought to be friends of Czechoslovakia, and there was truth in this. They also saw clearly the strategic importance of Czechoslovakia at the crossroads of central Europe, both in 1938 and six years later in the context of a post-war European settlement.

What cast a certain chill on their relations with Beneš was his love affair with the Russians. This had started with the Munich crisis in 1938, when the Soviet government gave Beneš – and the world – to understand that it was ready to put its mutual aid treaty with Czechoslovakia into effect, certainly if France and Britain acted and possibly even if they did not. Since Soviet intentions were never put to the test, most Czechs believed this and felt they could put no firm faith in the western democracies and must rely in future on the Soviet Union.

Naturally, neither Churchill nor Eden much liked this, feeling that since Britain was the wartime home of the Beneš government and, from 1940, of the Czechoslovak armed forces, there should be special ties between Britain and Czechoslovakia. Eden in particular resented Beneš's wooing of the Soviet Union in 1943. Churchill was less involved, and had perhaps excessive respect for Beneš as a wise man – a sort of central European Smuts – whose views on Russia were based on special knowledge and so (especially when he took a rosy view about Anglo-Soviet relations) worth special respect.

*

One of Beneš's strongest traits was dogged persistence, together with equally dogged optimism. These won him a series of political successes in the early war years, though where Britain was concerned he was perhaps helped more than he realised by Jan Masaryk, the son of the founder of the Czechoslovak state, T. G. Masaryk. He was the opposite of Beneš, an attractive extrovert personality, mercurial in his moods, with a strong sense of humour and just as strong a streak of melancholy; he had many personal friends in London and did a lot to ease Beneš's quest for recognition as head of a continuing Czechoslovak state.

This was achieved gradually by a series of steps. Britain's decision to take the final step – full recognition – Beneš owed chiefly to the Russians. When Hitler attacked Russia the Soviet government, which at the time of its pact with Germany had shut down the Czechoslovak legation in Moscow, now wanted friends where it could find them. It proposed to Beneš a restoration of close and friendly relations, saying it was ready to recognise the continuity of the Czechoslovak republic and aimed to see it restored, and also recognised Beneš as its president.

Eden could not let the Russians steal a lead. He told the War Cabinet on 14 July 1941 that in the light of the Soviet move to give full recognition he thought Britain should do the same; this need not commit Britain to any particular boundaries. The War Cabinet agreed but said the assent of the Dominions should first be obtained. But Beneš was able to wield a potent argument for speed, urging that Britain should announce recognition at the same time as the Soviet Union; 'this would avoid undue emphasis being placed' on the Soviet action. The War Cabinet, when Eden told them this, agreed to announce recognition the next day, 18 July.[1]

However, the British still lagged behind the Russians over the continuity of the Czechoslovak state and its future frontiers, so the Soviet Union had yet another claim on Czechoslovakia's gratitude and devotion. The U.S. recognised the Beneš government on 31 July, and thereafter, although there were a good many American voters of Czech or Slovak origin, took no very special interest in Czechoslovak affairs. It was left to the British and the Russians to compete for Beneš's favours, which, he must have thought, suited him well.

But in 1942 Beneš already began to feel a little of the Soviet iron hand beneath the velvet glove. In 1940, at a time when he himself had still a much lower status among the exiles in London than the Polish prime minister, Sikorski, he had started talks with him about a Polish–Czechoslovak confederation. Eden and the Foreign Office were very keen on the idea, believing that in east and central Europe confederations could in future be the best bulwark against fresh German aggression and also, if necessary, against Soviet expansion, though this was seldom put down on paper.

When Eden put the idea of confederations to Stalin in December 1941, he seemed mildly benevolent. But early in 1942, after Sikorski and the young King Peter of Yugoslavia made some rather foolish public remarks, the Russians became suspicious, and Soviet diplomats started dropping heavy hints to the British and more direct warnings to the exiled governments about confederations. But the Foreign Office did not want to drop the idea, and when Molotov came to London to negotiate the Anglo-Soviet treaty Eden tried to reassure him, seemingly with some success.

But privately Molotov told Beneš that the idea of a Polish–Czechoslovak confederation was still suspect: it would be necessary to 'modify' the government of Poland, and there must be certainty that it would not be directed against the Soviet Union. In reply Beneš said he would be 'neutral' in the territorial and other differences between Poland and the Soviet Union.[2] Sikorski for his part told Eden that Beneš was 'behaving badly'; though he professed to be as strongly anti-Communist as Sikorski himself, 'he was under Communist influence and seemed to be adjusting his policy away from Poland towards the Soviet Union'.[3] Later in 1942 Masaryk told Eden dolefully that the Poles thought Beneš a lackey of the Russians, while the Russians saw him as the Poles' friend; he was tired of being kicked by both sides.[4]

The British did not give up their hope of fostering confederations. Eden had originally meant to take it up again with Molotov on his return to London on his way home from the U.S. In the event, he tackled him on another question which had just blown up – a plan for a Soviet–Yugoslav treaty providing for post-war political co-operation. Eden did not like this: he had been holding off requests from Greeks and Poles for treaties of this sort with Britain. There was also the danger that the Russians, by binding the central and east European governments with bilateral treaties covering the post-war period, would be able to block the formation of confederations (as, indeed, Stalin ultimately did).

Eden therefore proposed to Molotov that Britain and the Soviet Union, in the spirit of the new Anglo-Soviet treaty, should both refrain from concluding treaties covering the post-war period with the smaller European Allies. Otherwise there might be a treaty-making race and both big powers might end the war with a string of possibly conflicting commitments to smaller European countries. Molotov seemed taken aback by Eden's proposing such a 'self-denying ordinance', but promised to report it to Moscow. In July 1942 Moscow appeared to sanction the plan, or, at least, consultation before either Britain or the Soviet Union made any treaty with a smaller ally.[5]

Eden thought this was a firm undertaking. At the same time he felt free to go on backing confederations, since the Russians were being disagreeably noncommittal rather than definitely forbidding. Talking to Masaryk in January 1943, Eden suggested that he himself should tell the Russians that he definitely favoured a Polish–Czechoslovak confederation, and a treaty between the two as a first step. Masaryk did not dissent.[6]

Even after the Katyn tragedy had caused a rupture in Polish–Soviet relations, Churchill and Eden did not give up hope of helping the Poles out of trouble by linking them with Czechoslovakia. In April Sikorski told Churchill he was in difficulties with the Czechs since, though he was willing to declare that a Polish–Czechoslovak confederation should not be pointed against Russia, Beneš would not move without Russia's consent; Churchill tried to cheer him by saying he heartily agreed with federation plans.[7]

By this time, however, Beneš had decided to play a lone hand, unhampered by the London Poles. Overestimating Czechoslovakia's importance to Russia and Britain, he overplayed it and got into difficulties. Different accounts were given later by the Czechoslovak and British sides of what actually happened. The Czechoslovak account was that in April 1943 the Soviet government agreed in principle to a proposal made by Beneš that a Soviet–Czechoslovak treaty of alliance should be concluded on the lines of the 1942 Anglo-Soviet treaty, and this was 'immediately' brought to the notice of the British and U.S. governments.[8] The British account was that on 5 May, just before going to the U.S., Beneš told the British ambassador accredited to his government, Philip Nichols, that, as a result of conversations he had initiated, the Soviet Union had said it was ready to give 'informal assurances' that it would respect Czechoslovakia's independence and territorial integrity and would not interfere in its internal affairs; also, that it was willing in principle, thought not ready to commit itself, to consider a triple pact with Poland and Czechoslovakia. No British comment was made. (The idea of a triple pact was, of course, attractive.) But when Beneš was in the U.S., Press reports appeared that he intended to conclude a treaty with the Soviet Union. Nichols, according to the British account, asked the Czechoslovak Foreign Ministry whether this was true and was told that the possibility of such a treaty being proposed could not be excluded, but no decision would be taken till Beneš came back from the U.S.[9]

When the Foreign Office heard that it was a purely Czechoslovak–Soviet pact, rather than a triple pact, that Beneš was pursuing, they were annoyed with Beneš for not telling them and worried that the Russians had apparently thrown overboard the self-denying ordinance of 1942. Eden's first move was to ask Beneš personally, when he got back from the U.S., whether he was planning to sign a treaty with the Soviet Union when he went to Moscow shortly. Beneš said it was possible and depended on the position in Moscow; Eden then told him about the self-denying ordinance: in view of this, Beneš's proposal would 'give rise to difficulties' from the British point of view. These 'difficulties' were explained to Beneš twice more before the end of June.[10]

On 25 June Beneš told the Soviet ambassador to his government, Bogomolov, that the British were making difficulties. On 28 June Eden took the matter to the War Cabinet and got them to agree that he should remind Molotov of the self-denying ordinance, but say that, if he insisted on going ahead, Britain might agree to the proposed Soviet–Czechoslovak treaty if it was the first instalment of a triple treaty including Poland later on; otherwise there should be no exceptions.[11] But before Eden could act, Bogomolov told Beneš that, because of British objections, the Soviet government, though in principle favouring a treaty, thought it best to go slow and postpone Beneš's Moscow visit.[12]

This was, of course, a blow to Beneš's hopes and pride and caused anti-British feelings among pro-Russian (not necessarily Communist) Czechs in London; Masaryk, however, tried to be helpful. Molotov, when reminded of the self-denying ordinance, said there was no provision for any such thing in the Anglo-Soviet treaty; he had been expecting Eden to follow up his original approach with a formal proposal and since none had come he had assumed the whole idea had been dropped.[13]

Eden was determined to rescue his self-denying ordinance, telling the War Cabinet in September that he intended to raise it formally at the coming Foreign Ministers' conference in Moscow. By this time he was gloomy about the chances of an eventual triple pact including Poland, since Polish–Soviet relations were still ruptured and the London Poles were unlikely to join any pact as poor relations coming late to the feast.[14]

Before Eden left for Moscow, the British–Czechoslovak wrangle had become public property. After an innocuous statement by Eden in the

House of Commons, the Czechoslovak government gave the Press a statement saying there seemed to be two different interpretations of the Eden–Molotov understanding and, anyhow, the proposed Czechoslovak–Soviet treaty should not be barred by it. Eden summoned Masaryk to reprove him; Masaryk said he had had a difficult time with his colleagues over the statement, and his view had not prevailed. The British then set out their version of the wrangle for the benefit of the U.S. and Soviet governments: this virtually accused Beneš of concealing his true intentions until personally challenged by Eden, and restated British 'reserve' about the treaty project.[15]

In the curiously balmy air of Moscow this 'reserve' melted away. On 23 October Molotov told Eden that Soviet–Czechoslovak negotiations had ended in complete agreement on a treaty, and gave him the text. Eden told the Foreign Office that he thought it as good as could be expected, and if Polish–Soviet relations could be renewed there was no reason why Poland should not join at once; so if Molotov would accept the general principle of the self-denying ordinance he would not object to the treaty, though he would urge that the Poles should be brought in as soon as possible.

The next day Eden reported to London his success over the London-based European Advisory Commission; and in a matter of hours after that he reported that, feeling that the Russians resented the British-imposed delay on the treaty with Czechoslovakia, he had told Molotov that he had no objections to it. So Molotov was to invite Beneš to Moscow, telling him that he now had Eden's blessing; but Molotov would wait until the next day, so that Churchill could be told first. As for the self-denying ordinance, Molotov had gone 'some way to meet us'.

Churchill acquiesced without question. There was little else he could do at that stage, even if he had wanted – and he probabaly did not. The next day Eden revealed one reason why he had given in so quickly and easily: Molotov had blamed Beneš for all the trouble, saying that the initiative for a treaty had come from him. Eden commented: 'If so, this was within a very few weeks of Russia's breaking off relations with Poland'; Beneš's part seemed to have been to tell half-truths to either side and so make a good deal of unnecessary mischief: 'I trust we shall offer Beneš no bouquets.'[16]

In London Cadogan was clearly rather shocked at Eden's total surrender, minuting to Churchill that what Eden had done ran counter to what had been agreed in the War Cabinet; 'no doubt the Foreign Secretary found it necessary to give way . . . in view of wider considerations'. Eden would 'presumably' not have forgotten the very firm line he himself had taken with Beneš, or the help he had been given by Masaryk; what had now been done would 'increase Dr Beneš's already exaggerated idea of his own importance and political wisdom, and will make him very hard to manage in future, and correspondingly weaken Masaryk's position'. Cadogan could now see little point in the self-denying ordinance, which the Russians would probably use against Britain.

Churchill did not defend Eden against Cadogan's implied criticism, but told Cadogan to communicate directly with Eden: 'I approve the substance of your message.'[17] The self-denying ordinance sank without trace. Beneš went to Moscow, signed the treaty, and told the British embassy that the Russians were now 'free from any signs of revolutionary exclusiveness or wish to interfere with systems different from their own'; no one had shown the slightest wish to influence him over the future ordering of Czechoslovak internal affairs. The Russians had not 'excluded' the resumption of relations with the Poles, but were in no hurry.[18]

In spite of a certain sourness over the treaty, Churchill and Eden were ready to forgive Beneš. For his part Beneš, having got his way over the Soviet treaty, was clearly eager to get back into British good graces and restore the balance. In Cairo, on his way back to London, he let it be known that Stalin had charged him with a message of 'fraternal embrace' to Churchill. He also let it be known he was convinced that the warmth of Stalin's feelings for Churchill was entirely genuine; he had hoped to deliver the message himself but did not wish to intrude when Churchill was convalescing from pneumonia.[19]

Churchill swallowed the bait and invited Beneš to visit him in North Africa. In the Foreign Office Sargent commented: 'He *will* have a swelled head when he gets back'; Eden added, 'I fear so.' Beneš hurried to Churchill, who then reported to Roosevelt: 'Beneš has been here and is very hopeful about the Russian situation. He may be most useful in trying to make the Poles see reason and in reconciling them to the Russians, whose confidence he has long possessed.' To Eden Churchill wrote that Beneš had given a glowing account of the Soviet mood after Tehran: 'Beans [*sic*] says that we really all of us got together . . . and the atmosphere is absolutely friendly and quite different from former times.' 'Beans' had also expounded Stalin's view on the Polish frontier. This did not go down well in the Foreign Office where Frank Roberts commented tartly: 'Dr Beneš should be given no further encouragement from us to play the mediator. He is profoundly disliked and mistrusted by the majority of Poles.'[20]

Nevertheless, Eden, after he himself had seen Beneš, reported his views without criticism to the War Cabinet: Beneš thought 'a new Russia was arising with a nationalist bent', and meant to co-operate with the U.S. and Britain after the war. Stalin had promised Beneš that when the Russian armies entered Czechoslovakia they would work through the local authorities.[21]

Visions of Beneš meditating between Russians and Poles, or even between British and Russians, soon faded. As the Soviet armies approached the old Czechoslovak frontier, he was more occupied with coming to terms with his own Communists in London, in Moscow and at home.

In the late summer there came the rising in Slovakia, close on the heels of the Warsaw rising, and at this point the Czechs turned to the British. At the end of August they asked the Chiefs of Staff for help, through supply drops and bombing of communications centres. Both Eden and the Chiefs of Staff thought it best to be cautious until they knew more about Soviet intentions, since Slovakia was in the Russian sphere of operations. If supplies were to be dropped, the Russians should do it, and it was up to them to give air support.[22]

While the Foreign Office were trying to find out what the Russians thought, a new and surprising request came from the Czechoslovak commander-in-chief, General Ingr, asking for British help in promoting a rising of the Czechoslovak 'Home Army' in Bohemia and Moravia, including the establishment of a base in Italy from which arms for 10,000 men could be delivered in six nights, and enough aircraft to deliver arms for up to 60,00 men within ten to fourteen days from the start of the rising, together with ammunition, food and medical stores. This was a very large order. Once again the Chiefs of Staff thought – and the Foreign Office agreed – that the same answer should be given as in the case of Slovakia; it was up to the Russians to carry out the proposed air operations – all the more so since co-ordination had apparently been established between the leaders of the Slovak rising and the Soviet forces on the Dukla Pass.[23]

However, the British did not wish to give the impression that they had no interest in Czechoslovakia, so the Chiefs of Staff and the Foreign Office agreed that General Ingr should be encouraged to carry on sabotage and other similar underground activity, and that, as in the past, S.O.E. should help in this. The British obviously feared a repetition of the Warsaw tragedy, and the first draft of the reply to Ingr referred specifically to this.

In the final draft the lesson of Warsaw was implicitly stressed: it would be most unwise to call for a large-scale rising in Bohemia and Moravia until the Russians were on the borders and plans could be fully co-ordinated with them.[24]

Beneš, so Cadogan later told Churchill, took this British refusal badly, and was anxious, for political reasons, to keep a balance between help received from Russia and from the West.[25] He was perhaps beginning to feel that he had thrown himself too eagerly into the waiting Russian arms.

In mid-October three Slovak delegates made their way to London and were told why Britain felt unable to help. Later that month there were renewed and urgent requests from both Beneš and Masaryk for British aid to Slovakia; Russian help had not been enough to prevent reverses, the main Resistance centre, Banska Bystrica, had fallen, the Soviet armies were still one hundred miles away. The Americans had dropped a small quantity of arms in the early days but had decided against trying again. The Foreign Office asked the Chiefs of Staff to reconsider sending supplies, but they stood firm and Cadogan himself minuted to Churchill: 'Our help would be ineffective. We should get no thanks for it but would only incur a share of responsibility for this premature rising, about which we were not consulted. . . . The small contribution we could make would only prolong the agony.' Churchill made no comment.[26]

Over the Slovak rising and over plans for a rising in Bohemia and Moravia the British stood firmly aside. But neither Churchill nor Eden had washed their hands of Czechoslovakia. Beneš on his side was beginning to feel the Soviet grip tightening. In January 1945 Molotov announced that the time had come for the Czechoslovak government to recognise the provisional Polish government set up under Soviet auspices. Masaryk told the Foreign Office that 'although no actual threat had been made M. Molotov had made it quite clear that the Soviet government intended their wish to be fulfilled at once unconditionally'. Masaryk thought that if Beneš refused the Russians might set up a committee in Slovakia as a rival body. He turned down a Foreign Office request that he should postpone a decision for a few days.[27]

At the end of February most of the exiled government set out for Slovakia, while Beneš himself was to visit Moscow. At this point Churchill and Eden began to feel fresh interest in Czechoslovakia and determined to get a British foot inside the door. In late March the Soviet government – ostensibly on practical grounds – refused to allow British and U.S. diplomatic missions to go to Slovakia to join the Beneš government, now established in Košice. Eden complained to the Soviet ambassador, Gusev, on 28 March and Clark Kerr, in Moscow, was instructed to tell the Russians that 'in view of the particularly close and friendly relations which have been maintained with the Czechoslovak government here throughout the war, it will be impossible to explain satisfactorily to public opinion the absence of any British representative in Czechoslovakia after the government's return' – especially since a Soviet ambassador was already there.[28]

Churchill, provoked by the Soviet ban, immediately raised the question : what would happen if the Americans reached Prague first, as then seemed likely: 'Will the Russians then tell them whether the American ambassador may take a toothbrush or not, or will it be the western Allies who will determine the character of the United Nations representation in the delivered capital?'[29]

In late April Eden, before leaving for the San Francisco conference, arranged for a letter to be sent to the U.S. ambassador, Winant, stressing how important and valuable it would be politically if American armed forces could press forward and liberate Prague. Sargent, temporarily in charge at the Foreign Office, told Churchill a few days later that the Czech ministers who had been left behind in London were delighted by the arrival of U.S. troops on the Czechoslovak border and had said that 'their Communists were correspondingly depressed'. Sargent added : 'The liberation of Prague and as much of the territory of western Czecho-slovakia as possible by the Americans might make the whole difference to the post-war situation in Czechoslovakia and might well influence that in nearby countries.'[30]

Churchill took up the cause with great vigour, getting Eden to raise the matter with Stettinius, who agreed with the British view, and himself raising it with Eisenhower, who disappointingly replied that he had never thought of going to Prague; his objective was to get to Linz, in Upper Austria, before the Russians. Churchill always hesitated to try to overrule Eisenhower, but he got the Chiefs of Staff to suggest to their U.S. colleagues that a message should be sent to him pointing to the political importance of Prague. The Chiefs of Staff followed this up by proposing instructions to Eisenhower that in Czechoslovakia he should 'advance over as wide an area as logistics permit to meet the Russians in order to accept maximum surrender [of Germans]'. On the same day Churchill sent Truman a message that the liberation of Prague and as much as possible of western Czechoslovakia by U.S. forces 'might make the whole difference to the post-war situation'.[31]

Washington was unwilling to put pressure on Eisenhower, but he himself – perhaps prompted by his earlier talk with Churchill – reported that he might make an 'initial move' to Pilsen and Karlovy Vary (well to the west of Prague). Then, hearing from the Russians that they were planning operations 'into the Vltava valley' (the Vltava runs through Prague), Eisenhower informed Moscow that he was about to thrust into Czechoslovakia and seize Budejovice, Pilsen and Karlovy Vary and was prepared 'if the situation so dictates' to advance to the line of the Vltava and Elbe rivers. (This would have brought the Americans into the heart of Prague.) From Moscow came an immediate veto : Soviet forces were to clear both banks of the Vltava, east and west; the Americans were not to move east of the Budejovice–Pilsen–Karlovy Vary line. Eisenhower accepted this. Churchill, prompted by Sargent, sent Eisenhower a most immediate private and confidential message : 'I thought you did not mean to tie yourself down if you had the troops and the country was empty.' Eisenhower did not reply.[32]

Expecting immediate help from either west or east, the Resistance organisation of Prague rose against the Germans. Sargent told Churchill on 8 May that according to S.O.E. the Germans were taking very strong measures : 'Unless help can be brought to them in the near future there will be a repetition of what took place in Warsaw.' (The only help the resisters got was from a Vlasov formation – the renegade Russians recruited by the Germans.) On 10 May Eisenhower let Churchill's staff know that he regarded the 'Pilsen line' as a bargain which could not be upset; in any case, the question was now academic since the Russians had reached Prague. S.O.E. confirmed this.[33]

On 6 June the newly arrived British ambassador reported from Prague that any mention in public speeches of the part the western powers had played in the war met with vociferous applause; but 'the failure to advance as far as Prague is not understood and will continue to rankle'.

The ambassador added that the Czechs seemed curiously apathetic and gave an impression of being cowed under the Russian occupation.[34] Prague had escaped the tragedy that devastated Warsaw at the time of the rising, but a longer Czechoslovak tragedy was beginning. Perhaps it started as early as 1943 when Eden gave way so easily to Molotov over the Soviet–Czechoslovak treaty; this may have been taken in Moscow as a signal that the British were willing to let Czechoslovakia slip into the Soviet sphere in post-war Europe. At the last moment Churchill, Eden and the Foreign Office tried to retrieve the situation but, having accepted American military command, they lacked the power.

CHAPTER TWENTY

The Balkan no-man's-land

The Balkan peninsula with its hinterland was an especially sensitive area in Anglo-Soviet relations. A century earlier it had already been a sort of no-man's-land between Britain and Russia. Russia was a great land power striving for access to the Mediterranean and so to the oceans. Britain was an empire to which Mediterranean sea communications were very important (as also, later, was Middle East oil). So there had been past conflicts of interest, and in the Second World War Stalin took over Tsarist policy, aiming to use local Communists, Slav brotherhood and the Red Army to extend Soviet influence and power.

The British had certain economic interests – Romanian oil, the Trepča mines in Yugoslavia – but they were not important; before 1939 they had passively watched Germany penetrate and dominate the area economically. With Yugoslavia and, to a lesser extent, Romania there were ties of sentiment dating from the First World War, in which the other countries of the area, Bulgaria and Hungary, had been on the enemy side. In the Second World War ties with Yugoslavia were renewed by the anti-Axis Belgrade coup of March 1941 and the brief and disastrous Balkan campaign of the following month. But ties with Yugoslavia were not so strong as with Greece which, geographically and otherwise, was seen as a special British responsibility and interest. However, Eden, because of his Balkan excursion in early 1941, did feel a certain personal involvement in Yugoslav affairs.

Churchill was always passionately interested in the strategic possibilities of fighting the Germans in the Balkans, either through orthodox military operations, or air attack, or through S.O.E. contacts and support for local Resistance movements. The aim could be to turn the southern flank of the German eastern front, or to hold down German troops away from the main fighting fronts, or to carry out strategic deception. The strategic decisions taken at Tehran virtually ruled out orthodox military methods except in Greece, but air attack, commando raids, guerrilla warfare and S.O.E.'s political contacts still offered exciting prospects. About hopes of long-term British influence in the area, Churchill gradually became pessimistic but never wholly resigned.

Eden, because of the professional feud between the Foreign Office and
S.O.E., was never willing to admit that S.O.E.'s contacts could be valuable
channels of British influence, seeing S.O.E.'s activities almost purely as a
political embarrassment, particularly to his attempt to cultivate friendly
relations with the Soviet Union and get Soviet co-operation in dealing
with the problems of the area.

Eden's idea was to keep the initiative in British hands while working
closely with the Soviet Union and avoiding anything that would rouse
Soviet suspicion and resentment. He was attempting a more or less impossible feat. Even so, once military operations were ruled out there was
little alternative, except total abandonment of the area apart from Greece.
Yet even this could hardly be done : S.O.E.'s political contacts in Romania
and Hungary, even at one moment in Bulgaria, gave hope of detaching
these countries more quickly than by any other method and so shortening
the war.

The policy of combining British initiative with co-operation with Russia
could be clearly seen in Yugoslavia. In the autumn of 1941, when wireless
contact had been made with the strongly monarchist Serbian officer,
Colonel Draža Mihailović, plans were made, in which S.O.E. were involved,
for a joint Yugoslav–Soviet–British mission to be flown in; these were
vetoed by the Yugoslav exiled government authorities.[1] A purely
Yugoslav–British mission was landed on the Adriatic coast, and news
then arrived in London of fighting between Mihailović and the Communist-
led partisans under Tito. Both the exiled government and Eden (somewhat
unrealistically) asked the Soviet government to help stop the strife and
get the partisans to accept Mihailović's leadership. This produced no
results, but in the spring of 1942, when communication with Mihailović
had been interrupted, Eden asked the Russians if they could help in
restoring contact. The reply was that the Russians had no contact.

In July 1942 the Russians told the exiled government and Eden that
they had evidence that Mihailović was collaborating with the Italians
and with Nedić, head of the German-installed puppet government of
rump Serbia. This was one of the factors – though not at all the only
one – which made the British reconsider their policy of backing Mihailović
as sole Resistance leader, and to think of making contact with the
partisans. Churchill was keen on this because of his strategic ideas for
developing war in the Mediterranean; Eden was keen on it because it
would enable him to keep in step with the Russians and nip parliamentary
criticism in the bud (and also annoy some of the high-ups in S.O.E.).
Early in 1943 Eden asked the Russians if they could help in contacting the

partisans but again got a negative answer, so S.O.E. successfully sent in missions of their own, and good relations with Tito were established, in the first place by William Deakin and a few months later by Fitzroy Maclean.[2]

Towards the end of 1943 the British came to the conclusion – Churchill with some enthusiasm, Eden very reluctantly – that they must break with Mihailović and give all material aid to Tito. Eden had a preliminary talk with Molotov at the Moscow conference in October, and the policy of all-out aid to Tito got top-level, three-power approval at Tehran.

This still left the British with the problem of what to do with the young King Peter – they worried very little about the existing royal government – and also how to win over the Serbs, believed to be still strongly monarchist at heart, to fight with the Communist Tito. Eden approached the Russians and in December 1943 the Soviet ambassador told him officially that his government agreed on the need for 'a basis of collaboration between the two sides' and would do everything possible to further this aim.[3] This was a unique and encouraging response; and against this background of apparent Soviet complacency Churchill and Eden spent a surprising amount of time and energy in January and February 1944 fighting one another on the question whether the British should first break with Mihailović and then ask Tito to receive King Peter at his headquarters, as Churchill wanted, or the other way round, as Eden wanted. They were both chasing a chimera since Tito would not have the king at his headquarters and, if he had done so, the king would have been quite incapable of exercising power and authority.

The outcome of this futile Churchill–Eden wrangle was a decision to abandon Mihailović without any prior undertaking from Tito, and to force King Peter to appoint a neutral exiled politician, Dr Ivan Šubašić, to try to reach agreement with Tito on a mixed government, including acceptable exiles, to take power in Belgrade when it was liberated. Churchill kept Stalin informed of this process, and Stalin seems to have seen it as a necessary but trivial evil which (as it did) would end in Tito's supremacy; in any case, he was helpful rather than the reverse.

Over Yugoslavia, therefore, the decencies of outward Anglo-Soviet co-operation were preserved. In Bulgaria, where the Soviet Union kept a legation throughout the war, it should in theory have been the Russians who took the initiative, all the more since the Communist Party was vigorous and well-organised. In practice they no doubt did; but when Eden asked Molotov (in October 1943) for information and co-operation, he got only a very thin and unrevealing written statement in reply. So, after S.O.E.'s efforts to make contact with the Resistance through their friends in the left-wing Agrarian Party had failed, it was through Tito's local commanders in Serbia that two British officers eventually got in touch with the Fatherland Front, the organisation favoured by the Russians and dominated by Communists, though Agrarians, Socialists and anti-monarchist army officers also belonged to it.

The Russians could hardly object to this. But they were very touchy about British contacts in Romania and Hungary: in Romania, throughout the war, with the traditional political parties – the National Peasant Party and in particular its leader, Iuliu Maniu, and the smaller Liberal Party – and through them with the young King Michael; in Hungary, from August 1943, with the 'surrender group' formed by certain ministers and senior officials with the backing of the prime minister, Miklos Kállay, and the vague approval of the regent, Miklos Horthy. These were, of course, all 'bourgeois' politicians, even if they had the sympathy of some left-wing groups; but they were important because they were in a position actually to influence their country's actions, which the tiny and hounded Communist Parties in both countries could hardly do. Eden hoped the Russians would see the practical point of working with them to shorten the war; this they certainly did, but they did not like the British communicating with them, obviously suspecting them of conducting sinister anti-Soviet machinations. This the British had no intention of doing; nevertheless, the mere fact of having contact with the British inevitably encouraged the 'bourgeois' politicians to hope that the British would have some influence on their country's post-war fate and would not leave them entirely to the mercy of the Soviet Union.

Eden did his best to keep the Russians happy, consulting them early in 1943 about Maniu; he eventually got the answer that, though the Russians themselves did not want to contact Maniu, they did not mind the British keeping in touch. In the following October Molotov was more negative in what he said about Maniu, though it was not clear whether he wanted the British to break off all contact, and Eden does not seem to have taken him that way. In the spring of 1944 Molotov agreed to Prince Stirbey going to Cairo as representative of the Romanian opposition, and meeting Soviet, British and U.S. representatives to discuss Romania's breaking with Germany. In all this Eden kept saying that the decisive voice must be the Soviet Union's.[4]

Over Hungary Eden was ready to take a rather more independent line.

When the 'surrender group' sent a representative to Istanbul in August 1943 Eden duly informed the Russians and asked for their approval of the proposed British reply to the group. Molotov wanted a very stern reply, Churchill did not: he was very much interested and did not want to nip the Hungarian development in the bud by forcing the group into premature open action. Eden followed Churchill's line. At the Moscow conference Molotov showed his bad temper over this; Eden was apologetic and said the Soviet Union should have a 'deciding voice', which prompted the Foreign Office to comment that this was the first time Eden had said such a thing about Hungary, though he had said it often about Romania. Back in London Eden stuck to his point, and at the end of December banned the despatch of a S.O.E. mission to the 'surrender group'. In March 1944 the Germans, knowing that something was brewing, occupied Hungary, and leading members of the group were imprisoned or had to flee.[5]

April 1944 was a crisis month in Anglo-Soviet relations over south-east Europe. Pressure of events pushed Churchill and Eden to face the choice between a major showdown with the Russians, or some sort of working arrangement which was likely to shock the Americans. On 3 April Churchill, talking to the War Cabinet about Soviet activities in Italy, said that the British 'were not claiming to interfere in the handling of the situation in conquered or liberated countries in eastern Europe'.[6]

Over Romania for the moment things were going smoothly; Molotov, after telling the British, issued a statement that the Soviet Union had no intention of taking any Romanian territory or changing the existing social order, and drafted very reasonable armistice terms. Greece was the trouble spot, with the mutinies in the Greek forces in Egypt. Cadogan, in Eden's absence, wrote to Churchill on 15 April that the Soviet news agency was implicitly attacking British handling of the mutinies; the Russians had in the past taken only a limited interest in Greece but now seemed determined to intervene. He suggested that Churchill should send Molotov a message about it.[7]

Churchill agreed, and wrote to Molotov asking that the Soviet news agency should stop its agitation over Greece: 'This is really no time for ideological warfare. I am determined to put down mutiny. . . . In spite of my political views, which you have always known, I allow nothing to stand between British policy and the supreme objective, namely, the defeat of the Hitlerites. . . . I wish you all success . . . in your

Romanian negotiations in which . . . we consider you are the predominant power.'[8]

So Churchill was always feeling his way towards a division of responsibility, if not spheres of influence. Molotov replied, expressing great reserve about Greek matters but saying the Soviet news agency would be asked to check its facts more carefully. Churchill thanked him, promised more information about Greece, and asked whether there was anything Molotov wanted done about Romania : 'We regard you as our leaders in Romanian affairs.'[9]

Molotov sent a very cold answer : from what Churchill had said in Parliament, it appeared that 'the British government control Greek affairs and the Greek government in the most direct manner'; the Soviet government could not then accept any responsibility for Greek affairs or for British action. And what were the British going to do to put greater pressure on the Romanians?[10]

On the day when Churchill received this Molotov sent another and far more unpleasant message about two British officers whom S.O.E. had dropped into Romania in December 1943 in order to contact Maniu; they had immediately been captured and held prisoner by the Romanian government, which had, however, used them as a channel of communications with the British in Cairo – who told the Russians everything that passed. Molotov now suddenly declared that these officers were in reality a 'semi-official British mission' to the Romanian government, using their own radio cyphers, which meant that there was a definite British–Romanian agreement concluded behind the back of the Soviet Union.[11]

This totally unfounded charge of ill faith seemed to Churchill an attack on his personal honour. He drafted, very late at night, an impassioned reply : 'In all this Romanian business I am working with you and Stalin. . . . You are absolutely mad if you suppose we are in any intrigue with Romania. . . . Of course, if you do not believe a single word we say, it really would be better to leave things to run out as they will.'[12] (Four months later Molotov, talking about this incident with Clark Kerr, said his relations with Churchill had always been so good that he felt able to say what was in his mind even if it was not agreeable; this had been 'the only misunderstanding he had had with the Prime Minister'.[13])

The storm caused by Churchill's wounded feelings and injured honour was something Eden had to deal with when he came back from sick leave. On 2 May he told the War Cabinet (in quite a different context) that eastern Europe and the Balkans would be largely dominated by the

Russians after the war. On 4 May Churchill sent him two minutes about 'the brute issues between us and the Soviet government' in Italy, Romania, Bulgaria, Yugoslavia and, above all, Greece. He put the question, 'Are we going to acquiesce in the Communisation of the Balkans and perhaps of Italy? . . . If our conclusion is that we resist Communist infusion and invasion, we should put it to them pretty plainly.' In another minute he suggested that Clark Kerr might be recalled from Moscow : 'Evidently we are approaching a showdown with the Russians.'[14]

On the same day Eden saw the Greek ambassador, who was worried about Soviet intriguing with Greek Communists against Papandreou, the man the British wanted to head a new Greek government; could not the British get the Soviet government to help them in Greece, or, at least, refrain from hindering them? Eden said he hoped to discuss the matter with the Soviet ambassador before long.[15]

At this point Eden was clearly trying to head Churchill off the idea of a showdown with the Russians, and on to the idea of the kind of working arrangement Churchill had himself foreshadowed in his exchanges with Molotov. On 5 May Eden asked Gusev to call and had a fairly friendly talk on Romania and Greece. He said he hoped the British explanation about the two officers in Romania had cleared up that matter; Britain, as he had often said, thought the Soviet Union 'should take the lead in our joint efforts to get Romania out of the war'. No more British parties would be sent to Romania for the time being and, in any case, the Russians would be consulted.

Eden then turned to Greece, saying he was 'gravely concerned'. There was a danger that Britain and the Soviet Union would diverge. Britain was backing Papandreou, a good democrat and a republican who wanted to bring all parties, including Communists, into a broad-based government. He would like the Soviet government to support him publicly; if not, they might at least tell the Greeks privately that it was EAM's duty to join Papandreou's government. The Soviet Press was supporting EAM against the Greek government; if this went on the world would see there was a split between Britain and Russia. Greece, Eden said, was in the British theatre of command, so he felt entitled to ask for Soviet help there, just as the British gave help to the Russians in Romania, which was in the Soviet sphere of military command.[16]

From this it seems clear that what Eden was proposing at this time was not any formal political agreement but a working arrangement, not unlike the understanding that Eisenhower, as Supreme Commander in Europe, later had with the Soviet general staff. There was nothing dramatic and no obvious reason why his suggestion should have led inevitably to a post-war division into spheres of influence.

Eden certainly did not see it in this light. Four days after seeing Gusev he replied to Churchill's two minutes of 4 May proposing a showdown with Russia. Eden was against this: 'It will not be easy to show that they have embarked on a policy of Communising the Balkans and Italy even if we suspect that this is their long-term objective.' If the Russians seemed to be supporting Tito and EAM, they were only following in Britain's footsteps; they had not yet shown their hand in Bulgaria or Romania except to say that they did not intend to alter Romania's social structure. But he agreed with Churchill that the time had come to consider 'the after war effect of these developments'.[17]

In talking to Gusev on 5 May, therefore, Eden was still thinking on a short-term practical basis. He did not even think it necessary to mention the matter to the War Cabinet. It was the Russians who dramatised and formalised the whole affair. On 18 May Gusev told Eden that the Soviet government agreed to his suggestion about Romania and Greece but, before giving any final assurance, wanted to know whether he had consulted the Americans and whether they had agreed. Eden replied that he didn't think the Americans had been consulted, but could not imagine they would dissent.[18]

It can only be guesswork whether the Russians made this move because they saw that Eden's suggestion could be the starting-point for a post-war carve-up, for which U.S. blessing was needed, or simply because they saw a chance to make mischief between the British and Americans – Stalin had discovered the pleasures of this game at Tehran. However this may be, they succeeded on both counts.

After seeing Gusev, Eden told the War Cabinet what was going on in a fairly off-hand way, saying he was sure there would be no difficulty with the Americans. The War Cabinet took note 'with satisfaction'.[19] At the same time Churchill, in a long message to Roosevelt on various problems, wrote that he had found it practically impossible to continue correspondence with the Russians, but he had noticed that after each rude message they seemed to do pretty well what was asked:

For instance . . . although Molotov was most insulting about Romania, they have today told us they accept the broad principle that they take the lead in the Romanian business and give us the lead in Greece. I am quite content with this. A portent of the Soviet policy is to be found in the gushing message which I have received from the representatives of EAM.[20]

Roosevelt did not react in any way to this information and perhaps did not even notice it. Churchill also seemed to forget that he had written it, for on 24 May he wrote to Eden that he would like to telegraph to Roosevelt about the arrangement with Gusev: 'He would like the idea especially as we should keep in close touch with him.'[21]

In the Foreign Office, however, there had already been some misgivings about it, one official minuting on 23 May: 'It is the thin end of the wedge towards spheres of influence.' Now, prompted by Churchill's minute, they sent a telegram to Washington stressing that the British had 'no desire to carve up the Balkans into spheres of influence'; the arrangement was just 'a useful device for preventing divergence of policy'.

There followed a deplorable British muddle which made the Americans think Churchill and Eden were behaving in a most underhand way. On 30 May Halifax spoke to Hull about the 'arrangement', but, knowing Hull would hate it, did not tell him Eden had already spoken to Gusev: 'I represented your suggestion as fruit of your own independent reflections.' Even so, Hull was very nervous about 'spheres of influence'. Before Halifax's report of this interview arrived in London, Churchill had sent Roosevelt a message informing him (for the second time, but more formally) of the arrangement with Gusev, presenting it as natural in the existing military situation, since Romania fell within the sphere of the Soviet armies and Greece within the sphere of the Allied Mediterranean Command. He also said there was no question of spheres of influence. Hearing of this, Halifax sent a personal telegram saying he was now in a 'slight difficulty': he had purposely not disclosed to Hull that Eden had already spoken to Gusev 'because I thought we were more likely to get the Americans along with us in that way'.[22]

Halifax's would-be skilful diplomacy caused more than a 'slight difficulty'. Tetchy messages between Roosevelt and Churchill were exchanged during June about the 'arrangement', culminating with a reproof from Roosevelt: 'I hope matters of this importance can be prevented from developing in such a manner in the future.' This stung Churchill to a passionate reply. He thought Roosevelt had agreed that the Russians, 'the only power that can do anything in Romania', should direct things there; the Greek burden rested almost entirely on the British: 'It would be quite easy for me, on the general principle of slithering to the left, which is so popular in foreign policy, to let things rip, when the King of Greece would probably be forced to abdicate and EAM would work a reign of terror. . . . I cannot admit that I have done anything wrong.' (Churchill's first draft had been still more passionate, but Eden persuaded him to leave out the more violent phrases, for instance: 'If I do not have your confidence and help within the spheres of action in which are Greece, I will be very glad to resign the burden which will become unendurable.'[23])

After this, Roosevelt agreed to a three months' trial of the 'arrangement'. But then Stalin decided to string things out. The Red Army was preparing a summer offensive which might carry it well into the Balkans, so there was no reason for him to tie his own hands. He decreed that the Soviet Union must make its own direct approach to Washington, since the Americans had 'some doubts'. Churchill wrote to Eden: 'Does this mean that all we had settled with the Russians now goes down through the pedantic interference of the U.S.?' Eden told the War Cabinet that the arrangement he had hoped for had broken down, and this could only add to the difficulties in a rapidly changing situation. The State Department's reply to Moscow's enquiry was so obscure and hedged about that Churchill asked Eden if it meant that everything was thrown into the pool again. Eden replied that it meant that 'the Americans would still agree to a three months' trial, but it is obvious also that they would much prefer that the Russians should turn the whole scheme down'. There might, he said, still be a chance of getting the Russians 'to recognise our predominant position in Greece', but he was not hopeful.[24]

By this time it was 8 August. Later that month King Michael of Romania carried out a coup which opened to the Red Army the way to Bulgaria and through Bulgaria to Yugoslavia; it also opened the way into Hungary. Churchill and Eden, together in Quebec in September, were particularly worried about Bulgaria as a potential threat to Greece, but even more worried about Greece itself. Eden telegraphed to the Foreign Office about the need for assurance that 'the Soviet Union recognises the predominant position of H.M.G. in all arrangements for Greece now and after the actual state of war has ended'. As for Yugoslavia, the Soviet government should be asked to agree to 'close consultation' and a common interest in a strong, united and independent state.[25]

So if in May Eden had been thinking of a short-term working arrangement over Greece and Romania, the events of the summer – Stalin's exploitation of Anglo-U.S. differences, the Red Army's sweep into southeast Europe – had changed things; both he and Churchill were now thinking in the longer term, about something very like a carve-up into spheres of influence. The outlines of a 'percentage agreement' could already be seen.

*

While Churchill was wrangling with Roosevelt over the 'arrangement' with Gusev, he was quarrelling with him even more passionately over Alexander's plan for a military operation through Istria and the Ljubljana Gap towards Vienna. He deeply resented the U.S. veto, but had to accept it in the end. But when he met Tito on 12 August he asked whether Tito would 'send a force to the north-east corner of Italy if we were able to reach the area by the east coast of Italy'. Tito said he would certainly favour an operation against the Istrian peninsula in which his forces would take part. Soon after, a British officer reported hopefully about the co-operation of the Slovene partisans in the event of a landing in Istria.

In Moscow in October Stalin, rather surprisingly, proposed a British invasion of Istria and a joint Anglo-Soviet attack on Vienna, but since he also suggested an Allied advance through Switzerland he probably did not mean it seriously. At Yalta Stalin again raised the plan with Churchill and Eden; but by this time any troops that could be spared from Italy were needed in France.[26] Eden and Macmillan later wrote regretfully and reproachfully about the U.S. veto on the plan and its post-war political impact on central Europe. But the Chiefs of Staff were always, at best, lukewarm. Probably it would never have worked.[27]

By the autumn of 1944 one of Churchill's motives in continuing to champion an Istria–Ljubljana Gap–Vienna operation was certainly the political one of checking Soviet power in south-east Europe. But by then he knew that the odds were against its ever coming off. He felt he must try other methods of setting a limit to Soviet expansion. He and Eden agreed that it was urgent to talk to Stalin face to face; and they proposed this to Stalin without first getting Roosevelt's blessing. Roosevelt, pre-occupied with the November presidential election, at first seemed happy enough to steer clear of any politically embarrassing entanglements, merely agreeing amiably to Churchill's request that Harriman, now U.S. ambassador in Moscow, should 'assist' him and Eden in their undertaking. But then, prodded by Hopkins, he decided that he must keep control over events, and instructed Harriman to participate in the talks as his 'observer'. When Churchill heard this he told Roosevelt he would be glad to have Harriman at all 'principal conferences' but this should not prevent 'private têtes-à-têtes between me and U.J. or Anthony and Molotov'. He promised to keep Roosevelt informed of 'everything that effects our joint interests'.[28]

What Churchill did not know at that moment was that Roosevelt had also sent Stalin a message – which Hopkins had helped him draft – stressing that he chose to regard the Anglo-Soviet talks 'merely as a preliminary to a conference of the three of us'; there was literally no question, military or political, in which the U.S. was not interested.[29] But even if he had known, Churchill and Eden were clearly set on acting independently for once, without any of the American 'pedantry' which had made so much trouble over Eden's 'arrangement' with Gusev in the summer.

In Moscow the two men behaved slightly like schoolboys playing truant. Harriman was a good friend but they did not want him there all the time. At their first meeting with Stalin and Molotov on 9 October there was an almost conspiratorial mood; Stalin encouraged it, telling them of Roosevelt's message. Churchill said he would welcome Harriman at a number of their talks, but did not want this to prevent 'intimate talk' between Stalin and himself; 'Harriman was not quite in the same position as they were'. Stalin, who seemed to be egging Churchill on to be anti-American, said he had 'noticed some signs of alarm' in Roosevelt's message and on the whole did not like it: it seemed to demand too many rights for the U.S., leaving too little for the Soviet Union and Britain, who after all had a treaty.

Churchill said he was 'not worrying much about Romania', that was very much a Russian affair, but Greece was different: 'Britain must be the leading Mediterranean power' and he hoped Stalin would let him have the first say about Greece in the same way as Stalin about Romania. He then threw caution to the winds and produced what he called a 'naughty document' showing a list of the south-east European countries with the proportion of interest in them of the great powers. This was the famous sheet of paper giving the percentages for the Soviet Union and 'the others': 90–10 in Romania, 10–90 in Greece, Yugoslavia 50–50, Hungary 50–50, Bulgaria 75–25. Churchill said the Americans would be shocked if they saw how crudely he had put it; but Stalin was a realist, he himself was not sentimental, and Eden was 'a bad man'. Churchill added that he had not consulted the British Cabinet or Parliament.

Stalin, so Churchill wrote later, ticked the paper after a slight pause. There followed an inconclusive wrangle about Bulgaria: Churchill said British interest there was greater than in Romania, and so Britain must be more than a 'spectator', as she was in Romania. Stalin said if Britain was interested in the Mediterranean, then Russia was equally interested in the Black Sea, and Bulgaria was a Black Sea country; he asked for the figures in the 'naughty document' to be amended.[30] Churchill suggested that Eden and Molotov should be left to deal with this. When the two met next day Molotov tried to beat Eden down to 90–10 for Bulgaria and 75–25 for Hungary, in Russia's favour. In the haggling the percentages became somewhat unreal and even absurd.[31]

It is difficult to say how seriously Churchill himself took them. But he was quite clear that what he had done would get him into trouble with Roosevelt and possibly with the War Cabinet and Parliament. Churchill and Stalin sent Roosevelt a joint message next day, which referred only in the vaguest way to the south-east European countries. Harriman was told 'in bits and pieces over several days'.[32]

On 11 October Churchill sent Roosevelt a message saying that nothing would be settled about the Balkans 'except preliminary agreements between Britain and Russia'. The next day he drafted a long letter to Stalin, explaining that the percentages were 'no more than a method by which in our thoughts we can see how near we are together and then decide upon the necessary steps'. They would be considered 'crude and even callous if they were exposed to the scrutiny of the Foreign Offices and diplomats all over the world'. They should not therefore be put in any public document, certainly for the present.

This letter was a clear sign that Churchill was worried that Stalin might make mischief with the 'naughty document', either by sending details to Roosevelt in an inauspicious form, or even by publishing it. Harriman found Churchill working in bed; Churchill read him the letter, and Harriman said he was sure Roosevelt and Hull would both repudiate it. Eden came in at this point and heard what Harriman had said. The letter never went and Harriman believed that his warning prevented Churchill from sending it.[33]

Churchill did, however, write a memorandum for the War Cabinet on the percentages, presenting them as drably as possible: they were mainly intended to prevent the threat of civil war and British–Soviet conflict, and also to produce 'a joint and friendly policy towards Marshal Tito'. They did not commit the U.S. and were only 'an interim guide for the immediate wartime future'.[34]

Their immediate use was as a counter for Eden in haggling with Molotov about the role of the British – and Americans – in the armistice commissions in Bulgaria, Romania and Hungary. The resulting arrangements meant in practice that Soviet control was nearly 100% effective. But the mere presence of British and U.S. missions did, for some months – in Hungary rather longer – give some confidence and courage to the non-Communist political parties there. In the long run the western governments could do nothing, however, to prevent their liquidation.

The one concrete achievement of the percentage agreement was that there was no open Soviet intervention in Greece during the civil war, perhaps no undercover intervention either. Churchill believed that Stalin had stuck to his word and that this in itself justified the 'naughty document'. There is no evidence that Eden disagreed: he hardly could, since he had, probably unintentionally, started the whole business on 5 May 1944. Churchill certainly regarded Eden as his partner and fellow-conspirator in hatching the 'naughty document'; he wrote to him in December 1944: 'Remember the percentages we wrote out on paper. . . . You and I took great responsibility.'[35]

What is also certain is that Stalin did not receive overlordship of Romania, Bulgaria, Hungary and, for a time, Yugoslavia from Churchill and Eden as a gift on a plate on 9 October 1944. He had already made sure of it through the victories of the Red Army in August and September and early October, with unacknowledged help from Tito's partisans, King Michael of Romania, S.O.E. and the strategic doctrines of the U.S. Chiefs of Staff.

CHAPTER TWENTY-ONE

In search of a Soviet policy

One of the oddest incidents in Anglo-Soviet relations was the great public welcome given to Churchill at the Bolshoi Theatre when he and Eden visited Moscow in October 1944. Stalin had already broken all precedents by going to the British embassy to dine with them. At the Bolshoi, when Churchill appeared with Stalin – who then retired into the shadow letting Churchill stand alone – there was enormous cheering and applause which – according to Harriman and his daughter – went on for 'many minutes'.[1]

This notable public demonstration of friendship for the old imperialist enemy, Churchill, and for Britain, must have had some political meaning. For some time past Stalin had committed himself in his public speeches and statements to friendship with the western Allies, leaving the hostility, jibes and suspicions to come out in his private messages to Churchill or indirectly through the Soviet Press. Now he was advertising his friendship in an even more personal way, standing with Churchill to take the applause. Churchill – as when he received public welcomes in Rome or Paris – was moved, and later described the scene as 'a rapturous ovation from the entire audience'. Eden, looking on from the back of the box, described it more coolly as 'much polite clapping and enthusiasm', adding that when he and Churchill went to wash their hands during the interval Churchill suddenly became excited by an idea to help him solve the Polish problem, and made the audience wait quite a while for his return.[2]

Whether rapturous or merely polite, Churchill's welcome raised the fundamental question: did Stalin perhaps really want friendship with Britain and, if so, on what terms?

Since 1941 the Foreign Office had been trying in fits and starts to tackle this central problem of Anglo-Soviet relations, which underlay disputes about the Soviet frontier, Poland, Czechoslovakia or south-east Europe. In early 1942 the Foreign Office – rather than Eden himself – had some very gloomy thoughts, inspired partly by Polish and Yugoslav exiled politicians, about Stalin's ambitions to build an east European empire. They saw British military operations in south-east Europe as probably the only way of forestalling him. Then came the Anglo-Soviet treaty, with the unhoped-for bonus that it completely left aside the difficult frontier question and provided for post-war co-operation. Since the idea had sprung from Cadogan's brain, the Foreign Office took pride in the treaty and set out to try to make it work, perhaps with special zeal because the Americans were not in it.

In spite of many setbacks and disappointments, the Foreign Office went on hoping, especially the Northern Department responsible for relations with the Soviet Union. In August 1943 Maisky, just back from a visit to Moscow, said to Eden that there were two ways of organising Europe after the war: a division into spheres of influence or, as his government would greatly prefer, each big power should admit the right of the others to an interest in all parts of Europe, which would mean Soviet interest in France and the Mediterranean. The Foreign Office and Eden himself were all for the second solution.[3] At the Moscow Foreign Ministers' conference Soviet agreement to a European Advisory Commission seemed to show that the Russians were sincere about it, even though Molotov stone-walled all Eden's suggestions about co-operation in central and south-east Europe.

Churchill for his part was determined not to let the three-power idea cut across effective military planning and this brought him briefly into conflict with Eden. In the summer of 1943 Churchill was having to fight for his Mediterranean strategy against the American military chiefs and also to resist strong public and private Soviet pressure for the earliest possible second front in the west. In June he telegraphed to Clark Kerr that, whatever the Russians' suspicions of Britain might be, 'nothing will induce me in any circumstances to allow what at this stage I am advised and convinced would be a useless massacre of British troops. . . . They have never been actuated by anything but cold-blooded self-interest and total disdain of our lives and fortunes.' Above all he was determined not to have the Russians in on military planning until the Anglo-American dispute was settled. When Clark Kerr suggested that the Russians should be invited to the next Anglo-American top-level meeting, Eden told Churchill that this would be the least troublesome of all the bad alternatives. But Churchill would have none of it: 'It would be better to call the meeting off altogether. I would far rather put up with Stalin's bad manners than be deprived of the means of carrying on this war effectively by consultation between Great Britain and the U.S.'[4]

The Russians did not take part in the first Quebec conference; nevertheless, the Anglo-American strategic argument was not finally settled. When Eden was in Moscow in October he suddenly became an enthusiast for three-power staff talks bringing in the Russians. There had been many signs, he telegraphed to Churchill, that the Russians were sincere in their desire for permanent friendship with the British and Americans. Uncle Joe, Molotov and Co., he was sure, did not for a moment imagine that there could be any sort of full Anglo-American staff meeting on the war in Europe without their being invited. The presence of a Russian representative need not be embarrassing: 'I would pledge my head that if you were there you would soon have the Russians eating out of your hand.' Three days later Eden wrote with the same faith and hope: 'So far as I can judge the mood of these incalculable people they are now in the current to move with us in all matters, provided they can be made to feel that they are in all things our equals and that we are holding nothing back. . . . I do not think that any of us sufficiently understood hitherto, I know that I have not, how much these people have suffered from a feeling of exclusion.'[5]

Eden was preaching with the fervour of the newly converted and some of it may have rubbed off on Churchill, who telegraphed to Roosevelt at the beginning of November: 'I am influenced by the prodigious results of the Moscow conference.' He yielded to Roosevelt's pressure and accepted the idea of a three-power staff meeting in Cairo.[6] This did not take place because Roosevelt had also invited the Chinese to Cairo; but for the same reason Churchill was cheated of any Anglo-American staff talks in advance of Tehran, so that he had to fight his strategic case there under Stalin's nose, with Stalin casting the deciding vote.

Early in 1944 both Eden and Churchill relapsed into gloom about Russia, but Churchill still believed he could achieve something by the direct approach to Stalin. Infuriated by Soviet Press reports of supposed British moves for a separate peace with Hitler, he wrote to him:

Even the best friends of Soviet Russia in England are bewildered. . . . I am sure you know that I would never negotiate with the Germans separately. . . . We have never thought of making a separate peace even in the years when we were all alone and could easily have made one without serious loss to the British empire and largely at your expense.[7]

But by the beginning of April he had concluded that appeals to Stalin did not work. He advised Eden 'to relapse into a moody silence' in Foreign Office contacts with Moscow, and said he would do the same over Stalin: 'I write the above without the slightest wish to go back on our desire to establish friendly relationships with Russia, but our and especially *my* very courteous and even effusive personal approaches have had a bad effect.' Eden agreed that 'we should give personal messages between you and Stalin a rest', but added: 'Exasperating as recent Russian behaviour has been, I feel we ought not to jump to the conclusion that they have decided to go back on the policy of co-operation. . . . I would be inclined to drift a little before considering a showdown.'[8]

At this time the Foreign Office were trying to counteract the alternating extremes of optimism and gloom of their masters, and work out a balanced and coherent policy towards the Soviet Union. On 1 April Sargent, inspired by a minute written by Geoffrey Wilson of the Northern Department, wrote that it would be a mistake to jump to the conclusion that the policy of co-operation with Moscow had broken down; when the Russians were guilty of discourtesies and blunders, they should be made to realise that the British resented them. But the one way not to show disapproval was by forming 'a sort of united Anglo-American front'. On this Eden commented: 'I don't feel so good about Russians as this'; he shared Sargent's valuation of Anglo-Soviet understanding, but he had growing fears that Russia had vast aims which might include the domination of eastern Europe and even the Mediterranean and the 'Communising' of much else.[9]

Undeterred, Geoffrey Wilson tried to analyse the reasons for Soviet hostility: traditional suspicion of foreigners; loose anti-Soviet talk by British officers, especially in the Middle East, and by members of the military mission in Moscow, which undoubtedly got back to the Russians; people in Britain who wanted to let the Germans down lightly; the use by the exiled Poles of British money and paper for anti-Soviet propaganda. 'A Russian', he argued, 'would probably draw the conclusion that important elements in Britain and the U.S. were deliberately following a policy of trying to save Germany from destruction, uniting Europe in an anti-Bolshevik crusade and . . . using Poland as the spearhead or jumping-off ground for an attack on the Soviet Union.' Moreover, the machinery of the Combined Chiefs of Staff led to 'Anglo-American hobnobbing on political questions' from which the Russians were excluded and this made them suspect plots: 'Recent intercepts regarding France show this process at work.'

The Russians, Wilson went on, wanted to co-operate, if only because it was the best way of finding out what the British and Americans were up to; but they watched very carefully for any falling short by the British, at the same time trying to reinsure in eastern Europe where they considered they had special interests. This fed British and American suspicions and a vicious circle was immediately created: 'It is idle to speculate on who started the process.' There should be far more careful selection of personnel who were to come in contact with Russians: 'We know from the document which came into our hands at Archangel how minutely the Russians tabulate the virtues and vices of the foreigners with whom they deal and it can be assumed that all remarks made in all sorts of unguarded moments are carefully recorded and passed on to Moscow.'

Gladwyn Jebb, the post-war planner, declared Wilson's diagnosis excellent: if a tough line was taken towards the Germans, there was no reason to despair of a perfectly amicable arrangement with the Bolsheviks. Cadogan also called it 'a very good paper', adding that the problem was that there were no Russians below the very top level bold enough to take responsibility as useful talking partners, and Churchill and Roosevelt could not always be travelling all the way to Tehran. Even Eden approved, and pondered sending Wilson's minute to Churchill.[10]

In June Eden put to the War Cabinet a paper drafted by the Foreign Office, mainly intended to explain his approach to Gusev for an arrangement over Greece and Romania. This said there were disturbing signs of a Soviet intention to acquire a dominating influence in the Balkans but this did not necessarily mean that they wanted to Communise the Balkan countries. The British aim should be to avoid any open clash of interests or conflict with the Russians, but to use every opportunity to spread British influence. The exception was Greece where an effort should be made to build up a regime which would 'definitely look to Great Britain for support against Russian influence'. A subsequent paper dealing with central Europe suggested much the same policy – avoiding a direct challenge to Russia, but spreading British influence – in Poland, Czechoslovakia, Hungary and Austria.[11]

These papers did not conflict with Wilson's diagnosis that the Russians were trying to 'reinsure' in eastern Europe, though they expressed Soviet intentions more bleakly. In August Wilson made a fresh suggestion: in order to put teeth into the Anglo-Soviet treaty in the post-war period, the Russians would almost certainly want regular staff talks with the British, whether or not a world organisation came into being.

He also pointed to differences between the Foreign Office and the service departments revealed in a paper produced by the Chiefs of Staff and the Post-Hostilities Planning Committee, on which the Foreign Office was represented. The military, Wilson wrote, said that the only power in Europe which could be a danger in the foreseeable future was the Soviet Union. This was quite right. But they then went on to say that the only way to meet that danger was to organise now, and had therefore argued for the dismemberment of Germany on the ground that 'we might then be able to use the manpower and resources of north-west Germany in an eventual war against the Russians'. In other ways, too, the military had shown that the Russian danger was in the forefront of their minds.

Sargent took the matter up with Eden, telling him of Foreign Office misgivings about the Chiefs of Staff argument that 'the dismemberment of Germany would be to our long-term strategic advantage in the event that we should require German assistance against a hostile U.S.S.R.'; 'a wide circle of military gentlemen' must be talking along these lines and if it was not already known to the Russians they were unlikely to remain ignorant for long. Also, the Chiefs of Staff were refusing to take account of political factors such as the Anglo-Soviet alliance and if this went on it would be senseless for the Foreign Office to be represented in preparing plans.

Eden was shocked, and minuted, 'This is very bad.'[12] He took the matter up with Ismay. The paper which emerged from the Post-Hostilities Planning Staff in November was purged of the passages about using German manpower against Russia which had so worried Wilson in August. It still foresaw a threat from Russia, but after 1955 rather than earlier. The threat would be so grave that Britain had a vital interest in remaining friendly with Russia. Failing that, methods must be found to delay a Soviet advance into western Europe, to give time for the deployment of British and Allied forces, especially those of the U.S. There were strong reasons for forming a west European group with France, Belgium, Holland, Denmark, Norway and possibly Sweden, Spain, Portugal and Iceland. All that was said of the Germans was that the British should not evacuate their occupation zone unless the Russians did theirs, and in case of 'a breakdown in our relations with the U.S.S.R.' the British should be ready to reoccupy their zone.

Eden passed this paper to three senior members of the Foreign Office only. Cadogan wrote that he hoped the report would be put in some secure pigeon-hole; Eden agreed.[13] (It would be interesting to know if the paper was taken out of its pigeon-hole when planning started for the 1948 Brussels Treaty and the Atlantic alliance of 1949.) In any case the Foreign Office attitude to it showed that throughout 1944 they did their best to make Anglo-Soviet co-operation work, eschewing evil thoughts and thinking good thoughts. On the whole Eden agreed with them (especially when it was a matter of inter-departmental warfare).

Reports that came in during the winter of 1944–5 of what was going on in the countries where the Red Army was now in control – Poland, Romania and Bulgaria – made it harder to eschew evil thoughts; but the Foreign Office still wanted to pin their faith on post-war co-operation with Russia, even if it meant deciding just how much to throw to the wolves, or, rather, where to draw a line limiting Soviet westward expansion and what sort of behaviour to accept without a murmur within the Soviet realm.

In March 1945 Sargent thought the Soviet Union might go so far as to annex Romania, but still believed an open clash should be avoided, and Eden seemed to agree. In mid-March Sargent argued the case for giving up Romania and Bulgaria : 'Would it not be better to abandon a position which has become untenable, and, without protest . . . to accept tacitly the governments which the Soviet authorities have set up. . . ? The British public are not likely to know what is going on in countries in Russian occupation, for censorship will prevent correspondents from reporting the true facts.' This was an 'unheroic course', but it would be a mistake to endanger 'our fundamental policy of post-war co-operation with the Soviet Union for the sake of an issue which, even if it is not entirely academic or quixotic, is at any rate not vital to British interests'. Another official, Douglas Howard, put it even more strongly : 'I fail to see how we are to prevent the Russians doing what they want in Romania, Bulgaria and Hungary and to some extent Yugoslavia, and the sooner we recognise it, and by so doing decrease the suspicion which is poisoning Anglo-Soviet relations, the better.'[14]

Eden could hardly go as far as this. It would, in any case, have been impossible to abandon Poland, which from the point of view of political opinion in Britain was still a very live and sensitive issue in the spring of 1945; there was also a good deal of interest in Yugoslavia. But at this time Eden's energies were directed to the building of a world organisation with the Soviet Union as an essential founder; other things came second.

Churchill, in the closing months of the war, was racked by uncertainty over Russia. His doctor (Lord Moran) noted in his diary on 30 October 1944 that he seemed torn between two lines of action, whether to try to get Roosevelt to take a firmer line with Stalin, or to make his own peace with Stalin : 'At one moment he will plead with the President for a common front against Communism and the next he will make a bid for Stalin's friendship. Sometimes the two policies alternate with bewildering rapidity.'[15] There was some truth in this.

At Yalta, where Roosevelt told Stalin that U.S. troops would leave Europe in two years, Churchill got little encouragement to think the

Americans could be induced to take the lead in standing up to the Russians in Europe – or that he could successfully follow the alternative of winning over Stalin on his own. But after Yalta he tried to get Roosevelt to take the lead. Over Romania he minuted to the Foreign Office at the beginning of April: 'I hope the Americans will react. . . . We should then support them, quietly but steadfastly.'[16] Churchill felt inhibited over Romania because of the percentage agreement; over Poland he had no such inhibitions, but he still wanted to push Roosevelt forward rather than play a lone hand. Eden at this time wanted him to act jointly with Roosevelt over Poland but to lay off his separate approaches: 'The Russians are behaving so abominably in every respect . . . that I hope you will not mind my suggesting that it might be as well that you should cut down your personal messages to Stalin to a minimum.'[17]

The one moment when there seemed to be a real meeting of minds between Churchill and Roosevelt was a week before Roosevelt died. It was caused by Stalin's extreme offensiveness over the Berne negotiations about the surrender of the German army in Italy, which had hurt Roosevelt's pride. Churchill wrote to him in early April:

We must always be anxious lest the brutality of the Russian messages does not foreshadow some deep change of policy. . . . On the whole I incline to think it is no more than their natural expression when vexed or jealous. For that very reason I deem it of the highest importance that a firm and blunt stand should be made. . . . I believe this is the best chance of saving the future. If they are ever convinced that we are afraid of them and can be bullied into submission, then indeed I should despair of our future relations with them and much else.

Roosevelt replied: 'We must not permit anybody to entertain a false impression that we are afraid. Our armies will in a very few days be in a position that will permit us to become "tougher" than has heretofore appeared advantageous to the war effort.'[18]

But when it came to pushing the Anglo-American armies as far east as possible, or, later, delaying their withdrawal westwards to the agreed line, so as to bargain with Stalin from strength, the greater toughness which Roosevelt had promised did not show itself, and Churchill failed to get his way.

One thing which may have softened Churchill's own feelings about Russia in the last weeks of war was his wife's long-delayed visit to the Soviet Union as creator of the very successful 'Aid to Russia' fund in Britain. A few days before she left, he asked Eden for his unprejudiced opinion: 'I suppose it is all right Clemmie going on her journey. . . . I incline to her going as arranged.' So he had his personal fears, but Mrs Churchill went and spent April in Russia. Soon after her arrival Clark Kerr reported that she had done 'a week of exacting work triumphantly performed'. Later in April Eden passed on to Churchill the news that Harriman was 'loud in praise of Clemmie's achievement in Moscow . . . she had made a valiant and tactful contribution to Anglo-American relations with Russia at a most critical time'.

Churchill saw that the visit had political meaning. He telegraphed to her: 'The ambassador will show you my telegrams to Stalin. Our personal relations are very good at present but there are many difficulties as you will see. You should express to Stalin personally my cordial feelings and my resolve and confidence that a complete understanding between the English-speaking world and Russia will be achieved and maintained for many years, as this is the only hope of the world.[19]

So in April 1945 Churchill still had some hope of friendship with Stalin, even if it was a badly battered hope, and his wife's warm welcome in Russia must have revived it a little. But when victory in Europe came he was, by his own account, filled with apprehension for the future: 'I could not rid my mind of the fear . . . that the real and hardest test still lay before us.'[20] Both he and Eden wanted a fresh meeting of the Big Three. Churchill wrote to Eden at the end of May that there 'we shall have to raise the great question of police government versus free government, it always being understood that the intermediate states must not pursue a hostile policy to Russia'.[21] (That was easier said than done. By this time the impact of the Red Army and the local Communists on the 'intermediate states' had been such that if there were to be governments friendly to the Soviet Union they were almost bound to be 'police governments'.)

Churchill's only hope was still to get the Americans to take the lead. He wrote to the Foreign Office in June: 'It is beyond the power of this country to prevent all sorts of things crashing at the present time. The responsibility lies with the U.S. and my desire is to give them all the support in our power. If they do not feel able to do anything, then we must let matters take their course.'[22]

Within a few weeks Churchill and Eden had been voted out of power, and it was left to the Labour government to make a last effort at political compromise with Stalin, and then to manoeuvre the U.S. into taking the lead.

In July 1945 Clark Kerr wrote to Eden in terms which – perhaps he did not realise it – implied a fundamental criticism of Churchill and Eden:

> It is a melancholy truth that the Russians are still uncertain about ourselves. I mean how far we are ready to go to back our friends and to stand up in good time for our principles and what we conceive to be our vital interests. About this I feel that we should leave them in no doubt, for when they are in doubt they tend to be a danger. . . .

Clark Kerr added: 'It would be prudent in us to pass speedily on to enlighten our own public opinion.'[23]

It was true that the signals which Churchill and Eden had sent to Stalin in their various disputes were confusing, at least for a man like Stalin. In Moscow in 1941 Eden had seemed quite confident that he would be able to fix matters quickly over the Soviet western frontier, but then all sorts of difficulties had loomed up and the frontier question was left open. In 1943 Eden made a fuss over the projected Soviet–Czechoslovak treaty and then suddenly gave way. At the end of 1943 Churchill seemed quite ready to do a deal on the Curzon line and gave Stalin Lwów into the bargain – yet he would not or could not effectively bully the London Poles into submission. In October 1944 Churchill must have seemed in Stalin's eyes to be clinching a private deal over south-east Europe, with a little perfunctory haggling to save face; yet soon after the British were taking a high moral line about what the Russians were doing in Romania and Bulgaria. It was not surprising if at the end of all this Stalin perhaps felt that Churchill and Eden did want friendship with Russia but could not make up their minds what price they would or could pay; in these circumstances Stalin could safely gamble on keeping British friendship on his own terms and without paying any price for it.

Certainly Stalin and Molotov seemed genuinely surprised when Bevin, as Labour Foreign Secretary, started being tough, and by October 1945 it was being said in Moscow that such a thing could never have happened in Churchill's day.[24]

Clark Kerr also had a point about the ignorance of the British public. During the war years it was understandable if Churchill and Eden were afraid of giving German propagandists useful material, or lowering morale at home and in the forces, or running into storms in Parliament. But if they had taken the risk of explaining their difficulties with Stalin more openly, stating them factually and without drama, they would have been in a stronger position to deal with Stalin, and he might have understood them better and taken them more seriously.

Yet even then he might not have listened if the Americans had been saying something different.

PART FIVE

Afterthoughts

CHAPTER TWENTY-TWO

Kings, Princes and Archdukes

It was sometimes hard to tell whether Churchill's devotion to kings, princes and archdukes was serious, or a piece of private romanticism, based on a vivid sense of history, and sometimes ostentatiously flaunted to annoy others, notably Eden and, in particular, the Foreign Office, which he once accused of marked prejudice against all kings. Once, too, writing to Eden that the Greeks might actually want their king back, he added: 'The above is for your eyes alone, and should not be shown to the Republican Guard at the Foreign Office.'[1]

At times this passion, or hobby, of Churchill's certainly embarrassed Eden and produced heavy sighs from the Foreign Office. Once it even put him at odds with King George VI. But it was not a cause of personal conflict with the republican Roosevelt, who, though he might think it politically convenient that Washington should on occasion publicly deplore Churchill's monarchist leanings, himself enjoyed foreign royalty as a pleasing pastime. In 1944 Pierson Dixon of the Foreign Office heard Churchill say: 'I have had many kings on my hands. I have fought hard for George and Peter, the king of Italy slipped through my fingers. President Roosevelt supports me: he likes to keep kings on their thrones.'[2] With Stalin, too, Churchill had no quarrel over monarchs. As a realist Stalin was quite ready to see that kings could have their wartime uses, and he gave a high Soviet award to King Michael of Romania for his anti-Axis coup. In the case of the young king of Yugoslavia, Stalin told Tito: 'Take him back temporarily, and then you can slip a knife into his back at a suitable moment.'[3]

Of Churchill's deep devotion and respect for the British monarchy there was no question whatever. This was something that Eden, too, took for granted. The monarchies of north-west Europe were not a problem, except for King Leopold's decision to remain in Belgium under German occupation, but that was a matter for the Belgians to deal with in their own time. In south and south-east Europe Churchill might wish to preserve the monarchies but was prepared to bully exiled monarchs with little mercy when pushed to it. The Italian monarchy might be a desirable institution, but Victor Emmanuel was valued chiefly as a figurehead who could command the loyalty of the navy and be used to block the ambitions of the politicians; once he had served the purpose he could be allowed to disappear.

King Peter of Yugoslavia, hardly more than a boy and young for his age, aroused a certain sentimental feeling in both Churchill and Eden. Eden was keen that he should be taught the English way of life and perhaps he would help to spread British influence in post-war Yugoslavia. The problem was how to get him back there. Churchill and Eden wrangled in the summer of 1943 over his projected marriage with a Greek princess, Alexandra. Eden was told that a wartime marriage would offend the Serbs and harm his chances of keeping the throne, so he wanted the wedding to be postponed. Churchill thought this nonsense and told Eden that the Foreign Office was living in the reign of Louis XIV instead of 'the lusty squalor of the 20th century', and that he would advise Peter to go to the nearest register office and take a chance; so what. Eden replied : 'If you think me incapable of handling even this minor Balkan domestic imbroglio the remedy is in your hands. So what.'[4]

Soon after, Eden sent Peter to Cairo, leaving behind him the sorrowing Alexandra, who wrote a pathetic letter to dear Mr Churchill asking to be allowed to go to Cairo, too. Churchill was in favour of letting her go to Cairo and get married there, and was obviously startled and somewhat upset when, in November 1943 on his way to Tehran, he got a telegram from King George VI, who was Peter's godfather, saying he did not think the marriage would be a very wise one : 'I am not at all sure that the girl is fitted to be his wife.' He hoped Churchill would dissuade Peter from immediate marriage. Churchill replied almost huffily, though 'with humble duty', that he had not been aware of the king's view or that the lady in question was not regarded as suitable : 'I had myself thought that the marriage should take place and that the lady should come to Cairo for the purpose. . . . In these circumstances it would probably be better for the Foreign Secretary . . . to be the channel through which Your Majesty's wishes should be communicated.'[5] Churchill did not want to eat his own words, so handed the job to Eden.

However, George VI decided to do it himself and telegraphed to Peter in Cairo, through the ambassador to the Yugoslav government, telling him he was doing good work in the Middle East and it was his duty to stay there : as his godfather, he strongly urged him to give up the idea of marrying before the Orthodox Christmas had been celebrated : 'I know this is hard but I feel bound to advise you as to the best interests of your dynasty and your country.' The Orthodox Christmas passed, and King

George VI was still worried that perhaps Peter was being forced into marriage and was not really in love. A British officer attached to the young king was asked to say what he thought his real feelings were : 'If he is in love we do not wish to be an obstacle, but if he is in doubt and wants to get out of the marriage we can provide him with plenty of good excuses.' The answer was not a wholehearted yes, but positive enough for marriage plans to go ahead,[6] and Peter came back to London for the purpose.

By this time Eden as well as Churchill was ready to bless the marriage; but Peter then found hmself under remorseless pressure from both of them to throw over Mihailović, and to form a new government with the aim of coming to terms with Tito. Early in 1945 he was put under even more ruthless pressure to agree to the appointment of a regency on terms acceptable to Tito; he was stubborn, but he had to yield. The monarchy was thereafter voted out of existence.

If for King Peter the war years were not entirely pleasant, they were a good deal pleasanter than for his uncle Prince Paul who, as Prince Regent, and in what he believed to be Peter's interest and Yugoslavia's good, had signed the Tripartite Pact with Hitler in March 1941. Deposed by the coup of 27 March, he left the country and was thereafter treated by both Churchill and Eden with scorn and disapproval which bordered on vindictiveness; he had always been very pro-British, and now he found himself an outcast, in spite of his relationship by marriage with the British royal family. Obviously a deposed prince regent merited no special consideration.

The Habsburg archdukes stood far higher in Churchill's esteem, and this was an embarrassment to Eden which he must have found particularly irritating, all the more since it was Roosevelt who helped to fire Churchill's enthusiasm. The last reigning Habsburg king and emperor had a large family; his sons Otto, Felix, Karl Ludwig and Robert were all active during the war, with Otto co-ordinating their operations from the U.S. Duff Cooper admired them almost as much as Churchill, and once wrote to him that it seemed unlucky that the Habsburgs, having produced so many regrettable specimens in the past, should at last have turned out these 'admirable young brothers, of which any dynasty may be proud'.[7]

Otto had a strong urge to mix in the affairs of the countries which had once been part of the Habsburg realm. Between 1935 and 1937 he had persuaded the hard-pressed Austrian Chancellor, Kurt von Schuschnigg, to come to several secret meetings with him : if these had become known they might have given Hitler an excuse for armed intervention and caused great resentment in Austria's bitterly anti-Habsburg neighbours, Czechoslovakia and Yugoslavia. At the final crisis of Schuschnigg's relations with Hitler, Otto wrote proposing that he himself should take over the office of Chancellor and defy Hitler. Schuschnigg refused; Hitler occupied Austria; Otto protested publicly. He had staked his claim to a political role in the anti-Hitler camp.

When France fell Otto was in Lisbon. Churchill proposed to Halifax that Otto should come to London, 'where we can control him, and make any use of him possible'. Halifax was against it because of the inevitable Czech and Yugoslav suspicions; it would be better if Otto went to the U.S.[8] His younger brother Robert was, however, already in London, and made a habit of appealing directly to Churchill, who was much more receptive than the Foreign Office to Otto's ideas about creating a Danubian federation or 'United States of Central Europe', comprising the old Habsburg lands, and more.

In 1941 and 1942 Robert was campaigning in London for the formation of an Austrian armed unit, and Otto in the U.S. for an Austrian legion. The Foreign Office wanted Churchill to squash Robert's proposal, but he wrote to Eden in December 1942 that it would be a very good thing to have an Austrian unit: 'I am extremely interested in Austria and hope that Vienna may become the capital of a great confederation of the Danube.' Eden, who had minuted earlier that month, 'we want nothing to do with the Habsburgs', replied that a Danubian federation with Vienna as its capital would cause consternation among the Polish, Czech and Yugoslav Allies, and concluded: 'I do not see any future for the Habsburgs.'[9]

Churchill, in his inner thoughts, still cherished the Habsburg dream. When he was in Quebec in August 1943 Otto asked to see him, adding that he had direct messages from central Europe which he wanted to impart. Churchill wrote to Eden: 'I should rather like to see him. What do you say?' Eden replied that he could see no harm in it; personally he saw no hope for the Habsburgs, who would be 'a bar to any union of Austria and the old successor states, which is what we want to see'.[10]

Churchill (without Eden) did see Otto, who later told John Wheeler-Bennett, then attached to the British information services in the U.S., that he had received the 'greatest encouragement' from Churchill whose views on the future structure of central Europe were most satisfactory; Churchill had, however, told him that he was hampered by 'those in his Cabinet who were prepared to make a surrender to Russia'. They had differed only on one point: Otto wanted Croatia to be part of a central European federation, Churchill wanted to restore the kingdom of Yugoslavia with its old frontiers. As for Hungary, Otto said the British were in touch with people who could not 'deliver the goods'; instead, they should get the regent Horthy to agree to resign and name a successor 'agreed upon in advance as friendly and amenable to the western powers'. (Otto did not say whether he meant himself.) All in all, he thought the English blind to the Bolshevik danger; it was only Churchill who saw it.[11]

Otto no doubt greatly dramatised what Churchill had said. All the same Churchill, in the light of his friend Roosevelt's sympathy for Otto – Roosevelt had also seen him – may well have gone far beyond what Eden would have approved. In any case, he plunged into the fray, tackling Eden on the reluctance of the Foreign Office to grant a visa to the archduke Karl Ludwig whom Otto wanted to send to Lisbon 'to make certain contacts'; for this purpose a British visa was needed. Churchill telegraphed to Eden, now back in London: 'I cannot see why this modest request should not be granted. . . . I really see no reason . . . why we, the leading monarchical country, should seem more allergic to royalty than the republic of the U.S.' No one could tell how central Europe would turn; while it would be silly to try to force any kind of king or emperor on them, it would be equally unwise to try to knock any such chance on the head. One of the greatest mistakes after the First World War was 'the destruction by ignorant hands of the Austro-Hungarian empire'; perhaps now 'those disillusioned peoples may see a way out of their troubles through some symbolic chief'. (That could only mean Otto.) Churchill ended with a plea:

> Do not discuss it with your colleagues, for I have no doubt you could easily beat everything on the head. Please try to have a little confidence in my insight into Europe gathered over so many years. . . . If the Wittelsbachs had been substituted in Germany for the Hohenzollerns there would have been no Hitler and no war. Be kind to me in this small matter and let the poor devil have his visa.[12]

This telegram was marked 'for your eye alone'. It put Eden in an awkward spot. The Foreign Office were against giving Karl Ludwig a visa and had told the Americans so; Eden agreed. Faced with Churchill's plea, the Foreign Office were caustic, minuting that there were only small pro-Habsburg elements in Hungary or Austria; in Hungary, a Habsburg attempt at mediation could be disastrous to the contacts the British had just established with the 'surrender group'; the Habsburg name stank with the Czechs, Yugoslavs and Russians. Strang commented: 'The Ruritanian brothers take themselves very seriously.' But the conclusion was that it was not worth pressing the Foreign Office view against the Prime Minister over the visa for Karl Ludwig. Eden answered Churchill that this might lead to complications with the Hungarian 'surrender group' but he supposed it would do not great harm.[13]

The visa did lead to trouble. Karl Ludwig arrived in Lisbon and conveyed a message from Otto to Budapest implying that he had Anglo-American blessing for a plan for the regent Horthy to step down and make way for Otto. This caused a good deal of confusion. At first S.O.E.'s contact in Budapest reported that the Hungarian prime minister was about to send back a message asking Otto to consider himself the only constitutional representative of Hungary if there were a German occupation. Soon after there came a report in the opposite sense – that the Hungarian government might withdraw its offer of unconditional surrender as a result of 'interference and misinformation from Otto Habsburg', who had told the Hungarians that 'Washington' had promised Otto restoration to the throne of Hungary. The Foreign Office agreed with S.O.E. on a prompt reply that the British were giving no support to the Habsburgs in either Austria or Hungary and 'we should be surprised if American policy were different'. The matter was cleared up and negotiations with the 'surrender group' got back on the rails, but went more slowly than the British had hoped. Frank Roberts of the Foreign Office commented that this was in part due to 'the over-friendly remarks to the Archduke Otto by President Roosevelt and the Prime Minister, which were passed on to Budapest'.[14]

When Churchill was again in Quebec in September 1944, Otto's A.D.C. asked whether 'His Imperial Majesty Otto of Austria' could see him. Churchill had him to lunch. At this moment the Hungarian regent was making last desperate efforts to make contact through the western Allies with the Russians. Otto gave Churchill a copy of a letter he had just given to Roosevelt proposing that he should go in utmost secrecy to the Swiss–French border and work with a former Hungarian diplomat to bring the Budapest government at once to terms with the western Allies, with the aim of saving Hungary from Communist domination: 'Irrespective of my future role, my sole desire at present is to accomplish sincere reconciliation of the much suffered Danubian nations [sic].' If a general rising in Austria were demanded, he would wish to be informed and would then ask for the necessary arms for 'my people'.[15]

Churchill had these documents sent home to Eden, who was to say what he thought. Before Eden could do this, an article appeared in the

U.S. Press saying that, with Churchill's approval, Otto was travelling to London. This was a complete distortion of what Churchill had said to Otto.[16] Foreign Office comments were inevitably acid: Otto's interference in Hungarian matters could only do harm and the tone of his message, with its insistence on surrender to the Anglo-Soviet powers only, was 'deplorable'; his support in Austria and Hungary was negligible. Eden agreed: 'Personally I don't want to have anything to do with Otto.' Cadogan passed on all these views to Churchill in Eden's name.[17]

Churchill let the matter lie. By March 1945 Hungary was lost to Otto, but he still had hopes of Austria and wrote to Churchill from Paris asking for arms, explosives, radio equipment and money for non-Communist Resistance organisations in Austria with which he claimed to be in contact; he himself and his brothers were trying – so far unsuccessfully – to get to Switzerland so as 'to join our country as soon as the action inside will start. . . . We will not give up.'[18] On this Ismay wrote that the Foreign Office felt that, whether or not there were effective monarchist groups in Austria, 'we have grounds for mistrusting the Habsburgs' intentions for seizing power in Austria after the war'. This provoked Churchill to lecture the Foreign Office:

> This war would never have come if, under American and modernising pressure, we had not driven the Habsburgs out of Austria and Hungary and the Hohenzollerns out of Germany. By making these vacuums we gave the opening for the Hitlerite monster to crawl out of its sewer on to the vacant thrones. No doubt these views are very unfashionable.

If there was any chance of helping Otto and his brothers, he added, he did not see why there should be difficulties. Eden, in reply, tried to be sympathetic about the dissolution of the Habsburg empire but went on: 'To attempt now to put back the clock by embarking on substantial military assistance to the Habsburgs would in my view be both impracticable and dangerous.' Especially at a moment when the British were trying to get the Russians to agree to joint arrangements for Austria, it was particularly important not to arouse Russian suspicions.[19]

Churchill subsided for the moment, but burst out yet again when he read that the Belgian Prince Regent was much annoyed because Otto had turned up in Brussels. He telegraphed to the newly arrived British ambassador:

> The principle of constitutional monarchy, provided it is based on the will of the people, is not – oddly enough – abhorrent to the British mind. Personally, having lived through all these European disturbances and studied carefully their causes, I am of the opinion that if the Allies at

the peace table at Versailles had not imagined that the sweeping away of long-established dynasties was a form of progress . . . there would have been no Hitler. . . . This is a personal view, but perhaps you would like to meditate upon it.[20]

It is certain that Churchill believed deeply in constitutional monarchy based on the will of the people. It is much less certain whether he seriously believed in a Habsburg restoration, however rosy and romantic the idea might seem. He could not have imagined that Beneš or Stalin – or Tito – would ever have swallowed it. It looks more as though the Habsburg game was one which he found fascinating, especially when he could play it with his friend Roosevelt. He knew it could be dangerous; but he also knew that Nurse – that is, Eden and the Foreign Office – would stop him when he went too far and drag him, moaning and protesting a little, back into the real world. After all, that was one of Eden's important duties in his relations with Churchill; and it was why Churchill kept on asking for Eden's opinion even when he knew the answer would be 'No.'

CHAPTER TWENTY-THREE

Open Verdict

If Stalin, Roosevelt and de Gaulle were in the foreground of Eden's war-time dealings with Churchill, in the background there was the towering shadow of Hitler. Neither Churchill nor Eden seemed to have much interest in Hitler as a man, nor in the forces which gave him power – the collapse of confidence in orthodox capitalism and parliamentary democracy which followed the world economic crisis. To Churchill Hitler was simply an evil that must be destroyed; as for the future, 'first catch your hare'. Eden seemed to share Churchill's view of Hitler; his solution for the future was a bigger and better League of Nations.

Yet it was Hitler who gave Churchill his chance to become a very great war leader. Without him, Churchill would have remained a great aristocratic eccentric, a highly gifted journalist and historian, but too erratic and self-willed to get to the top as a politician. Eden would have remained a highly competent but uninspired Conservative with special knowledge and skill in foreign affairs.

Hitler's challenge to the world made Churchill fulfil his potential to the utmost limit, and turned character traits which could be a liability into supreme assets. One of his staff who worked closely with him in the war[1] later used two words in particular to describe him: pugnacious and changeable. The fact that Churchill was a born fighter and enjoyed fighting could in ordinary times be a handicap to himself and a nuisance to others; in war it was an invaluable virtue. His changeability sprang from his extraordinarily fertile brain, always eagerly exploring new possibilities and spawning new ideas; this could lead to time-wasting pursuit of fantasies, but could also in desperate times make him a dynamic driving force.

Churchill's unique personal achievement was that he gave back to ordinary people in Britain (and elsewhere) their belief in themselves and their way of life, and destroyed the myth of Hitler as the irresistible conqueror. He did this by appealing to older traditions and more primitive instincts than devotion to the particular economic and political system existing in Britain in the 1930s (even though he himself believed in these). He jeered at Hitler as well as cursing him as evil. He also caricatured himself and so made people laugh with him and respond to his patriotic rhetoric. He made people feel they were taking an active part in an extraordinary though grim adventure, rather than passively suffering an unbearable tragedy.

These were things Eden could not do, or help Churchill to do. But the experience of working closely with Churchill charged Eden with an energy and drive which, while they lasted, made him able to meet challenges and bear strains he could not normally have done. His war years as Foreign Secretary are thought by many to have been the peak of his achievement.

Churchill needed someone to direct his pugnacity to useful ends and away from futile or destructive purposes, and to control his changeability by persuading him to discard his wilder fantasies and concentrate on what was possible and worth while. In foreign affairs Eden was the man who had to do the job. The difficulty was that he, too, could be carried away by a passing mood, a sudden enthusiasm, or an attractive-looking 'policy' that would never work. Yet there was some advantage in this: if Eden had been nothing but a wet blanket, Churchill would not have stood him for long. As things were, Churchill took from Eden a great deal of opposition and frustration over his pet ideas or stubborn prejudices, and still liked him and trusted him.

In the spring of 1944 it was rumoured that, to take some of the burden off the exhausted Eden, Churchill might make Cadogan Foreign Secretary.[2] He was certainly an experienced and resourceful practitioner of traditional diplomacy and also the man who produced the draft of the Atlantic Charter at a moment's notice and invented the innocuous version of the Anglo-Soviet treaty; he was not afraid of Churchill, who respected him. But Cadogan was not a politician and did not like politicians; and a man who could not instinctively see the political dimension of a course of action – as Eden could – would have been of much less use. (Eden, moreover, had more first-hand knowledge of Europe and European politicians than either of his two senior officials, Cadogan and Sargent, whose lack of personal experience in this field perhaps explained some of the more unrealistic 'policies' that they sponsored.)

At the end of it all Britain came out of the war financially bankrupt but with a large fund of good will in many countries. De Gaulle had deep grievances, but the French, in spite of British bombing, were more kindly disposed than ever before. Britain was not, in fact, totally subservient to the U.S., in spite of the war debts; and more Americans than before respected and even liked the British. Neither Eden nor even Churchill could claim sole credit for these things. Nor, on the other hand, could they bear sole blame for their failure to turn Stalin into a benevolent and kindly uncle or to stop him imposing his own brand of despotism in central and south-east Europe. Perhaps no one could have stopped him. In fitful and uncertain fashion and with very little help from elsewhere, Churchill and Eden did at least try.

Notes

The sources given in the following notes are for the most part documents in the Public Record Office. The Prime Minister's papers are denoted by the prefix PREM 3; the Foreign Office papers have the prefix FO 371; the Avon Papers have the prefix FO 954; Cabinet documents have the prefix CAB 65 or CAB 66. The Inverchapel Papers come under the class of Private Collections and so have the prefix FO 800. Sources other than the P.R.O. papers are self-explanatory or refer to the Bibliography.

Introduction

1. Woodward, *British Foreign Policy in the Second World War*, I, xxx
2. FO 371/44001 Churchill minute M.647/4 28.5.44
3. PREM 3/211/16 Eden minute PM/44/288 27.4.44

Chapter 1

1. Thomas Barman, B.B.C. diplomatic correspondent, to author, 1974
2. CAB 129/13 C.P.(46)369 23.9.46
3. Woodward, III, 109
4. Churchill, *Second World War*, I, 119; Gilbert, *Winston S. Churchill*, V, 635
5. Ed. James, *Chips: The Diaries of Sir Henry Channon*, 146
6. Ed. Harvey, *The Diplomatic Diaries of Oliver Harvey 1937–40*, 255
7. Harvey, 244
8. Avon, *The Reckoning*, 55
9. Harvey, 305
10. Churchill, *Second World War*, I, 216
11. Gilbert, 696
12. Churchill, *Second World War*, I, 217
13. *The Listener*, 13.1.77
14. FO 954/7 (467–72, 482) Churchill letter 3.9.37; Duff Cooper letter 5.9.37; Eden letter 3.9.37; Churchill letter 20.9.37
15. Churchill, *Second World War*, I, 231
16. Churchill, *Second World War*, I, 361; Gilbert, 1107
17. Avon, 62
18. Roy Jenkins, *Asquith*, 404
19. de Gaulle, *War Memoirs: Unity 1942–44*, 57
20. Avon, 97
21. Boyle, *Poor, Dear Brendan*, 246
22. Avon, 97
23. Ibid., 127
24. Ibid., 129
25. Ibid., 129

26. Ibid., 182
27. Ibid., 182
28. Churchill, *Second World War*, II, 504
29. Ibid., I, 215
30. Lord Blake in *The Sunday Times*, 16.1.77
31. Avon, 144
32. Ibid., foreword
33. FO 954/4 (145) Salisbury letter 20.2.42
34. e.g. Channon Diaries, 302–3, 333
35. Taylor, *Beaverbrook*, 540
36. Churchill, *Second World War*, IV, 337
37. Vernon Bartlett and William Forrest talking to author, 1976
38. *The Sunday Times* (James Margach) 9.7.76
39. Harold Macmillan, *The Past Masters*, 174
40. Lord Blake in *The Sunday Times*, 16.1.77
41. Lord Strang to author, 1975
42. Ed. Dilks, *Sir Alexander Cadogan: Diaries*, 497
43. Sir Frank Roberts to author, 1975
44. Churchill, *Second World War*, IV, 733, FO 371/43795, Churchill minute M.602/4 22.5.44
45. FO 954/9 (612) Churchill note to Cadogan M.656/5 23.6.45, FO 954/14 FO 389 to Algiers February 1944
46. Sir John Colville to author, 52.2.76; *see also* pp. 45–6, 64–5 below
47. FO 954/7 (517–18) Eden minute 10.1.41
48. FO 954/22 (274), Eden minute to Cadogan 5.1.45
49. FO 954/26 (620), Churchill minute M.315/5 8.4.45
50. Cadogan Diaries, 710
51. FO 954/9 (252), Eden note undated (?15.6.41), Churchill ditto
52. Cadogan Diaries, 374, 376
53. Cadogan Diaries, 478
54. Avon, 332, 364, Cadogan Diaries, 460–1
55. Avon, 364
56. *The Listener*, 13.1.77

Chapter 2

1. and 2. Sir John Colville; ed. Sir John Wheeler-Bennett, *Action This Day*, 60
3. Wheeler-Bennett, 60–1
4. Woodward, I, xlix–lii
5. Thompson, *Churchill and Morton*, 96, 154
6. Foot, *S.O.E. in France*, 140 ff.
7. Lord Strang
8. CAB 65/7 WM(40)163 12.6.40
9. CAB 66/26 WP(42)295 14.7.42
10. PREM 3/176, Amery letters to Churchill 13 and 14.6.40, Colville minute 16.6.40, Vansittart note 16.6.40
11. CAB 65/7 WM(40)169 16.6.40
12. CAB 65/7 WM(40)171 18.6.40
13. CAB 65/7 WM(40)176 22.6.40
14. PREM 3/174/2 de Gaulle letter to Churchill 23.6.40, J.M. minute on text of statement
15. CAB 65/7 WM(40)186 28.6.40

16. CAB 65/8 WM(40)219 5.8.40
17. PREM 3 120/10 Morton minute to Churchill 3.9.41
18. PREM 3 186A/5 Churchill minutes 23 and 25.7.40, Halifax minute 25.7.40
19. PREM 3 186A/5 Churchill minute M.229 26.10.40
20. Murphy, *Diplomat among Warriors*, 76–7
21. PREM 3 186A/5 Eden minute 10.1.41
22. PREM 3 186A/5 Eden notes 20 and 28.1.41
23. PREM 3 187 Lisbon 41 17.1.41
24. PREM 3 187 Morton minute 6.2.41, Eden letter 5.2.41, Ismay minute 25.2.41
25. PREM 3 120/10 Churchill letter 4.3.41
26. PREM 3 186A/5 Churchill minutes M.149 12.2.41 and D59/1 19.2.41
27. Murphy, 69–70, 76
28. PREM 3 187 Eden minute PM/41/107 9.9.41, Churchill minute 30.11.41
29. PREM 3 187 President to P.M. T.139/2 12.1.42
30. PREM 3 187 Churchill minute M.21/2 31.2.42, Eden minute PM/42/13 5.2.42
31. PREM 3 187 Churchill minute on Washington 3730 16.7.42, Eden minute 23.7.42

Chapter 3

1. PREM 3 120/10 Churchill letter 3.4.41, telegram T.101 22.4.41
2. PREM 3 121/5 WP(44)288 1.6.44
3. Ibid.
4. PREM 3 120/1 undated note
5. PREM 3 120/5 P.M.'s personal tel. T.519 27.8.41
6. PREM 3 120/2 Brazzaville 345 29.8.41
7. PREM 3 120/5 Churchill minute M. 862/1 1.9.41
8. CAB 65/19 WM(41)88 1.9.41
9. PREM 3 120/5 Morton minute 1.9.41
10. PREM 3 120/5 Churchill letter 2.9.41
11. PREM 3 120/5 record of de Gaulle–Morton interview 2.9.41
12. PREM 3 120/5 de Gaulle letter 3.9.41
13. PREM 3 120/5 Morton minute 9.9.41
14. PREM 3 120/2 record of meeting between P.M. and de Gaulle 12.9.41
15. PREM 3 120/4 Benson minute to Martin 22.9.41
16. PREM 3 120/4 Morton note dictated by telephone 23.9.41
17. PREM 3 120/4 note of meeting between P.M. and de Gaulle 23.9.41
18. PREM 3 120/4 J.M. minute to P.M. 23.9.41
19. PREM 3 120/4 Churchill minute M.924/1 23.9.41
20. PREM 3 120/4 Morton minute to P.M. 24.9.41
21. PREM 3 120/4 Bessborough to Churchill 25.9.41
22. PREM 3 120/4 Colville to Bessborough 26.9.41
23. PREM 3 120/4 Churchill minute M.935/1 26.9.41
24. PREM 3 120/4 Eden minute PM/41/119 26.9.41
25. PREM 3 120/3 record of a meeting 1.10.41
26. Foot, 230–1
27. FO 954/8 (202–5) records of Eden–de Gaulle conversations Z2065/97/G 5.3.42, Z2087/97/G 10.3.42

Chapter 4

1. FO 371/31873 diary of events, report by Naval Liaison Officer F.S. *Surcouf* 1.1.42
2. FO 371/31872 TAUT 241 27.12.41

3. FO 371/31872 GREY 170 30.12.41
4. FO 371/31872 TAUT 376 4.1.42, TAUT 377 4.1.42, W. B. Mack minute 5.1.42
5. FO 371/31872 GREY 315 12.1.42
6. WM(42)4 12.1.42, FO 371/31872 TAUT 499 12.1.42
7. FO 371/31872 TAUT 502 12.1.42, GREY 330 14.1.42
8. FO 371/31873 Z521/3/17 16.1.42
9. WM(42)5 14.1.42
10. FO 371/31873 Eden note (unsigned) 14–15.1.42, FO 371/31874 Churchill minute to Roosevelt 14.1.42
11. WM(42)9 19.1.42
12. FO 371/31873 Eden minute PM/42/3 20.1.42, note of conversation with de Gaulle 22.1.42
13. FO 371/31873 Churchill to Roosevelt T.104/2 23.1.42
14. FO 371/31873 Washington 511 28.1.42, FO 371/31874 Washington 778 10.2.42
15. PREM 3 120/10 Churchill minute 16.1.42
16. PREM 3 121/10 Bessborough 'secret paper' undated, with covering minute to P.M. dated 6.2.42
17. PREM 3 395/18 Z277/74/17 7.1.42, Churchill minute 23.1.42
18. PREM 3 120/7 Peake No. 51 Saving 7.4.42, Churchill minute 9.4.42, Eden minute PM/42/67 10.4.42, Churchill minute 11.4.42
19. PREM 3 120/7 Eden minute PM/42/115 27.5.42, Churchill minute 30.5.42
20. CAB 65/30 WM(42)71 2.6.42
21. PREM 3 120/7 Eden despatch to Peake 258 Z4718/298/17 4.6.42
22. PREM 3 120/7 Eden minute PM/42/125 4.6.42, Churchill minute M.231/2 5.6.42, Press notice 11.6.42
23. PREM 3 121/5 WP(44)288 1.6.44
24. PREM 3 120/10 Eden despatch to Peake 13.6.42
25. PREM 3 120/10 Minister of State Cairo 797 10.6.42, Churchill minute 13.6.42
26. PREM 3 120/7 T.L.R. minute to Churchill 29.7.42, Morton minute 5.8.42
27. PREM 3 121/5 WP(44)288 1.6.44
28. Ibid.
29. CAB 66/25 WP(42)233 1.6.42
30. CAB 66/25 WP(42)235 2.6.42
31. CAB 66/25 WP(42)239 5.6.42
32. CAB 66/25 WP(42)247 9.6.42
33. CAB 66/26 WP(42)285 8.7.42
34. CAB 66/26 WP(42)295 14.7.42
35. CAB 66/27 WP(42)349 8.8.42
36. CAB 66/28 WP(42)298 4.9.42
37. PREM 3 120/10 Morton minute 11.9.42, Morton letter to Lawford 14.9.42
38. PREM 3 120/10 CFR(42)37
39. CAB 66/29 WP(42)426 23.9.42
40. CAB 66/29 WP(42)450 7.10.42
41. de Gaulle, 37–9
42. FO 954/8 (290–3) record of meeting between P.M. and Secretary of State and de Gaulle Z7530/5123/G 30.9.42
43. PREM 3 120/10 Harvey minute to Morton 8.12.42
44. PREM 3 121/5 WP(44)288 1.6.44
45. PREM 3 120/10 Morton minute 30.10.42
46. PREM 3 120/10 Eden minute PM/42/254 3.11.42, Churchill minute 4.11.42
47. Sir John Colville to author, February 1975
48. Avon, 348

49. FO 954/8 (314, 315) Bracken letter 13.11.42, Eden letter 13.11.42
50. Avon, 348
51. de Gaulle, 56–8
52. Ibid.
53. Avon, 350
54. PREM 3 120/8 Cadogan minute 21.11.42
55. PREM 3 120/8 F.N.P. to President 205 T.1564/2 22.11.42
56. de Gaulle, 59
57. PREM 3 120/8 minute to P.M. 24.11.42
58. PREM 3 120/8 draft and amendments
59. Hansard, 25.11.42, Col. 730
60. e.g. PREM 3 120/8 T.L.R. minute 28.11.42
61. PREM 3 120/8 F.D.W.B. minute 4.12.42
62. PREM 3 120/8 T.L.R. minute 28.11.42, Churchill minute on this 28.11.42
63. PREM 3 120/10 U.S. Secret Ref. 261625

Chapter 5

1. Churchill, *Second World War*, IV, 819
2. FO 954/8 (336–9) Randolph Churchill letter 28.12.42
3. PREM 3 181/8 FO 30 to Washington 2.1.43
4. PREM 3 181/8 FO 343 to Washington 15.1.43
5. FO 954/8 (359–62) record of Eden–de Gaulle conversation 17.1.43
6. de Gaulle, 79
7. CAB 66/50 WP(44)288 1.6.44
8. PREM 3 120/10 Morton minute to P.M. 18.3.43, Churchill minute 19.3.43
9. PREM 3 120/10 Washington 1736 13.4.43, FO 2470 and 2495 to Washington 15.4.43
10. CAB 65/38 WM(43)53 13.4.43
11. de Gaulle, 100
12. CAB 65/38 WM(43)75 23.5.43
13. Ibid.
14. CAB 65/38 WM(43)75 ALCOVE 370, 371, 372 23.5.43
15. Avon, 386
16. Ibid., 363–4
17. Ibid., 367
18. Churchill, *Second World War*, V, 193
19. de Gaulle, 113
20. Avon, 388
21. FO 954/8 (428, 429), FO 565 to Algiers 17.4.43, Algiers 587 20.4.43
22. PREM 3 181/11 Algiers 898 5.6.43
23. PREM 3 181/11 F.N.P. to President 300 T.740/3 6.6.43
24. PREM 3 181/11 FO 889 to Resident Minister Algiers 6.6.43
25. PREM 3 121/1 Churchill minute M.371/3 12.6.43 and attached guidance, F.D.W.B. minute 12.6.43
26. PREM 3 181/11 Washington 3183 and 3184 12.7.43
27. PREM 3 181/11 Washington 3199 13.7.43
28. PREM 3 181/11 P.M. to Halifax T.1037 15.7.43
29. Barclay, *Ernest Bevin and the Foreign Office*, 13
30. Hansard, Vol. 391, No. 92, Cols. 892–3
31. Ibid.
32. FO 954/9 (5), Algiers 24 3.1.44

Chapter 6

1. PREM 3 181/2 President to P.M. 288 T.839/3 17.6.43
2. Avon, 394
3. CAB 65/38 WM(43)87 21.6.43
4. FO 954/8 (478–9) FO 1061 to Algiers 20.5.43
5. FO 954/8 (483) Algiers 1032 22.6.43
6. PREM 3 181/11 Moscow 526 20.6.43, Churchill minute M.403/3 21.6.43, Churchill to Stalin T. 875A/3, 751 to Moscow 23.6.43
7. PREM 3 181/11 P.M.'s personal telegram T.894A/3 26.6.43
8. PREM 3 181/8 WP(43)291 2.7.43
9. PREM 3 181/8 Churchill minute M.443/3 5.7.43
10. PREM 3 181/2 Algiers 1143 6.7.43
11. PREM 3 181/2 P.M.'s telegram T.969/3 7.7.43
12. PREM 3 181/2 F.N.P. to President 348 T.979/3 8.7.43
13. PREM 3 181/2 Algiers 1263 21.7.43
14. PREM 3 181/2 President to PM. T.984/3 8.7.43
15. PREM 3 181/8 Eden minute PM/43/225 13.7.43, Churchill letter 13.7.43
16. Avon, 397–8
17. PREM 3 181/8 Eden's draft memorandum
18. PREM 3 181/8 WP(43) [sic]
19. CAB 65/35 WM(43)99 14.7.43
20. de Gaulle, 105
21. PREM 3 184/6 Selborne letter to Churchill 18.6.43
22. PREM 3 184/6 Morton minute 18.6.43
23. PREM 3 184/6 Churchill minute M.386/3 19.6.43
24. PREM 3 184/4 Selborne minute to P.M. 24.6.43
25. PREM 3 184/4 Churchill minute M.446/3 5.7.43
26. PREM 3 184/4 Selborne minute 6.7.43, Churchill minute 7.7.43
27. PREM 3 181/11 Eden minute PM/43/215 9.7.43
28. PREM 3 181/11 Churchill minute M.457/3 11.7.43
29. PREM 3 181/11 Eden minutes PM/43/222 12.7.43, PM/43/233 16.7.43
30. PREM 3 181/2 F.N.P. to President 373 T.1077/3 21.7.43
31. PREM 3 181/2 President to P.M. 321 T.1085/3 22.7.43
32. PREM 3 181/2 Attlee minute 23.7.43, Churchill minute 23.7.43
33. PREM 3 181/2 P.M. to Mackenzie King T.1118/3 26.7.43, Eden minute PM/43/249 28.7.43, Churchill minute M.538/3 30.7.43
34. PREM 3 181/2 Eden minute PM/43/255 1.8 43, F.N.P. to President 399 T.1182/3 3.8.43
35. PREM 3 181/2 President to P.M. T.1198/3 4.8.43
36. PREM 3 181/2 Churchill minute 5.8.43
37. PREM 3 181/9 Algiers 1441 11.8.43
38. PREM 3 181/9 Churchill letter to Roosevelt 15.8.43
39. PREM 3 181/9 WELFARE 395 25.8.43, WELFARE 424 25.8.43
40. PREM 3 181/9 CONCRETE 605 27.8.43

Chapter 7

1. Macmillan, *The Blast of War*, e.g. 337, 358
2. Cooper, *Old Men Forget*, 315, PREM 3 273/1 Duff Cooper letter 13.9.43
3. PREM 3 273/1 Churchill letter to Eden 3.10.43
4. PREM 3 273/1 Churchill letter 14.10.43
5. Cooper, 315

6. PREM 3 181/4 Z10180/5/9 27.8.43
7. PREM 3 181/4 Churchill minute M.703/3 16.10.43
8. PREM 3 273/1 Duff Cooper letter 18.10.43
9. PREM 3 273/1 Churchill letter to Duff Cooper 19.10.43
10. PREM 3 273/1 FROZEN 984 29.12.43, FROZEN 1009 31.12.43
11. PREM 3 273/1 FROZEN 1027 1.1.44
12. Cooper, 315
13. See p. 74 above, PREM 3 181/4 Z10180/5/9 27.8.43
14. PREM 3 181/11 P.M.'s personal telegram T.745/3 6.6.43, Eden minute PM/43/156 8.6.43, Churchill minute 8.6.43
15. PREM 3 181/11 Georges letter 27.6.43
16. PREM 3 181/11 note by Morton 19.12.43
17. PREM 3 181/11 FROZEN 340 5.12.43
18. PREM 3 181/11 note by Morton to Makins 19.12.43
19. PREM 3 181/11 Algiers 2747 21.12.43, PREM 3 182/3 Algiers 102 to Tunis 22.12.43
20. PREM 3 181/11 Tunis 30 to Algiers 23.12.43
21. PREM 3 181/10 Duff Cooper despatch to Eden 19, 16.1.44
22. PREM 3 177/6 Churchill letter to Duff Cooper 12.2.44, Ismay minute 16.2.44
23. FO 954/8 (336–9) Randolph Churchill letter 28.12.42
24. PREM 3 182/3 FROZEN 779 21.12.43
25. PREM 3 182/3 FROZEN 780 21.12.43
26. PREM 3 182/3 Roosevelt to Eisenhower 5456 and 5457 22.12.43
27. PREM 3 182/3 FROZEN 814 23.12.43, FROZEN 813 23.12.43
28. PREM 3 182/3 GRAND 759, 760 23.12.43
29. PREM 3 182/3 Algiers 109 23.12.43
30. PREM 3 182/3 GRAND 817 24.12.43
31. PREM 3 182/3 FROZEN 875 25.12.43
32. PREM 3 182/3 President to P.M. 425 T. 2064/3 27.12.43
33. PREM 3 182/3 GRAND 859 27.12.43
34. PREM 3 182/3 e.g. FO 104 to Algiers 29.1.44
35. FO 954/9 (22) Duff Cooper letter to Eden 27.1.44
36. PREM 3 182/3 Churchill minute M.224/4 4.3.44
37. PREM 3 182/3 Algiers 1644 29.9.44, Millard letter to Colville 2.10.44, Churchill minute to Eden 13.10.44

Chapter 8

1. PREM 3 181/11 Churchill to Macmillan T.1447/3 29.9.43
2. PREM 3 181/11 Makins letter to Mack 18.10.43
3. PREM 3 181/11 FROZEN 340 5.12.43
4. Murphy, 209
5. PREM 3 177/6 Macmillan to Eden 4.10.43
6. PREM 3 177/6 Morton minute 9.10.43
7. PREM 3 177/6 Eden minute PM/43/300 9.10.43, Grigg minute 11.10.43, Cadogan minute PM/43/315 12.10.43, Churchill minute M.682/3 13.10.43
8. PREM 3 177/6 GRAND 424 3.12.43, GRAND 437 3.12.43. GRAND 471 4.12.43, GRAND 494 5.12.43
9. PREM 3 177/6 GRAND 522 7.12.43
10. PREM 3 177/6 GRAND 471 4.12.43, FROZEN 382 7.12.43, Algiers 48 to Tunis 11.12.43
11. PREM 3 177/6 SHAEF B15 19.1.44 Churchill minute 21.1.44
12. PREM 3 177/6 Ismay minute 24.1.44

13. PREM 3 177/6 Washington CITIZEN 31 22.1.44, DON 146 24.1.44, Churchill minute 25.1.44
14. PREM 3 177/6 Churchill minute M.33/4 26.1.44, Eden minute 30.1.44
15. PREM 3 177/6 Eden minute PM/44/53 9.3.44
16. PREM 3 177/8 Soviet *aide-mémoire* 25.3.44
17. PREM 3 177/8 Eden minute PM/44/191 31.3.44, Churchill minute M.329/4 31.3.44
18. PREM 3 178/8 Morton minute 5.4.44
19. PREM 3 121/2 President to P.M. 518 T.762/4 8.4.44, P.M. to President 643 T.795/4 12.4.44, President to P.M. 521 T.810/4 4 14.4.44. PREM 3 182/2 President to P.M. 542 20.5.44
20. PREM 3 121/2 President to P.M. 518 T.762/4 8.4.44, P.M. to President 643 T.795/4 12.4.44
21. de Gaulle, 172, PREM 3 181/10 P.M. to President 559 T.176/4 30.1.44
22. PREM 3 121/3 President to P.M. 521 T.810/4 14.4.44
23. PREM 3 121/2 P.M. to Duff Cooper Extreme Priority T.820/4 14.4.44
24. PREM 121/2 Algiers 444 15.4.44, P.M. to Duff Cooper 353 T.835/4 16.4.44, P.M. to Roosevelt 653 T.887/4 20.4.44, President to P.M. 527 T.897/4 21.4.44
25. PREM 3 121/2 P.M. to President 656 T.912/4 22.4.44
26. PREM 3 121/2 President to P.M. 530 T.933/4 24.4.44
27. PREM 3 121/2 P.M. to President 657 T.936/4 24.4.44
28. PREM 3 121/2 P.M. to President 692 4.6.44, President to P.M. 552 4.6.44 (delayed)
29. PREM 3 182/2 Eden minute PM/44/347 16.5.44, Churchill minute 17.5.44
30. PREM 3 182/2 WM(44)66 19.5.44
31. PREM 3 182/2 P.M. to President 678 T.1095/4 19.5.44, President to P.M. 542 T.1100/4 20.5.44
32. PREM 3 182/2 Churchill minute M.610/4 23.5.44
33. FO 954/9 (142, 165) Attlee letter 31.5.44, Eden letter 5.6.44
34. de Gaulle, 226–8, FO 954/9 (59–62) record of conversation at luncheon and after 4.6.44
35. FO 954/9 (166 ff.) Eden minute PM/44/409 5.6.44
36. FO 954/9 (173–4) Eden minute PM/44/413 6.6.44
37. FO 954/9 (176–8) Bevin letter 6.6.44
38. FO 954/9 (180) Dixon minute 6.6.44
39. Avon, 454
40. CAB 65/42 WM(44)73 7.6.44
41. Churchill, *Second World War*, VI, 13
42. FO 954/9 (231–2) Churchill letter to Eden 13.6.44
43. de Gaulle, 232, Avon, 456
44. PREM 3 182/2 Eden minute PM/44/455 26.6.44
45. PREM 3 182/2 Eden minute PM/44/508 8.7.44, Churchill minute M.816/4 10.7.44
46. PREM 3 121/3 Algiers 1436 12.8.44
47. PREM 3 121/3 Churchill minute M(K)1/4 12.8.44
48. PREM 3 177/8 note from Mrs Churchill to Mr Churchill
49. Cadogan Diaries, 634–5
50. PREM 3 177/7 HEARTY 100 14.10.44
51. PREM 3 177/7 HEARTY 171 18.10.44
52. Leahy, *I was There*, 321
53. PREM 3 177/7 DRASTIC 180 T. 1941/4 20.10.44
54. PREM 3 177/7 A.M.S.S.O. to TOLSTOY 21.10.44
55. PREM 3 194/5 P.M. to President 822 T.2122 15.11.44

NOTES

Chapter 9

1. PREM 3 173/1 FO 4293 to Moscow 16.11.44 T.2127/4, Stalin to P.M. T.2153/4 22.11.44 and T.2233/4 2.12.44
2. PREM 3 173/1 Churchill draft reply 3.12.44, WM(44)161 4.12.44, FO to Moscow 4573 5.12.44
3. PREM 3 173/1 Stalin to Churchill T.2287/4 7.12.44, T.2342/4 10.12.44
4. PREM 3 173/1 Roosevelt to Churchill T.2273/4 and T.2275/4 6.12.44
5. PREM 3 173/1 Moscow 3675 10.12.44
6. PREM 3 173/1 Churchill minute M.1206/4 11.12.44
7. PREM 3 173/1 Washington 6591 10.12.44, Churchill minute M.1223/4 18.12.44
8. PREM 3 173/1 Churchill to Stalin T.2394 18.12.44, T.2433 27.12.44
9. Avon, 494, PREM 3 194/5 Eden minute PM/44/732 29.11.44, PREM 3 173/1 Churchill minute M.1259/4 31.12.44; *see also* pp. 214–16, 291 below
10. PREM 3 173/1 Duff Cooper despatch U.232/1/70 6.1.45, despatch 29.12.44
11. PREM 3 173/1 Churchill minute to Eden 5.2.45
12. FO 954/9 (455, 456–7) Eden minutes PM/45/23 12.1.45, PM/45/32 16.1.45
13. FO 954/9 (458–60) Churchill letter 19.1.45, FO 954/2 (161) Churchill minute M.113/5 25.1.45
14. PREM 3 194/5 JASON 229 8.2.45
15. PREM 3 185/2 FLEECE 354 9.2.45
16. PREM 3 173/3 Duff Cooper 177 Saving 5.4.45, Paris 565 6.4.45
17. PREM 3 173/3 Churchill minute M.298/5 6.4.45
18. PREM 3 173/3 Eden minute PM/45/161 7.4.45
19. PREM 3 173/3 Churchill minute M.306/5 8.4.45
20. PREM 3 173/3 Eden minutes PM/45/165 8.4.45, PM/45/172 10.4.45
21. PREM 3 173/3 Paris 621 18.4.45
22. PREM 3 173/3 FO 732 to Paris 20.4.45
23. PREM 3 173/3 FO 842 to Paris 30.4.45
24. PREM 3 121/5 President Truman to P.M. 60 6.6.45, P.M. to Truman 77 7.6.45
25. PREM 3 121/5 Cadogan minute PM/45/274 18.6.45
26. PREM 3 121/5 Paris 862 11.6.45, Cadogan minute PM/45/275 18.6.45
27. PREM 3 121/5 Cadogan minute PM/45/275 18.6.45
28. FO 954/9 (612) Churchill note to Cadogan M.656/5 23.6.45
29. cp. Strang, *Home and Abroad*, 71 ff.

Chapter 10

1. PREM 3 469 F.N.P. to President T.45 6.4.41
2. CAB 65/19 WM(41)84 19.8.41
3. PREM 3 473 P.M. to President 879 T.46/5 7.1.45
4. PREM 3 467 President Roosevelt to Churchill 11.9.39, Naval Person to President 5.10.39
5. PREM 3 471 P.M. to President 296 T.718/3 26.5.43
6. PREM 3 471 President to F.N.P. 252 T.18/3 3.1.43, F.N.P. to President 253 T.21/3 3.1.43
7. e.g. PREM 3 471 F.N.P. to President 298 T.723/3 31.5.43
8. PREM 3 470 F.N.P. to President 90 T.764/2 27.5.42, President to P.M. T.789/2 1.6.42
9. PREM 3 472 President to P.M. 662 T.2214A/4 30.11.44, P.M. to President 842 T.2230/4 3.12.44
10. Avon, 367
11. Harriman and Abel, *Special Envoy*, 191

319

12. PREM 3 486/3 President to P.M. 18.3.42
13. Sherwood, *The White House Papers of Harry L. Hopkins*, 744–5
14. Harriman and Abel, 224
15. PREM 3 471 F.N.P. to President 477 T.1767/3 29.10.43
16. PREM 3 471 P.M. to President 480 T.1783/3 30.10.43
17. Avon, 424
18. CAB 65/40 WM(43)169 13.12.43
19. FO 371/38675 British Consul General Chicago letter 11.3.44, N. Butler minute 8.4.44
20. PREM 3 472 P.M. to President 692 T.1192/4 4.6.44, P.M. to President 712 T.1342/4 23.6.44
21. PREM 3 472 P.M. to President 816 T.2086/4 8.11.44
22. PREM 3 473 P.M. to President 914 T.298/5 18.3.45
23. PREM 3 473 P.M. to President 927 T.367/5 30.3.45, President to P.M. 731 T.376/5 1.4.45
24. PREM 3 470 F.N.P. to President 62 T.519/2 1.4.42, PREM 3 472 HEARTY 18 T.1914/4 10.10.44
25. Harriman and Abel, 353
26. PREM 472 President to P.M. 506 T.618/4 21.3.44, P.M. to President 635 T.698/4 1.4.44
27. PREM 3 486/3 Roosevelt to Churchill 18.3.42
28. Taylor, 504, 544
29. PREM 3 472 P.M. to President 635 T.698/4 1.4.44
30. Harriman and Abel, 277
31. Ismay, *Memoirs*, 248–9
32. PREM 3 469 President to P.M. T.132 1.5.41, Churchill minute M.498/1 2.5.41, amended draft message T.139 4.5.41
33. PREM 3 486/2 Churchill letter to Roosevelt 20.10.41
34. Churchill, *Second World War*, IV, 739
35. Ante Smith Pavelić, *Kairska Afera*, 88
36. PREM 3 310/15 President to P.M. 393 T.1699/3 22.10.43, P.M. to President 470 T.1705/3 23.10.43
37. PREM 3 471 F.N.P. to President 449 T.1571/3 10.10.43
38. FO 954/10 (378–80) Churchill minute M.446/4 19.4.44
39. FO 954/17 (20) President to P.M. 577 T.1399/4 2.7.44
40. FO 954/17 (29–30) J. M. Martin letter to P. Dixon 17.7.44 and attached draft
41. Gowing: *Britain and Atomic Energy 1939–45*, 439–40, 444–7, 345; *Independence and Deterrence*, 5, 7
42. PREM 3 476/9 Washington 1509 30.3.43
43. CAB 66/21 WP(42)48 28.1.42

Chapter 11

1. Channon Diaries, 259
2. Churchill, *Second World War*, II, 199
3. Churchill, *Second World War*, II, 107–8
4. CAB 65/7 WM(40)135 23.5.40
5. CAB 65/7 WM(40)137 24.5.40, WM(40)138 25.5.40
6. PREM 3 468 Lawford letter to Colville 28.2.41, Colville to Lawford 28.2.41, unsigned and undated draft with handwritten heading, 'Lord Halifax's draft'
7. Churchill, *Second World War*, II, 78–9, CAB 66/7 WP(40)169 26.5.40
8. Churchill, *Second World War*, II, 79

9. CAB 66/13 WM(40)142 C.A. 27.5.40
10. Cadogan Diaries, 291
11. Birkenhead, *Halifax*, 458
12. CAB 65/13 WM(40)145 28.5.40
13. Churchill, *Second World War*, II, 87–8
14. Churchill, *Second World War*, II, 109–11
15. PREM 3 468 F.N.P. to President 15.5.40, President to F.N.P. 17.5.40, F.N.P. to President 20.5.40, Churchill minute 20.5.40
16. PREM 3 468 Washington 834 28.5.40 [*sic*]
17. CAB 65/13 WM(40)142 C.A. 27.5.40, CAB 65/7 WM(40)141 27.5.40, CAB 65/13 WM(40)145 28.5.40
18. CAB 65/13 WM(40)168 16.6.40
19. Sherwood, 473
20. PREM 3 483/6 WP(40)466 8.12.40
21. PREM 3 476/10 Eden minute PM/41/9 13.5.41, Churchill minute 15.5.41
22. CAB 65/19 WM(41)71 17.7.41
23. CAB 65/19 WM(41)84 19.8.41
24. CAB 65/19 WM(41)86 25.8.41
25. PREM 3 476/3 S. Africa (H.C.) 1339 4.11.41
26. Avon, 285–6

Chapter 12

1. PREM 3 361/1 Lisbon 321 26.6.40, Ismay minute 12.7.40
2. PREM 3 361/1 Churchill minute 24.7.40
3. PREM 3 361/1 Makins minute 25.7.40
4. FO 954/27 (486) Madrid 485 29.3.44
5. PREM 3 405/1 Madrid 301 Saving 22.10.40
6. Templewood, *Nine Troubled Years*, 256
7. FO 954/27 (96–100) Hoare letter 24.12.40
8. FO 371/43793 Churchill minute 29.5.44
9. PREM 3 361 C.O.S. minute 23.3.41, extracts from minutes of C.O.S. meeting 24.4.41
10. PREM 3 469 President to P.M. T.132 1.5.41, Churchill minute M.498/1 2.5.41, F.N.P. to President T.139 4.5.41
11. PREM 3 469 Washington 2406 28.5.41, F.N.P. to President T.237 29.5.41
12. PREM 3 361/1 P.M.'s minute 11.8.41, PREM 3 458/5 record of conversation between P.M. and President 11.8.41, notes of meeting in P.M.'s cabin 11.8.41, PREM 3 361/1 P.M.'s minute 11.8.41
13. FO 954/27 (306, 338) FO 1195 to Madrid 23.10.42, FO 1281 to Madrid 4.11.42
14. FO 954/27 (363) Cadogan minute 18.11.42
15. FO 954/21 (93–4, 109 ff.) Campbell letters 15.4.42, 18.8.42, PREM 3 362/7 handwritten note in Eden's writing, unsigned and undated
16. PREM 3 362/2 Rio de Janeiro 115 12.2.43
17. PREM 3 362/2 Lisbon 254 13.2.43, Lisbon 256 14.2.43
18. PREM 3 362/2 FO 1278 to Washington 25.2.43
19. PREM 3 362/2 C.O.S. (43)73(O) 22.2.43
20. FO 954/21 (157) Washington 1485 29.3.43
21. CAB 65/38 WM(43)84 C.A. 10.6.43
22. PREM 3 362/7 F.N.P. to President 305 T.777/3 11.6.43
23. PREM 3 362/11 Lisbon 1150 10.7.43

24. PREM 3 362/7 Eden minute PM/43/83 24.6.43, PREM 3 362/11A Churchill minute M.453/3 11.7.43
25. PREM 3 471 F.N.P. to President 347 T.967 7.7.43
26. PREM 3 471 F.N.P. to President 363 T.1031/3 14.7.43, President to P.M. 317 T.1040/3 15.7.43, F.N.P. to President 367 T.1041/3 16.7.43, F.N.P. to President 392 T.1151/3 31.7.43
27. PREM 3 362/11A F.N.P. to President 364 T.1035 15.7.43, PREM 3 362/8 Churchill minute M.514/3 24.7.43, Churchill minute 25.7.43 written on Campbell letter to Eden 20.7.43
28. PREM 3 362/9 Eden minute PM/43/244 27.7.43
29. PREM 3 362/9 President to P.M. 335 T.1159/3 31.7.43
30. PREM 3 362/9 Lisbon 1403 31.7.43
31. PREM 362/9 Jacob minute 2.8.43, extract from D.O.(43)7 2.8.43
32. Avon, 400
33. FO 954/21 (275) P.M.'s telegram T.1359 20.9.43
34. PREM 3 471 President to P.M. 376 T.1525/3 7.10.43, P.M. to President 444 T.1545/3 8.10.43
35. PREM 3 362/10 Eden minute 18.1.44
36. PREM 3 362/10 Ismay minute 18.1.44
37. PREM 3 472 P.M. to President 549 T.81/4 19.1.44
38. PREM 3 362/10 Lisbon 131 and 134 24.1.44
39. FO 954/27 (427) Churchill minute M.581/3 6.8.43, Eden minute FS/Q/3 19.8.43
40. FO 954/27 (440 ff., 445–6, 459) Hoare letter 20.10.43, Cadogan minute PM/43/383 4.11.43, Eden minute 27.1.44
41. PREM 3 405/7 Madrid 222 10.2.44
42. PREM 3 405/7 P.M. to President 577 T.299/4 13.2.44
43. PREM 3 405/7 President to P.M. 467 T.316/4 15.2.44, Eden minute PM/44/79 17.2.44, Madrid 269 17.2.44, Washington 851 19.2.44, P.M. to President 586 T.355/4 21.2.44
44. PREM 3 405/7 President to P.M. 478 T.380/4 23.2.44
45. PREM 3 405/7 P.M. to President 631 30.3.44
46. PREM 3 502/2 Madrid 480 29.3.44, Eden minutes PM/44/186 29.3.44, PM/44/190 30.3.44
47. PREM 3 505/2 P.M. to President 649 T.849 17.4.44, President to P.M. 529 T.903/4 22.4.44
48. PREM 3 472 P.M. to President 655 T.909/4 22.4.44, President to P.M. 531 T.960/4 25.4.44
49. Sherwood, 465
50. FO 954/27 (472) Madrid 286 21.2.44
51. PREM 3 472 P.M. to President 692 T.1192/4 4.6.44
52. CAB 66/57 WP(44)622 C.A. 4.11.44
53. CAB 66/58 WP(44)651 C.A. 15.11.44
54. CAB 65/48 WM(44)157 27.11.44
55. FO 954/27 (350) Churchill minute M. 1172/4 2.12.44
56. FO 954/27 (550, 570) Churchill minutes M.1172/4 2.12.44, M.52/5 11.1.45

Chapter 13

1. Churchill, *Second World War*, VI, 562
2. PREM 3 471 F.N.P. to President 344 T.958/3 5.7.43, President to P.M. 304 T.961/3 6.7.43, F.N.P. to President 346 T.966/3 7.7.43
3. CAB 65/37 WM(43)42 C.A. 18.3.43; *see also* PREM 3 242/11A Morton minute 27.7.43

NOTES

4. PREM 3 471 President to P.M. 334 T.1153/3 30.7.43, F.N.P. to President 394 T.1163/3 31.7.43
5. PREM 3 242/11A Report on Mission to Italy, 14–17 September 1943
6. FO 800/320 Loraine to Halifax 30.5.40, PREM 3 242/11A Report on Mission to Italy 14–17 September 1943
7. PREM 3 243/5 Washington 4019 4.9.43 CONCRETE 807 9.9.43, WELFARE 677 9.9.43
8. PREM 3 243/5 CONCRETE 925 17.9.43
9. PREM 3 243/5 F.N.P. to President 425 T.1440/3 28.9.43, 431 T.1470/3 1.10.43
10. PREM 3 273/1 Churchill letter to Eden 3.10.43
11. PREM 3 243/5 Eden minute 8.10.43, Sforza letter to Churchill 11.10.43, draft record by Cadogan 12.10.43
12. PREM 3 243/5 Churchill minute M.742/3 25.10.43
13. PREM 3 242/8 Algiers 2085 19.10.43, Cadogan draft reply 19.10.43, Churchill minute M.723/3 21.10.43
14. PREM 3 471 P.M. to President 495 T. 1875/3 6.11.43 (for final draft see PREM 3 242/8)
15. PREM 3 471 President to P.M. 415 T.1913/3 9.11.43
16. PREM 3 242/8 Algiers 2274 8.11.43
17. PREM 3 242/8 Washington 415 26.1.44, Washington 641 8.2.44
18. PREM 3 243/5 Eden minute PM/44/52 8.2.44, P.M. to President 573 T.263/4 9.2.44, President to P.M. 464 11.2.44
19. PREM 3 242/8 Messages to Macfarlane and Wilson 16.2.44
20. PREM 3 242/8 NAF 622 18.2.44, P.M. to General Wilson T.350/4 20.2.44, P.M. to Wilson T.358/4 21.2.44
21. PREM 3 242/8 P.M. to President 593 25.2.44
22. PREM 3 242/8 Eden minute PM/44/99 24.2.44
23. PREM 3 242/8 NAF 634, NAF 635, Churchill minute M.196/4 1.3.44, Eden minute PM/44/121 2.3.44
24. PREM 3 242/8 P.M. to President 610 T.486/4 8.3.44
25. PREM 3 242/8 Churchill minute M.255/4 10.3.44, T.L.R. minute to P.M. 11.3.44, FO 690 to Moscow 12.3.44
26. PREM 3 472 P.M. to President 618 T.515/4 13.3.44, President to P.M. 498 T.547/4 13.3.44
27. CAB 65/45 WM(44)35 15.3.44, PREM 3 242/8 P.M. to President 621 T.564/4 15.3.44
28. PREM 3 242/8 President to P.M. 502 T.588/4 18.3.44
29. PREM 3 242/8 P.M. to Macmillan through 'C' T.590 18.3.44
30. CAB 65/40 WM(43)147 27.10.43
31. PREM 3 472 P.M. to President 545 16.1.44, President to P.M. 444 19.1.44
32. PREM 3 472 P.M. to President 608 T.478/4 7.3.44
33. FO 371/43304 Eden minute on Wilson minute of 31.3.44
34. FO 371/43792 Halford note to Caccia 25.3.44
35. Macmillan, 488–9, Murphy, 202
36. FO 371/43792 Naples 34, 35 21.4.44, Naples 37 22.4.44, P.M. to Charles T.923/4 23.4.44, Macmillan, 495, CAB 65/42 WM(44)51 17.4.44
37. FO 371/43636 Churchill minute M.498/4 4.5.44, Eden minute PM/44/323 9.5.44
38. FO 371/43792 Naples 157 24.5.44, Churchill draft telegram, FO 194 to Naples 1.6.44
39. FO 371/43793 Eden minute PM/44/377 27.5.44, Churchill minute 29.5.44, Eden minute PM/44/411 6.6.44
40. FO 371/43793 Naples 178, 181 31.5.44, Eden minute on above

NOTES

41. FO 371/43793 Naples 220, 221 10.6.44
42. FO 371/43793 Dew minute 10.6.44, Cadogan minute 10.6.44, WM(44)75 12.6.44
43. PREM 3 243/12 Churchill minute M.705/4 10.6.44, P.M. to Charles 260 T.1249/4 10.6.44, P.M. to Macfarlane 261 T.1255/4 11.6.44, P.M. to President 699 T.1247/4 10.6.44
44. PREM 3 243/12 Attlee minute 13.6.44
45. PREM 3 243/12 Churchill minute M.711/4 13.6.44, WM(44)76 13.6.44
46. PREM 3 243/12 Stalin message T.1265 11.6.44, P.M. to President 703 14.6.44
47. PREM 3 243/12 Algiers 776 12.6.44, Eden minute PM/44/444 16.6.44, Algiers 785 13.5.44
48. PREM 3 243/12 Churchill minute M.722/4 16.6.44, President to P.M. 562 T.1293/4 16.6.44, P.M. to Stalin T.1302/4 17.6.44, WM(44)79 16.6.44
49. PREM 3 243/12 Churchill minutes M.735/4 20.6.44, M.754/4 25.6.44
50. Avon, 485
51. FO 954/14 (245) Rome 237 19.8.44
52. CAB 65/53 WM(44)126 22.9.44; FO 954/14 GUNFIRE 304 22.9.44, FO 8377 and 8404 to Washington, Washington 8197 23.9.44, FO 8438, to Washington 23.9.44
53. PREM 3 243/5 FO 10307 to Washington 6.12.44
54. Macmillan, 558
55. PREM 3 243/5 Churchill minute M.1136/4 23.11.44, Rome 901 22.11.44, FO 1114 to Rome 23.11.44
56. FO 954/14 (312) FO 10250 to Washington 3.12.44; cp. PREM 3 243/5 Churchill draft telegram to Halifax 2.12.44, Churchill minute to Private Office 3.12.44
57. Sherwood, 830
58. PREM 3 472 P.M. to President 845 T.2263/4 6.12.44
59. PREM 3 472 President to P.M. 669 T.2274/4 6.12.44
60. PREM 3 241/7 Churchill note on Eden minute 9.1.45
61. FO 954/14 (383–7, 440, 441–3, 444) Cadogan minute PM/AC/45/3 14.4.45, Churchill minute M.609/5 15.6.45, Cadogan minute PM/45/264 15.6.45, Churchill minute M.617/5 16.6.45

Chapter 14

1. FO 954/11 (108–12) Leeper letter to Eden 24.7.43
2. PREM 3 211/4 Cairo (Leeper) 211 18.8.43
3. PREM 3 211/4 Churchill minute M.(Q)20/3 19.8.43
4. FO 371/37198 CONCRETE 419 20.8.43, PREM 3 211/4 Eden memorandum 21.8.43, S. Africa (H.C.) to Canada (H.C.) 20.8.43
5. PREM 3 211/4 WELFARE 490 31.8.43, Cairo (Leeper) 250 7.9.43, WELFARE 670 8.9.43, un-numbered telegram 13.9.43
6. PREM 3 211/5 Eden minute PM/43/283 30.9.43
7. PREM 3 211/5 Myers draft as amended by Churchill; Auty and Clogg (eds.), *British Policy Towards Wartime Resistance in Yugoslavia and Greece*, 161–2
8. PREM 3 211/6 Churchill minute 3.1.44 on Cairo (Leeper) 335 2.11.43, Selborne minute 4.11.43
9. PREM 3 211/6 GRAND 102 19.11.43, WP(43)522 17.11.43
10. CAB 65/36 WM(43)155 16.11.43, Cadogan Diaries, 575, CAB 65/40 WM(43)160 22.11.43
11. PREM 3 211/6 GRAND 102 19.11.43, PREM 3 211/7 FROZEN 67 22.11.43, PREM 3 211/15 Brief for Secretary of State – major talking-points with the King of the Hellenes, Morton minute 2.12.43, Churchill note 3.12.43
12. PREM 3 211/15 Eden minute to P.M. 5.12.43

13. PREM 3 211/15 King George letter 6.12.43
14. PREM 3 211/15 Leeper minute 7.12.43
15. Avon, 430
16. PREM 3 212/1 CLASP 89 17.8.44
17. PREM 3 211/9 Churchill minutes M.76/4 6.2.44, D.45/4 14.2.44
18. PREM 3 211/11 Cairo (Leeper) 148 8.3.44 and 154 13.3.44, Eden minute PM/44/167 17.3.44, PREM 3 211/16 George II letter to Churchill 5.4.44, George II letter to Smuts 22.3.44, Eden handwritten minute 9.4.44
19. PREM 3 211/11 Cairo (Leeper) 198 3.4.44
20. PREM 3 211/11 draft telegram from P.M. to Cairo (Leeper) sent as T.723 5.4.44, Churchill minute 6.4.44, Sargent minute 6.4.44, FO 131 to Cairo (Leeper) 7.4.44, Cairo (Leeper) 228 7.4.44, Sargent minute 7.4.44
21. PREM 3 211/11 P.M. to Paget 082040 Z 8.4.44, FO 134 to Cairo (Leeper) 8.4.44, P.M. to Cairo (Leeper) 138 T.765/4 9.4.44
22. CAB 65/42 WM(44)47 11.4.44, WM(44)51 17.4.44
23. PREM 3 211/11 Cairo (Leeper) 248 12.4.44, P.M. to Leeper and all principals concerned T.808/4 14.4.44, PREM 3 472 P.M. to President 648 T.840/4 16.4.44
24. PREM 3 472 President to P.M. 523 T.861/4 18.4.44, P.M. to President 651 T.865/4 18.5.44, P.M. to President 664 T.946 24.4.44, President to P.M. 532 T.964/4 26.4.44
25. PREM 3 212/1 Eden minute PM/44/502 7.7.44, Churchill minute 8.7.44, Eden minute PM/44/509 8.7.44, Churchill minute M.863/4 15.7.44
26. PREM 3 212/1 WM(44)103 C.A. 9.8.44
27. PREM 3 212/1 WM(44)103 C.A. corrigendum 13.8.44
28. PREM 3 212/1 CLASP 56 15.8.44
29. PREM 3 212/1 CHAIN 56 16.8.44, CHAIN 78 17.8.44, CHAIN 114 18.8.44, CLASP 127 19.8.44, CHAIN 143 21.8.44
30. PREM 3 212/1 Cairo (Leeper) 634 30.8.44, FO 954/11 Eden despatch to Leeper 202 R 14473/9/G 7.9.44
31. PREM 3 472 P.M. to President 755 T.1625/4 17.8.44, CLASP 23 President to P.M. 608 26.8.44
32. PREM 3 212/9 Eden minute PM/44/622 27.9.44, Churchill minute M.981/4 29.9.44
33. PREM 3 212/9 Eden minute PM/44/639 4.10.44, Churchill minute 6.10.44
34. FO 954/11 (332, 334) Attlee letter to Eden, Eden letter 7.12.44
35. FO 371/43697 FO 10307 to Washington 6.12.44
36. PREM 3 212/5 note dictated by P.M. 10.12.44, Sherwood, 832–3
37. PREM 3 212/5 Churchill letter to Hopkins 11.12.44
38. PREM 3 472 President to P.M. 673 T.2354/4 13.12.44
39. FO 371/43698 Athens (Leeper) 593 13.12.44
40. PREM 3 472 P.M. to President 851 T.2358/4 14.12.44
41. PREM 3 472 P.M. to President 855 T.2379/4 17.12.44
42. CAB 65/48 WM(44)169 C.A. 16.12.44
43. Ibid.
44. CAB 65/48 WM(44)169, WM(44)171, WM(44)173
45. PREM 3 472 P.M. to President 858 T.2340/4 24.12.44, President to P.M. 680 T. 2345A/4 27.12.44, FO 371/43698 Athens 593 13.12.44
46. PREM 3 472 P.M. to President 864 T.2449/4 30.12.44, 870 T.2461/4 31.12.44
47. FO 954/11 (415–6, 536, 543) Churchill minutes M.29/5 7.1.45, M.314/5 8.4.45, Eden minute PM/45/174 11.4.45
48. PREM 3 211/11 Churchill minute M.354 2.4.44

Chapter 15

1. FO 954/22 (197) FO 6398 to Washington 24.9.43
2. PREM 3 472 President to P.M. 474 T. 368/4 23.2.44, P.M. to President 613 T.506/4 and 614 T.507/4 9.3.44, President to P.M. 509 T.652/4 25.3.44
3. FO 954/22 (199) FO 1492 to Washington 19.2.44
4. CAB 66/47 WP(41)109 15.2.44
5. PREM 3 472 P.M. to President 583 T.348/4 20.2.44, President to P.M. (unnumbered) T.378/4 22.2.44, P.M. to President 591 T.388/4 24.2.44, President to P.M. 485 T.444/4 3.3.44, P.M. to President 601 T.453/4 4.3.44
6. FO 371/44574 Halifax letter to Bevin 12.12.45, FO 954/22 (168–71) Washington 1470 28.3.43
7. CAB 65/44 WM(44)153 22.11.44, PREM 3 472 P.M. to President 827 T.2154/4 22.11.44
8. PREM 3 472 President to P.M. T.2176/4 24.11.44, P.M. to President 835 T.2196/4, 836 T.2201/4 28.11.44
9. PREM 3 473 President to P.M. 717 T.291/5 16.3.45
10. PREM 3 472 P.M. to President 730 T. 1447/4 14.7.44, President to P.M. 613 T.1709/4 1.9.44, President to P.M. 651 T.2133/4 19.11.44, P.M. to President 832 T.2186/4 26.11.44, CAB 65/48 WM(44)155 29.11.44
11. CAB 65/46 WM(44)43 3.4.44; for a different angle on this matter, see Lord Zuckerman, *From Apes to Warlords* (Hamish Hamilton, 1978)
12. CAB 65/46 WM(44)57 27.4.44, WM(44)61 2.5.44
13. PREM 3 472 P.M. to President 669 T.1044/4 7.5.44, President to P.M. 537 T.1067/4 11.5.44, CAB 65/46 WM(44)69 30.5.44
14. PREM 3 473 P.M. to President Truman No. 2 T.472/5 14.4.45, Truman to P.M. No. 5 T.500/5 17.4.45
15. Harriman and Abel, 266
16. PREM 3 476 W.O. paper, 'Anglo-American Relations in Washington in the Autumn of 1942'
17. FO 954/22 (174–5) WP(43)233 record of a conversation at British embassy, Washington 22.5.43, and Annex B.
18. FO 954/22 (180–1) Halifax letter to Eden 28.5.43
19. CAB 66/40 WP(43)398 20.9.43
20. Gladwyn, *Memoirs*, 130 ff.
21. CAB 65/42 WM(44)58 27.4.44
22. PREM 4 33/4 *passim*
23. FO 954/22 (156–60) STRATAGEM C/6 1.2.43
24. FO 954/22 (168–71) Washington 1470 28.3.43
25. FO 954/22 (174–5) WP(43)233 record of a conversation in Washington 22.5.43
26. CAB 65/42 WM(44)58 27.4.44
27. Avon, 443
28. CAB 65/48 WM(44)157 27.11.44
29. FO 954/10 (378–80) Churchill minute M.446/4 19.4.44
30. FO 954/10 (375, 378–80) Attlee minute 25.1.44, Churchill minute 26.1.44, Churchill minute 19.4.44
31. Churchill, *Second World War*, V, 330, Harriman and Abel, 273
32. PREM 3 472 FROZEN 1038 T.5/4 1.1.44, FO 954/10 (378–80) Churchill minute M.446/4 19.4.44 PREM 3 434 record of meeting at Kremlin 9.10.44
33. CAB 65/46 WM(44)68 C.A. 25.4.44
34. Harriman and Abel, 386
35. Avon, 476, Colville, *Footprints in Time*, 166
36. PREM 3 434 record of meeting at Kremlin 9.10.44

NOTES

37. FO 954/7 (520–3) Churchill minute M.461/2 18.10.42, Eden minute PM/42/229 19.10.42
38. FO 954/22 (168–71, 172) Washington 1470 28.3.43, FO 2077 to Washington 30.3.43
39. FO 954/22 (270–3) Churchill minute M.22/5 4.1.45
40. Avon, 341
41. Strang, *Home and Abroad*, 205 ff.
42. Ibid.
43. FO 371/40581 Halifax letter to Eden 30.5.44, Strang minute 10.6.44, Jebb minute 7.6.44
44. Spaak, *The Continuing Battle*, 76–7
45. FO 954/22 (222–3) Eden despatch to Bland, Oliphant and Collier 19.7.44, Spaak, 82–3
46. Avon, 492
47. Churchill, *Second World War*, VI, 222, 224; see p. 116 above, p. 291 below
48. Strang, *Home and Abroad*, 218
49. PREM 3 472 P.M. to President 832 T.2186/4 26.11.44

Chapter 16

1. PREM 3 472 P.M. to President 562 T.187/4 1.2.44
2. FO 954/26 (37) FO 1764 to Washington 18.3.43
3. CAB 66/21 WP(42)48 28.1.42
4. CAB 65/51 WM(45)26.5 C.A. 6.3.45
5. FO 800/302 'Russia – seven years later' (paper by George Kennan, Moscow 1944)
6. PREM 3 396/14 Sargent minute PM/OS/45/60 2.5.45
7. FO 800/302 G. M. Wilson letters to Clark Kerr 19.3.44, 15.5.44
8. Ullman, *Anglo-Soviet Accord*, 114–15
9. FO 371/44304 G. M. Wilson minute 19.4.44
10. CAB 65/39 WM(43)114 11.8.43 CONCRETE 85 10.8.43
11. Djilas, *Conversations with Stalin*, 77
12. Churchill, *Second World War*, IV, 434
13. FO 954/24 (192) FO 324 to Algiers 6.4.44
14. FO 371/43304 Churchill minute M.338/4 1.4.44, CAB 65/48 WM(44)157 27.11.44, CAB 65/51 WM(45)22.1 C.A. 19.2.45
15. FO 954/1 (440) Churchill minute M.562/5 2.6.45
16. FO 954/25 (362) Moscow 104 20.8.42, Djilas, 70,106
17. Deane, *The Strange Alliance*, 160, 154 ff.
18. Ullman, (quoting Hankey's diary for 18.11.20) 420, Churchill, *The World Crisis: The Aftermath*, 163, 80
19. Avon, 55
20. FO 371/43506 Clark Kerr letter 31.8.44
21. PREM 3 395/16 Moscow 4 to Cairo 22.2.41, FO 364 to Athens 23.2.41
22. PREM 3 395/16 Churchill minute M.461/1 22.4.41, Eden minute 22.4.41, CAB 65/18 WM(41)48 8.5.41
23. CAB 65/18 WM(41)61 19.6.41, Eden, 269
24. Avon, 270
25. CAB 65/18 WM(41)62 23.6.41
26. Leahy, 52
27. Strang, *Home and Abroad*, 158
28. FO 371/43304 Eden minute 18.2.44
29. CAB 65/10 WM(41)62 23.6.41, CAB 65/34 WM(43)75 23.5.43, WM(43)77 24.5.43

NOTES

30. FO 371/39398 Churchill minute M.330/4 31.3.44
31. Taylor, 474
32. Taylor, 522
33. FO 800/302 Warner letter to Balfour 25.1.44
34. FO 371/48192 R 5063/5063/67 Sargent minute 13.3.45
35. FO 954/1 (440) Churchill minute M.562/5 2.6.45
36. FO 800/302 Eden letter to Clark Kerr 19.6.44
37. FO 800/302 Warner letter to Balfour 25.1.44, Wilson letters to Clark Kerr 19.3.44, 15.5.44
38. FO 954/3 (371–2) FO 1952 to Washington 25.3.43
39. PREM 3 354/8 memorandum of conversation between P.M. and Sikorski 15.4.43, cp. Churchill's attitude to Stalin during Warsaw rising.

Chapter 17

1. PREM 3 395/16 Moscow 381 18.4.41
2. PREM 3 395/16 Eden minute PM/41/59 4.7.41, Eden note 9.7.41
3. CAB 65/23 WM(41)90 C.A. 5.9.41, PREM 3 469 F.N.P. to President T.544 5.9.41
4. CAB 65/19 WM(41)95 22.9.41, WM(41)100 6.10.41, WM(41)102 13.10.41
5. CAB 65/23 WM(41)90 C.A. 5.9.41
6. PREM 3 395/17 Kuibyshev 27 26.10.41, FO 47 to Kuibyshev 28.10.41
7. PREM 3 394/4 FO 188 to Kuibyshev 21.11.41, Stalin to Churchill T.866 23.11.41
8. CAB 66/20 WP (41)288 (revise) 29.11.41, CAB 65/24 WM(41)124 C.A. 4.12.41
9. PREM 3 394/4 HAUGHTY T.955/1 10.12.41
10. PREM 3 394/4 Moscow HECTIC 15 17.12.41
11. CAB 65/25 WM(41)131 C.A. 19.12.41
12. PREM 3 394/5 HAUGHTY 85 20.12.41
13. PREM 3 399/7 TAUT 390 5.1.42, GREY 261 8.1.42
14. CAB 66/21 WP(42)48 28.1.42
15. CAB 65/29 WM(42)17 6.2.42
16. PREM 3 399/1 WP(42)71 7.2.42, Taylor, 510–11, PREM 3 399/8 Beaverbrook letter 17.3.42
17. PREM 3 395/12 memorandum by Minister of Production 18.2.42, Bridges minute 19.2.42, Churchill minute 22.2.42
18. PREM 3 399/1 and 2 Washington 971 19.2.42, Washington 1013 20.2.42
19. CAB 65/25 WM(42)25 25.2.42
20. PREM 3 470 F.N.P. to President 40 T.340/2 7.3.42
21. PREM 3 399/8 Washington 1438 11.3.42, Washington 1477 13.3.42
22. PREM 3 399/8 Beaverbrook to Stalin 19.3.42, Beaverbrook letter to Churchill 17.3.42, Churchill to Stalin T.431/2 20.3.42
23. PREM 3 399/8 Washington 1921 1.4.44, Washington 2252 16.4.42
24. PREM 3 399/8 Stalin to Churchill 22.4.42, President to F.N.P. 139 T.607 22.4.42, F.N.P. to President 78 T.620/2 24.2.42
25. PREM 3 399/8 extract from report by P.P.S. 24.2.42, Lord Simon letter 8.5.42, Churchill minute 8.5.42, Eden minutes PM/42/88 11.5.42, PM/42/89 12.5.42, Churchill minute 13.5.42
26. FO 954/19 (425 ff., 428) F. D. Brown letter to Lawford 15.5.42, Eden minute PM/42/98 16.5.42
27. PREM 3 399/8 Morton note 21.5.42, Churchill minute 21.5.42
28. PREM 3 399/8 Stuart minute 22.5.42
29. FO 954/19 (428) Eden minute PM/42/98 16.5.42
30. PREM 3 399/6 Churchill M.657/3 6.10.43

31. PREM 3 399/4 fifth meeting with Soviet delegation 24.5.42
32. CAB 65/30 WM(42)67 26.5.42
33. CAB 65/30 WM(42)68 26.5.42, WM(42)73 C.A. 11.6.42, cp. PREM 3 399/4 and 5, seventh meeting with Soviet delegation 9.6.42
34. CAB 65/31 WM(42)118 25.8.42, PREM 3 470 F.N.P. to President 134 T.1119/2 28.8.42
35. CAB 65/38 WM(43) 53.2 C.A. 13.4.43
36. Ismay, 327
37. CAB 66/41 WP(43)438 5.10.43
38. PREM 3 399/6 Churchill minute M.647/3 6.10.43, CAB 66/41 WP(43)447, CAB 65/40 WM(43)137 8.10.43
39. FO 371/39393 record of conversation at Soviet embassy, Tehran C3031 1.12.43
40. PREM 3 399/6 Churchill minute M.(S)31/4 16.1.44
41. PREM 3 399/6 Eden minute PM/44/21 25.1.44
42. PREM 3 485/8 Churchill minutes M.322/5 31.3.44, M.336/4 1.4.44, Eden minute PM/44/201 5.4.44

Chapter 18

1. FO 371/39393 Churchill minute M.226/4 4.3.44
2. FO 371/39414 HEARTY 51 12.10.44
3. PREM 3 352/12 CLASP 24.8.44, FO 954/20 Beaverbrook letter 26.8.44
4. CAB 65/19 WM(41)74 24.7.41, WM(41)76 31.7.41
5. PREM 3 354/8 Churchill letter 16.2.43, Churchill minute M.224/3 3.4.43
6. PREM 3 354/8 Cadogan minute PM/43/109 31.3.43, FO 503 to Moscow 6.5.43
7. PREM 3 354/8 memorandum of conversation between P.M. and Sikorski C 4230/910/G 15.4.43
8. PREM 3 354/8 Moscow 292 20.4.43
9. CAB 65/34 WM(43)62 29.4.43, PREM 3 354/8 Stalin message 21.4.43
10. CAB 65/34 WM(43)56 19.4.43
11. CAB 65/34 WM(43)59 27.4.43
12. PREM 3 354/8 Churchill message to Stalin T.581/3 25.4.43, Stalin message T.593/3 26.4.43
13. PREM 3 354/8 report prepared by Bracken and revised by Churchill 25.4.43
14. PREM 3 354/8 Churchill minute M.323/3 28.4.43
15. PREM 3 354/8 FO 459 to Moscow 30.4.43 (endorsing minor amendments to Churchill message of 28.4.43)
16. PREM 3 354/8 Moscow 327 1.5.43
17. PREM 3 354/8 Churchill to Clark Kerr T.633/3 2.5.43, Moscow 333 3.5.43, Moscow 355 8.5.43
18. CAB 66/41 WP(43)439 5.10.43
19. FO 371/39393 record of conversation at Tehran C 3031 1.12.43
20. A valuable paper on this subject was given by Jozef Gerliński at the Conference on Exiled Governments in London during the Second World War, 25.10.77
21. CAB 65/46 WM(44)47 11.4.44, FO 371/39398 Harrison minute 7.4.44
22. FO 954/20 (168) Churchill minute M.537/4 8.5.44
23. PREM 3 352/12 AMSSO to 30 Military Mission 4131 2.8.44, AMSSO to AFHQ 3.8.44
24. PREM 3 352/12 CLASP 111 18.8.44
25. Ibid.
26. PREM 3 352/12 C11639/8/G 30.8.44
27. PREM 3 352/12 Stalin message T.1629/4 16.8.44, CLASP 121 18.8.44

28. PREM 3 352/12 CORDITE 10.9.44
29. PREM 3 352/12 CHAIN 34 14.8.44, CLASP 54 15.8.44
30. PREM 3 352/12 CLASP 82 16.8.44, WM(44)107 C.A. 16.8.44
31. CAB 65/47 WM(44)107 C.A. 16.8.44, PREM 3 352/12 CHAIN 110 18.8.44, PREM 472 President to P.M. 601 T.1640/4 CLASP 132 19.8.44, P.M. to President 762 T.1641/4 20.8.44
32. PREM 3 352/12 CLASP 163 22.8.44, CLASP 165 22.8.44, CAB 65/47 WM(44)110 24.8.44
33. PREM 3 352/12 CLASP 185 T.1662/4 23.8.44, CLASP 189 23.8.44, CLASP 210 24.8.44, CHAIN 209 25.8.44
34. CAB 65/47 WM(44)111 28.8.44
35. FO 954/20 (298) Raikes letter to Eden 30.8.44
36. PREM 3 352/12 Roberts record of Churchill–Mikolajczyk meeting 1.9.44, draft message from P.M. to President 3.9.44
37. CAB 65/47 WM(44)115 C.A. 4.9.44, PREM 3 352/12 FO 2855 to Moscow 4.9.44
38. PREM 3 352/12 P.M. to President 779 T.1740/4 4.9.44, President to P.M. 619 T.1746/4 5.9.44
39. PREM 3 352/12 CORDITE 89 10.9.44 (repeating Moscow 2379 9.9.44)
40. Ibid., PREM 3 352/12 CORDITE 180 13.9.44
41. CAB 65/47 WM(44)122 11.9.44, WM(44)123 18.9.44
42. FO 371/39414 HEARTY 51 12.10.44
43. CAB 65/47 WM(44)117 C.A. 5.9.44, for Bevin's Polish contacts see also CAB 65/51 WM(45)7 22.1.45
44. FO 371/39414 HEARTY 123 16.10.44
45. CAB 65/51 WM(45)7 22.1.45, WM(45)10 26.1.45
46. CAB 65/51 WM(45)22.1 C.A. 19.2.45, WM(45)23.2 C.A. 21.2.45
47. FO 954/20 (410, 411) FO 512 to Athens 12.2.45, Cairo 363 17.2.45
48. CAB 65/51 WM(45)26.5 C.A. 6.3.45
49. PREM 3 473 P.M. to President 910 T.285/5 13.3.45, President to P.M. 718 T.292/5 16.3.45
50. PREM 3 473 P.M. to President 929 31.3.45, P.M. to President 945 T.444/5 11.4.45, President to P.M. T.448/5 12.4.45

Chapter 19

1. CAB 65/19 WM(41)69 14.7.41, WM(41)71 17.7.41, an authoritative account of earlier British moves towards recognition was given by Sir William Barker in a paper at the Conference on Governments in Exile in London during the Second World War, October 1977
2. FO 954/4 (16) Eden despatch to Nichols C 6483/1257 25.6.42
3. FO 954/19 (438) Eden despatch to Dormer C 5813/151/G 8.6.42
4. FO 954/4 (20) Eden despatch to Nichols C 10614/151/G 2.11.42
5. FO 371/33882 record of 7th meeting with Soviet delegation N/3000/G 9.6.42, FO 371/36955 Warner minute 9.7.43
6. FO 954/4 (21) Eden despatch to Nichols C 1212/859/G 29.1.43
7. PREM 3 354/8 conversation between P.M. and Sikorski C 4230/910/G 15.4.43
8. PREM 3 114/2 Czechoslovak government memorandum 1.10.42
9. PREM 3 114/2 British memorandum 16.10.43
10. FO 954/4 (24) Eden despatch to Nichols C 7084/416/G 16.6.43
11. CAB 65/38 WM(43)89 28.6.43, CAB 65/39 WM(43)93 5.7.43
12. FO 954/4 (26, 27) Eden despatches to Nichols C 7363/2462/C 25.6.43, C 7493/2462/G 30.6.43

NOTES

13. FO 371/36955 FO 1019 to Moscow 2.8.43
14. PREM 3 114/2 WP(43)423 28.9.43
15. PREM 3 114/2 Eden statement in House of Commons 22.9.43, British memorandum 16.10.43, FO 954/4 Eden despatch to Nichols C 11655/2462/G 7.10.43
16. PREM 3 114/2 Moscow 1155 23.10.43, Moscow SPACE 75, SPACE 78 24.10.43, SPACE 86 25.10.43
17. PREM 3 114/2 Cadogan minute PM/43/355 25.10.43, Churchill minute 26.10.43
18. PREM 3 114/2 GRAND 679 19.12.43
19. PREM 3 114/3A FROZEN 1048 1.1.44, FO 954/4 Sargent and Eden minutes on FO 9 to Algiers 2.1.44
20. PREM 3 114/3A FROZEN 1048 1.1.44, PREM 3 472 FROZEN 1120 6.1.44, FO 371/39385 FROZEN 1104 4.1.44, Roberts minute 7.1.44
21. CAB 65/45 WM(45)4 10.1.44
22. PREM 3 114/3A COS(W)312 6.9.44, COS(44)880(o) 5.10.44
23. PREM 3 114/3A COS(44)880(O) 5.10.44
24. PREM 3 114/3A COS(W)380 16.10.44, DRASTIC 12 16.10.44
25. PREM 3 114/3A Cadogan minute PM/44/672 31.10.44
26. Ibid.
27. PREM 3 114/3A FLEECE 29.1.45
28. FO 954/4 (44) Eden despatch to Clark Kerr N 3411/3411/12 28.3.45, PREM 3 114/3A FO 1805 to Moscow 13.4.45
29. PREM 3 114/3A Churchill minutes M.334/5 14.4.45, M.344/5 16.4.45
30. PREM 3 114/3A Sargent minute PM/OS 45/21 22.4.45
31. PREM 3 114/3A COS(W)822 30.4.45, PREM 3 473 P.M. to President Truman 24 T.687/5 30.4.45
32. PREM 3 114/3A J.S.M. 766 1.5.45, PREM 3 473 Truman to P.M. 21 T.717/5 1.5.45, PREM 3 114/3A SHAEF FORWARD to Military Mission Moscow ASCAF 337 4.5.45, Moscow to AGWAR MS 24193 5.5.45, SHAEF FORWARD to Military Mission Moscow ASCAF 6.5.45, Sargent minute PM/OS/45/76 6.5.45, P.M. to Eisenhower T.807/5 7.5.45, Churchill to P.O. 10.5.45
33. PREM 3 114/3A T.L.R. minutes to P.M. 4.5.45, 10.5.45
34. PREM 3 114/3A Prague 24 6.6.45

Chapter 20

1. Amery, Approach March, 259–60
2. Sir William Deakin, Major-General Sir Fitzroy Maclean
3. Clissold, Yugoslavia and the Soviet Union, 15–21, 32 ff.; Deakin, The Embattled Mountain, 139, 204–6; Auty and Clogg, passim; Barker, British Policy in South-east Europe in the Second World War, 157–64, 170–2
4. Barker, 255–8
5. Barker, 251–9
6. CAB 65/46 WM(44)43 3.4.44
7. FO 371/43984 Millard to Colville 2.4.44, FO 1067 to Cairo 2.4.44, PREM 3 374/13A WM(44)47 C.A. 11.4.44, PREM 3 211/16 Cadogan minute PM/44/248 15.4.44
8. PREM 3 211/16 Churchill draft 16.4.44
9. PREM 3 211/16 Molotov to P.M. T.913A/4 22.4.44, P.M. to Molotov T.938/4 23.4.44
10. PREM 3 211/16 Molotov to P.M. T.1004/4 delivered by Gusev 29.4.44, scrambled to Chequers 30.4.44
11. FO 371/43999 FO 1310 to Moscow 30.4.44
12. FO 371/43999 Churchill draft message 1.5.44

13. FO 800/302 Clark Kerr letter to Eden 8.9.44
14. CAB 65/44 WM(44)61 2.5.44, FO 371/43636 Churchill minutes M.497/4 and M.498/4 4.5.44
15. FO 954/11 (210) Eden despatch 99 to Leeper R 7170/9/G 4.5.44
16. FO 371/44000 Eden despatch to Clark Kerr R 7214/9/G 5.5.44
17. FO 371/43636 Eden minute PM/44/323 9.5.44
18. FO 371/43636 FO 1560 to Moscow 25.5.44
19. FO 371/43636 WM(44)65 18.5.44
20. PREM 3 472 P.M. to President 678 T.1095/4 19.5.44
21. FO 954/23 (359) Churchill minute 24.5.44
22. FO 371/43636 Howard minute 23.5.44, FO 4638 to Washington 25.5.44, FO 954/23 (361) Washington 2860 30.5.44, PREM 3 472 P.M. to President 687 T.1161/4 31.5.44, FO 954/23 (363) Washington 2983 4.6.44
23. PREM 3 472 President to P.M. 565 22.6.44, P.M. to President 712 T.1342/4 23.6.44, PREM 3 66/7 draft message from P.M. to President 23.6.44
24. PREM 3 66/7 President to P.M. 570 T.1364/4 27.6.44, FO 371/43636 FO 2079 to Moscow 12.7.44, Stalin to P.M. T.1453/4 15.7.44, PREM 3 66/7 Churchill minute M.813/4 9.7.44, WM(44)89 10.7.44
25. PREM 3 79/1 GUNFIRE 247 17.9.44
26. FO 371/44261 record of P.M.–Tito meeting at Naples 12.8.44, FO 371/44263 Broad letter to Macmillan 26.8.44 Bryant, *Triumph in the West*, 294, 304, 313, 340, Leahy, 321
27. Avon, 467, Macmillan, 511, General Sir Ian Jacob to author 1976, Nigel Nicolson, *Alex*, 260–2
28. Sherwood, 825, PREM 3 472 President to P.M. 626 T.1881/4 4.10.44, P.M. to President 791 T. 1891/4 5.10.44
29. Sherwood, 825–6
30. FO 800/302, draft record of meeting in Kremlin 9.10.44; the final record omits reference to the 'naughty document'
31. PREM 3 434 record of meeting at Kremlin 9.10.44, meeting at Kremlin 10.10.44
32. Harriman and Abel, 357
33. PREM 3 66/7 Churchill letter to Stalin 11.10.44, Harriman and Abel, 358
34. PREM 3 66/7 memorandum by P.M. 12.10.44
35. PREM 3 374/13A Churchill minute M.1207/4 11.12.44

Chapter 21

1. Harriman and Abel, 362
2. Churchill, *Second World War*, VI, 205, Avon, 487
3. FO 371/36955 FO 1019 to Moscow 2.8.43, FO 371/36956 Harvey and Eden minutes 15.9.43
4. FO 954/26 (93, 112–13, 114–15) Churchill to Clark Kerr 16.6.43, Eden minute PM/43/258 31.7.43, Churchill minute M.533/3 31.7.43
5. FO 954/26 (187, 188, 192) Moscow SPACE 112 29.10.43, Moscow SPACE 144 31.10.43, Moscow SPACE 158 2.11.43
6. PREM 3 471 F.N.P. to President 484 T.1813/3 1.11.43, 500 T.1929/3 11.11.43
7. FO 954/26 (259–61) FO 192 to Moscow 24.1.44
8. PREM 3 396/14 Churchill minute M.338/4 1.4.44, Eden minute PM/44/207 5.4.44
9. FO 371/43304 Sargent minute 1.4.44, Eden minute 3.4.44
10. FO 371/43305 Wilson minute 19.4.44, Jebb minute 13.5.44, Cadogan minute 14.5.44, Eden minute 15.5.44

11. FO 371/43636 WP(44)304 7.6.44, FO 371/39051 draft cabinet paper by S. of S. 7.7.44
12. FO 371/43306 Wilson minute 10.8.44, Sargent minute 18.8.44, Eden minute 23.8.44
13. FO 954/22 247–51, 266) PHP(49)(O) Final 9.11.44, Cadogan minute 11.12.44, Eden minute 13.12.44; *see also* p. 116 and pp. 214–16 above
14. FO 371/48539 undated Sargent minute of March 1945, FO 371/48192 Sargent minute R5063/5063/67 13.3.45, Howard minute R7333/81/67 30.4.45
15. Moran, *Winston Churchill: The Struggle for Survival*, 206
16. PREM 3 374/13A Churchill minute 6.4.45
17. FO 954/26 Eden minute PM/ 45/133 24.3.45
18. PREM 3 473 P.M. to President 934 T.406/5 5.4.45, President to PM 736 T.413/5 6.4.45
19. FO 954/26 (591) Churchill minute M.256/5 25.3.45, FO 954/2 (224) Washington 2773 21.4.45, FO 2347 to Moscow 2.5.45
20. Churchill, *Second World War*, VI, 495–6
21. FO 371/48192 Churchill minute M.532/5 29.5.45
22. FO 371/48193 Churchill minute M.635/5 17.6.45
23. FO 371/47883 Clark Kerr despatch to Eden 10.7.45
24. FO 371/47883 Roberts letter to Warner 30.10.45

Chapter 22

1. PREM 3 374/13A Churchill minute 25.10.44, FO 954/11 (525) Churchill minute M.242/5 20.3.45
2. Dixon, *Double Diploma*, 115
3. Churchill, *Second World War*, VI, 551, Dedijer, *Tito Speaks*, 234
4. FO 371/37625 Churchill minute M.451/3 11.7.43, Eden minute 11.7.43
5. FO 371/37625 Princess Alexandra letter 18.11.43, Cadogan minute 13.11.43, GRAND 71 18.11.43, FROZEN 43 19.11.43
6. FO 954/33 (396) FO 83 to H.M. ambassador to Yugoslav government Cairo 23.11.43, FO 954/34 (22, 25) FO 104 to H.M. ambassador 9.2.44, H.M. ambassador to Yugoslav government Cairo 140 12.2.44
7. PREM 4 33/5 Duff Cooper letter 23.5.45
8. PREM 4 33/5 Churchill minute 24.6.40, Halifax minute 27.6.40
9. FO 371/30911
10. PREM 4 33/5 Otto letter 17.8.43, Churchill minute 18.8.43, Eden minute FS/Q/2 19.8.43
11. FO 371/34453 Wheeler-Bennett minute 1.10.43
12. PREM 4 33/5 Cadogan minute 5.9.43, WELFARE No. [*sic*] 5.9.43, WELFARE 641 7.9.43
13. FO 954/1 (110–14) Allen minute 9.9.43, Harrison minute 9.9.43, Roberts minute 9.9.43, Strang minute 10.9.43, Harrison minute 15.9.43, PREM 4 33/5 CONCRETE 846 10.9.43
14. FO 371/34452 Threlfall letters 16.11.43, 23.11.43, 26.11.43, FO 371/34453 Roberts minute 12.12.43
15. PREM 4 33/5 Count Eltz letter 14.9.44, Otto letter to Churchill and enclosures 17.9.44, Churchill minute 18.9.44
16. PREM 4 33/5 Washington 5522 10.10.44, Churchill minute thereon
17. FO 371/39254 Allen minute 25.9.44, Harrison minute 28.9.44, Roberts minute 29.9.44, Eden minute 30.9.44, PREM 4 33/5 Churchill minute PM/44/663 28.10.44
18. PREM 4 33/5 Otto letter 1.3.45

19. PREM 4 33/5 Ismay minute 7.4.45, Churchill minute M.311/5 8.4.45, Eden minute PM/45/186 13.4.45
20. PREM 4 33/5 Brussels 106 Saving 9.4.45, P.M. to ambassador Brussels T.642/5 26.4.45

Chapter 23

1. General Sir Ian Jacob to author, 1976
2. Cadogan Diaries, 611–12

Select Bibliography

Main sources other than official documents

Churchill, Winston S., *The Second World War*, vols. I–VI (Cassell, 1948–54)
Avon, Earl of (Anthony Eden), *The Reckoning* (Cassell, 1965)
Woodward, Sir Llewellyn, *History of the Second World War: British Foreign Policy in the Second World War* (H.M.S.O. 1970–6)

Memoirs, biographies, diaries

Birkenhead, Earl of, *Halifax* (Hamish Hamilton, 1965)
Boyle, Andrew, *Poor, Dear Brendan* (Hutchinson, 1974)
Bryant, Arthur, *The Turn of the Tide, 1939–43* (Collins, 1957)
—, *Triumph in the West* (Collins, 1959)
Colville, John, *Footprints in Time* (Collins, 1976)
Cooper, Alfred Duff, *Old Men Forget* (Hart-Davis, 1953)
Deane, John R., *The Strange Alliance* (John Murray, 1947)
Dilks, David (ed.), *Sir Alexander Cadogan: Diaries, 1938–45* (Cassell, 1971)
Dixon, Piers, *Double Diploma: The Life of Sir Pierson Dixon, Don and Diplomat* (Hutchinson, 1968)
Gaulle, Charles de, *War Memoirs: Unity 1942–44* (Weidenfeld and Nicolson, 1959)
Gilbert, Martin, *Winston S. Churchill*, vol. V (Heinemann, 1976)
Gladwyn, Lord, *Memoirs* (Weidenfeld and Nicolson, 1972)
Harriman, W. Averell, and Abel, Elie, *Special Envoy to Churchill and Stalin, 1941–46* (Hutchinson, 1976)
Harvey, John (ed.), *The Diplomatic Diaries of Oliver Harvey, 1937–40* (Collins, 1970)
Hoare, Samuel, *Ambassador on Special Mission* (Collins, 1946) *see also* Templewood, Viscount
Hull, Cordell, *Memoirs* (Hodder and Stoughton, 1948)
Ismay, Lord, *Memoirs* (Heinemann, 1960)
James, Robert Rhodes (ed.), *Chips: The Diaries of Sir Henry Channon* (Weidenfeld and Nicolson, 1967)
Leahy, William D., *I Was There* (Gollancz, 1950)
Macmillan, Harold, *The Blast of War: 1939–45* (Macmillan, 1967)
—, *The Past Masters* (Macmillan, 1975)
Moran, Lord, *Winston Churchill: The Struggle for Survival, 1940–45* (Constable, 1966)
Murphy, Robert, *Diplomat among Warriors* (Collins, 1964)
Sherwood, Robert E., *The White House Papers of Harry L. Hopkins* (Eyre and Spottiswoode, 1949)
Stettinius, Edward R., *Roosevelt and the Russians* (Jonathan Cape, 1950)
Strang, Lord, *Home and Abroad* (André Deutsch, 1956)
—, *Prelude to Potsdam: Reflections on War and Foreign Policy* (International Affairs, vol. 46, July 1970)
—, *Special University of London lecture, 16 March 1965* (unpublished)
Taylor, A. J. P., *Beaverbrook* (Hamish Hamilton, 1972)

Templewood, Viscount, *Nine Troubled Years* (Collins, 1954)
Thompson, R. W., *Churchill and Morton* (Hodder and Stoughton, 1976)
Wheeler-Bennett, Sir John (ed.) *Action This Day: Working with Churchill* (Macmillan, 1968)

Other historical works

Amery, Julian, *Approach March* (Hutchinson, 1973)
Auty, Phyllis, and Clogg, Richard (eds.), *British Policy Towards Wartime Resistance in Yugoslavia and Greece* (Macmillan, 1975)
Barclay, Sir Roderick, *Ernest Bevin and the Foreign Office, 1932–69* (published by the author, 1975)
Barker, Elisabeth, *British Policy in South-east Europe in the Second World War* (Macmillan, 1976)
Churchill, Winston S., *The World Crisis: The Aftermath* (Thornton Butterworth, 1929)
Clissold, Stephen, *Yugoslavia and the Soviet Union, 1939–73* (Oxford University Press, 1975)
Deakin, F. W. D., *The Embattled Mountain* (Oxford University Press, 1971)
Dedijer, Vladimir, *Tito Speaks* (Weidenfeld and Nicolson, 1953)
Djilas, Milovan, *Conversations with Stalin* (Hart-Davis, 1962)
Foot, M. R. D., *History of the Second World War: S.O.E. in France* (H.M.S.O., 1966)
Gowing, Margaret, *Britain and Atomic Energy, 1939–45* (Macmillan, 1964)
—, *Independence and Deterrence* (Macmillan, 1974)
Spaak, Paul-Henri, *The Continuing Battle* (Weidenfeld and Nicolson, 1971)
Ullman, Richard Henry, *Anglo-Soviet Relations, 1917–21*, vol. 3, *Anglo-Soviet Accord* (Princeton University Press, 1973)

Index

Abyssinia, 162–3
Admiralty, 35, 44–5, 50, 127
Adriatic, 166, 273
Aegean, 136
Africa, 208
Alexander, Field-Marshal Sir Harold, 120, 136, 196, 282
Alexandra, Princess (of Greece), 300–1
Algiers, 37, 69, 74–5, 79, 84, 91, 93, 95–6, 98, 100, 110, 173
Alsace-Lorraine, 82
Amery, Leo, 17, 34
Anvil, 104, 136
Archangel, 290
Arciszewski, Tomasz, 258
Argentina, 126, 131, 147, 151, 202, 205
Asia, 208
Asquith, Herbert, 20
Athens, 17, 186, 189, 193–7
Atlantic; Ocean, 147–8, 151, 154; Charter, 205, 234–6, 238, 243–4, 255, 308; Alliance, 216, 291
Atomic energy/bomb, 137, 204
Attlee, Clement, 10, 24, 52–3, 72–3, 87, 94, 97, 99, 107–9, 139, 142–3, 161, 176, 178, 181, 186, 194, 199, 205, 207, 209, 216, 228, 235, 237, 258
Australia, 145, 205, 207
Austria, 17, 207, 213, 290, 301–2, 304–5
Austro-Hungarian empire, 303
Avon, Countess of, 11
Avon Papers, 10
Azores, 148, 150, 152–7

Badoglio, Marshal Pietro, 163–71, 173–7

Baldwin, Stanley, 226
Balkans, 11, 23, 135–6, 174, 184, 192, 203, 205, 207, 225–6, 229, 234, 272, 277–8, 280–1, 290
Baltic States, 103, 225–6, 233, 235, 239, 242–4
Banska Bystrica, 269
Barclay, Sir Roderick, 77
Bari, 168
Battle of Britain, 146
Beaverbrook, Lord, 20, 22–3, 26, 199–202, 228–9, 233–4, 236–9, 246, 255–6, 291
Beirut, 58
Belgium, 140, 203, 215, 299, 305
Belgrade, 272, 274
Berle, Adolph, 165–6
Berlin, 137, 216
Beneš, Eduard, 261–9, 306
Bessborough, Earl of, 45–7, 54, 59
Bevan, Aneurin, 67
Bevin, Ernest, 10, 24, 47, 59, 72–3, 107–9, 120, 196, 221, 228, 234–5, 237, 258, 259
Bir Hacheim, 56
Birmingham, 141
Bizerta, 7
Black Sea, 225, 283
Bogomolov, Alexander, 65–6, 170, 265
Bohemia, 268–9
Boisson, Pierre, 74, 95–8, 102
Bolshoi Theatre, 286
Bonaparte, Napoleon, 116
Bonomi, Ivanoe, 168, 175–8, 180
Boothby, Robert, 67, 77
Bor-Komarowski, General, 257
Bordeaux, 35

Morgenthau Plan, 25, 211
Morocco, 57
Morrison, Herbert, 25, 32, 34, 38,
    43–7, 49, 54, 62–5, 67, 70, 84, 93–4,
    187, 222, 228, 234, 237, 258
Morton, Major Desmond, 25, 32, 34,
    38, 43–7, 49, 54, 62–5, 67, 70, 84,
    93–4, 187
Moscow, 222, 224, 226–7, 233–5, 249,
    252–6, 262, 264–5, 268–9, 278, 281–2,
    287, 289–90, 294–5; Eden visit
    (1941), 232, 234, 241, 244; Churchill
    visit (1942), 224, 241; Foreign
    Ministers' Conference (1943), 93,
    100, 102, 156, 168, 170, 172, 186,
    213, 242, 265–7, 274, 276, 287–8;
    Churchill–Eden visit (1944), 111,
    209, 282–6; de Gaulle visit (1944),
    114–16, 215–16
Moulin, Jean, 83
Munich agreement, 90, 95, 149,
    239–40, 261
Murphy, Robert, 37–8, 49, 81, 167,
    173
Muselier, Admiral Émile, 43–6, 48, 50
Mussolini, Benito, 18, 28, 39, 77, 87,
    140–4, 149, 162–5, 178, 181
Myers, Brigadier Edmund, 183, 185,
    188

Nedić, General Milan, 273
Netherlands, 215, 291
New York, 177
New Zealand, 201, 205
Newfoundland, 50, 145
Nichols, Philip, 264, 271
Niger, River, 57
Nile, River, 135
Normandy, 131, 202, 210
Norway, 215, 291
Nyon, 19

Office of Strategic Services (O.S.S.),
    135, 192
Orel, 231
Ottawa, 51
Overlord, 95, 97, 99–101, 104, 131,
    136, 168, 202–3, 209–10, 231

Pacific Ocean, 134, 201, 208
Pan-American Airways, 157
Papandreou, George, 191–4, 197, 278
Paris, 112, 286
Passy, Colonel (Dewavrin), 43–7
Paul, Prince, Regent of Yugoslavia,
    301
Peake, Charles, 55–7, 61, 65, 67
Pearl Harbor, 28, 50, 134, 147
Persia, see Iran
Pétain, Marshal Philippe, 33–4, 36–7,
    39, 59, 82
Peter, King (of Yugoslavia), 135, 263,
    299–301
Peyrouton, Marcel, 95, 97–8, 102
Philip, André, 70
Pilsen, 271
Pleven, René, 34
Poland, 11, 103, 286; exiled
    government, 65, 242, 245–55,
    257–60, 295; and Soviet Union,
    228–9, 235, 242–4, 246–60, 263–4,
    286, 292; and Anglo-Soviet treaty,
    240–1; Katyn, 248–51, 254, 264;
    Curzon line, 247–8, 251–2, 258, 295;
    and U.S., 242, 246–7, 254–6, 259–60,
    289, 291, 293, 295; Warsaw rising,
    251–7, 268, 271; underground army
    in, 251–5; and Czechoslovakia,
    262–7
Political Warfare Executive (P.W.E.),
    62
Popov, Colonel Grigory, 197
Portugal, 11; and Azores, 148–58;
    post-war role, 291
Potsdam conference, 260
Prague, 19, 270–1
Press, the; and Eden, 24; and
    Churchill, 24, 28, 75–6, 83; and
    de Gaulle, 56, 65, 68, 75–8, 83; and
    U.S., 171; and Soviet Union, 229–30,
    233, 292; and Czechoslovakia, 265
Prince of Wales, 151
Prussia, 209; East Prussia, 248

Quadrant, 87–8